Democratic Reform
in Africa

£16

Also published by
James Currey & Ohio University Press

Ethnicity & Democracy
in Africa
EDITED BY BRUCE BERMAN,
DICKSON EYOH & WILL KYMLICKA

Democratic Reform in Africa

Its Impact on Governance & Poverty Alleviation

Edited by
MUNA NDULO

Professor of Law, Cornell Law School
& Director of the Institute for African Development
Cornell University

JAMES CURREY
OXFORD

OHIO UNIVERSITY PRESS
ATHENS

James Currey Ltd
73 Botley Road
Oxford OX2 0BS
www.jamescurrey.co.uk

Ohio University Press
19 Circle Drive, The Ridges
Athens, Ohio 45701
www.ohio.edu/oupress

© James Currey Ltd 2006
First published 2006

1 2 3 4 5 10 09 08 07 06

ISBN 10: 0-85255-945-3 (James Currey cloth)
ISBN 13: 978-085255-945-1 (James Currey cloth)
ISBN 10: 0-85255-946-1 (James Currey paper)
ISBN 13: 978-085255-946-8 (James Currey paper)

ISBN 10: 0-8214-1721-5 (Ohio University Press cloth)
ISBN 13: 978-0-8214-1721-8 (Ohio University Press cloth)
ISBN 10: 0-8214-1722-3 (Ohio University Press paper)
ISBN 13: 978-0-8214-1722-5 (Ohio University Press paper)

British Library Cataloguing in Publication Data
Democratic reform in Africa : its impact on governance & poverty alleviation
 1. Democratization – Africa – Congresses 2. Democracy – Africa – Congresses 3. Poverty –
 Africa – Congresses 4. Africa – Politics and government – 1960- – Congresses 5. Africa –
 Economic conditions – 1960- – Congresses 6. Africa – Social conditions – 1960- – Congresses
I.Ndulo, Muna
320.9'6

Library of Congress Cataloging-in-Publication Data
Democratic reform in Africa : its impact on governance & poverty alleviation / edited by Muna Ndulo.
 p. cm.
 Includes bibliographical references and index.
 ISBN 0-8214-1721-5 (alk. paper) – ISBN 0-8214-1722-3 (alk. paper)
 1. Democracy—Africa. 2. Africa—Politics and government—1960- 3. Poverty—Africa. I. Ndulo,
Muna.
 JQ1879.A15D39 2006
 320.96–dc22   2006045335

Typeset in 10/11½pt Monotype Plantin
by Avocet Typeset, Chilton, Aylesbury, Bucks
Printed and bound in Great Britain by
Woolnough, Irthlingborough

Contents

1

MUNA NDULO
Introduction
Good Governance:
The Rule of Law & Poverty Alleviation

2

JOHANN KRIEGLER
Democratic Reform
in Africa

3

JOEL BARKAN
Democracy in Africa:
What Future?

4

ANN SEIDMAN & ROBERT SEIDMAN
Legal Drafting for Democratic Social Change
& Development

5

PENELOPE ANDREWS
The South African Constitution
as a Mechanism for Redressing Poverty

Acknowledgements

This book is the result of a conference entitled: 'Democratic Reform in Africa: Impact on Governance and Poverty Alleviation' held at Cornell University, 24–26 October 2002 and sponsored by the Institute for African Development, Cornell University, in collaboration with the Poverty, Inequality, and Development Initiative, Cornell University and the Center on Democratic Performance, Binghamton University. The conference was born out of the need to examine the impact of democratic reform on governance and poverty alleviation in Africa. It was noted that a wave of democratic reform had swept across Africa during the last three decades of the twentieth century, in part because of the failure of authoritarian rule to promote sufficient economic development and respect for human rights. Some would argue that democracy is now well on the way to becoming a global entitlement, one that is increasingly promoted and protected by the collective international process. There has also been a new approach to the question of governance in Africa on the part of the international community. Economic aid and other forms of financial assistance are progressively being made conditional on good governance. Africans themselves in the New Partnership for African Development (NEPAD) have acknowledged the relationship between governance and economic development and have devised standards for economic and political governance.

It was also noted that democratic reform in Africa has been slow, difficult, and at times painful. Nevertheless, sufficient time has passed for those interested in political and economic development to begin to assess what progress, if any, Africa has made in recent years in addressing the need for the consolidation of democratic reform and the resolution of considerable developmental challenges. While the link between governance, development and poverty is gradually being accepted, some key interrelationships between elements of the two sectors remain open to debate. This symposium was designed to highlight the types of issues that cut across both the political and economic reform spectra, and to identify how well they are being addressed. It was also designed to identify obstacles to democratic reform and areas of future focus. To accomplish this goal, the symposium had two main key subtexts. The first was the examination of institutions and their role in governance and poverty alleviation, and the second focused on key actors in the processes of both democratic reform and economic development.

The symposium aimed to contribute to policy analysis of law and development, and on how to increase the level of control disadvantaged populations exercise over their lives. It also analyzed successful civil society strategies that employ the law to advance good governance and poverty reduction. This book is a collection of the papers presented at the conference. Each chapter is written by a person with considerable knowledge and expertise on the particular subject. The varied backgrounds of the speakers reflected the conference's interdisciplinary focus, which makes the papers contained in this book invaluable educational material.

The Conference and this book could not have been achieved without the help of many people. In particular, I would like to thank Jackie Sayegh, who did an excellent job in organizing the conference, without which this book would not have been possible. I would also like to thank Edward McMahon of the Center for Democratic Performance, Binghamton University and Ravi Kanbur of the Poverty, Inequality, and Development Initiative for their collaboration in holding the conference. I am also grateful to my research assistants Sonia Gioseffi, Gabriel Ristorucci, Alexis Boyce and Lauren Harris, who worked tirelessly and diligently in preparing the manuscript for publication.

Contributors

PENELOPE ANDREWS BA, LLB (Natal), LLM (Columbia) is Professor of Law at the City University of New York. She previously worked at the NAACP Legal Defense and Educational Fund in New York before serving as Chamberlain Fellow in Legislation at Columbia Law School. Professor Andrews teaches in the areas of anti-discrimination law and policy and Aborigines law. She has also taught at the University of Melbourne, Australia and at the University of Maryland, USA.

DOUGLAS G. ANGLIN BA (Toronto), M.A. D.PHIL (Oxon) is Professor Emeritus of Law at Carleton University, Canada. He was founding Vice Chancellor of the University in Lusaka, Zambia. He served as Adviser to the South African Council of Churches during the transition period from Apartheid to democratic rule (1992–4), and has participated in numerous election-monitoring processes including those in Nigeria, South Africa, and Namibia.

REGINALD AUSTIN BA, LLB (Cape Town), LLM (London)has served as Director of the sub-Saharan Africa program, International IDEA, as Director of the Legal and Constitutional Affairs Division of the Commonwealth Secretariat, and as Chief Electoral Officer of the Electoral Unit of the UN Observer Mission in South Africa (UNOMSA), the UN Mission to Cambodia and the UN Mission in Afghanistan (UNAMA). In his home country, Zimbabwe, he was involved in the Constitutional Conference leading to the country's independence and was Professor of Law and Dean of the Law Faculty at the University of Zimbabwe.

JOEL D. BARKAN AB (Cornell), PhD (UCLA) is Professor of Political Science at the University of Iowa in Iowa City. As a specialist in politics and development policy in sub-Saharan Africa, he served as the Regional Democracy and Governance Advisor for East and Southern Africa to the US Agency for International Development from 1992 to 1994. His knowledge of the politics of developing countries is the result of three decades of teaching, research, and government service in Ethiopia, Ghana, Kenya, Lesotho, Namibia, Nigeria, South Africa, Tanzania, Uganda and Zambia.

KATE K. FLETCHER BA (Harvard) is an associate in the Africa Division of Human Rights Watch. She graduated *magna cum laude* in Social Studies from Harvard College in 2000. Her senior thesis, 'Second Sight in this American World', looked at the politics of identity through paintings by contemporary African-American artists. In 1998, she went to Nepal for the Carr Foundation to evaluate NGO work aimed at preventing child labor in the Kathmandu valley. She has also worked as an investment banking analyst at JPMorgan Chase & Co.

JOHN HATCHARD LLB, LLM (London) is Professor of Law at the Open University, United Kingdom. He has also taught law at the Universities of

Zambia, Zimbabwe, Buckingham University, UK and at the School of Oriental and African Studies, London. He is associate editor of the *Journal of African Law* and Secretary of the Commonwealth Legal Education Association.

ROBERT B. KENT BA (Harvard), LLB (Boston), LLD (Roger Williams) is Professor Emeritus at Cornell Law School. He is an expert in alternative dispute resolution, civil procedure, conflict of laws, constitutional law, federal courts and international litigation. After receiving his LL.B from Boston University, where he served as Editor-in-Chief of the *Boston University Law Review*, Professor Kent worked for two years in private practice, and then began teaching at his alma mater. He has served as Professor of Law and Dean of the University of Zambia, and also as Distinguished Visiting Professor at the Roger Williams University School of Law.

JOHANN CHRISTIAAN KRIEGLER LLB (Pretoria) was until recently a Justice of the Constitutional Court of South Africa. During his years at the Bar he was actively involved in the promotion of human rights and the development of institutions for their defense. He drafted the constitution of the Christian Institute, became National President of Verligte Aksie, and was the founding Chairman of Lawyers for Human Rights. For some years, he served on the Transvaal Board of the Urban Foundation and was a founding trustee of the Legal Resources Centre. He is currently a Board Member of the University of South Africa Law Faculty and of the University of Pretoria Institute for Human Rights Studies, and a trustee of a number of charitable trusts.

THOMAS R. LANSNER BA (Hobart College), MIA (SIPA) is an adjunct professor at the Columbia University School of International and Public Affairs. He writes regularly on international affairs and has served as a consultant on media, elections, human rights and democratization issues to numerous non-governmental organizations and political parties. For 10 years, he was a correspondent in Africa and Asia for the *Observer* (London), the *Guardian*, and the *Far Eastern Economic Review*.

BRIAN LEVY BA (Cape Town), PhD (Harvard) is Sector Manager of the Public Sector Reform and Capacity Building Unit in the Africa Region of the World Bank. Prior to taking up this position, he worked in both operational and research groups within the Bank. His operational work focused on southern Africa, including Namibia, Mozambique, South Africa, Zambia, and Zimbabwe, and his research is on the approaches to strengthening the institutional foundations of market-based development with particular emphasis on the fundamental institutional underpinnings of government capacity.

COLLEEN LOWE-MORNA BA (Princeton), MA (Columbia) is executive director of Gender Links. She joined the Commonwealth Secretariat in 1991 and later served as Chief Program Officer of the Commonwealth Observer Mission to South Africa. Following South Africa's first democratic elections in 1994, she became advisor on gender and institutional development to the Commonwealth Fund for Technical Assistance. She subsequently served as founding CEO of the South African Commission on Gender Equality.

DANIEL MANNING BA (Wisconsin), JD (Boston) is currently the Director of Litigation for Greater Boston Legal Services (GBLS), where he has worked since 1973. GBLS is a non-profit law firm that provides free legal assistance to low-income people on civil matters such as housing, employment, immigration, disability and family law. He has also served as a consultant advising legal service organizations in developing and transitional countries around the world, including Albania, Bangladesh, Bosnia and Herzegovina, Cambodia, China, Croatia and South Africa, among others. He has worked as a consultant on behalf of the World Bank, the UK Department for International Development, the UNDP, USAID and the Open Society Institute.

MUNA NDULO LLB (Zambia), LLM (Harvard), D.Phil (Oxon) is Director of Cornell University's Institute for African Development and teaches the common law and African legal systems, human rights, constitutions, election monitoring, international development, and legal aspects of foreign investments in developing countries. He was Dean of the University of Zambia School of Law, and from 1986 to 1996 served as Legal Officer with the UN Commission for International Trade Law. He was Political Adviser to the UN Mission in South Africa, and has served in UN Missions in East Timor, Kosovo and Afghanistan.

ANN W. SEIDMAN BA (Smith College), MS (Columbia), PhD (Wisconsin) is a recognized expert in the area of law and development. Her research includes economic development, planning policy and strategy studies in southern and eastern Africa, and she is the author of numerous textbooks on Africa and development issues.

ROBERT B. SEIDMAN BA (Harvard), JD (Columbia)is Professor Emeritus at the School of Law, Boston University, and a renowned specialist on law and development and legislative drafting. He has taught law at the Universities of Ghana, Lagos (Nigeria), Zambia, Dar es Salaam, Zimbabwe, and Witswatersrand (South Africa), as well as having worked as a consultant to various governments in Asia and Africa.

PETER TAKIRAMBUDDE LLB (Makerere), LLM, JSD (Yale) is the Director of the Africa Division of Human Rights Watch. He previously served as Professor of Law and Dean of the Faculty of Law and Social Sciences at the University of Botswana.

TSATSU TSIKATA LLB (Ghana, Legon), BCL (Oxford) is a former Chief Executive of the Ghana National Petroleum Company, and a former Law Lecturer at the University of Ghana, Legon.

List of Acronyms & Abbreviations

ACHPR	African Charter on Human and Peoples' Rights
ACHPR	African Commission on Human and Peoples' Rights
ACHPR	African Court of Human Rights and Peoples' Rights
ADB	African Development Bank
ANC	African National Council
ANC	African National Congress
APF	Africa Partnership Forum
APR	Africa Peer Review
APRM	African Peer Review Mechanism
AU	African Union
BBC	British Broadcasting Corporation
BSAC	British South Africa Company
CAHRCs	Commonwealth African human rights commissions
CAR	Central African Republic
CAS	Country Assistance Strategy
CDD	Center for Democracy and Development
CEDAW	Convention for the Elimination of All Forms of Discrimination Against Women
CEMAC	Central African Economic and Monetary Union
CHRAJ	Commission on Human Rights and Administrative Justice
CHRCs	Commonwealth human rights commissions
CMAG	Commonwealth Ministerial Action Group
CNN	Cable New Network
CODESRIA	Council for the Development of Social Sciences in Africa
CSO	civil society organization
CSSDCA	Conference on Security, Stability, Development and Cooperation in Africa
DANIDA	Danish International Development Agency
DFID	Department for International Development
DRC	Democratic Republic of the Congo
ECA	Economic Commission for Africa
ECOMOG	Economic Community of West African States Monitoring Group
ECOSOCC	Economic, Social and Cultural Council
ECOWAS	Economic Community of West African States
EISA	Electoral Institute of South Africa
ERP	Economic Recovery Program
ESAP	Economic Structural Adjustment Program
EU	European Union
FIDA	International Federacion of Women Lawyers (Spanish acronym)
FOWODE	Forum for Women in Democracy
GBI	Gender Budget Initiative
GDP	Gross Domestic Product
GEAR	Growth, Economic, and Redistribution Program
HDR	Human Development Report'
HIPC	Heavily Indebted Poor Countries
HRC	human rights commission
HSGIC	NEPAD Heads of State and Government Implementation Committee
ICCPR	International Covenant for Civil and Political Rights

ICRC	International Committee of the Red Cross
ICSECR	International Covenant for Social, Economic, and Cultural Rights
ICTs	information and communication technologies
IDASA	Institute for a Democratic Alternative in South Africa
IDEA	Institute for Democracy and Electoral Assistance
IDS	Institute for Development Studies
IFI	international financial institution
IFJ	International Federation of Journalists
IMF	International Monetary Fund
IPU	Inter Parliamentary Union
LRC	Legal Resources Center
MAP	Millennium Partnership for the African Recovery Program
MDC	Movement for Democratic Change
MECs	members of executive councils
MISA	Media Institute of Southern Africa
MNR	Movement for National Resistance
MoU	Memorandum of Understanding
MP	Member of Parliament
NAI	New African Initiative
NCA	National Constitutional Assembly
NDI	National Democratic Institute for International Affairs
NEPAD	New Partnership for Africa's Development
NGLS	Non-Governmental Liaison Service
NGO	non-governmental organization
NHRI	national human rights institution
NIBMAR	No Independence Before Majority Rule
NPP	National Progressive Party
NWICO	New World Information and Communications Order
OAU	Organization of African Unity
ODA	official development assistance
OECD	Organization for Economic Cooperation and Development
OSISA	Open Society Initiative for Southern Africa
OTI	Office of Transition Initiatives
PAF	Planning and Finance
PAMSCAD	Program of Actions to Mitigate the Social Costs of Adjustment
PAP	Pan-African Parliament
PELCRA	Port Elizabeth Land and Community Restoration
PF	Patriotic Front
PRSP	Poverty Reduction Strategy Paper
PSC	Peace and Security Council
RAF	Royal Air Force
RDP	Reconstruction and Development Program
RF	Rhodesian Front
ROCCIP	Rule, Opportunity, Capacity, Communications Interest, Process and Ideology
RTLM	Radio Télévision Libre des Milles Collines (Rwanda)
SADC	Southern African Development Community
SAL	Social Action Litigation
SAPs	Structural Adjustment Programs
Sida	Swedish International Development Agency
SPA	Special Program for Africa
TAC	Treatment Action Campaign
TGNP	Tanzania Gender Networking Program

UANC	United African National Council
UDHR	Universal Declaration of Human Rights
UDI	Unilateral Declaration of Independence
UGBI	Uganda Gender Budget Initiative
UN	United Nations
UNDP	United Nations Development Program
UNESCO	United Nations Educational, Scientific and Cultural Organization
UNHCR	United Nations High Commissioner for Refugees
UNICEF	United Nations International Children's Emergency Fund
UNIFEM	United Nations Development Fund for Women
UNIP	United National Independence Party
UNOMSA	United Nations Observer Mission in South Africa
UNSITC	United Nations Standard International Trade Classification
UNTAG	United Nations Transition Assistance Group
UPP	United People's Party
USAID	United States Agency for International Development
VOA	Voice of America
WACC	World Association of Christian Communications
WBI	Women's Budget Initiative
WDR	World Development Report
WEI	Women's Empowerment Index
WSI	Women's Self-Reliance Index
WTO	World Trade Organization
ZANLA	Zimbabwe National Liberation Army
ZANU (PF)	Zimbabwe African National Union (Patriotic Front)
ZANU	Zimbabwe African National Union
ZAPU	Zimbabwe African Peoples Union
ZCTU	Zimbabwe Congress of Trade Unions
ZIPRA	Zimbabwe Peoples Liberation Army
ZUM	Zimbabwe Unity Movement
ZUPO	Zimbabwe United Peoples Organization

Foreword

ROBERT KENT

It is with great pride and pleasure that I write a preface to this book. The question of governance and poverty alleviation is a matter that has exercised my mind ever since I came to be involved with Africa. The publication of a book on this issue is a good opportunity to reflect on where we have been, where we are, where we are going, and the problems of governance in Africa. As superannuated teachers are apt to do, I turn anecdotal, with three stories bearing on these so-called reflections. The first involves the late Professor Kwamena Bentsi-Enchill, the founding Dean at the University of Zambia School of Law and the man to whom I am ever grateful for having brought me to Africa. When I first arrived in Lusaka, Zambia, Kwamena was about to return to Ghana. He was deeply concerned about constitutionalism in his country, and he engaged in exercises in constitutional drafting. Desirous of avoiding fragmentation into many parties, he proposed the initial assignment of all voters by lot to one or other of just two parties. When I expressed skepticism, he replied with his customary vigor, 'You must remember one thing.' 'What's that, Kwamena?' 'You have something, you and the British, which very few others have.' 'What is that?' 'Mechanisms for the orderly transfer of political power', he replied with great conviction.

The second involves my early observation that there were more Mercedes in Lusaka than I had ever seen before. I soon came to the realization that in many, if not most, instances these were indicia of government office holding. This brought home the need to address the question of power and wealth and the consequential economic and social importance of public office to individuals in the midst of poverty. Constitutional stability is important. A few years ago, Muna Ndulo and I wrote about the constitutions of Zambia, four in 32 years, hardly a settled state of affairs. A constitution is often thought of in terms of rights, but at root a constitution is a charter for the exercise of political power. There are two features that seem crucial. One is a matter of substance: the two-term limit for presidents, a structural barrier to the formation of presidential dynasties. The other is the amending process, too often possible by a parliament alone, and, even with a provision requiring a super majority, much too easy to achieve in a president-dominated legislative body. A good structure must contain provision for a popularly elected convention and above all, for submission of an amendment to a referendum. In Zambia's recent history, President Frederick Chiluba's attempt to eliminate the two-term limit by constitutional amendment was thwarted by outcries from civil society, from the populace. But structure alone cannot insure fair elections, as experiences in several African elections apparently demonstrate.

The third came later, when I read an address of an American public figure I had come to admire. He expressed enthusiasm for the recent emergence on the African continent of what he called 'market democracies'. I found the term troubling. The concept of market democracy is for me related to globalization, something hard to define. Muna Ndulo has written recently of much African perception of globalization as a false god foisted on weaker states by the capitalist center of the West, as an ideology of predatory capitalism. This accompanies what is widely perceived as a 'retreat from Africa' on the part of the United States and other Western nations. What is needed is well-targeted aid viewed by Africans as helpful, not as designed for the benefit of multinational corporations. Attention to governance cannot alone lead to the alleviation of poverty, but good government is essential to development in dealing with poverty. Among the most important aspects of good governance are holding the executive in check, accountability, and increase in parliamentary effectiveness. Some have expressed hope in the future of Africa based on their assessment of the emergence of a second-generation leadership and its potential, but it is here that I have a concern. The institutions of higher learning in Africa, including but not limited to law schools, are in trouble economically and in terms of staffing. How well prepared with respect to education will the next generations of African leaders be? This is an area in which developed countries, especially the United States, can help, not by reassuming administrative direction, but by furthering opportunities for Africans to study in developed countries and by augmenting, through talented people, the teaching cadres of African institutions.

The diversity of the subject-matter so well articulated in the chapters in this book brings a singular but profound richness to the book and readily makes available an illuminating, penetrating, and perceptive analysis of the various aspects of governance and its impact on poverty and development. I hope that the book will provide a useful analysis of the interconnectedness of governance, poverty, and economic development and, in doing so, will serve to emphasize the urgency of addressing the obstacles to good governance in Africa.

1

MUNA NDULO
Introduction
Good Governance:
The Rule of Law & Poverty Alleviation

ANY publications have been written focusing on good governance, and particularly on its political dimension. This book
explores the concept of good governance, the rule of law and,
with a view to examining the extent to which good governance is a vehicle for
poverty alleviation, the consolidation of economic development. One of the
most important political and legal conceptions in good governance is the
concept of the rule of law. At the dawn of the twenty-first century, nations of virtually every region in the world recognize the role of the rule of law and the protection of human rights in their own political and legal systems as a critical factor
in nation-building and good governance. The rule of law has become a central
focus of domestic and international efforts to promote good governance.

The question arises as to what is meant by the rule of law and in what ways it
can assist in nation-building, the promotion of good governance, and the protection of human rights. To some the rule of law calls for the elimination of wide
discretionary authority from government processes. To others the rule of law
means the existence of formal rules which do not involve a choice between particular ends or particular people, and which are there for the use of everyone, for
the purpose for which people will decide to use them (Ocran, 1984). The
concept assumes the existence of inalienable rights and liberties which governments should not touch or violate. Predominant among such rights are property
rights, the right to free expression, freedom of association, equality before the
law, due process, and protection against discrimination. To some extent, the
essence of the rule of law lies in its juxtaposition to 'the rule of men'. This aphorism is not meant to express the utter absurdity that laws are capable of governing society without the help of men. Rather, it seeks to state the following basic
principles: that all state power ought to be exercised under the authority of law,
and that there should be rules of law governing the election and appointment of
those who make and execute policy, as well as the manner in which such policies are made and executed, in such a way as to ensure rationality and fairness
in the decision-making process (Hart, 1961). This state of affairs is thus contrasted with a regime of caprice or arbitrariness in which acts or omissions are
traceable to the whims of the particular man (or woman) in power at a given
time.

The rule of law connotes the use of state power, through rules of law for the
establishment of the economic and social system agreed upon by the people via
constitutionally sanctioned representative institutions or other acceptable surro-
gates. Typically the division and regulation of state power is established through
the national constitution. In this sense a national constitution is a charter of government. It is a body of fundamental principles by which a society organizes a

government for itself, defines and limits its powers, and regulates the relations between its organs *inter se* and with the citizen. The rule of law implies the assurance of some sort of predictability in the conduct of state officials by the prior existence of a basic law covering the subject-matter that falls within their fields of operation. It demands the precise definition of the roles and status of such public officials by law. It commends the creation of control devices to ensure that public officials abide by these norms, and if they do not, that their actions are invalid. It embraces procedural guarantees necessary to assure fairness in the adjudication of disputes and the application of sanctions, without hamstringing the administration of justice or frustrating the imposition of basic order in the community. It demands equality of treatment before the law of all persons in the application of a general rule to all cases where, according to its content, the rule should be applied. Unifying all the elements of the juridical quest for legitimacy are the demands for the existence of legal barriers to governmental arbitrariness, defined as the absence of legal authority for acts done, and the demand for some procedural safeguards, especially during trials of individuals alleged to be in conflict with the law. It means that the government, in all its actions, is bound by rules fixed and announced beforehand, which make it possible to foresee with certainty how authority will use its coercive power in given circumstances, and thereby allow an individual to plan his or her affairs on the basis of this knowledge.

The aim of the rule of law is to limit, thereby checking the arbitrary, oppressive, and despotic tendencies of power, and to ensure the equal treatment and protection of all citizens irrespective of race, class, status, religion, place of origin, or political persuasion. It implies a legal framework that is fair, that is enforced impartially (particularly in regard to human rights, public security and safety), and that legitimizes state actions. Authority is legitimate if there is an established legal and institutional framework, and if decisions are to be taken in accordance with the accepted institutional criteria, processes, and procedures.

In every country a national constitution articulates the vision of the society, defines the fundamental principles by which the country is organized, and distributes power within it, and plays an important role in nation-building and consolidating the national state. The idea of a constitutional democratic government, or constitutionalism, connotes a government defined, regulated and limited by a constitution. Constitutional democracy is founded upon the notion of checks and balances, namely that different institutions – the legislature, the judiciary, and the executive – while operating independently of one another, act to check each other's operations and balance each other's power. In essence, all three institutions are duty-bound to uphold the rule of law. This necessitates the precise definition of the roles of each institution and that of public officials (Nwabueze, 1993b). In the absence of role definitions, decisions are either not taken, or they are taken by persons without authority to do so, or else by the top leadership of the state apparatus who know little or nothing about the situation. In a constitutional democracy, it is not enough to assure predictability. Control devices to curb bureaucratic excesses are also necessary, on at least two grounds: first, in the absence of such controls, bureaucrats will most probably use their power arbitrarily to sabotage the program of the administration through corruption and abuse of office; and, second, such powers may be used either in outright violation of the rights of citizens, or in more indirect acts of bureaucratic insensitivity. If a government constituted by a written constitution can have only such powers as are granted by its constituent instrument, then we must accept, as a practical consequence, that the constitution, in granting powers, can also, and must by necessary implication, limit them. In other words, the constitution is something antecedent to government and connoting a system of fundamental principles according to which a nation or state is governed. In this sense a constitution embraces not only a frame of government, but also the relations of the government to the individuals that compose the nation or state.

A government operating under a written constitution has no more power than is granted to it by the constitution, either expressly or by necessary implication (Nwabueze, 1993a). It has been pointed out that the mark of good governance consists, above all else, in its effect in nurturing and promoting the best qualities in the people – the habits of obedience to government as the constituted authority, its laws and its interposition in the settlement of disputes and the redress of grievances; the habits of integrity, probity, fairness, self-restraint, and discipline in the conduct of social relations and public affairs; the spirit of enterprise, hard work, self-reliance and inventiveness in the pursuits and activities of life; and the quality of public–spiritedness and patriotism in matters affecting the interests of the community. In general terms, therefore, constitutional democracy concerns the following principles: (a) the use of the constitution as the supreme and fundamental law of the land to regulate and limit the powers of government, and to ensure the efficacy of such limitations in actual practice – the rule of law; (b) the assurance that the legitimacy of the government is regularly established by requiring that governmental powers are assumed or exercised only with the mandate of the people, given at periodic intervals through free and fair elections that are executed and administered according to the constitution and well-defined electoral laws, and in the context of a system-wide pluralism; and (c) the protection of fundamental human rights of the people (Paul, 1988). However, the effectiveness of constitutionalism as an element of the rule of law depends on how the limitations imposed on the government by the constitution are interpreted and enforced.

The best form of government is that which tends to foster in the people such qualities as initiative and inventiveness, and to steady improvement in their overall intellectual and moral qualities, since on these depends in turn the success of government in maintaining and promoting economic development and the well-being of the society. It is the good qualities of the people that supply the moving force that operates the machinery of the government. Judged by this criterion, a government of absolute or unlimited power is intrinsically bad, being inherently incapable of nurturing and promoting the best qualities in the people. Its inherent effect, not merely its natural tendency, is to create indifference, apathy, and passivity in the people. These negative qualities are necessarily 'implied in the very idea of absolute power' and result inevitably from the lack of public participation in the government. An absolute government creates other far worse evil traits in and propensities among the people. First, it divides rather than unites them. A still worse evil is the capacity of absolute power to corrupt (Nwabueze, 1993c). The famous saying of Lord Acton that 'power corrupts and absolute power corrupts absolutely' represents a universal political truth, founded upon universal experience. Repression of individual liberty is inseparable from a dictatorship. In a dictatorship, all expressions of opinion, all associations, and all political activities, which are critical of its rule, are viewed as hostile to the interests of the state and dangerous to its security, and must therefore be repressed.

In sum, good governance entails first and foremost a government that lives up to its responsibilities by ensuring the effective delivery of public goods and services, the maintenance of law and order, and the administration of justice. It also involves the creation of an efficient and dynamic market that secures economic growth and property, as well as a vibrant civil society which facilitates interaction between the state and economic and social actors within it. Democratic governance and the rule of law advance the protection of human rights at both the international and national levels. Thus, international instruments for the promotion and protection of human rights within the UN system are replete with admonitions that popular political participation must be free (International Covenant on Civil and Political Rights; African Charter on Human and Peoples' Rights). While the various instruments do not describe a particular methodology for ensuring such freedom, their essence is clear: to be free, participation in the political process of a country must be conducted in an atmosphere characterized by the absence of intimidation and the presence and respect of a wide range of fundamental human rights. It means that all men and women should have a voice in decision-making, either directly or through legitimate intermediate institutions that represent their interests. Such broad participation is built on freedom of association and speech, as well as capacities to participate constructively in the running of the affairs of the state. While the Universal Declaration of Human Rights enunciates the basic human rights, the International Covenants on Civil and Political Rights and on Economic, Social and Cultural Rights elaborate upon each of the rights contained in it. Regional conventions, such as the African Charter on Human and Peoples' Rights and the European Convention on Human Rights, further contribute to their elaboration and protection in their respective regions.

Governments are organized around institutions that engage in the delivery of goods and services and ensure government accountability. As widely recognized, institutional effectiveness and accountability are central to good governance and the rule of law (UNDP, 1997a; Armstrong, 1994; World Bank, 1992, 1994a; IMF, 1997). Without effective and responsive institutions that are undergirded by sustained constitutional structures and behavioral norms that guide the actions of decision-makers, political representation and all its attributes will not be sustainable. Weak, unproductive, and unaccountable public institutions have arguably been largely responsible for the failure of governance and the general economic decline in much of Africa (World Bank, 1989: 60). Transparency is an in-built *modus operandi* in the conception of good governance. It relies on free flow of information processes and access to institutions. For there to be effective transparency, institutions and information have to be accessible to those concerned with them, and enough information has to be provided to understand and monitor them. Decision-makers in government, the private sector, and civil society organizations should be held accountable to the public, as well as to institutional stakeholders. The indices for institutional effectiveness, among others, are the following: (i) respect for the rule of law on the part of all the actors in the political process; (ii) independence and capacity of the judiciary; (iii) mechanisms for self-regulation and external oversight of the activities of the executive and legislative organs; (iv) transparency, accountability of oversight bodies, and mechanisms for the active participation of civil society and the private sector in decision-making; (v) the extent and degree of decentralized structures and decision-making; (vi) gender representation in all spheres of decision-making; (vii) effective delivery mechanisms and capacity for servicing the poor; and (viii) independence of the legislatures in drafting and enacting relevant legislation.

Outline of the Book

This book is organized in fifteen chapters. In Chapter 2 Kriegler begins with a general review of the state of governance in Africa. He makes the unwelcome observation that most African countries are not developing but rather regressing. In the face of this, and the history which led up to it, he first argues that democratic reform must be seen as African – by Africans for Africans. Second, he highlights the importance of real access to foreign markets. Third, drawing on Amartya Sen, he argues that democratic reform is essential to attaining economic progress. Fourth, he posits that democratic reform and economic development must be rooted in a favorable social context. Fifth, he believes that Africa must be built from the 'bottom up', as opposed to the top-down efforts of international donors. He also recommends ensuring that recipients of aid have the capacity to use it in desirable ways. His seventh point is a warning that the climate developing in Africa is not sympathetic to civil rights and individual freedoms. Finally, he briefly reviews NEPAD, arguing that, to make NEPAD's peer review effective, the potential for deal making or 'back scratching' should be eliminated.

In Chapter 3 Barkan reviews the conflicting evidence concerning the state of democratization in Africa, arguing that, while expectations for widespread democracy must be tempered, many states have great democratic potential and should be nurtured. He first examines the views of the 'optimists', who point to trends in the re-emergence of African civil society and governmental reforms, and contrasts these with the 'realists', who remind us that only one-fifth of African nations are classified as 'free', that African civil society, while stronger, is still relatively weak, and that African governments are still mired in corruption. He argues, however, that both of these views are correct, and that, rather than speaking in terms of 'free' and 'not free', a more nuanced view is required. He sets out a scale of five different categories, from consolidated and semi-consolidated democracies, to aspiring democracies, to authoritarian or semi-authoritarian regimes, to nations mired in civil war, and concludes that the optimists' expectations may be warranted for the consolidated and semi-consolidated democracies, and that while progress may be more protracted in the other states, they deserve our support rather than our pessimism.

Chapter 4 by Ann and Robert Seidman challenges the notion of a deadlock between the clear predictability of law and the creative experimentation necessary for development. Applying their legislative theory to African institutions, the Seidmans begin by describing Africa's historical difficulties of poverty, vulnerability and poor governance. To explain these problems, they look to the institutions of many African countries and especially the legislative institutions of post-colonial governments, many of which, while led by Africans after independence, continued to rely on legislative methods designed by the colonialists, resulting in a lack of accountability and participation, which led to corruption. In addition, there was a tendency to merely copy legislation from the colonial power, which led to ineffective laws. The Seidmans then set out their own legislative theory, beginning with a review of the historical debates surrounding law and development, and prescribe that the drafter focus on the elements of rule, opportunity, capacity, communication, interest, process, and ideology – 'ROCCIPI'. They argue that laws should be designed as solutions to social problems, and that the heart of the rule of law is an injunction against arbitrary rule-making, requiring that executive discretion be limited and exercised according to considerations related to the public interest. Thus, the limits imposed by the rule of law can provide a resolution to the supposed deadlock.

In Chapter 5 Penny Andrews examines the use of the South African Constitution as a mechanism to address poverty, reviewing the Constitutional Court's emerging strategies for enforcing social and economic rights and addressing some of the extra-constitutional impediments to fulfilling those rights. Unlike most other constitutions, the South African Constitution is premised on the idea that South Africa is an unjust society in which inequality is deep and systematic. The Constitution therefore protects an extensive list of rights, and creates government obligations with respect to both positive and negative rights. Moreover, in the recent *Grootboom* and *Treatment Action* cases the Constitutional Court held that social and economic rights are, in fact, enforceable, and ordered the government to adopt reasonable policy measures that better provided for healthcare and housing. Andrews also highlights the many structural obstacles to realizing social and economic rights, such as the economic inequalities resulting from apartheid and the 'market friendly' privatization policies; extra-legal strategies therefore have to be pursued as well as constitutional litigation.

Chapter 6 argues against the 'full belly thesis' – namely, that civil and political rights are secondary to economic development, an idea espoused explicitly or implicitly by much of the international development community. Takirambudde and Fletcher contend that civil and political rights are not luxuries, but rather fundamental elements of durable economic success. This is because sustainable poverty alleviation can take place only where civil society institutions can pressure the government to respond to the needs of its citizens; civil society, however, can work to enforce accountability and transparency where certain human rights, such as the rights of association, expression, and the freedom of the press, are sufficiently protected. Takirambudde and Fletcher also consider the varieties of, constraints upon, and problems with the myriad forms of civil society action. 'Civil society' is often highly fragmented, representing disparate and politicized elements of society. This does not necessarily mean that it will be representative, however, and many organizations are not participatory and may exclude the poor or other ethnic groups. Furthermore, government policies and regulations can effectively restrict civil society action, and many civil society institutions operate with very limited budgets and are often seriously understaffed. Nonetheless, civil society organizations have an important role to play in poverty alleviation.

In Chapter 7, Ndulo examines the benefits and drawbacks of the devolution of power to regional or local governmental units, and reviews some of the challenges to devolution in Africa. Devolution can bring political benefits by increasing opportunities for participation and reducing the potentially corrupting concentration of power in the central government, as well as economic benefits through the greater accountability of local governments and efficient regional formations. Yet it can also prove divisive if sub-national units are partitioned along ethnic or religious lines. In addition, there is the risk of creating inefficient government by unnecessary duplicating, prolonging existing inequalities between regions, and hindering the development of consistent national economic policy. Most African states, however, have highly centralized governments, a situation that has in part resulted in governments that focus too much on control and not enough on public participation. In critiquing this state of affairs, Ndulo examines the colonial and post-colonial history of the continent, models of the relationships between the center and regional units in a devolved government, and the fiscal arrangements and dispute resolution mechanisms between national and sub-national governments, and recommends recognizing devolution of power in the constitution, taking care not to draw regional lines on divisive bases, and ensuring that the resulting regional units are adequately funded.

In Chapter 8 Tsikata examines Ghana's 'success story', analyzing the relationship between economic reform, decentralization and democratization, and the interaction between national authorities and international financial institutions. He notes that while the IMF and World Bank have often touted Ghana as a star pupil, one of its most important economic reforms, the multiple exchange-rate regime, was undertaken against IMF/World Bank advice. Similarly, it instituted a poverty alleviation program with the assistance of UNICEF decades before poverty alleviation became a buzzword among international lenders. Nonetheless, with strict IMF/World Bank conditionalities, the country was left with little room to maneuver. These restrictions did not prevent Ghana from deepening its commitments to democracy, however, and Tsikata notes the political successes it has enjoyed – seeing the national government change hands during an election, decentralizing political power and holding regular district-level elections. Thus, the country's future lies less in complying with the mercurial programs of the IMF and World Bank and more in confronting the challenges of local governance and effective management.

In Chapter 9 Hatchard assesses the contributions and potential of Human Rights Commissions in Commonwealth Africa, arguing that these 'in vogue' institutions should be strengthened and their mandates protected. Unlike courts, which can only adjudicate claims brought before them, the Human Rights Commissions can actively investigate human rights violations, press for broad changes, and educate the public about human rights issues. Furthermore, they command compulsory powers and influence unavailable to non-governmental organizations. The Commonwealth Commissions are nascent institutions, however, and Hatchard points to new difficulties they face in promoting respect for human rights and overseeing a state's compliance with international obligations. He recommends strengthening their independence and effectiveness, developing transnational links between them, and providing training for Commission personnel.

In Chapter 10 Levy examines economic and governance data drawn from 21 African countries, arguing that economic reform has improved the performance of many African economies, but that these hard-won gains are far from stable.

He begins by setting out a 'governance diamond' modelling the interactions between institutions, political interests, the economy, and the bureaucracy. He then reviews the economic history of Africa, from the neopatrimonial downward spiral to the structural adjustment programs of the 1980s and '90s, which he finds had generally positive effects – specifically, increased patterns of GDP growth, higher trends in agricultural and industrial value added, improved relations between business and government, enhanced bureaucratic quality and credibility, and general improvements in governance. While he thus finds that many countries have broken free of patrimonialism, he also warns that African economies lack the diversified economic base and inclusiveness that is necessary to sustain a 'virtuous spiral'. Using the governance diamond model, he points to political institutions as supporters for sustained economic development, and recommends reducing excessive centralization of state institutions, strengthening judicial independence and performance, improving accountability in the use of public resources, translating political priorities into practical policies, strengthening administrative capacity of the bureaucracy, using formal checks and balances, and checking corruption.

Lowe-Morna provides a brief overview of gender and governance in Africa in Chapter 11. Beginning by examining what we mean by 'governance', and the state of women's representation in the world's legislatures, she argues that women should be *equally* represented, on the grounds of the efficiency of participation by all parties, an empowerment approach to poverty reduction, and equity. She then examines the framework developed by Thenjiwe Mtintso, who argued that cultural, economic and social constraints could be overcome by means of quotas and shifting societal attitudes. Lowe-Morna then examines indices for measuring women's empowerment and the political and constitutional strategies African nations have used to increase it; she finds an increased chance of women getting elected under proportional representation. She also looks at ways of supporting women candidates and at their position after they are elected, including a critique of parliaments' gender-unfriendly practices and sexist environment. Finally, she examines the important role women can play in legislative reform and analyzing budgets from a gender perspective.

In Chapter 12 Manning examines the role of legal service organizations in Africa and their importance in advocating and enforcing the rights of poor people and pressuring the government on legal reform. His basic premise is that a justice system cannot effectively advance the interests of the poor unless it is possible for the government to hear them. Thus, legal service organizations can provide a voice for poor people in the justice system, and can work to educate them on their rights. Moreover, by enforcing their rights against landlords, employers, bureaucrats, or spouses, they can help people think differently about their role in society and contribute towards the creation of a culture of rights. Manning also examines some of the core values of legal services work: client loyalty and zealous advocacy, independence, and knowledge of the law and culture, and reviews the work of three African legal services organizations – FIDA and the Legal Resources Centre in Ghana, and the Legal Resources Centre in South Africa.

In Chapter 13 Lansner reviews the role of the media in democratic development and surveys efforts to enhance it in countries under authoritarian rule or in transition. He argues that active and open media can serve a number of important purposes in democratic development, including acting as a watch-dog over the state, providing civic fora to debate issues, and promoting human rights – roles that are all the more difficult in transitional and authoritarian countries, where media freedoms are not respected and 'nation-building' is often used as an excuse to exercise control. He notes that access to the media, the cultural suitability of its content, and emerging information and communication technologies are crucial issues. In addition, he examines some of the positive media efforts to influence democracy and good governance. In contrast to Rwanda, where the media were used to incite genocide, 'peace media' projects have been started in the Democratic Republic of the Congo, Burundi, and a number of other countries. Similarly, media campaigns in Benin helped that country avoid violence during its 1996 presidential election. Community radio projects have also helped deliver development information, such as the use of drama to impart AIDS awareness in South Africa and Uganda. Lansner also warns, however, that continued support for and engagement with the media in developing countries are required, as commercial survival is often difficult and many countries lack established traditions of press freedom. Finally, he reviews the approaches and guidelines used by a number of governmental and non-governmental organizations which fund media projects, and stresses the importance of civil society in monitoring and evaluating media performance.

In Chapter 14 Austin raises the question of why Zimbabwe, after several cycles of negotiations and constitution-making involving a broad range of participants, has failed to develop a durable constitution. He begins by carefully examining Zimbabwe's historical circumstances, starting with the British South Africa Company's settlement of what is now Harare and tracing the country's history through the post-World War II period during which oppressive practices leveled against the black population, including inequitable land policies, had given way to guerrilla war. This lasted until the Lancaster House conference in 1979, where representatives from the white government, the leaders of the liberation movement, and the British government met to simultaneously achieve a cease-fire and to fashion a new constitution. While the war was brought to an end, the constitution agreed upon lacked strong support; in particular, it protected the inequitable distribution of land in the hands of white farmers. By the 1990s, the Zimbabwe government had still not fulfilled its revolutionary promise of land reform, it was forced to enact a painful structural adjustment program, and it was under public pressure to revise the constitution. This led to its controversial land reform program and the establishment of a Constitutional Commission in 1999. Like the Lancaster House conference, however, the Constitutional Commission process also became polarized and generated little consensus, in part because the Act creating it gave great discretion to the President. In analyzing this long and complex history, Austin draws a number of lessons to be considered in constitution-making. First, the peace-making and the constitution-making processes should not be conflated, as can be seen from the Lancaster House conference. Second, military and ideological conflicts can have significant effects on the constitution-making process. Third, the process of constitutional debate should be made transparent, with advance consultation, public participation, and proper management of expectations. Fourth, the international community's support is important, but their close assistance is not always helpful. Fifth, appeals to international law can be helpful, and human rights abuses should be dealt with.

In Chapter 15, Anglin first reviews areas where peer review mechanisms have been employed by intergovernmental bodies. In particular, the OAU/AU has been generally effective in coping with coups and its election monitors are now firmly established, although it is unclear whether member nations are committed to the enforcement of the African Charter on Human and Peoples' Rights. The history of NEPAD's African Peer Review Mechanism is briefly given, including the resistance the program encountered from other NEPAD heads of state. Anglin then considers the leadership of peer review by a group of committed states, its purpose of achieving development through good governance, and contentious governance indicators by which such a review would operate. He notes that the process is still unclear as the institutional structure is not yet firmly established, and he reviews the planned process of investigation, assessment, and monitoring compliance. He also points to a number of potential constraints, notably the AU's continued resistance, funding, the need to involve civil society, relationships with G8 development partners, and ensuring impartiality. Thus, although peer review constitutes a dramatic break with the past supported by a solid minority of African leaders, an increase in political will is necessary to ensure its future.

2

JOHANN KRIEGLER
Democratic Reform in Africa

T HE time for politically correct platitudes about 'developing' countries in Africa has passed. Such characterizations are more often than not misnomers, if not lies. Most African countries are *not* developing but regressing, that is, regressing in terms of criteria that are most important for gauging the quality of life – infant mortality, life expectancy, per capita income, GDP and, of course, the incidence of HIV/AIDS. Many countries have negative economic growth, while others wallow close to a zero per cent growth rate. When colonial Europeans spoke of 'Darkest Africa' it may have been Victorian melodrama, but now large swathes of Africa are truly benighted. War, famine, pestilence and death are not merely apocalyptic specters but a stark reality for all to see. In the Great Lakes region, the Horn, and the Western Bulge, strife has brought bloodshed and misery for millions of helpless bystanders. The most lasting and the most telling legacy of Africa's involvement with the developed world since World War II is the AK 47, with the landmine a close second.

In the face of such odds, it would be easy to despair, simply to give up, and join erstwhile compatriots who have settled in Palm Springs or Perth. However, cynicism about the immobility of Africa is a cheap shot and desertion is an easy way out. I would rather try to determine what has gone wrong and what can be done to avoid such missteps in the future.

The United States is wounded and preoccupied with its hurt, urging others to join in the endeavor to seek and destroy its evanescent enemies. Europe is taken up with its own affairs and the incorporation of several relatively undeveloped new members. Asia has never paid much attention to happenings in Africa. If, therefore, we wish to maintain interest, the opportunities such as those offered by the Democratic Reform in Africa conference must be grasped. I preface what follows with a disclaimer: my views are based largely on South African society, though I do have personal knowledge of most southern African countries and have a keen interest in the affairs of the continent generally.

Particularly since the demise of the communist bloc, African intellectuals have adopted a form of black consciousness. The frequent response of pan-Africanists to a call for 'democratic reform in Africa' is: For heaven's sake, go back whence you came and let us be. Have you not reformed us enough? You came to us from across the water with a great message of hope from your god. Some came in the name of Islam, others as missionaries for Christianity. The message was peace and love. First you took our daughters and our sons; then you told us that it was bad to go about in the heat with only our loins covered. Christian missionaries forced us to give up polygamy, tribal initiation, reverence for our forebears, and obedience to our chiefs. Colonial administrators told us

11

to change our system of land tenure, family law customs, and rules of inheritance. You 'reformed' our means of production, introduced channels of marketing, imposed a poll tax, a land tax, a cattle tax – you name it, you taxed it. To pay these taxes, our fathers and mothers left us to work in your fields, your homes, your factories and your mines. You ravaged our fields, destroyed our pasturage, and denuded our forests, stripping the continent of raw materials and leaving slagheaps. Then, exhausted by World War II, you replaced your district commissioners and magistrates and governors with technical advisers, foreign aid dispensers, trade commissioners, and bankers. When you offer more 'development aid,' our response is a resounding 'Thank you, but no thank you.'

Obviously this is a one-sided picture, but it represents the perspective of a significant number of the African intelligentsia, and is important for that reason alone. Moreover, there is enough truth in it to warrant its being taken seriously. In any event, I believe that elements of this thinking color opinions in the corridors of power in most African countries. It was effectively the leitmotif of the New Partnership for African Development (NEPAD) and the motivation for NEPAD's enthusiastic adoption at Abuja in 2001. Arguably with more reason than Americans, Africans are suspicious of foreigners with strange accents and different pigmentation.

I therefore submit that when considering democratic reform in Africa, the first basic proposition is that such reform must be, and must manifestly be seen as, African – by Africans for Africans. The days of Africans wagging their tails for their masters' approval are long past. Furthermore, well-meaning condescension is likely to be counter-productive. Happily, there is a new-found resilience and self-reliance, a confident assertiveness. Meanwhile, whether one calls it xenophobia or the wisdom of centuries of bitter experience, fresh gifts from across the water are likely to be regarded with suspicion.

This raises an ostensible conundrum. Poverty cannot be alleviated in Africa only from within. However, the contradiction is apparent, not real. The northern hemisphere, more specifically the United States and the European Union, has a vital role to play in uplifting the poverty-stricken regions of Africa. This role that they can, and I suggest should, play is more subtle and indirect, and at a much lower level than heretofore. In particular, it should be played more sincerely.

The second proposition is that, instead of handouts or displays of kindliness, Africa needs access, real access, to foreign markets. Fulsome platitudes about humanitarian concern for the starving peasants of Africa are all well intended, but the truckloads of grain that accompany them push those very peasants out of the marketplace. If you wish to subsidize farmers directly, why not African farmers instead of yours? It would certainly be cheaper. The parable of teaching a man to fish should be adapted: as you fish in his or her lake, permit him or her to fish in yours.

But trade is not my immediate focus. Rather, my concern is democracy as the engine for development in Africa. I claim no expertise in economics, political science, or the compound field of development studies. Since I am unable to pass a professional judgment on economists, I asked my research assistant to confine her investigations to Nobel laureates, and was delighted with the two she came up with. Not only can I understand Amartya Sen and Joseph Stiglitz; they also make eminent sense to me. Although neither is concerned with Africa in particular, their principal observations are singularly appropriate. I adopt them gratefully and without major reservations. Their expertise and reputations are beyond question, and I find the cogency of their reasoning compelling.

In agreement with Professor Sen (Sen, 1999a), I maintain that a functioning democracy with a relatively free press is immune to a famine of any significant duration or extent. The data garnered and analyzed by Professor Sen establish a definite causal nexus between unresponsive government and famine. In the case of famine and other national disasters, any powerless, voiceless group is certain to suffer the impact most severely. Civil rights and freedoms create and ensure opportunities of participation and are crucial, not only in precluding inequitable distribution of disadvantage, but in guaranteeing equal economic rights. These in turn are vital to broad-based economic growth. An informed, empowered, and vocal populace serves government as a ubiquitous forecaster, informant, critic, and corrective, through anticipating and signaling threats, and monitoring governmental responses, as well as gauging the government's adequacy in applying appropriate remedial strategies. With real dialogue between governors and governed, responses to societal crises – not only those related to food supply or distribution – can be rapid and flexible, less costly, and more effective.

Obviously, what is good for the husbanding of food supplies is equally valid for other socio-economic needs, such as public health and housing. A society where those in need have access to and are taken seriously by those who distribute the limited resources is truly democratic. Whether society maintains this responsiveness through regular elections or in some other manner is not important. Responsiveness itself is the prophylactic. The third proposition is, therefore, that democratic reform is an essential tool to attaining economic progress.

However, I also accept and endorse Professor Stiglitz's caveat (Stiglitz, 2002), namely, that one cannot foster economic development in a vacuum. For an economy to flourish, especially where none was before, a suitable framework of political, legal and ethical norms must exist. A market economy cannot exist without sanctity of contract. If a man's word is not his bond, business cannot survive. Without a legal structure for amassing capital, entrepreneurship is impossible. And, of course, progress is doomed without a system of known or knowable rules applied impartially by competent tribunals. The fourth proposition, therefore, is that democratic reform and economic development must be rooted in a favorable social context. Civil society must be ready, willing, and able to nurture and sustain reform.

China has been able to liberalize its economy while keeping a tight rein on politics. Indeed, some of the Pacific Tigers maintain a tight hold on politics in order to promote rapid economic development, but their economic development has faltered. Although it is not difficult to refute this latter proposition, we are concerned with African economic and social development in the context of that continent's unique history and its current challenges. Analogies can be useful but attention must be paid to significant differences. For reasons that I hope to make clear, the wise philosopher-king option is not a realistic choice for African societies struggling to escape the vicious circle of poverty, illiteracy, disempowerment, hunger and disease.

Mercantile tradition is poorly developed in most of sub-Saharan Africa. The region once had a merchant class like the canny Chinese and Indian émigrés whose shops became mini stock exchanges from Hong Kong to Singapore, Jakarta, Denpasar and Fiji. But the Indians in Uganda were ejected by Idi Amin, while apartheid in South Africa compressed their cousins into residential and commercial ghettos. Despite the heroic efforts of those who fought in the South African freedom struggle, and notwithstanding the steadfast adherence of the African National Congress and the South African government to non-racial ideals, a persistent undercurrent of animosity exists towards 'Indians'. Likewise, despite the reforms of Museveni in Uganda and the blooming of laissez-faire capitalism in Kenya, acceptance of the Indian businessmen as fully indigenous remains incomplete. Consequently, they are not the obvious option for the promotion of stable business communities at the grassroots level.

Tragically, Zimbabwe and South Africa also have had a massive outflow of Jewish talents and skills during the last two decades. Commerce and industry, the professions, and the arts have suffered particularly heavily, but the loss has also been painful at the level of small business. The gap has been partially filled by immigrants from West Africa and by an upcoming class of more or less honest business people, which form the building blocks of a truly African small business community.

I lay stress on small business because, like Stiglitz, I believe that we must build from the bottom up; this is the fifth basic proposition. I invite the skeptics to examine the track record of top-down efforts in Africa over the last 40 years. The World Bank, the International Monetary Fund, the UN through its food, refugee, and development agencies, the International Red Cross, many individual governments through their agencies such as USAID, DFID, Sida, and Danida, and countless non-governmental agencies, church groups and other organizations have spent billions of dollars and countless effort; however, the signs are pitifully few and very far between. To paraphrase: never before in the field of human endeavor has so much been done by so many with so little effect.

My submission is that, unless the international community adopts a radically new approach, future efforts will be equally fruitless. True enough, the World Bank has now realized that a human being is not merely a producer/consumer/economic entity, and it has popularized the concept of good governance to articulate the wider scope of its prescripts for assistance. There is also good reason to accept that the Bank now regards human rights as a desideratum for favorable consideration of pleas for assistance. However belated, this continued movement away from the formalism of the so-called Washington consensus is to be welcomed. Government no longer needs to be minimalist and non-interventionist. On the contrary, it is now accepted that government has a role to play in promoting economic progress.

However, the point I wish to make does not pertain to the role of government. Rather, my plea is for intervention at a sub-governmental level, that is, at the level of civil society. In South Africa, Zimbabwe, Namibia and Malawi, donor agencies, especially those from the Nordic countries, have supported human rights activists and their liberation movements since the 1970s. With the advent of democracy in these countries, however, foreign funding largely diverged to the newly elected governments of these fledgling democracies. The switch highlights a fundamental flaw in prior attempts to bring about human development in sub-Saharan Africa. Unhappily, it is also a feature of NEPAD and augurs little success as currently formulated. Establishing a viable economy requires infrastructure, which is more than roads, railway lines, and electricity, but requires 'social capital'.

Development aid pumped into government agencies can be harmful. As a trustee of development charities, as an administrator of donor funds, as a deputed observer and as a judge, I have witnessed when citizens' dissatisfaction with official action (or rather inaction) has led to litigation. Without governmental capacity to administer such funds competently, the beneficence becomes a curse, and this is basic proposition number six. Before providing development funds to governments, donors need to ascertain the recipient's capacity to convert the money into desirable objectives. Administrators often become evasive, unco-operative, deceptive, and corrupt. Funds that are desperately needed at the grassroots and that could be delivered by the tried and tested NGOs simply choke government agencies.

In Africa, with its particular history of top-down administration, democratization of government is a precondition for meaningful development. Colonial rule was elitist and centralist, with power percolating through a tightly controlled hierarchy of administrators of the central will. Then Africa was blessed with great leaders, patriots, and freedom fighters. But these founding fathers of independent post-colonial states were concerned with national liberation, not personal freedom. Human rights and the dignity of the individual were not high on their agendas. On the contrary, faced with the task of holding together the rickety diversities bequeathed to them by their colonial predecessors, as a rule these national liberators readily resorted to the same elitist and centralist models they had fought to remove. In addition, the continent was (and still is) ravaged by wars, which destroyed the material and human infrastructure essential for survival and development. Governments increasingly introduced repressive measures of central enforcement and human rights remained a chimera. Proposition number seven must therefore be in the form of a warning: generally, the climate in 'developing' Africa is not sympathetic to civil rights and individual freedoms.

To an extent, the intervention of foreign agencies has nudged several countries in the direction of democracy. A non-violent, free, and fair electoral process with honest attempts at ballots is indispensable, but the process itself is not enough. Likewise, a legislative assembly with a speaker and rules of procedure does not suffice; neither do formal courts with bewigged judges. These aspects by themselves do not ensure a genuine democracy.

One applauds the creation, under the NEPAD Protocol, of the African Peer Review Mechanism (APRM) to measure the performance of participating governments against a set of norms for good political and economic governance. The problem is that the mechanism and the standards are vague, the sanctions are imprecise; the reciprocal assessment of governments is done by politicians and the technocrats in government.

The assessment feature permeates the basic fabric of NEPAD, underscoring what its skilled and dedicated initiators have learned from Africa's troubled history. Like most prior development plans in Africa, no role is allocated to the people. The APRM makes no mention of the elements of civil society that will ultimately bear the consequences if the dream of pan-African development fails.

The approach, again, is that of a top-down intergovernmental operation, channeling all resources through, and conferring all significant authority on, central governments. Involvement and mobilization of special interest groups would enhance the prospects of success. These groups include women's groups, trade unions, professional associations, churches, chambers of commerce, and youth organizations.

The process should also involve mechanisms for ensuring transparency and accountability. The present form of the APRM allows for too much intergovernmental latitude to provide a meaningful guarantee of governmental compliance. Recent experience with the rulers of delinquent regimes suggests that criticism from the opposition is unlikely. Broadly speaking, proposition number eight is that NEPAD, and, more particularly, good governance, requires eliminating the potential for mutual back scratching.

States should consider affording a role in the implementation and policing of the APRM to national legislatures and judiciaries. This can serve as a stepping-stone towards full involvement of civil society in what is civil society's business. Reform that leaves the people behind cannot be democratic and is unlikely to succeed.

One last area of African society should be considered in the context of democratic reform: traditional authorities, which are a common feature in most, if not all, countries in southern and West Africa and directly affect the daily lives of tens of millions of people. Political discourse generally ignores traditional authorities, and reformers generally denigrate these vestiges of pre-colonial social and political structures as outmoded and reactionary. This criticism has some truth to it, and colonial governors (and some modern politicians) have perverted these structures to their own ends. The local government level also has an unavoidable tension between the power and status of duly elected public representatives and traditional authorities. Before a serious claim of democratic reform can be made and before the continent can be said to have addressed its socio-economic and political problems comprehensively, this vital societal component needs to be included. Basic proposition nine is that traditional leadership can be a powerful agent for good or for evil and should not be ignored in development planning.

3

JOEL D. BARKAN
Democracy in Africa:
What Future?

Government is like a T-shirt. If you do not change it from time to time, it begins to stink!

(A Ghanaian taxi driver commenting
on the outcome of the 2001 election)

A decade ago, seasoned observers of African politics, including Larry Diamond and Richard Joseph, argued that the continent was on the cusp of its 'second liberation' (Diamond, 1992, 1993). The rising popular demand for political reform across Africa, the holding of multi-party elections, the alternation of power in several countries, and negotiations for a new political framework in South Africa led these scholars to conclude that the prospects for democracy were high. Today, these same observers are not so sure. They describe the current democratization experience in terms of *electoral democracy*, *virtual democracy*, or *illiberal democracy*, instead of the real article, and are far more cautious about predicting the future (Joseph, 1998). What is the reality? Has the process of democratization in Africa stalled? Where is Africa heading in respect to further democratic change?

African Governance before the 1990s

The first liberation in Africa was the transition from colonial to independent rule that swept the continent, except in the south, between 1957 and 1964. In the perspective of the West, the process of decolonization was supposed to have been a transition to democratic rule (Apter, 1958). It established more than 40 new states with democratic constitutions, following the holding of multi-party elections for new African-led governments. The regimes established by this process soon collapsed or reverted to authoritarian rule, a process which Samuel Huntington has termed a 'reverse wave' of democratization (Huntington, 1991). By the mid-1960s, military coups in roughly half of all African countries had toppled the elected governments.

In the remainder countries, elected regimes degenerated into one-party rule in what became a familiar scenario. The political parties that embodied the nationalist movement and won large majorities in elections held immediately before independence formed the first governments of the new states. Leaders of these parties then destroyed or marginalized the opposition through a combination of carrots and sticks. The result was a series of clientelist regimes that were the instruments for neo-patrimonial or personal rule by the likes of Mobutu Sesse Seko in the former Zaire, Daniel Moi in Kenya, and Paul Biya in

Cameroon. Parties built their regimes around a political boss, rather than a strong party apparatus and a coherent program or ideology (Jackson and Rosberg, 1982; Bayart, 1993; Bratton and van de Walle, 1997).

This pattern and its military variant, such as Sani Abacha in Nigeria, became the model pattern of African governance from the mid-1960s until the early 1990s. Both depended on a continuous and increasing flow of patronage and 'slush' money for their survival, as little else bound these regimes together. This situation, which I call inflationary patronage, gave rise to unprecedented levels of corruption, unsustainable macroeconomic policies (persistent budget and current account deficits), and state decay, especially through decline in the civil service and in the delivery of social services. It is a structural and normative legacy with which most African governments still struggle, and is why the process of democratization, especially democratic consolidation and the emergence of liberal democracy, has been a halting one (for example, in Nigeria).

A Decade of Democratization?

The second liberation began in 1991 with the historic multi-party election in Benin which resulted in the defeat of the incumbent president, and Malawi and Zambia replicated this process the same year. These elections raised expectations, held out the prospect of restoring democracy, and improved governance across the continent. By the end of 2000, all but five (Comoros, Congo-Kinshasa, Equatorial Guinea, Rwanda, and Somalia) of sub-Saharan Africa's 47 states had held multi-party elections.

Together with the new states of the former Soviet Union, Africa became the last region to be swept in the so-called 'Third Wave' of democratization. And like many of the successor states of the former Soviet Union, the record has been mixed. In marked contrast to the democratic transitions that occurred during the 1970s and '80s in Southern and Eastern Europe and in Latin America (excluding Mexico), most transitions in Africa have *not* been marked by the breakthrough of a founding election that brought a definitive end to an authoritarian regime and a group of political reformers to power. While this has been the pattern in a small number of states, most notably in Benin and South Africa, the more typical pattern has been a process of protracted transition (Barkan, 2000) – a mix of electoral democracy and political liberalization combined with elements of authoritarian rule and, more fundamentally, the perpetuation of clientelist rule.

In this context, politics is a struggle between three types of protagonists: (i) *incumbent authoritarians* attempting to retain power by permitting greater liberalization and elections, combined with the selective allocation of patronage to those who remain loyal; (ii) *insurgents*, who seek the spoils of office via electoral means (i.e. 'patronage seekers'); and (iii) *reformers* committed to establishing democratic rule as well as structurally reforming the state and the economy. The boundaries often blur between the incumbent authoritarians and the insurgents, and between the insurgents and the reformers. The level of cohesion among these groups is usually low. Political alignments are usually very fluid. The consolidation of a liberal democracy is therefore unlikely until a significant number of reformers ascend to power. Even in countries where reformers have come to power, as in South Africa, in Benin under Soglo, and most recently in Kenya under Mwai Kibaki, the patronage seekers constitute a significant minority, and the contest between them and the reformers continues after an election. The challenge of reformist governments is to balance genuine moves towards reform, while distributing some minimum level of patronage in the form of jobs or contracts to keep the new coalition intact.

The result is what Tom Carothers (2002) has termed a 'gray zone' of politics – countries with limited progress towards democracy beyond elections and countries where, if the consolidation of democracy does occur, it unfolds over a long period, perhaps decades. This does not necessarily mean that the third wave of democratization is over in Africa. Rather, we should expect the transition to be similar to those that occurred in India or Mexico. In India, the party that led the country to independence did not lose an election for three decades, and the periodic alternation of power between the parties did not occur for four decades. In Mexico, the end of one-party rule and its replacement by an opposition party committed to democratic principles played out over five elections spanning thirteen years, rather than in a single founding election. This pattern appears in Africa, as incumbent authoritarians have returned to power in two-thirds of founding and second elections, but each iteration of the electoral process usually results in an incremental though significant advance in developing civil society, 'fairness' of elections, and an overall liberalization of the political process.

Most African polities fall into the 'gray zone,' as confirmed by the *Freedom in the World* annual survey (Freedom House, 2002). Of the 47 states that comprise sub-Saharan Africa, the survey classified 23 as 'partly free' with respect to the extent of their political freedoms and civil liberties. It classified only 8 (Benin, Botswana, Cape Verde, Ghana, Mali, Mauritius, Namibia, and South Africa) as 'free', while it deemed 16, including 5 war-torn societies (Burundi, Congo-Kinshasa, Liberia, Sierra Leone, and Sudan) as 'not free'.

The overall picture revealed by these numbers is sobering: less than a fifth of all the countries are classified as 'free,' and of these, only two or three (Botswana, Mauritius, and perhaps South Africa) are consolidated democracies. On the other hand, if one excludes states mired in civil war, a fifth are 'free', and a fifth 'not free', while three-fifths fall in between. Most states, the four-fifths of those not enmeshed in civil war, are 'partly-free' or 'free'. This is a significant advance on their condition a decade ago. Only a handful are consolidated democracies, but few are the harsh dictatorships that dominated Africa from the mid-1960s to the beginning of the 1990s. As noted by E. Gyimah-Boadi, an astute Ghanaian observer of democratization on the continent, 'Illiberalism has persisted, but is not on the rise. Authoritarianism is alive in Africa today, but is not well' (Gyimah-Boadi, 1998).

Optimists vs. Realists: Two Shades of Gray

Since the status of democracy in the continent varies greatly from one country to the next, one should resist generalizing all 47 states of sub-Saharan Africa. One size does not fit all. Notwithstanding this reality, those who track events in Africa have divided themselves into two distinct camps in generalizing about the continent: optimists and realists (or, as others might say, Afropologists and Afropessimists).

OPTIMISTS

Those who take an optimistic view include US government officials responsible for Africa, especially former members of the Clinton administration; those involved in efforts to promote democratization abroad; members of the Congressional Black Caucus; and the staff of some Africa-oriented non-governmental organizations. Optimists trumpet the fact that nearly 90 per cent of all African states have held multi-party elections. They note that most African countries have held competitive elections twice, and that some, including Benin, Ghana, Kenya, Senegal, and Zambia, have held three elections, with at least one resulting in a change of government. The optimists further note that election quality has improved in some countries, with respect to the efficiency of electoral administration and, more significantly, with respect to being 'free and fair'. Electoral commissions seem to be more independent, even-handed and professional in their administration of recent elections than in the early 1990s. Opposition candidates and parties have greater freedom to campaign, and suffer less harassment from incumbent governments. The presence of election observers, both foreign and domestic, is now widely accepted as part of the process. Perhaps most significant, citizen participation has been fairly high, if not spectacular, averaging just under two-thirds of registered voters (Bratton, 1998).

Recognizing that elections are a necessary but insufficient requisite for the consolidation of democracy, the optimists also point to significant changes in eight related spheres. First, the re-emergence, proliferation, and maturation of civil society organizations after their systematic suppression during the era of single-party and military rule. Second, the re-emergence of an independent and free press, including the privatization of the broadcast media in a number of countries. Third, a rising assertiveness of the legislature to play a larger role in the policy-making process and to exercise greater oversight of the executive branch. Fourth, the strengthening of the judiciary and the rule of law in some countries, including Tanzania (Widner, 2001); human rights abuses, in both their number and degree, have also declined, except in countries wracked by civil war. Fifth, countries have experimented with federalism through the delegation or devolution of authority from the central government to local authorities in order to enhance governmental accountability to the public and to diffuse the potential for ethnic conflict (most notably in Nigeria, but also in Ethiopia, Ghana, Tanzania, Uganda, and South Africa).

Sixth, members of the governing elite show a more rapid circulation than during the era of authoritarian rule. In country after country, the iterative holding of multi-party elections has resulted in a significant turnover of members of the national legislature and local government bodies, which is often as high as 50 per cent (far higher than in the US). While the quality of elected officials at the local level remains poor, members of the national legislature appear to be younger, better educated, and more sophisticated in their approach to politics than the older generation they have displaced. Although further research is needed to confirm any sea change in the composition of these bodies, it would also appear that new MPs are more likely than their predecessors to be democratic reformers focusing on public policy issues and less likely to be patronage seekers (Barkan, 2000, 2003). This group is also more active than their predecessors in asserting the legislature's independence vis-à-vis the executive and in seeking to strengthen the committee system.

Seventh, some countries, such as Kenya and perhaps Nigeria, are experiencing the coming to power, usually at the second echelon of power, of a new generation of African leaders. This is a new age cohort of political activists, and should *not* be confused with the so-called 'New Leaders of Africa' about which much ink was spilled in the early and mid-1990s, and who represented a new breed of authoritarian rulers in Africa, one that embraces macroeconomic reform and curtails human rights abuse but is not democratic.[1] They were economic reformers, not political reformers, and all have been (or were) in power for more than a decade. By contrast, the new generation of African leaders is just that – an emerging group of individuals in their early thirties to mid-forties whose presence was not apparent as recently as the 1990s. Some members in this group won elections to the national legislature and represent the new breed of parliamentarians mentioned above.

Others have assumed leadership positions in civil society organizations that are qualitatively different from the initial manifestation of civil society that began the process of democratic reform. In the late 1980s and early '90s, nearly all civil society organizations that ventured into the political arena were urban-based and concerned mainly with opening up the political space. These were human rights organizations and organizations concerned with promoting the rule of law, such as election observer organizations. By contrast, the new generation of civil society leaders is more interested in taking advantage of the political space won by transforming civil society into the political process or by organizations that seek to influence the content of public policy. They are interest groups similar to those found in established democracies, groups that organize to promote the economic or professional interests of their members. Interest-based organizations are beginning to emerge in the countryside, like cocoa farmers in Ghana and coffee and tea farmers in Kenya. The new generation of leaders is also prominent in invigorating the press and professional organizations, such as those for lawyers and accountants.

Finally, public opinion across Africa appears to prefer democracy to authoritarian alternatives. Surveys undertaken for the Afrobarometer project in 12 African countries between 1999 and 2001 found that 69 per cent of the respondents regarded democracy as 'preferable to any other kind of government', while only 12 per cent agreed with the proposition that 'in certain situations, a non-democratic government can be preferable'. Moreover, 58 per cent of all respondents stated that they were 'fairly satisfied' or 'very satisfied' with the 'way democracy works' in their country (Afrobarometre, 2001). Like the Ghanaian cab driver quoted at the beginning of this chapter, most if not all Africans now believe that democracy is 'the only game in town'. Internalizing the value of democracy is essential for its consolidation (Linz and Stepan, 1996).

REALISTS

Realists take a far more cautious view of what is occurring on the continent. They are mainly critics of what they contend was a moralistic approach to US foreign policy during the Clinton administration because it often (though not consistently) stressed democratization as a foreign policy goal. They are also critical of those engaged in democracy promotion and the 'industry' that has emerged to nurture democracy abroad. Realists, correctly, put less emphasis on elections and more emphasis on the nature of political life between them.

When considering the quality of elections plus the same eight developments that optimists cite as examples of democratic advancement, realists note that all are present in less than a half-dozen countries. They also see much less progress than optimists do in regard to any of the eight spheres when considered individually. First, holding regular multi-party elections across the continent has resulted in alternating the government in only one-third of the countries that have held elections. Moreover, only about half of these elections are regarded as 'free and fair', with those who lost accepting the results. It is also debatable whether recent elections have been of a higher quality than those held in the early 1990s (Bratton, 1998); a few have, but many have not.

Second, the re-emergence of civil society and the press is a significant advance on the era of authoritarian rule, when the government barely tolerated or systematically suppressed both. But civil society remains very weak in Africa compared with other regions, and is concentrated in the urban areas. Political parties are especially weak, and rarely differentiate themselves from one another on the basis of ideology or policy. Apart from the church and the presence of farmer organizations and/or community self-help groups in a smattering of countries (Kenya, Côte d'Ivoire, Ghana, Nigeria, and South Africa), civil society barely exists in rural areas, which is where most of the population reside.

Third, the press, especially the print media, is similarly concentrated in the urban areas, and thus reaches a relatively small proportion of the entire population. Only the broadcast media penetrates the countryside, but it is largely state-owned. Although private broadcasting, especially TV and FM radio, has grown in recent years, stations cater almost exclusively to an urban and peri-urban audience. With few exceptions, AM and short and/or medium wave broadcasting is the chief means of informing the rural population and remains a state monopoly.

Fourth, while the legislature holds out the promise of becoming an institution of countervailing power in some countries, it remains weak and has yet to exercise an effective check on executive power. Fifth, the judicial system in most countries also remains weak, either because it lacks capacity (too few magistrates and poor infrastructure to keep pace with the number of cases to be tried), and/or because of corrupt members. Human rights abuses also continue without judicial intervention, though less frequently and with less intensity than a decade earlier. Sixth, only a small number of states have attempted to experiment with federalism, though experimentation is promising and clearly on the rise.

Seventh, while the circulation of political elites has increased with elections, this may contribute not to consolidating democracy but instead to instability in the political system. High turnover in the legislature may also lessen efforts to strengthen this institution. The emergence of a new age cohort of younger leaders as both aspiring politicians and civil society leaders is apparent in only a minority of countries (Kenya and South Africa). Finally, the extent to which Africans have internalized democratic values is hard to judge. Although the Afrobarometer surveys indicate broad support for democracy, the results also suggest that such support is shallow – 'a mile wide and an inch deep' (Bratton, 1998). Only 23 per cent of the respondents in each country described their country as 'completely democratic' (ibid.).

ASSESSMENT OF POSITIONS

Both optimists and realists are correct in their assessments; but how can both views be valid? The answer is that both present only one side of the story. On a continent where the record of democratization is one of partial advance in over half of the cases, those assessing progress towards democracy or the lack of it tend to dwell on either what the countries have accomplished or they have yet to achieve. These diverging assessments are proverbial examples of those who view the glass of water as 'half-full' compared to those who see it as 'half-empty'. Optimists and realists also draw their conclusions from slightly different samples. Whereas optimists focus mainly on states that are 'partly free' or 'free', realists concentrate on states that are 'partly free' or 'not free'.

The perspectives of both optimists and realists are valid, as there are several Africas rather than one. Indeed, at least five Africas cut across the three broad categories in the Freedom House survey. Each of these five Africas presents a different context for analyzing the pursuit of democracy:

(i) States with a *consolidated democracy* or a *semi-consolidated democracy*. This is a much smaller group of states than those classified as free, and currently consists of only two or three cases, Botswana, Mauritius, and perhaps South Africa.

(ii) *Aspiring democracies*, consisting of approximately 15 countries, including the remaining five the Freedom House classifies as 'free' but which are not yet consolidated democracies and roughly 10 classified as 'partly free' but their transition to democracy has not stalled. All these states have made slow but continuous progress towards a more liberal and institutionalized form of democratic politics. Included in the group are Benin, Ghana, Kenya, Mali and Senegal, and possibly Madagascar, Malawi, Nigeria, Tanzania and Zambia.

(iii) *Semi-authoritarian states*, which are those classified as 'partly free' but their transition to democracy has stalled. This category also consists of approximately 13 members, such as Uganda, the Central African Republic and Zimbabwe.

(iv) *Authoritarian regimes*, which are states that are 'not free' and have little or no prospect of a democratic transition in the near future. About 10 countries make up this group, such as Angola, Cameroon, Chad, Eritrea, Ethiopia, Rwanda and Togo.

(v) *States mired in civil war* or those that can easily slip back into war – Burundi, Congo, Liberia, Sierra Leone, Sudan and perhaps Côte d'Ivoire.

Conditions Inhibiting Democratization

A number of conditions peculiar to the continent make Africa a difficult place in which to sustain democratic practice, and explain why Africa lags behind other regions in the extent of its democratic advancement. These conditions also explain why political party organizations are weak, and why leaders and followers usually base their ties on clientelist relationships between patrons and members of their entourage. They create pressure for more patronage, a situation that undermines electoral accountability and leads to corrupt practice.

First, Africa is the poorest of the world's principal regions, with per capita income averaging $490 per year (World Bank, 2000a: 19). This condition does not affect the emergence of democracy, but does affect its sustainability (Przeworski et al., 1996). On average, democracies with per capita incomes of less than $1,000 last eight and a half years, while those with per capita incomes of over $6,000 endure for 99 years or more. The reasons for this are straightforward. Relatively wealthy states are in a much better position to allocate some of their resources to most or all groups making claims on them, while poor states are not. The result is that politics in poor countries is more likely to be a zero-sum game, a pattern that does not foster bargaining and compromise between competing interests, nor a willingness to play by democratic rules.

Second, almost all African countries remain agrarian societies. With few exceptions such as South Africa, Gabon, and Nigeria, 65–90 per cent of the population reside in the rural areas where most of them are peasant farmers. Most Africans consequently maintain strong attachments to their local place of residence and to fellow citizens in their community. Norms of reciprocity shape social relations to a much greater degree than in industrial urban societies. In this context, Africans usually define their political interests, that is to say, their interests as citizens vis-à-vis the state, in terms of where they live and their affective ties to their neighbors rather than basing them on their occupation or socioeconomic class. With few exceptions (Botswana and Somalia), African countries are multi-ethnic societies where each group inhabits a distinct territorial homeland. The fact that residents of different areas are often members of different ethnic groups or sub-groups accentuates the tendency of Africans to define their political interests in terms of where they live.

Third, the African state provides a much larger proportion of wage employment, particularly middle-class employment, compared with states in other regions. Few countries have a middle class that is not dependent on the state for its own employment and reproduction. In this context, people view and seek political office for the resources it confers – for one's own personal consumption and/or for one's clients' consumption, which thus enhances one's own status. In the words of a well-known Nigerian party slogan, 'I chop, you chop', which literally means, 'I eat, you eat' (Bayart, 1993).

Likely Scenarios/What Future?

Given these realities, what is the future for further democracy on the continent? The answer varies greatly by type of polity. Over the next decade, the small handful of states currently classified as consolidated or semi-consolidated democracies are likely to gain a small number (perhaps up to half a dozen) of additional members. This category, however, will remain the smallest of the five Africas, if for no other reason than the limited number of people that a party can realistically consider as candidate members. These include countries classified as 'free' in the Freedom House surveys, but which have yet to experience a turnover, especially a double turnover, of elected government. Indeed, even

Botswana and South Africa have yet to pass this test.

Within the current category of aspiring democracies, one can reasonably expect a process of further political liberalization and the growth of civil society including the emergence of interest group politics to challenge and cut across the continuation of clientelist politics. Civil society can also better organize itself in the countryside. The legislature and judiciary are likely to become stronger and more independent institutions. The amount of electoral turnover of government will increase, if for no other reason than that some countries like Kenya, Tanzania and Zambia have adopted term limits at the presidential level. Some members of this category will be promoted to the consolidated democracy category. All or nearly all should see improvements in their performance.

Among semi-authoritarian states where democratization has stalled, the prospects for progress are much lower. This Africa also consists of approximately 13 polities, all of which are in the lower range of the 'partly free' category. As a result, there is a limited amount of political space open in these polities for the growth of civil society and the press, as well as for electoral politics. One should not write off this category. Rather, one should acknowledge that democratization in these states will be a particularly protracted process.

Prospects for the fourth and fifth Africas, states classified as authoritarian regimes of the old school and those mired in civil war, are obviously the least promising. The immediate challenges in authoritarian countries are halting human rights abuses and beginning a meaningful political liberalization, which are the first steps towards democratization. The first challenge in countries mired in civil war is obviously to stop the fighting and reconstitute the state. State decay is probably the biggest problem for these two groups, and it must be addressed before any genuine democratization process can begin.

In conclusion, one can be cautiously optimistic about democratization prospects in one-third to one-half of the states on the continent, but one must be realistic about the prospects in the remainder, especially those in the bottom third. Future progress is likely to be incremental and played out over a period of at least a decade or more.[2] Moreover, progress will not occur on a linear basis through a series of well-defined stages, but will be uneven and halting. This is because further progress, especially in the third Africa of semi-authoritarian states and, to a limited extent, the fourth Africa, will be an outcome of the continuous three-cornered struggle between authoritarians, patronage seekers, and true reformers. One must also expect some erosion and/or reversals among states currently regarded as semi-consolidated democracies and aspiring ones.

Finally, it is important that US policy-makers and those in other established democracies that seek to support the process appreciate these constraints and are honest about the varied nature of the challenge. The most difficult task is to nurture the process in states in the third and fourth categories. Indeed, the tendency is to over-celebrate progress in the first and second Africas, while retreating from the challenge in the third and fourth categories. Such an approach, however, will undermine both the accomplishments to date and the prospects for further democratic advancement. Foreign policy critics who stress democracy should reflect on the fact that the development of Western democratic systems evolved over more than a century. While one can appreciate the sense of impatience among many realists, this is no time to walk away from the Ugandas and Zimbabwes, no matter how halting the process may be.

Conclusion

Staying the course in support of protracted transitions is also the most realistic approach to both democratic development and rebuilding weak states, as the recent experience of Kenya makes clear. In an era when the defeat of terrorism has become the prime objective of US foreign policy, the retreat from support for democratic development and the forming of alliances with incumbent authoritarians resembles US African policy during the Cold War. In the context of contemporary Africa, however, such an approach is unlikely to work. Terrorists establish havens in failed or weak states (Afghanistan and Somalia), not in strong ones. Building strong and accountable states in the context of open and democratic societies is the most effective way of denying such havens.

Notes

[1] The label was usually applied to Jerry Rawlings of Ghana, Meles Zanawi of Ethiopia, Afewerki Issyas of Eritrea, and Paul Kagame of Rwanda, all of whom came to power through a military coup or insurgency. All subsequently donned civilian clothes and 'won' elections that were neither completely 'free' or 'fair'.
[2] Ghana and Kenya are two good examples.

4

ANN SEIDMAN & ROBERT B. SEIDMAN

Legal Drafting for Democratic Social Change & Development

AFTER Africa's nations won independence, newly installed populist governors sat in the seats of power. They ruled through the old, inherited institutions that were authoritarian, non-developmental, and frequently racist, and unless they cannily exercised their power to modify those institutions to facilitate development, nothing would change. At independence, a fatal race emerged as to which would change the other first: the new governors or the old institutions?

In most, if not all African countries, governments did introduce new laws giving discretion to administrators to build new schools, roads, and hospitals – even to set up new industries – to fulfil their people's basic needs. A decade or so later, as economic crises deepened, these governments, seeking to restore the market's invisible hand, cut back sharply on development spending and privatized state industries. Unemployment mounted. As their living standards sank below poverty levels, more and more Africans struggled for bare survival. Everywhere, the new governors faced accusations of corruption, the misuse of state power to benefit themselves and their cronies. The old institutions appeared to have won the fatal race – hands down.

For some scholars, this failure seemed to confirm the prophecies of the 'Deadlock of Law and Development.' The new nations confronted a paradox. On the one hand, law – when used properly – must provide stability and predictability in social relations. As Dicey famously proclaimed, predictability abhors government officials' exercise of discretion. The rule of law requires bright line rules that dictate precisely how those officials must behave (Hayek, 1944). *Per contra*, development requires social transformations, and these require entrepreneurship, creativity, and experimentation (Dresang, 1971) – everything to which, these nay-sayers claim, law stands unalterably opposed. These theorists seemed to insist that a country might have law, or it might have development – but not simultaneously. Their dire predictions seemed to be even worse: without the rule of law, governments aiming to develop descended into the pits of corruption. African efforts to induce development through law appeared to be impossible, thus defining Africa's apparent law and development deadlock.[1]

This chapter denies the existence of this deadlock. It argues that Africa's governors did not lose the fatal race because they tried to reshape the institutions through law. They lost it partly because they did not understand that, to carry out development, institutional transformation constituted their principal task (and as a result they attempted precious little institutional change), and partly because those leaders who occasionally did try to transform institutions had no theory to guide them in their use of law.

This chapter proposes a legislative theory and methodology to guide the instrumental use of law and the legal order to facilitate the institutional changes required to foster development, and procedures designed to resolve Africa's seeming deadlock. Using legislative theory's problem-solving methodology (see below, Box 4.2),[2] the chapter begins by describing the social problem as to how Africa's new governors apparently lost the fatal race.

I: Africa's Multiple Agonies: Poverty, Vulnerability, and Poor Governance

The process of solving a social problem begins by describing the nature and scope of the problem's superficial appearance. This section first characterizes African poverty, dependency and poor governance. It then demonstrates that what superficially appears as a problem in resource allocation in fact reflects the role of problematic institutions. Finally, it briefly reviews the way African governments initially sought to use law to address the overriding obstacles to development.

POVERTY, DEPENDENCY, AND RESOURCE ALLOCATION

Figure 4.1 models the distorted resource allocations that define Africa's massive poverty, and its continuing dependence on the developed world (Seidman and Seidman, 1994: 28). As in the colonial era, in most post-independence African countries a wealthy minority, often associated with transnational corporate enterprises, employed low-cost labor to produce and export Africa's mineral and agricultural products to developed country markets. African workers, seeking to escape neglected hinterlands, worked for a quarter or less of the wages paid for comparable work in the industrialized countries of the North (Seidman, 1990: 133b). As the twentieth century drew to an end, a few variations on the colonial pattern emerged. A tiny handful of industries employed unskilled workers to

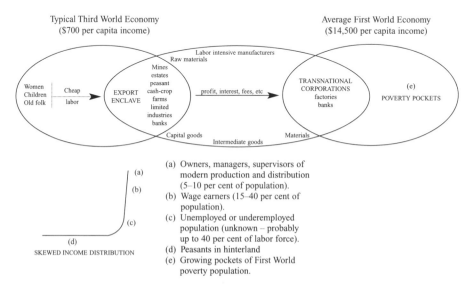

Figure 4.1 The Fried Egg Model

assemble and process cheap consumer exports – shoes, textiles, even last-stage assembly of imported parts for radios and automobiles – importing the machinery, equipment, parts and materials. After independence, homegrown African elites still bought imported luxury consumer items: cars, television sets, and even clothing (Seidman and Seidman, 1994).

Although the value of some countries' exports exceeded that of their imports, almost every year African countries paid out, in the form of high-priced imports, profits, interest, dividends, and 'invisible exports' (like insurance, shipping costs, and capital flight), more than they earned. For many, if not most, net capital outflows still exceed net inflows (see IMF, *International Financial Statistics*). Africa's poor majority still struggled for survival at the mercy of the rich and powerful, vulnerable to pestilence, drought, and brutal ethnic conflicts.

Africa's rich resources, however, never did (and do not now) misallocate themselves. Instead, social, economic, and political institutions, inherited from a century and more of colonial rule, defined the scope and nature of these distortions.

INSTITUTION AND RESOURCE ALLOCATION

A country's institutions define it (March and Olsen, 1989: 2). Understanding a country's institutions is integral to understanding the processes of development (ibid., n. 12; Sjostrand, 1993: 9–12). An institution consists of a set, or interrelated set, of repetitive patterns of social behaviors (Homans, 1967: 507; Uphoff, 1986: 9).[3] A bank counts as an *institution* not because it has a brass plate on its door, but because of the repetitive patterns of behaviors of its tellers, sweepers, president, secretaries, and other functionaries. In Africa, the inherited banking institutions' several repetitive patterns of behaviors combined to ship Africa's surpluses overseas, instead of directing them to investment within the continent, and to make loans to multinational corporations and large farmers, instead of to peasants. Thus Africa's banks contributed to the continent's dependence and poverty.

Other institutions combined to perpetuate many, if not most, African countries' deplorably poor governance: corrupt officials, inefficient sewage and water systems, roads that sometimes did not last through the first rains, and a court system rife with bribery. To change the way in which an African country's institutions reinforced its dependency, perpetuated its poor governance, and impoverished (and still impoverish) its people, its governors must find a way to change its inherited institutions' dysfunctional patterns of social behaviors. To lead the way to development, a government must use the legal order to transform the institutions that together cause its people's impoverishment.[4]

II: The Role of Law in African Development

Africa's new governors came to power promising to use state power to improve their people's lives. The first sub-section below explains why they turned to the law as their instrument of change; the second characterizes (in heroically general terms – Africa is, after all, a big place) – the kinds of laws they enacted; the third describes the methodologies the new law-makers typically adopted to design those laws' *details*.

WHY LAW AS THE INSTRUMENT OF DIRECTED SOCIAL CHANGE?
As their instrument of choice to bring about behavioral change, *every* government turns to the law for at least three reasons:

First, for very practical reasons governors must use *rules* to communicate their prescriptions to public employees and the general public. In every government larger than a tiny village, a few governors must induce a large number of public employees and the general public to behave in prescribed ways. Inducing that behavior constitutes the very essence of governing. By putting its prescriptions into the form of rules, governments communicate the behaviors prescribed to their addressees.

Second, positive law's so-called *ultra vires* rule holds that a public official may not so much as lift an official little finger unless authorized by a law. To ensure that officials implemented their policies, Africa's governors had to enact them in the form of law.

Third, at its core, the rule of law prescribes a government, not of men, but of *laws*. To give themselves and their policies legitimacy in the public eye, governors express publicly avowed policies not only in speeches and exhortations but also in *law*. To govern, Africa's new governors had no choice but to use law to induce desired new behaviors. Yet strangely, in most countries, they enacted precious few new laws.

How Africa's new governors exercised state power through law
Most newly independent African states initially used laws not to transform institutions, but to increase expenditures on social services – education, health, roads, and water supply. A few did try to create genuinely new institutions. Typically, they enacted laws that effectively granted broad discretion to administrative officers, frequently through government development corporations or analogous structures.

Expanding social services
The newly independent governors took office under laws deeply rooted in colonial practice. Every country's constitution or its earliest statute provided that, until amended or repealed, existing laws, the former colonial laws, remained in effect. The new constitutions changed the institutions that recruited and selected the governors, but introduced few other institutional changes (cf. Nzongola-Ntalaja, 1987).

Save at the fringes, most of the new rulers did not change the received laws (Makgetla and Seidman, 1987). In most African countries, even today, except for blatantly discriminatory laws, the principal laws remain as they existed during the colonial era. The courts still defer to English precedents in private law areas – torts, property, contracts, insurance, and commercial law. Civil service codes changed only incrementally. The penal codes remained all but untouched, as did the legal foundations for most government institutions – courts, ministries, and parliament. Four years after independence, the Speaker of Parliament in Zimbabwe still wore a wig and a gown; the clerk dressed in satin knickers, the high kick of fashion in eighteenth-century England. Twenty years after independence, Zambia's Price Control Law, except in insignificant details, remained unchanged from the colonial statute (Seidman and Seidman, 1994: 37–8).

Many governments did expand social services (ibid: chap. 15). They increased the number of available schools, but did not change the structure of the education system; some did not even change the syllabuses of the colonial era. They improved curative health care for Africans, but, ignoring most professionals' advice, did not change the colonial institutions' propensity to spend most public health money on curative, rather than more efficient preventive, health care.

Few did anything to change the economic institutions that kept most Africans chained to unmechanized agriculture. The continued export of raw materials, coupled with limited industrial growth, drained investable surpluses abroad. In the former settler colonies, obscene divisions persisted between rich (mainly white) and poor (all black). Few laws were enacted to expand domestic trade and productive employment in a more balanced economy. Save at the margins, land tenure systems, banks and other financial institutions, or the trading systems that maintained dependence on crude agricultural and mineral exports to uncertain global markets, were rarely restructured. Even when the mines were nationalized (as in Zambia), the shares of the foreign companies were merely taken over and the old management left to operate the mines – much as before nationalization (Seidman, 1975; for other examples, see Seidman and Seidman, 1994: chaps 9–14).

Because the new governments failed to restructure law-making and law-implementing institutions to ensure the transparency, accountability and participation required for good governance, officials still, as in the colonial era, made arbitrary and increasingly corrupt decisions (for early examples, see Diamond, 1987; O'Brien, 1975). Too often, in Africa, as throughout the developing world, people lamented, 'We have good laws, but poor implementation' (Seidman et al., 2001: 125).

As a consequence of the increased competition resulting from the expansion in exports from other developing countries, their terms of trade worsened and African governments borrowed heavily overseas. By the late 1980s and '90s, most found themselves overwhelmed by foreign debt. Promising rescue, the international financial institutions (IFIs) dictated that they adopt neoliberal economic policies that relied on the market as the universal cure-all. Currency values fell; inflation soared; subsidies for social services dried up, and, in time, so did social services (Seidman and Seidman, 1994: chaps 14, 15).

Working in largely unchanged institutions, many bureaucrats continued to behave as they always had. In Zimbabwe, immediately after independence, the new Minister of Transport instructed his civil servants to prepare a ten-year road plan to provide access to the hitherto neglected African population. After some months, they produced a plan with not a single new road leading to unserved African communities. When the Minister inquired, the civil servants explained that existing regulations determined what new roads the Ministry might build; they had conscientiously applied these regulations and their formulas for estimated traffic, economic effect, and so on. Unsurprisingly, not a single African community qualified for a new road – after all, the former white, colonial administration had designed these regulations (interview with Minister, 1980). Multiply that by all the colonial regulations that, despite independence, continued to shape civil service behaviors throughout the continent!

Development corporations and analogous institutions

Some new African governments, frequently in the name of 'socialism,' did introduce laws which aspired to transform the productive system, but still used the legal forms of the colonial era, which, like those that established colonial development corporations and marketing boards in Kenya, Uganda, and Tanganyika (Ghai, 1977), granted considerable official discretion to aid settler enterprise. In Kenya, for example, a colonial industrial development corporation law of 1954 aimed to stimulate industrialization by providing 'soft' loans to colonialist (white) entrepreneurs.[5] In 1967, the newly independent Kenyan government revised the law to establish the Industrial and Commercial Development Corporation, and used it to help create a new black bourgeoisie (Amin, 1987). The new populist governments used both public corporations and government-owned shares in private corporations to take over and change the thrust of colonial corporations, and to start a clutch of new ones: marketing boards of all sorts, the National Construction Corporation,[6] the Transport Licensing Board, and the Kenya National Trading Company (1965), to name but a few.

Supposedly controlled by a government committed to a populist course, these so-called 'parastatals' served as the principal economic vehicles for implementing government policies. They acted mainly pursuant to private company law, which, transferred from imperial England to its former colony before the English had modernized it, required little transparency, accountability, and participation in the parastatal companies' decision-making (Gower, 1965). Indeed, governments typically justified the use of the company – either in its parastatal form or as an ordinary company with government-owned shares – to carry out government policy, rather than ministries, by explaining that it gave corporate managers the power to conduct business as they saw fit:

> We were giving this greater degree of managerial autonomy [to the public corporation managers] in order that we could get a higher degree of business efficiency and less red tape and bureaucracy.[7]

> The public corporation is based on the theory that a full measure of accountability can be imposed on a public authority without requiring that it be subject to ministerial control in respect of managerial decisions and multitudinous routine activities, or liable to comprehensive parliamentary scrutiny of its day-to-day working. The theory assumes that … a successful combination of political control and managerial freedom can be achieved by reserving certain powers of decision in matters of major importance to Ministers answerable to Parliament and leaving everything else to the discretion of the public corporation acting within its legal competency.[8]

As in Kenya, so elsewhere, populist governments appointed officials to run state corporations, assuming that they would use their discretionary powers to 'develop' the economy. These appointments invariably rested on the discretion of the appointing authority, usually a minister. As Kenya's experience illustrated, appointments to development corporations and marketing boards too often became sinecures for the deserving party faithful (Nowrojee, 1977: 175ff). In time – less time in some countries than others – the new corporate managers too often exercised their broad discretion, not in the public interest, but for their own power and wealth.[9]

For the vast majority of Africans, far from avoiding the impact of the economic crises of the 1980s and '90s, the institutions that were permitted to continue or that were introduced by the new governments perpetuated grinding poverty. They produced and reproduced miserable housing, poor education, non-existent health care, unending cold and hunger and pain, and unrewarded, unremitting labor. By the end of the century, median African incomes were reportedly lower than at the end of the colonial era.[10]

Thus the institutions won (and the people lost) the fatal race. Some academics argued that no other result could have occurred. Law, they said, far from being an instrument of social change, constitutes a conservative barrier against change. The contradiction between the imperatives of the law and the demands of development – demands for creativity, originality, entrepreneurship; in short, for discretion – inevitably led to the deadlock in law and development.

III: Why Did the Populist Leaders Fail to Deliver Development?

Africa's post-independence governments failed to enact laws to transform the received institutions in ways that produced either meaningful change or non-arbitrary governance. Why? To begin with, we discuss the widespread claim that, inherently, law cannot induce social change.

CAN LAW INDUCE DELIBERATE SOCIAL CHANGE?

Some authorities deny that law *can* induce deliberate social change, resting their claim on the plain fact that so few laws achieve their stated goals. This, they argue, reflects not accident (or lawmakers' inattention) but the reality that using law to induce social change *cannot* work (see Box 4.1). If law inherently cannot induce social change, law and development, of course, state a contradiction in terms; they stand in deadlock.

Box 4.1. Can Law Induce Social Change?
(Seidman et al.: 20–1)

Contrarian's Argument 1. Society makes law; law constitutes an artifact of society; law always drags behind society (Sawer, 1963; Reid, 1970). How can society's artifact change the society that made it?

An answer: 'Society' does not make law. Lawmakers make law. Within the limits of law, lawmakers can use law to bolster existing institutions, or to change them (Pound, 1942).

Contrarian's Argument 2. The ruling class controls both the law-making system and the economy. The ruling class will never introduce laws that disadvantage it (Williams, 1980: 255)

An answer: In every country's history, moments occur when *opponents* of the class that controls the economy control the law-making machinery. Immediately after the defeat of colonialism, in most African countries giant colonial companies still held controlling economic power. New populist parties held political power. These new parties had an opportunity to use law to change the inherited economic institutions. (Too often they failed, but this chapter argues that this reflected a lack of understanding of how to use law for democratic social change).

Contrarian's Argument 3. Law's function concerns dispute settlement. Laws declare rights and duties to instruct judges how to decide cases. Law has no function in behavioral change (Driedger, 1983).
An answer: Law has multiple functions. True, among them, it decides disputes. It also channels behaviors. In most countries, the education law does not have as its principal purpose dispute resolution, but rather to direct behaviors that are likely to produce and operate a school system. To facilitate development and transition, law has as its principal function inducing change in problematic social behaviors (Llewellyn, 1940).

Contrarian's Argument 4. The post-modern school of literary criticism – 'deconstructionism' – holds that a 'text' has no inherent meaning. A reader's own perceptions and values shape its meaning. A law's readers – its addressees – similarly interpret its text to suit their convenience without regard to what the law-drafter or the legislator intended (Singer, 1984).
An answer: Words constitute more than silly putty. Society exists because we can and do communicate with each other. We can draft a law sufficiently precisely to convey its core meaning to its addressees.

Contrarian's Argument 5. Only the rule's underlying political decision counts, not the technical process of stitching words together into a law. Design good policies, and legal technicians will draft good laws. Study policy, not law (Griffiths, 1976).
An answer: Of course a government must have sound policies. A policy, however, does not enforce itself. A lawmaker must ensure that a bill sufficiently translates a policy's generalities into the operative commands, prohibitions and permissions of the law.

Contrarian's Argument 6. Behaviors reflect multiple causes, of which the law constitutes only one. These causes interact in ways so complex that nobody can say whether or how law causes behavior. Unless one can do that, one cannot use law purposively. The law and development project becomes a mission impossible (Kidder, 1983).
An answer: Behavior never has a single, determinative cause (Seidman, 1978: chap 2; Chambliss, 1967: 703). In addition to a law's words, other non-legal factors influence behaviors. In assessing a bill, you must understand not only its words, but also the non-legal constraints and resources that influence its addressees' behaviors.

Everyday reality demonstrates that the contrarians' claims go too far. Sometimes, laws do work. Before an income tax law, nobody paid income tax. Without a national election law, people cannot vote in national elections. Sometimes laws do not work. In no country does a law forbidding sexual intercourse between unmarried people achieve 100 per cent conformity to its commands. The challenge remains to discover why some laws work, and others fail, and then to use that knowledge to write *effective* laws.[11]

WHY DRAFTERS FAILED TO DRAFT EFFECTIVE TRANSFORMATORY LAWS
This subsection argues that three interrelated factors contributed to African law-makers' seeming inability to draft, enact, and implement effective transformatory laws: (i) the received British legislative drafting myth; (ii) the unchanged nature of the drafting institutions of the executive branch (where most legislative proposals still originated); and (iii) the general ignorance of the new governments and the development community about how to produce laws to facilitate democratic social change.

THE DRAFTERS' IDEOLOGY
In Africa, in the crucial years immediately following independence when the fatal race still hung in the balance, almost all individuals who served as drafters were the same individuals (or their apprentices) who had drafted laws under the British. Without exception, every newly independent British colony came to Independence under a constitution negotiated as a settlement of the anti-colonial struggle. These constitutions in effect guaranteed continued employment of the remaining colonial civil servants – including the drafters, both in ministries and in the central drafting office. In Africa, as in Britain, these drafters had been trained almost entirely through an apprenticeship system, which indoctrinated the belief that drafters should focus on the form of legislation and its technical competence, not on its policy.

This ideology rested on two footings. First, for reasons that lay rooted in Britain's history of drafting,[12] central office drafters rejected the notion that they dealt with a bill's substance (Dickerson, 1986; Driedger, 1976; Ilbert, 1914; Russell, 1938; Thornton, 1987; Thring, 1902). Substance, they asserted, remained an aspect of 'policy' which the substantive ministry determined; central office drafters merely put into legal form the policy devised by ministry officials.

Derived from the analytical positivism of John Austin (1954), the second footing of the drafters' ideology rested on their belief that the law embodies the sovereign's command, to interpret which, one searches, not in the world of social science, but in a law library. Once a court determines the facts of a case, the discourse turns on the law's content, its doctrine. An eminent Canadian drafting expert declared:

> [A drafter] should always ask himself: 'What will courts say?' If the drafter succeeds in writing his statute so that the courts are left in no doubt as to its meaning it is altogether likely that the persons to whom it is directed and the persons who have to administer it will also understand it. (Driedger, 1953)

African drafters to a man (in Africa, only a few women became drafters) agreed. Both their self-perception and their notion of law's court-centered function convinced them that they had nothing to do with a bill as a recipe for the changed behaviors required to facilitate development. Their training convinced them that they had no business investigating how a bill might affect its addressees' behaviors. They therefore made no investigation of the problem, and drafted in the ways that came easiest. They copied similar laws;[13] they drafted in broad principles; they criminalized;[14] and they compromised between competing interests.[15] Their laws sometimes, though rarely, succeeded in inducing desired behavior. When a law did work, it did so not because of the drafters, but in spite of them.

DRAFTING INSTITUTIONS[16]
In the executive branch, a policy usually began its transition to a bill when a line ministry official instructed a civil servant to prepare a 'layman's draft'. Ministry officials believed that their task comprised, not developing a bill's detailed words, but articulating broad policy statements that did little more than propose a drafting priority for a bill dealing with a particular social problem. Without much attention to detail, these officials sent their layman's draft – a rough draft bill, sometimes only a memorandum describing what should go into the bill – to the central office drafters, who, making no effort to examine how their country's unique circumstances might affect the relevant social actors' behaviors, proceeded to put it into a technically 'suitable' form. In the end, the details of the bill – its all-important *design* – fell between two stools (Seidman et al., 1997). Nobody in the drafting process saw the necessity of researching the time- and place-specific factors likely to influence how people would behave in response to the bill. Without such research, whether the bill's details would induce the desired new behavior rested on mere conjecture. No more than the drafting institutions did the development community's prevailing paradigms of law and development require drafters to undertake required *behavioral* research.

THE PREVAILING PARADIGMS OF LAW AND DEVELOPMENT
The tiny academic community concerned with law and development, and, more importantly, the international aid community (including the international financial institutions), did nothing to encourage drafters to investigate the country-specific circumstances likely to influence problematic behaviors.[17] Making some more heroic generalizations, we suggest that the development community's views of law and development fell into three periods, each with its own dominant paradigm.

Modernization theory and development through executive discretion
During the early years of independence, two competing paradigms struggled for dominance:

(i) Development through executive discretion. Throughout the period of the anti-colonial struggle, the liberation movements' thinking focused on a monumental challenge: how to shake off the colonial chains that had kept them subordinated and exploited so long? The populist leaders apparently believed that by breaking those chains, they had conquered the hard part of the job. Once they had won 'the political kingdom', development came as dessert. In effect, liberation ideology seemed to hold, leave development to the leaders; they will know what to do. As in Kenya (see Leys, 1975), most new governments enacted laws that granted the leadership the discretion thought necessary to do the job.[18]

Unfortunately, no matter how ably they led the liberation movement, the leaders had little knowledge and less experience in the use of state power. Most of the grand, frequently *soi-disant* 'socialist' schemes of the first-generation African leaders led, not to development for the poor majority, but to coup and counter-coup, self-aggrandizement, corruption, and ultimately to the grip of the international financial institutions and their structural adjustment programs. As Kenya's 1970s development programs and Zimbabwe's new-millennium land reform efforts (Cass, 2003; see also Dicey, 1959; Hayek, 1944) demonstrate, no matter how laudable the government's declared objectives, unless carefully planned and expressed as rules that limit discretion, unharnessed exercise of state power tends towards the personal aggrandizement of well-placed officials. *(ii) Modernization theory applied to the law.* To counter the development-through-executive-discretion notion, the international financial institutions and the majority of law and development scholars turned to the law. Like law teachers and lawyers everywhere, they focused on law as experienced by practitioners in the courts (Dworkin, 1986).

This should cause no surprise. Lawyers everywhere practice in the courts or in the courts' shadow. Law teachers train their students to solve problems of the sort that practicing lawyers usually confront, that is, problems arising *within* an existing legal order.[19] From the practicing lawyers' perspective, the law appears as an all but immutable set of rules. To an extent, a good lawyer can tame that complicated system, and perhaps even change the law at the margin. Through the courts alone, however, a lawyer can very rarely change an institution's basic structure. Nevertheless, the World Bank and the IMF focused on the role of law in development, not primarily as an instrument for institutional transformation, but for dispute settlement in the courts.[20]

In the United States, the then-popular 'legal process' school of jurisprudence had its fountainhead in the work of Professors Hart and Sachs at Harvard. They taught that changes in the law came about from bargaining between interest groups, in which the state and its laws should remain governed by a set of neutral principles – a view which resonated easily with the then prevalent notions of modernization, which for lawyers, meant copying the 'legal' institutions and the laws of a 'modern' country (Galanter, 1966). Profoundly misunderstanding the potential instrumental role of law to achieve effective development, the first generation of African leaders mainly used law, not for institutional change, but to expand welfare schemes which, as terms of trade for their countries' exports worsened, proved unsustainable. Unable to exercise state power through law to change their inherited institutions, not a few misused their official discretion corruptly. In 1974, David Trubek and Marc Galanter (who between them constituted something close to a majority of the tiny law and development community) publicly abandoned their former views of the importance of law in the development process, and declared law and development dead.

The night-watchman state
The international financial institutions seemed to tease out a different lesson: any strengthened use of state power to aid development would be likely to foster, not development, but corruption. Changing their economic perspectives from Keynesian to those of the Chicago School, they adopted what became known as the 'Washington Consensus' (Williamson, 1999). Freed from the shackles of the law, markets would flourish. Markets could solve every problem. The ideal state became the night-watchman, a state that attended to law and order and collected taxes, and never sought to redistribute wealth through taxes or other devices, or to use its power to shape economic activity.

When they actually work in ways that more or less resemble the ideal-type competitive model, markets can match the output of goods and services with 'effective' – dollar-backed – demand (Samuelson, 1989). They do not, however, function to redistribute wealth – nor did the Washington Consensus pretend that they would. Instead, relying on the 'rising tide lifts all boats' principle to deal with poverty, they focused on increased efficiency within the distorted resource patterns shaped by the inherited institutions. At a USAID-supported conference in the early 1980s, when asked about the consequences of market-bound development for poor farmers, one USAID official claimed that equity should remain a 'second-order issue'.

Like developing countries elsewhere, most African nations fell under the international financial institutions' thrall. For a decade, neo-liberalism and notions of the night-watchman state dominated their law-making decisions. This consensus declared that governments ought not, and in any event could not, successfully use law in aid of development

Law in aid of the market
Sometime in the late 1980s the World Bank decided that the Douglass North (North, 1993, 1981; North et al., 1996; Instituciones, 1985) version of Law and Economics had it right; markets could not work without an appropriate legal framework (Wolfensohn, 2003). The state can and ought to use law to remove 'transaction costs', the flaws which made real-world market operations diverge from the economists' free market model (Trachtman, 1998: 193). With a rush, law and development scholars jumped into the breach. Once again IFI practitioners and law and development scholars sang in unison (World Bank, 1997a).

What most of these scholars taught, and most IFI practitioners preached, mainly consisted of a rehash of the earlier, academic law and development thesis: developing countries should adopt laws that expressed neutral principles, mainly expressed in 'businessmen's laws', largely copied from foreign countries (or from a new, recently discovered virtual jurisdiction called 'international best practice').[21] The new consensus served little better than the older ones. Development still eluded all three groups of players: African leaders, the IFIs, and law and development theorists in their consultant roles. In Africa as throughout the developing and transitional worlds, the institutions still won the fatal race – and the people lost (see Stiglitz, 2002, 1998).

IV: Resolving the Deadlock: Law as a Device for Making the Exercise of Rule-making Power Non-arbitrary

The first time around, in different degrees, every country in Africa lost the fatal race. The new populist leaders failed to transform the received institutions in ways that would solve the problems of poverty, vulnerability, and poor governance. Two sets of explanations purport to set out the reasons for this failure. One argues that the whole notion of development, in the sense of state-powered, forced-draft economic and social improvement for the mass of the population, ran aground on the deadlock in law and development. Development requires discretion and massive legal change; the rule of law requires their mirror image. Without the rule of law, they say, good governance becomes impossible; without good governance, efforts to use state power end up in corruption and 'failed states.' The alternative set holds that Africa lost the race because of lack of capacity to use law to bring about social change, myths of the drafter's passive role, the nature of the received drafting institutions, and the changing paradigm of the appropriate use of law in development. This section aims to provide a solution to overcome only two of the causal factors suggested: the governments' lack of capacity to use law instrumentally to bring about the social changes subsumed under the heading of development, and the deadlock explanation.

THEORY AND METHODOLOGY FOR LAW AND DEVELOPMENT

Legislative theory and methodology grounded in reason informed by experience suggest that social change through law does not lie beyond the reach of African governments. Legislative theory aims to guide drafters and others engaged in the law-making process in answering the key question: *Why do people behave as they do in the face of a law?* In so doing, it gives directions as to the kinds of country-specific evidence required to design a bill's detailed prescriptions for appropriate new behaviors. At the same time, problem-solving methodology informs as to the steps to be taken to structure the available evidence in order to design detailed legislative prescriptions that will induce the new behaviors needed to transform dysfunctional institutions.

How to predict the likely impact of a proposed law on society,[22] and to conceptualize its probable influence on behavior? Confronted by a law, social actors behave within the time- and place-specific constraints and resources of the environment within which they live and work,[23] among which the law – and its threats and promises – constitute only one (Seidman et al., 2001: 115–26). To understand why a person behaves in particular ways in the face of a rule of law and, conversely, to *predict* how s/he will behave in face of a new rule of law, drafters must examine these constraints and resources, involving not only legal but also social science research, which a focus on drafting techniques alone – a prevalent practice in Africa – tends to ignore. Moreover, no matter how well a foreign law on a similar problem may work in its native habitat, one cannot confidently expect that, if copied, it will induce similar behavior in the different circumstances prevailing in a given African country.[24] This leaves, however, a large, indeterminate residual category unexplained: the constraints and resources of the environment. By helping drafters to unpack that broad category into subjective and objective causal factors, legislative theory offers a more detailed guide for explaining a person's behaviors in the face of a rule of law.

Subjective factors include material incentives (here called *interests*), and the mish-mash of value-sets, myths, ideologies, and the like – what the sociologist Alvin Gouldner (1980) called, 'domain assumptions' – (here termed *ideology*) (see also Schutz, 1965). Punishments and other sanctions address material incentives; efforts to educate people into new ways of behavior address ideologies. Legislative theory specifies five categories of objective factors likely to influence the behaviors of a law's addressees. Ask: to what extent does the rule of law itself help explain the addressees' problematic behavior? Do the addressees have the *opportunity* or *capacity* to behave as required? (Or, conversely, the opportunity or capacity to misbehave?) Do the addressees know about the rule; have the authorities *communicated* it to them? Does the *process* by which the addressees decide how to behave help explain that behavior? (Seidman and Seidman, 1994: 122–5).

Rearranged, the first letters of these seven categories – rule, opportunity, capacity, communication, interest, process, and ideology – form the mnemonic

ROCCIPI. These categories serve to 'spark off' specific hypotheses as to the causes of relevant social actors' problematic behaviors in the face of existing law. They lay the basis for educated guesses about whether, in a specific environment, a bill will logically be likely to help overcome those causes and induce social actors to adopt the new behaviors prescribed.

A METHODOLOGY FOR DECIDING WHAT THE LAW OUGHT TO BE

Legislative theory's problem-solving methodology offers drafters a way of conceptualizing how to translate this kind of evidence into a bill's detailed prescriptions. Its four interrelated steps (ibid.: 76–83) enables drafters *logically* to structure the available evidence (i) to decide on a bill's detailed prescriptions (its design), and (ii) to *justify* those details. (Box 4.2 briefly reviews the three alternative methodologies available for deciding these details.)

BOX 4.2: THREE ALTERNATIVE WAYS TO DESIGN A BILL

i. ***Ends-means.*** Positivist social science draws a sharp line between propositions as to what is the case, and what ought to be the case. It insists that evidence about what *is* cannot warrant a proposition about what *ought to be* the case. Positivist social science teaches that to decide what the law ought to be requires a two-step methodology: (i) decide one's objectives or ends; in practice, ministers or higher officials tell drafters the bill's policy objectives; (ii) determine the means for achieving those ends; this requires investigating the costs and benefits of alternative solutions in the real world (Rubin, 1991).

For drafters, the ends-means methodology has two inherent weaknesses: (i) the values of someone in authority decide the bill's 'end', ends-means makes democratic participation difficult. (ii) Ends-means ignores the relationship between policy and a bill's detailed design. In reality, the drafter who decides the bill's details, i.e. its means, also shapes its policy – its ends. The discontinuity between ends and means, between values and facts, proves illusory.[25]

ii. ***Incrementalism.*** Incrementalists deny that, even with the most advanced computers, ordinary mortals can make an adequate cost-benefit analysis to compare even relatively simple policy alternatives (Lindblom, 1963). Since one can only guess at potential outcomes, one should adopt as the best option simply 'muddling through' (Lindblom, 1959: 79). To reduce the inevitable risks, measures that make the *least* change from the present situation should be taken. This solution, however, plainly will not transform the institutions that thwart development. (It may serve, however, if, after exhausting available research resources, the drafter can think of nothing better.)

iii. ***Problem-solving.*** Descended intellectually from John Dewey (1939: 47–8) and the American philosophical pragmatists, problem-solving specifies four logically interconnected steps: describing the social problem; proposing and warranting explanations of problematic behaviors; designing a solution (the bill's details); monitoring and evaluating the new law's implementation.

A map to guide the drafter in gathering and organizing the available relevant evidence and a methodology to tell him/her what steps to take to design a bill that nestles comfortably into the country's unique circumstances constitute the building blocks for a legislative theory. Legislative theory, however, only guides a drafter in writing instrumental bills, which directly prescribe the behaviors necessary to help resolve clearly specified social problems. Traditionally, most people view the rule of law as preventing arbitrary official behaviors. Applied to lawmakers, it must limit the kinds of laws that they may properly draft and enact. How and to what extent does the rule of law, or at least its core concerns, limit instrumental laws looking to the kinds of social transformation required for development?

V: Development and the Rule of Law

Legislative theory's problem-solving methodology directs drafters to design their bills' critical prescriptions to ensure that, logically, they will alter or eliminate the causes of the problem behaviors addressed. Thus stated, the instrumental use of the law, as a concept, has no inherent value content.

Development – forced-draft, government-led, deliberate institutional transformations – requires a whole blizzard of rule changes, whether made by delegation to an executive or administrative agency or by the legislature itself. The nakedly instrumental use of law, combined with the range of change required by the development process, triggers the warning signals raised by those who predict a deadlock of law and development.

Africa's post-independence experience seems to argue that the law and development deadlock inevitably thwarts dreams of development. Discretion and the corruption that it breeds lie at the opposite pole from the rule of law. Does that mean Africa must give up the dream of development?

This section proposes a resolution of that seeming deadlock. First, it examines the rather hazy doctrines that the concepts of the rule of law and good governance subsume, and concludes that, with respect to rule-making, at their heart, these enjoin an arbitrary rule-making process. Second, with respect to the executive branch, it examines procedural devices for making arbitrary rule-making less likely: transparency, accountability, participation, and decision by rule. Third, with respect to both the executive and the legislative branches, it examines in more detail the requirement of demonstrating that a new rule will probably meet the demand of non-arbitrariness, and thus serve the public interest.

To overcome many of the stickiest obstacles to development, government's strategy of choice frequently requires what the literature terms an 'intransitive' law (Diver, 1983; Rubin, 1989). In effect, this identifies a social problem, an agency to deal with it, and turns the problem over to the agency to write the detailed prescriptions required. This seems to raise the specter of the deadlock of law and development: a law granting implementing agency officials sufficient scope to draft rules prescribing behaviors appropriate for constantly changing circumstances seems almost inevitably likely to generate official rule-making behaviors that violate the rule of law. The claimed deadlock teaches the necessity of imposing limits on African governments' instrumental use of law to give them any chance of winning the fatal race. How to grant discretionary authority to officials, but still ensure that they exercise that discretion, not to feather their own nests, but to advance the public interest? How to do that both for officials acting under an intransitive law, and for the legislature itself?

THE HEART OF THE RULE OF LAW: AN INJUNCTION AGAINST ARBITRARY
RULE-MAKING
From a rule limiting adjudication to a rule limiting legislation. The terms 'rule of law' and 'good government' have become almost synonymous. They carry heavy burdens of value content. Who does not want a government under the rule of law? Who would reject good governance?

Neither of these terms has a clearly defined agreed meaning. As in the case of 'art' and 'pornography,' though we have difficulty in defining these terms, we would recognize these conditions when we see them. The rule of law 'belongs in the category of open-ended concepts which remain subject to permanent debate' (Grote, 1999). Nevertheless, both contain a core content.

Over time, the concept of the rule of law has not remained static ('Democracy and the Rule of Law Project'). We aim here to redefine it in terms of its core meaning, and use it to help overcome the obstacles to development.[26] This core meaning centers on *non-arbitrary* decision-making; for officials making subordinate regulations, and the legislature itself, this means rule-making utilizing *reason informed by experience.*

Historically, the rule of law aimed, not at rule-makers, but at adjudicators, those who decide disputes. In ancient days, people conceived of law as immutable, part of the natural, frequently divine order; the rule of law placed a curb on the ruler who, as the supreme adjudicator, must judge, not by whim, but pursuant to objective existing law (Thomas, 2003). Max Weber's ideal-type of legal-rational legitimacy focused on settling disputes pursuant to fixed rules, announced beforehand, with as little discretion as the very nature of words permits (Weber, 1947). A judge should function like a slot machine: insert the rule and the facts, and the judge simply grinds out the required decision. Jurisprudence in general has remained fixated on the judicial role. Almost all definitions of the rule of law aim at the judicial or executive roles. All insist that judges rest decisions on previously declared rules, and on the basis of the facts as they appear before them.

Under the versions of the rule of law developed for adjudication (which seemingly permitted small room for change in the laws), some authors also subsumed the rule-making function. Dicey's classical functional definition held that it prohibited a grant of discretion to government officials.[27] Hayek (1944) held the same notion. Protective of property rights, some held that laws defining these rights ought to remain immutable (Buchanan, 1972).

Already, however, beginning as early as the sixteenth and seventeenth centuries with the expansion of legislative activities, people began to question this definition as applied to the rule-making function. If, in their own discretion, the parliament made new laws, how did that differ from a judge who, in deciding cases, exercised judicial discretion? (Thomas, 2003) Today, confronting the phenomenon of development, the same dilemma plagues the concept of the rule of law.

In reality, if legal change conflicts with the rule of law, every government inevitably, from time to time, violates the rule of law. Over centuries, the United States has repeatedly used law in aid of what today we would denote as 'development'. When, in 1862, it sought to transform land tenures in the western frontier country, Congress enacted the Homestead Act; to achieve hydro-electric development of the Tennessee Valley, it used law to create the Tennessee Valley Authority; when it chose to transform industrial relations, it enacted the National Labor Relations Act; when it decided to change the securities markets, it enacted the Securities and Exchange Commission Act. When Germany wanted to change the conditions of industrial safety, it invented and introduced laws to establish the workmen's compensation system. Through law, Britain nationalized and then denationalized coal and other industries. If using law to institute deliberate social change violates the rule of law, the rule of law lives only in the imagination. When these countries enacted these laws, they never thought to test them against the dictates of the rule of law. Any lawyer can recite a dozen statutes that grant a great deal of discretion to government officers to make rules to fill in the details of statutes phrased in general terms. In England, they call these rules 'subordinate legislation'; in the continental system, implementing decrees; in the US, 'administrative regulations'. If Dicey and later Hayek and Buchanan had it right, every government has it wrong. The grant of administrative discretion to make subordinate legislation cannot *per se* violate the rule of law – or every government stands in violation of it.

In 1987, the General Counsel of the World Bank, Ibrahim Shihata, equated the Rule of Law with 'good governance'. He pointed out that even markets need rules, and that kleptocrat governments make poor investment climates. 'Good governance', he argued, required not only the effective use of government resources for development, but also

> ... good order, not in the sense of maintaining the status quo by force of the state (law and order) but in the sense of having a system, based on abstract rules which are actually applied and on functioning institutions which ensure the rules' application. Reflected in the concept of 'the rule of law,' this system of rules and institutions appears in different legal systems and finds expression in the familiar phrase, 'government of laws and not of men'. (Shihata, 1991)

In the 1990s, under the terms 'good governance,' the Rule of Law emerged as a leading theme in development.

What constitutes the underlying principle of the rule of law (or 'good governance')? (Chuen). As Shihata stated, whatever else the rule of law may denote, it denotes a government of laws, and not of men (see also Wolfensohn, 2003). It imposes limits on what those who wield state power may do with it. Historically those limits applied mainly to the adjudicatory function. What limits ought the rule of law to impose on those who exercise the rule-making function?[28]

As we have seen, development requires radical institutional transformation and therefore radical legal change. On the other hand, simply to permit whatever changes in the law seem desirable to those who hold power plainly defies good governance. No matter how many times the Prince proclaims that his whims constitute *law*, however codified, they never become laws that conform to the demands of the rule of law (Fuller, 1969). Are we not back at the paradox of the deadlock in law and development? In what sense can rule-making amount to anything other than 'government by men?'

Limits on discretionary rule-making: underlying premises. The essence of government by laws lies in the idea that law limits the behavior of the nation's governors. What limits ought the law to impose on officials who in their discretion make and promulgate the detailed rules that together constitute policy?

In all its applications, the rule of law seeks to further non-arbitrary government decision-making. In adjudication, this implies that judges hear both sides before deciding; that they decide by fixed rules, not ones dredged from the judge's subconscious. The same sorts of rules apply to administrative actions. In rule-making, the rule of law must have the same central thrust. It must require that rule-makers' decisions prove non-arbitrary.[29] That requires answers to two questions. First, what does 'non-arbitrary' mean? Second, why must discretion in development be non-arbitrary in order to seem tolerable and accord with good governance?

The meaning of 'non-arbitrary'. Presumably, in a democracy, law lodges rule-making discretion with an official for the benefit of all. Whether explicitly or implicitly, its ruling prescription requires the official to use that discretion in the public interest, (Pipkin, 1967; Habermas, 1996: 180), therefore not resting on considerations that appeal only to a person or a group whose interests or values coincide with those of the official making the rule. To meet the criterion of non-arbitrary, a decision ordaining a rule made by a legislature or a public official must rest, not on considerations of power, interest, or parochial ideology, but on considerations germane to the public interest.

To the extent that in making the rule the discourse of power influences the outcome, the decision merits the characterization 'arbitrary'. The same applies to legislation.

Of what does rational, non-arbitrary decision-making consist as applied to the rule-making exercise? So far as possible, it requires the rule-maker to: (i) discover and describe in detail (a) the problematic behaviors at which the new law aims, and (b) the causes of those behaviors;[30] and (ii) reflecting on those behaviors and their causes, use logic to devise a legislative solution – the bill's detailed design – that, (a) taking into consideration available capacities, (b) will alter or eliminate those causes and induce new behaviors likely to resolve the social problem effectively. In short, to avoid arbitrary rule-making, the drafter must adopt a problem-solving methodology that grounds the bill's design on reason informed by experience, facts, and logic.

Why does discretionary rule-making accord with good governance only if it is non-arbitrary? Why does requiring the use of reason informed by experience make discretionary rule-making by an official non-arbitrary and in accordance with good governance principles? Why *should* a rule-maker design, or a legislator assess, a regulation in terms of facts and logic? We suggest five reasons (Seidman and Seidman, 1994: chap. 3).

First, and most important, human experience teaches that, for making public policy, using facts and logic – not casting bones, examining a chicken's entrails, consulting a madwoman as the Oracle of Delphi, searching the stars or gazing at the decision-maker's navel to dredge up subjective values and attitudes – produces better results for the people subject to the policy (Kronman, 1990). Second, some claim that compromises among conflicting interest groups, if reached on a 'level playing field', constitute the true definition of the public interest. Habermas (1996: 180) calls our attention to an obvious reality: the discourse on legislation always simultaneously concerns two strands. One consists of the discourse of power, its outcomes at best shaped by the competing interest groups' compromise. Bargaining, not the best solution for the public, but the best solution for the winner of the bargaining process, inevitably emerges as the basis for the bill's design. In bargaining, the odds are that power and privilege come out on top. A compromise between interest groups contains no built-in assurance that the outcome will likely change the problematic behaviors at issue. It contains no built-in guarantee that the outcome will advance the public interest, or that it will not adversely affect especially the poor, women, children, the environment, human rights – all the interests usually with weak representation in the bargaining forum. In short, a bill whose provisions rest only on interest-group haggling does not rest on a process that assures non-arbitrary rule-making, and thus will not further the public interest. In contrast, Habermas observes that the second form of legislative discourse focuses on rational argument founded on observations of the real world, logically-ordered facts. Strangely – and perhaps counter-intuitively – such arguments trump those based solely on power.

Third, some argue that pluralism only sings in an upper-class accent when it produces its compromises on a rocky and uneven playing field. One can well question whether mere humans can ever construct a truly level playing field; power and privilege exist precisely because no level playing field cancels their inbuilt advantages. Moreover, no matter how even it is, a detailed rule based, not on a careful, logically constructed examination of the facts about the environment within which it will operate, but on a compromise between interest groups, has little chance of inducing appropriate new behaviors.

Fourth, Weber argues that legal-rational government, and thus the rule of law in most of its guises, excites a sense of legitimacy because the decision-making mechanism used enables an individual to predict that the state will act rationally, not arbitrarily, in connection with the citizen's affairs.[31] After all, Weber was speaking of 'legal-rational legitimacy'. To foster that legitimacy, good governance requires that those affected by a proposed rule participate in the rule-making process. Reliance on a discourse of power obviously excludes or diminishes some voices; power consists precisely of the capacity to exclude weaker stakeholders' inputs. *Per contra*, reliance on reason informed by experience makes it possible for any stakeholder, either individually or through representatives in government or civil society, to give the rule-maker inputs and feedback in the form of relevant facts and ideas.

Finally, discourse grounded in the public interest requires arguments that reach 'across the aisle'. Legislators must appeal not only to their own supporters, but also to those in the opposition (Pipkin, 1967). Arguments addressed to interests and values could do that only if the values and interests of the opposition coincided with those of the proponents. If at all, that might happen only in a micro-society. As people grow up and live in increasingly complex societies, however, they acquire our domain assumptions as it were by osmosis from their increasingly diverse social situations. The very meaning of the word 'society' differs for that of a resident of the inner city, compared with that of a cowboy on the Western plains, or an elite graduate of Harvard Law School (Chambliss and Seidman, 1971). Only arguments grounded in facts and logic – not inchoate values reflecting diverse groups' relative power – can appeal to the other side.

The teachings of human experience in making public policy; that by definition the rule of law cannot rest on the arbitrary exercise of power, the requirements that rule-makers base regulations on a solid, detailed understanding of relevant local circumstances; the advantages of participation by all stakeholders; and the nature of discourse in the public interest all argue that a rule-maker's exercise of discretion, as long as it rests on reason informed by experience, conforms with the requirements of the rule of law. Only then does it merit the characterization 'non-arbitrary'.

A requirement that officials make rules grounded in reason informed by experience imposes limits on rule-making, and ensures non-arbitrary rule-making. Thus, the rule of law places limits on rule-makers, administrative and legislative alike.

Some might argue that this proposition only plunges us into another linguistic tangle: What does it mean to say that the rule of law demands non-arbitrary rule-making?

OPERATIONALIZING NON-ARBITRARY RULE-MAKING[32]

How to ensure that a rule-maker's decision as to the content of subsidiary legislation will prove non-arbitrary? Here we must distinguish between rule-making under an intransitive law, and by the legislature itself. We discuss first rules concerning stated criteria and procedural requirements applicable only to the former, and in the following section, the requirement of a statement of the reasons for a rule, a requirement that applies as well to the legislature as to administrative officers making subordinate legislation.

The rule of law requirement that rules and rule-making prove demonstrably non-arbitrary suggests three kinds of procedural limits on an official engaged in making and promulgating subordinate legislation. The enabling act must clearly define the legitimacy of the source of the official's rule-making power; specify relevant criteria; and require transparent, accountable and participatory decision-making processes.

A legitimate grant of rule-making power

As the first test for the legitimacy of a new subordinate regulation, the rule-maker must act under a grant of power from a legitimate source, one formally authorized by constitution or statute (cf. Kelsen, 1961; re: the hierarchy of norms; Rose, 1959: 470). If no law granted an official the power to make regulations, whatever rule the official promulgated would remain illegitimate. Both the Constitution and positive law declare such a regulation void on *ultra vires* grounds (Wade, 1959). The official's decisions as to a particular rule must conform to the limits imposed by that grant of power. The sorts of issues a rule may address include the factors the rule-maker may consider; the parties who may participate in the rule-making process, and in what capacities; the kinds of rule-making procedures the official may use; and the remedies a rule may impose.

Stipulating criteria to limit factors rule-makers may take into account
Officials promulgating a regulation must have some degree of choice, some discretion; otherwise, why grant them law-making power? Yet unlimited discretion would leave citizens subject to the official's whim. To constrain a grant of discretionary rule-making power by the dictates of good governance requires limiting the rule-makers' substantive choices to those relevant to resolving the social problem specified.

Discretion involves choice. If the enabling law grants rule-makers a huge number of possible choices, it becomes all but impossible to hold them accountable; they may easily make their choice arbitrarily. Consider a football coach, with eleven men on the team. If the coach rules that all squad members must go to bed by 10:00 p.m. the night before the big game, and someone charges a player with partying until 12:00, the coach has a simple choice – yea or nay. In contrast, if the right guard says he wants to play any position other than right guard, just considering the eleven men on the first team, the coach has almost 40 million options!

To limit discretion's scope requires specifying criteria of relevance to the particular kinds of problem the rules aim to resolve. This reduces the number of factors a rule-maker must take into account.

In designing an intransitive law, how should law-makers decide what factors – what criteria of relevance – agency rule-makers should consider in making subordinate rules? The power to make regulations ordinarily grants a power to make regulations that tend to accomplish the statute's objectives. Some authorities therefore argue that a law's 'objectives' clause adequately limits the rule-making powers it grants to agency officials.[33] Yet, no one-size-fits-all objectives clause provides adequate criteria to guide a multi-tasked agency's rule-making officials in making rules.

In making these hypothetical emergency ward admission rules, only if an enabling law specifies a relatively small number of criteria can the rule-making authority justify a requirement to use some facts, and to exclude others. Instead of a set of overall agency objectives, an intransitive bill should specify criteria for the kinds of facts each set of regulations should require agency officials to consider.

How might a drafter determine what criteria to include in a law requiring an agency to make rules addressing a relatively narrow social problem? The problem-solving methodology emphasizes that a bill's detailed prescriptions must logically address the causes of the problematic behaviors that comprise the difficulty. In identifying hypotheses to explain the social problem, the drafter simultaneously may obtain ideas as to the criteria which the enabling law might require rule-making officials to take into account.

To limit official discretion the drafter should specify, not only the relevant criteria, but also rule-making procedures that prove consistent with good governance principles.

Procedural limitations
The detailed provisions necessarily depend on the particular circumstances likely to influence officials' decisions in implementing a particular law's objectives. Nevertheless, we review here the broad outlines of rule-making procedures likely to help ensure good governance. They include, first, the three preliminary

conditions for accountability – stakeholder participation, transparency, and institutions which can call the responsible official to account – and, second, the kind of justification an official must provide in order to make a decision accountable.

Stakeholder participation. A complex rule-making structure incorporates three sets of processes, input, feedback, and conversion processes.

In any society larger than a kin-bound village, the governors can no longer maintain face-to-face relationships with all those living in their jurisdiction (Seidman and Seidman, 1994: 58). Not all those with an interest in a new rule, or whom that rule may affect, can participate directly in the conversion processes. Sound decision-making about subordinate legislation requires that the decision-makers act on the most complete information available. Nobody knows as much about their own situation as the stakeholders. This makes it indispensable that the rule-makers receive stakeholders' inputs of facts and ideas, their feedback as to the existing rules' present impact on their lives, and the anticipated impact of a proposed rule. Without this, officials may too easily impose foolish, or – worse – corrupt bought-and-paid-for regulations.[34]

A statute delegating rule-making power to unelected administrative officials should especially ensure inputs from those groups and interests seldom heard in the halls of power: the poor, women, children, minorities, and advocates for human rights and the environment (Pareto, 1935). Without the *facts* that stakeholders uniquely can contribute, no assurance exists that rule-makers will weigh the evidence relevant to the enabling law's stipulated criteria.

Here, pardon a brief digression. Many years ago, in a small Connecticut town where we lived, the mayor had a serious hearing disability. He wore an old-fashioned hearing aid in his ear, keeping its battery in his coat pocket. On occasion, as chair of a public meeting on a proposed local ordinance he favored, he would call for comments from its supporters, and listen attentively. When they had finished, saying, 'We will now hear from those opposed to the proposal,' he very ostentatiously removed his earpiece and put it, together with its battery, on the table. The moral of the story: Participation becomes meaningless unless the decision-makers listen.

How to draft procedural regulations that ensure that the decision-maker will take the criticisms and suggestions of stakeholders seriously? Some jurisdictions meet this problem by notice-and-comment provisions. After advertising proposed new regulations and requesting comments, the agency making the subordinate legislation publishes the final regulations which must include changes suggested by comments received or, alternatively, the agency must explain in a note published with the regulations why it did not do so. In short, stakeholder participation constitutes an important means of ensuring that new rules meet the criterion of non-arbitrariness, and contribute to government's legitimacy.

Transparency. The enabling statute must ensure that, in addition to facilitating participation, the rule-making processes prove transparent. When rule-makers consider new rules, they must inform both stakeholders and those concerned with oversight (the legislature, bureaucratic superiors, the courts) about the issues and facts they take into account, and must state the reasons for their new rules' detailed provisions (see below). Only when informed of the logic and facts on which rule-makers ground their decisions, can stakeholders and supervisory agencies (including legislative committees) assess proposed rules and suggest constructive revisions more likely to serve the public interest.

Accountability. Good governance requires that rule-makers demonstrate that their rules do not emerge as a result of whim or private considerations, but that they follow criteria and procedures specified in the enabling statute designed to ensure non-arbitrariness. To ensure accountability, an intransitive law must specify devices to ensure that the rule-makers follow the stipulated procedures, and take into account the stipulated criteria, and no others.

To ensure accountability, the law must assign someone the power to reject or amend a new rule in the light of findings resulting from a review of the criteria and procedures which the rule-makers used in practice. The law may provide top-down supervision by an authority senior to the rule-maker and bottom-up supervision by a legislative committee, acting as the people's representative. It may even require a plebiscite or an election to enable the voters to show their views. Commonly used accountability procedures include submitting a rule to the legislature for approval, intra-agency appeals, and appeals to a court for review of the new regulation.

Whatever device an enabling statute employs, it must ensure that the rule-making officials used criteria and procedures that prove consistent with the essentials of good governance – participation, transparency, and accountability. For rule-makers acting under the authority of a more or less intransitive statute, this leaves open the final, all-important question: What counts as an adequate justification for the substance of a new rule made under an intransitive statute? Plainly, the responsible official must show that the head statute authorizes rule-making, that the decision took into account all of the permitted criteria, and that it followed the stipulated procedures.

The procedures mentioned in this section plainly do not apply to the legislature. Deputies have their authorization to enact statutes in the Constitution. Just as a rule-making official must confine the rules to the limits imposed by the authorizing statute, so the deputy must confine his/her law-making to the constitutional limits (see Wintgens, 2002: 24).

This leaves us with the question, 'What must the rule-making official show to demonstrate that the new rule substantively meets the requirement of good governance?

THE CONTENT OF THE JUSTIFICATION: ASSURING THAT THE RULE RESTS ON FACTS AND LOGIC

How can law-makers draft an enabling law which ensures that rule-makers base their proposed rules on reason informed by experience? Observing the procedural and substantive limits imposed by law of course constitutes the first step in raising the likelihood that the rules promulgated prove non-arbitrary. Their legalistic observance, while important, does not suffice, however. A rule-maker can claim the governing statute authorizes a proposed rule, too easily masking a decision based, not on reason informed by experience, but on calls of interest, of party, of clan, or perhaps of corruption. A legislator can demonstrate that a law, in fact enacted to further parochial interest, nevertheless meets the technical requirements of the constitution. Legalism alone does not guarantee that the new law meets the requirement of non-arbitrariness.

We have asserted that the rule of law limits law-makers to rules arising out of a non-arbitrary, rational decision-making process. Whether made by an administrative official under the authority of an intransitive law, or by the legislature within its constitutional authority, how can it be made likely that a new rule meets that demand of the rule of law? How to ensure that a new rule rests on facts and logic? How to make sure that a visitor, viewing the new rule through the veil of ignorance, would agree with it? How to prevent interest and 'values' from having the 'final cut' on the details of the rule and, because the devil does lie in the details, therefore on the policy the rule purports to embody?

We suggest that, when proposing an important new rule, the law should require that the drafter declare the reasons for the design of its specific prescriptions (Nino, 1996: 121–2, 129; Gutmann and Thompson, 1994: 161). This would enable both downward and upward reviewers to assess whether the rule would be likely to achieve its stated aims. It constitutes a minimum requirement for transparency, and ultimately, for accountability.

Because the very heart of the limits imposed by the rule of law on the law-making function lies in the requirement that the sponsor of a rule demonstrate that it rests on reason informed by experience, the key discourse concerning the rule of law with respect to rule-making centers on the appropriate form of such a justification, and procedures for making it likely that rule-givers will provide an adequate justification.

An adequate justification for a subordinate rule's detailed provisions should serve a purpose analogous to that, in the common law system, served by a judge's opinion. To assess the adequacy of a judge's decision, lawyers test the substantive adequacy of the opinion against criteria determined by the culture of judges and lawyers. In the case of important legislation or a rule made under an intransitive law, no equivalent standard currently exists. What standard seems appropriate to justify a rule in terms of the public interest? We have argued that it will not do to justify it merely in terms of pluralist bargaining, copying law from another country, 'international best practice', or in terms of the bill's general statement of objectives because it adheres to familiar forms of the criminal law. How to ensure justification in terms of reason informed by experience and thus ensure that, consistent with development's demand for change and discretion, lawmakers meet the requirements of the rule of law to avoid the deadlock of law and development?

Procedurally, a polity can meet the requirement of an adequate justification by requiring rule-making officials and drafters to accompany their proposed rule with a research report stating the facts and logic on which it rests. For intransitive law, the legislature can require such a report by stipulating it for each intransitive law, at least those raising important, development-oriented changes, or by enacting a general administrative procedure requiring it for all subordinate legislation of a stipulated rank. For the legislature itself, a parliamentary regulation can require a bill's drafter to accompany the bill with a written justification.

In either event, by rule, the deputies can stipulate the content of an adequate research report. Legislative theory and methodology suggest that the report should provide the available facts to warrant its description of the social problem, the behaviors that comprise that problem, and its explanations of the causes of those behaviors. It should demonstrate logically that, of the available alternatives, the rule's detailed prescriptions – including those for its implementation – are likely, at the least possible social cost, to alter or eliminate the causes of existing problematic behaviors and induce the desired new behaviors. Finally, the report must show that the new rule provides adequate mechanisms for monitoring and evaluating its implementation and social impact. In short, the research report should adhere to the problem-solving methodology suggested earlier.

Rule-makers and drafters should justify their drafts to demonstrate their non-arbitrary character and that they rest on reason and experience, on facts and logic. To do this, they should accompany important rules with a report that uses reason informed by experience to justify those rules' detailed prescriptions (see Seidman, 1992).

VI: Conclusion

Using legislative theory's problem-solving methodology, this chapter describes as a social problem the apparent difficulties of Africa's new populist governments in exercising state power through law to restructure the inherited institutions that have for so long impoverished the majority of Africans. In a few instances, in the name of 'development,' they enacted laws – typically adapting colonial models – that granted officials broad discretion to write their own rules. During the half century that the winds of change blew across the African continent, many of the new governments seemed to have lost the fatal race: instead of transforming the old institutions, they too often seemed to adapt to them – even, cynically, to profit from them – leaving Africa's economies and peoples, if anything, more impoverished and vulnerable than before. Some observers saw this as the inevitable result of what they called the 'deadlock of development administration'. They noted that development requires giving government officials freedom to experiment; but officials may use that freedom to act for personal gain, not in the public interest.

This chapter offers a different explanation. As evidenced by the experience of Anglophone Africa, a significant cause of officials' arbitrary, even corrupt, behaviors, was rooted in colonial drafting traditions and institutions that hampered the efforts of law-makers, especially legislative drafters, to design effective transformatory laws. In general, most simply adopted inherited drafting practices: copying laws, including those of the former colonial power; criminalizing deviant behaviors; or incorporating into their bills conflicting interest-group compromises. Given the realities facing African countries, none of these entropic practices could effectively alter the dominant inherited institutions' misallocation of Africa's rich agricultural, mineral and human resources.

Based on this analysis, the final part of the chapter offers an institutionalist legislative theory to guide law-makers in using reason informed by experience – logic and facts – to design more effective transformatory legislation. This theory rests on the premise that institutions consist of repetitive patterns of behavior. Its problem-solving methodology equips law-makers to analyze their countries' unique realities in order to discover the causes of the problematic behaviors and the dysfunctional institutions that block development. On this basis, law-makers can logically design a bill's detailed prescriptions for the effective implementation of measures that eliminate those causes and induce new behaviors. Using this theory as a guide, Africa's law-makers may find it possible to stipulate criteria and procedures for legislative grants of rule-making power consonant with the principles of good governance essential to the maintenance of the rule of law in conditions of development. By requiring transparency, accountability, and participation, the law's detailed prescriptions may limit officials' rule-making discretion to implementing measures likely to foster increasingly productive employment opportunities and improving the majority's quality of life.

In particular, both an intransitive law empowering an official to make detailed rules covering a broad sector of human activity – and indeed legislation itself – should use rule of law principles that impose constraints on the rule-making power. An intransitive law and legislative regulations should require the drafter to justify a new rule, at least one defined by legislated criteria as 'important', by accompanying it with a report that uses reason informed by experience to demonstrate that it is likely to help resolve the specified social problem in the public interest. The governing statute should require that a rule-maker state reasons for a rule. For an important rule, the law could require rule-makers and drafters, guided by legislative theory's problem-solving methodology, to organize available facts in a report that logically demonstrates that the rule's detailed prescriptions accord with rule of law principles. By imposing limits on the discretion of administrative rule-makers and legislative drafters, this kind of statute could help resolve the 'deadlock', which too long has thwarted efforts to use law for the institutional transformations essential to achieve effective development. The limits imposed by the rule of law, as interpreted to ensure non-arbitrary governance, provide a resolution to that deadlock.

Notes

[1] We derived the concept of the 'deadlock' in Law and Development from Schaffer (1969: 179).

[2] For a more detailed review, see Seidman and Seidman, (1994), Chapter 4 (hereafter. 'Seidman and Seidman'); Seidman et al. (2001: 88–94).

[3] This definition is contested. *Cf.* Sjostrand (1993: 9–12). ('Institution' means 'a human mental construct for a coherent system of shared (enforced) norms that regulate individual interactions in recurrent situations'; 'institutionalization' means 'the process by which individuals subjectively approve, internalize and externalize such a mental construct'; North (1993: 36). ('Institution' consists of formal rules, informal constraints (norms of behavior, conventions and self-imposed codes of conduct) and the enforcement characteristics of both'. 'Organizations' consist of 'groups of individuals engaged in purposive activity. The constraints imposed by the institutional framework (together with other constraints) define the opportunity set and therefore the kind of organizations that will come into existence' (ibid.: 37). 'The agent of change is the entrepreneur, the decision-maker(s) in organizations'; Johnson ('social institution' means a 'complex normative pattern that is widely accepted as binding in a particular society or part of society'), (quoted in Seidman and Seidman, 1994: 22). For analyzing the law-making enterprise, the behavioral definition seems more useful. Law always addresses behaviors; law can only transform institutions by changing behaviors. Problem-solving holds that the key question becomes, *why* do those behavioral patterns exist? A drafter ought to count as important not merely the clarity and elegance of a bill's words, but also their likely effectiveness in bringing about the prescribed behaviors, and those behaviors' effectiveness in resolving the social problem at which the law aims. To serve a drafter's needs, the definition of 'institutions' ought to reflect the requirement that a bill should not merely change the rules, but change behaviors.

These utilitarian considerations suggest two reasons for the definition of 'institution' used here: (i) Because the problem-solving methodology teaches to construct solutions on causes (or explanations), to build into the definition of 'institution' only one possible explanation for repetitive patterns of behavior (for example, that the normative pattern is 'widely accepted as binding', Johnson (1994: 22) tends to limit the investigation of explanations for those repetitive patterns, and thus contracts the range of possible legislative initiatives to change them. (ii) To confine the definition of institution to the rules that prescribe the behavior (as does North) can lead to focusing only on the rules as distinct from the behavior they will likely induce in the given circumstances; that is, it neglects the American legal realists' observation that the law-in-action systematically differs from the law-in-the-books. *See* Pound (1910). This ignores the potential use of law to change institutions and thus to foster development.

[4] Wunsch and Owolu (1990); Pound (1942). For a review of objections to the instrumental use of law, see Seidman and Seidman (1994: 42–4) and below, Section III.

[5] Government intervention in the economy via a government corporation went back at least 20 years into colonial history. The East African Industrial Management Board was set up in 1944 (by the Defence (East Africa Industrial Management Board) Regulations, 1944 (G.N. 434/1944), made under the Emergency Powers (Defence) Acts, 1939), and incorporated in 1952 (Defence (Industrial Management Corporation [Incorporated]) Regulations, 1952 (G.N. 678/1952), made under the Supplies & Services (Transitional Powers) Act, 1945, and the Order-in-Council of 1946). The Industrial Development Ordinance No. 63 of 1954 established the Industrial Development Corporation in Kenya, as the successor to the Industrial Management Board. Much of the information about the Kenyan experience is drawn from Nowrojee (1977).

[6] National Construction Corporation Act, No. 9 of `1967 created the Corporation as a company; it was reconstituted as a public corporation in 1972 (the National Construction Corporation Act, No. 9 of 1972).

[7] Herbert Morrison, in the House of Commons, 1954, *Hansard*, Vol. 423, col. 850.

[8] Robson (1962: 75–6). The new millennium's corporate scandals in the United States

revealed that, despite extensively amended regulations over almost three-quarters of a century under the New Deal's Securities and Exchange Commission Act, the transparency and accountability of private corporations proved insufficient (eg., see daily *New York Times* reports, September-December, 2002.)

[9] In Kenya, purchase of shares in government corporations owned under the company laws became a principal entry into the new elite, or (as some have called them) the bureaucratic bourgeoisie. See, generally, Leys (1975).

[10] No way exists to measure these accurately then or now. See UNDP's annual reports. In the 1990s, after falling copper prices had slashed Zambia's copper-dependent revenues, the newly elected President Chiluba implemented an IMF-crafted Structural Adjustment Program that restored state-owned corporations to private sector owners, without altering the country's inherited company and government secrecy laws. Real per capita GDP dropped by 20 per cent in 1991–5; by 1996, the percentage of people living in poverty had increased to 73 per cent. Meanwhile, Chiluba's government 'became self-serving and corrupt, and mainly responded to the needs of the political, bureaucratic, military and economic elite to the neglect of the social interests of the majority' (Osei-Hwedie, 2003: 5).

[11] 'Effective law' here means law that proves effectively implemented. See Otto (2002: 23).

[12] In 1869 Britain created the office of Chief Parliamentary Counsel as its first central drafting office. Where formerly bills could be sent direct to Cabinet, now they were sent for review in the central drafting office. The line ministries objected to this as a dilution of their power. The first Chief Parliamentary Counsel, Sir Henry Thring, sought to deflect this criticism by asserting, in effect, that the new drafting office dealt only with issues of form and legality, not of 'policy'. See Seidman (1981).

[13] For copying foreign law, African drafters had ample colonial precedent. See Seidman (1969: 47).

[14] Many, if not most, African governments have passed laws providing heavy criminal punishment for corruption. As elsewhere, these threats do little to reduce the opportunities for corrupt behavior.

[15] This strategy seems justified by pluralism, a theory that focuses on bargaining among interest groups as the basis of legislative activity. See Carnoy (1984: 47); Kesselman (1982). It resonates with the view that holds that 'legislation … is a matter of politics, and politics is not rational. Politics is a power game, which results in compromises framed in a legislative or statutory structure. This power game seems to have its own logic, and, most of the time, the results outweigh any other form of logic.' (Wintgens, 2002: 1).

[16] Wintgens (2002: chap. 2); Seidman et al. (1999: 1).

[17] This chapter offers an alternative view to the usual description of the law and development paradigm changes. In 1974, the legend goes, law and development received its death warrant in an article by David Trubek and Marc Galanter (1974). For a long time thereafter, nobody thought law had anything to do with development. Then suddenly the World Bank discovered 'good governance', and law and development was resurrected. See Tamanaha (1970: 470).

[18] In this they followed Western thought of the period. This expressed the New Deal solution for the analogous social problems generated by the great Depression of the 1930s.

[19] In the United States and some other common law countries, student texts on law consist almost exclusively of reports of cases. In the law schools at which we have taught or lectured elsewhere in the world, law teaching always focuses on dispute settlement as the central function of the law. The same seems true elsewhere. See Luc J. Wintgens, 'Legislation as an Object of Study of Legal Theory: Legisprudence,' in *Legisprudence: A New Theoretical Approach to Legislation*, ed. Luc J. Wintgens, Oxford: Hart Publishing, 2002. (At least until relatively recently, 'legal theory was almost exclusively focused on adjudication, legislation being almost completely neglected. Legal science generally [focused] on the person of the judge in his task of the application of rules. The creation of rules by the legislator was not the order of the day.')

[20] A major share of the IFIs' training budgets, therefore, went to strengthening develop-

ing countries' courts. *Cf.* Oxner (2003: 307); Tuori (2002: 99).

[21] See Seidman et al. (1999b). When the former Soviet countries entered the map of countries needing new legal order, the demand for law and development practitioners swelled.

[22] Ann Seidman et al. (2001: 17). Unless drafters know why people behave as they do in the face of a law, they can neither explain existing problematic behaviors, nor predict how those behaviors may change in the face of a new law's detailed prescriptions. See Erikson (2002).

[23] Barth (1966). People may respond to some laws without conscious choice; by definition, where laws prohibit negligent conduct or impose absolute liability. Laws relating to transformation, however, require that their addressees make conscious decisions.

[24] Call this the 'law of the non-transferability of law'; see Seidman (1978).

[25] Dewey (1939), instead, emphasized a continuum of ends and means.

[26] Solum (1994) 'The rule of law may not be a single concept at all; rather, it may be more accurate to understand the ideal of the rule of law as a set of ideas connected more by family resemblance than by a unifying conceptual structure.'

[27] To the extent that a law grants discretion to a government official, that official – not the law – determines how to exercise the state's reserved monopoly of violence. Prohibition of officials' discretion underpins the entrepreneurial classes' central claim on the law; already facing trouble trying to outguess the market, they do not want to have to outguess what some government official will decide as well. When they make investments or sign contracts, they desire predictability and certainty. For Dicey, and others, that constituted the rule of law's very essence. Development, however, requires that officials experiment, use initiative, and make choices – in a sense act entrepreneurially – i.e. that they have discretion. The very concept of state-led social change seems to deny predictability and certainty in the law.

[28] See Kritz (1996: 588). ('The rule of law does not simply provide yet one more vehicle by which government can wield and abuse its awesome power; to the contrary, it establishes principles that constrain the power of government, oblige it to conduct itself according to a series of prescribed and publicly known rules.')

[29] See generally, Wintgens (2002); Poplova (2003: 5) ('Clearly the rule of law doctrine's popularity does not stem from its conceptual precision. It emanates from the belief that a legal system based on the rule of law is more likely than other systems to guarantee the promulgation of nonarbitrary laws and their predictable application. Since both predictability and non-arbitrariness are believed to be associated with greater justice, a rule-of-law-based legal system becomes a justice-enhancing and thus desirable social arrangement.')

[30] The Dutch Directives for Regulations (1993) prescribes that 'Before deciding to introduce a regulation, the following steps shall be taken: (a) knowledge of the relevant facts and circumstances shall be acquired . . .'

[31] In all its definitions, legitimacy resides in the consciousness of the people (Ghai, 1986). Weber held that a government can rule either by power, or by authority (Weber, 1947; Roth and Witlich, 1978). In most governments, people come to recognize government's authority; they obey the laws, not because of compulsion, but because they believe they ought to obey them. The process of moving from rule by power to rule by authority Weber called the process of legitimization. A government that in fact meets the substantive demands of its citizens for a decent quality of life, for freedom in its various forms, for peace, can confidently expect that its citizens will recognize its legitimacy. Weber's ideal-type of legitimization seeks to explain the fact that incompetent, self-seeking, unjust governors sometimes – often – rule over citizens who, despite their rulers' dreadful behavior, nevertheless permit them to govern, to that extent conceding their legitimacy. In his ideal-type model, Weber taught that a state might acquire legitimacy by any of three means: by sacred or traditional legitimacy (the ceremonies surrounding the Crown in England, or the power of the Ayatollah in Iran); by charismatic legitimacy (a George Washington or a Vladimir Ilyitch Lenin); or by 'legal-rational' or 'bureaucratic' legitimacy. Of these, a state either has traditional legitimacy or a charismatic leader, or it does

not. No government *instanter* can either whip up a supportive thousand-year-old tradition or religious movement, or create a Washington or a Lenin. Government can only acquire legitimacy by legal-rational means. For Weber, legal-rational legitimacy rested on 'rationality, which facilitates the pursuit of purposive action through qualities of calculability and predictability' (Ghai, 1986: 181).

[32] For a general review of devices law-makers may consider to reduce the danger that legislators and officials will take advantage of their decision-making powers, see Seidman et al. (2001: chap 14).

[33] This kind of clause, of course, proves far better than stating no objectives at all; at least, it requires a judge to infer the law's objectives from the statute on its face. Self-evidently, the more general the statement of objectives, the more it grants relatively unchecked discretion to the rule-makers.

[34] Many theorists have emphasized the importance of Africans participating in the law-making process; see Nzongola-Ntalaja (1987); Amin (1990); Szentes (1990; Leys (1969).

5

PENELOPE ANDREWS

The South African Constitution as a Mechanism for Redressing Poverty

JUSTICE Albie Sachs of the Constitutional Court of South Africa raised the following question in a lecture he gave at Harvard Law School in 2000: 'What does it mean to live in a country with a wonderful constitution and an advanced comprehensive Bill of Rights, [when there is] such inequality, injustice, and poverty?' (Sachs, 2000a).

The quotation came six years after South Africa's most prominent citizen, President Nelson Mandela, set the tone for the first post-apartheid democratic government in South Africa by announcing very early on his government's commitment to improving the conditions of the majority of South Africa's population. In his Inaugural Address to a Joint Sitting of Parliament on 23 May 1994 he described the newly-elected government's commitment as follows:

> ... to create a people-centered society of liberty binds us to the pursuit of the goals of freedom from want, freedom from hunger, freedom from deprivation, freedom from ignorance, freedom from suppression and freedom from fear. These freedoms are fundamental to the guarantee of human dignity. They will therefore constitute part of the centerpiece of what this government will seek to achieve ... (Liebenberg, 2001: 405)

This chapter will address the issue of the use of the Constitution as a vehicle to address poverty in South Africa. The topic is propitious. The South African Constitution's embrace of a broad array of civil, political, cultural, and socio-economic rights sets it apart from most constitutional arrangements.[1] The Constitutional Court has in the past few years confronted the issue of the judicial enforcement of socio-economic rights, and has, in fact, begun to map out some strategies to give effect to the socio-economic rights listed in the Bill of Rights (De Vos, 2001: 258). The Court's decisions, specifically the *Grootboom*[2] and *Treatment Action Campaign*[3] decisions which dealt with the rights to housing and to health care, respectively, are in many ways landmark decisions, not just under South Africa's constitutional paradigm, but also internationally. Although the Indian Supreme Court has on occasion imposed duties on the Indian government to enforce socio-economic rights listed in the Indian Constitution, most constitutions do not provide for the justiciability of socio-economic rights (Tripathi, 1993). As the UN Economic and Social Council strives to develop a methodology on the implementation of social and economic rights, the Constitutional Court's decisions provide some useful pointers in this regard.

As many South Africans will attest to, and as many who have travelled to South Africa are aware, the country generates all kinds of contradictions – and in the process also stirs up contradictory emotions – of hope and despair, great personal warmth and tremendous sadness.

Shortly after one arrives in Cape Town, one is struck by several observations.

First, the miles and miles of informal settlements, until recently termed squatter camps. The second striking observation is the number of very expensive cars on the roads. Since the prices of luxury cars in South Africa are so very steep, the large numbers are really astounding. Closer to the city, one is struck by the number of notices on houses which warn of armed response in the event of a burglary.

These observations are not particularly novel, nor are they confined to South Africa. Similar images confront observers in Jakarta, Rio de Janeiro and Nairobi. Several historical, political, and economic factors have combined to produce a particular political geography of devastatingly poor communities existing amidst great wealth with a small buffer class in between (Sassen, 2002; Evans, 2002). Justice Kriegler, in an interview conducted in the 1980s, referred to the legal profession in South Africa at that time as 'an enclave of privilege in a sea of misery'. These words, in many ways, apply to all sectors of South African society today.

But despite obvious similarities with other developing countries, and some would argue even in the developed world, South Africa is different. Fifteen years ago the world was mesmerized as the tall dignified figure of Nelson Mandela emerged from prison, where he had spent most of his adult life. The world continued to be transfixed as he shepherded the country to an agreement on the most comprehensive constitution of the late twentieth century, including a detailed listing of rights (Friedman and Atkinson, 1994), and together with the ANC steered the country towards its first ever democratic elections in 1994 (Sparks, 1995).

South Africa provides the most compelling case study for considering the question of constitutional adjudication and review of social and economic rights. The legacy of colonialism and apartheid has resulted in a dualized or hybrid society both peculiar to South Africa, and also typical of many poor countries. Those countries may not have been blighted by the scourge of racism, but the ravages of other criteria utilized for dispossession, abuse, disenfranchisement, and exploitation have rendered similar consequences. It is widely known that the dualism or hybridity in South Africa has resulted in the heights of affluence and the depths of poverty sharing the national space – often amid huge tension. The grand narrative of reconstruction is in many ways unfolding on a global stage and at the center of the narrative is the core question of economic reconstruction (see Sachs, 2000b: 1381).

This chapter will address the following questions:

- What are the specific directives in the Constitution that provide for social and economic rights and what methods are in place with respect to their enforcement?
- How has the Constitutional Court given effect to these rights?
- What are the structural and extra-constitutional impediments to redressing poverty that the Constitution cannot address?
- What are the possibilities other than litigation for redressing poverty?

Social and Economic Rights: Constitutional Provisions

> Both liberty and equality are among the primary goals pursued by human beings through many centuries; but total liberty for wolves is death to the lambs, total liberty of the powerful, the gifted is not compatible with the rights to a decent existence of the weak and the less gifted ... Equality may demand the restraint of the liberty of those who wish to dominate; liberty ... may have to be curtailed in order to make room for social welfare, to feed the hungry, to clothe the naked, to shelter the homeless, ... to allow justice or fairness to be exercised. (Berlin, 1990: 12–13)

The South African Constitution displays an appreciation of the tensions between liberty and equality. Hence the listing of socio-economic rights is extensive. Included are environmental rights, the rights of access to land, housing, health care services, food, water and social security rights. Also included are rights to education and children's socio-economic rights.

What is particularly profound about social and economic rights in the Constitution is that they are subject to judicial review and enforcement. This makes the South African Constitution unique. Whereas most constitutions provide for the justiciabilty of classic civil and political rights – the right to vote or free speech – the South African Constitution rejects this bifurcated approach to rights. What the framers of the Constitution recognized is that all rights are interconnected and in fact depend on one another in mutually reinforcing ways (Sachs, 2000b). So, for example, the argument that access to food and shelter is more important than the right to vote rings hollow. As several commentators have pointed out and as demonstrated by the work of the Nobel laureate Amartya Sen, the existence of democratic institutions plays an indispensable part in the creation of access to life's basic necessities (Sen, 1999).

Subjecting socio-economic rights to judicial review and enforcement makes litigation an important tool. The Bill of Rights has jettisoned the historically stringent standing requirements in favor of more access to individuals and groups.[4]

Unsurprisingly, equality is at the core of the South African Bill of Rights. This principle, of course, is set against a backdrop of institutionalized racism, sexism, homophobia, and other forms of intolerance. The principle therefore is strongly associated with the norm of non-discrimination. In this sense the South African Constitution comports with global human rights developments since the passage of the Universal Declaration of Human Rights – the international endeavor to deal with the legacy of genocide, racial persecution and other egregious forms of rights denial based on race, ethnicity, religion, and other markers of identity.

But the Constitution also references human dignity, and states specifically 'everyone has inherent dignity and the right to have their dignity respected and protected' (Section 10). This adds a unique dimension to the rights endeavor and in particular traditional notions of equality; it links equality to dignity. This has been stated succinctly by Arthur Chaskalson, the Chief Justice of South Africa:

> There is also a close link between dignity and equality. No society can promise equality of goods or wealth. Nor could it reasonably be thought that this is what our Constitution contemplates. It recognizes that at the basic level of basic needs such as housing, health care, food, water and social security, profound inadequacies require state intervention... (Chaskalson, 2000: 202)

This notion, the interlinking of equality and dignity, though fairly fluid, envisions not just individual freedoms in the classical sense, but also, in President Mandela's words, freedom from want, hunger and deprivation.

These references to socio-economic rights in the Constitution make clear that the state provides these rights 'within its available resources', and that they do not confer an entitlement to 'claim the right on demand' (Sections 24–9). As far as the rights of access to housing, health care, sufficient food and water, and social security for those unable to support themselves and their dependants are concerned, the state is not obliged to go beyond available resources or to realize these rights immediately.[5] With respect to land reform, and particularly the pressing question of access to land, the Constitution acknowledges 'the nation's commitment to land reform, and to reform to bring about equitable access to all South Africa's natural resources' (Section 25(4)(a)). The Constitution requires the state to 'take reasonable legislative and other measures within its available resources to foster conditions which enable citizens to gain access to land on an equitable basis' (Section 25 (5))

Here other points may be worth noting about the South African approach to constitutionalism as compared with other models, particularly the American one. The first is, obviously, the respective points of departure. The underlying premise in South Africa is that South Africa is 'an unjust society in which inequality is built in systematically and deeply into the universe of constitutional adjudication' (Sachs, 2000a). In most constitutional democracies, and this is obviously the case in the United States, the assumption is that society is arranged fairly and that any derogation from the status quo has to be justified. The reverse pertains in South Africa: 'any defence of the status quo has to be justified, because the South African reality has been structured in a systematically unfair way'.[6]

The second point worth noting is that the South African Constitution obliges the government to provide a panoply of socio-economic rights. The Constitution therefore embodies both the negative model of constitutional law, that is, a proscription on state intrusion, as well as the positive listing of rights (see Klare, 1998: 146).

This positive duty imposed on the government and the constitutional access to the judiciary to enforce the rights create an identifiable role for the Constitutional Court. The Court is required 'not just to protect the status quo from undue unjustifiable intrusions by the state on people's rights, but it also has to ensure that the rights promised in the Constitution are actually achieved'.[7]

Another feature of the South African Constitution is the mandate to consider international and foreign jurisprudence. A cursory perusal of American jurisprudence suggests that US courts are self-contained and self-referential. Ironically, this mandate to consider international and foreign jurisprudence has not yielded much for the Court in its adjudication of socio-economic rights. In South Africa, to a large extent the script is being written at the outset by the Constitutional Court judges themselves, with very little to draw from in comparative jurisprudence.[8] Although the UN Economic and Social Council has articulated a global approach to the enforcement of socio-economic rights globally, it has done so not as a court of law, instead relying on compliance by member states (UN Economic and Social Council, 1987).

Constitutional Court's Interpretation of Social and Economic Rights

Since its establishment in 1995 the Constitutional Court has carved out a jurisprudence which clearly breaks from South Africa's ignominious legal past to pursue a legal future forged on principles of dignity, equality, and non-discrimination. To illustrate this point, I shall discuss the two most significant and recent cases of the Constitutional Court, which dealt respectively with the right to housing and the right to health care. In both cases the court rulings demonstrate that socio-economic rights can bring meaningful relief to the poorest in the country.

THE GROOTBOOM DECISION

In 2000 the Constitutional Court considered the enforcement of socio-economic rights provided for in the Constitution.[9] The case concerned an application for temporary shelter brought by a group of people, including a number of children, who were without shelter following their brutal eviction from private land on which they were squatting. The community lived in the most intolerable conditions; they had access to one tap and no sanitation facilities.

The Court considered the scope of the obligations imposed on the government to provide housing in terms of section 26 of the Constitution. Section 26 provides as follows:

(1) Everyone has the right to have access to adequate housing.
(2) The state must take reasonable legislative and other measures, within its available resources, to achieve the progressive realisation of this right.
(3) No one may be evicted from their home, or have their home demolished, without an order of court made after considering all the relevant circumstances. No legislation may permit arbitrary evictions.

This case is widely regarded as an international test case of the enforceability of social and economic rights. The Court affirmed that the government had a duty to adopt reasonable policy, legislative, and budgetary measures to provide relief for people who have no access to land, no roof over their heads, and who are living in intolerable conditions. The judgement also dealt in detail with the implications of children's socio-economic rights enshrined in Section 28, which provides, *inter alia*, for every child the right of nutrition and shelter.[10]

It is worth noting that the Court order provided no individual relief to the applicants, although the national government and the Western Cape government had agreed to provide them with various kinds of relief. It so happened that both the national and Western Cape governments failed to honour these agreements. Thus, several months later the Constitutional Court was forced to order them to do so.[11]

THE TREATMENT ACTION CASE

The *Treatment Action* case appeal to the Constitutional Court was directed at reversing orders made in a high court against the government, addressing perceived shortcomings in the government's response to an aspect of the HIV/AIDS challenge. The Constitutional Court found that the government had not reasonably addressed the need to reduce the risk of HIV-positive mothers transmitting the disease to their babies at birth. More specifically the finding was that

the government had acted unreasonably in, first, refusing to make an antiretro-
viral drug called nevirapine available in the public health sector where the
attending doctor considered it medically indicated, and, second, not setting out
a timeframe for a national program to prevent mother-to-child transmission of
HIV.

The case started as an application to the High Court in Pretoria on 21 August
2001. The applicants were a number of associations and members of civil
society concerned with the treatment of people with HIV/AIDS and with the
prevention of new infections. The principal actor among them was the
Treatment Action Campaign (TAC). The respondents were the national
Minister of Health and the respective members of the executive councils
(MECs) responsible for health in all provinces except the Western Cape.[12]

The South African government, as part of an array of responses to the pandemic, had devised a program to deal with mother-to-child transmission of HIV
at birth and identified nevirapine as its drug of choice for this purpose. The
program imposed restrictions on the availability of nevirapine in the public
health sector. This was challenged by the applicants who contended that the
restrictions were unreasonable because the Constitution mandated 'the state
and all its organs to give effect to the rights guaranteed by the Bill of Rights.'[13]
At issue was the public's right to access public health care services[14] and the
right of children to be afforded special protection.[15]

The second issue for the Court to consider was whether the government was
constitutionally obliged to plan and implement an effective, comprehensive, and
progressive program for the prevention of mother-to-child transmission of HIV
throughout the country. The Minister of Health attempted to demonstrate to
the Court the complexity of providing a comprehensive package of care throughout the country. The government's apparent reason for confining the provision
of nevirapine in the public sector to the research sites was to develop and
monitor the human and material resources nationwide for the delivery of a comprehensive package. This package consisted of testing, counselling, and dis-
pensing nevirapine and follow-up services to pregnant women at public health
institutions. The rationale was that the targeted research and training sites
would provide important information, which would guide the government in
developing the very best possible prevention program for mother-to-child transmission of HIV.

The immediate issue requiring the Court's attention, however, was what to do
about those mothers and their babies who could not afford private health care
and who did not have access to the research and training sites.

In a comprehensive judgement, the Court found that the government had not
reasonably addressed the need to reduce the risk of HIV-positive mothers transmitting the disease to their babies at birth. More specifically, the finding was that
the government had acted unreasonably, first by refusing to make an antiretro-
viral drug called nevirapine available in the public health sector where the
attending doctor considered it medically indicated and, second, by not setting
out a timeframe for establishing a national program to prevent mother-to-child
transmission of HIV. The Court ordered the government to do so.

Structural and Extra-Constitutional Impediments to Redressing Poverty

The 'rights revolution' in South Africa in many ways represents an important yardstick in the chronology of human rights activism of the twentieth century. The Constitution and its expansive Bill of Rights have arguably vindicated fifty years of global human rights endeavors that followed the establishment of the United Nations and the promulgation of the Universal Declaration of Human Rights and its progeny (Makau Wa Mutua, 2002). The South African Constitution contains the most comprehensive listing of rights in any national rights document. The drafters of the Bill of Rights were not coy about the aims of the document – to generate a transformative agenda with human rights at the core. The Constitution was designed to be a key instrument in moving the country from being one steeped in minority privilege to one embracing rights for all, and a symbol of the possibilities of human rights as a mode of political transformation (Liebenberg, 2001: 408–9). Sandra Liebenberg has noted thus:

> The apartheid legacy of social and economic deprivation is a major structural source of inequality in South African society. It also undermines human dignity and the freedom to participate fully in the democratic institutions and processes. South Africa has one of the worst records among comparable middle-income developing countries in terms of social indicators (health, education, safe water, fertility) and income inequality. Poverty in South Africa also has strong racial, gender, age and rural dimensions. (ibid.: 408)

The human rights project in South Africa is therefore extremely ambitious. The Portuguese scholar, Boaventura de Sousa Santos, has commented on the primacy of human rights as 'the language of progressive politics,' confidently providing an 'emancipatory script' (de Sousa Santas, 1997) for those seeking redress from unjust and abusive regimes, and increasingly for those who insist that there exists a state duty to address economic inequalities. Upendra Baxi, the Indian legal scholar and human rights activist, refers to the discourse of human rights as 'seeking to supplant all other ethical languages' (Baxi, 1998). This focus has to a large extent replaced the discourse of economic equity and redistribution. It is worth noting that this global project on rights has been analyzed and subject to quite thoughtful critique by international legal scholars (see, for example, Klug, 2000; Gathii, 2000).

The new constitutional dispensation, laudable and ambitious as it is as a model of transformation, is significantly impeded by the broader context of political transformation in South Africa. In other words, the economic legacy of apartheid and its hierarchy has essentially been frozen in the post-apartheid era. During the period of negotiations, which led to the drafting of the interim Constitution and the first democratic elections, it was apparent that a wider program of economic redistribution, an ideological staple of the African National Congress, was no longer possible. The property and other economic rights of whites had to be guaranteed in order to secure stability for the new government. In addition, the politics of economic redistribution had largely been discredited by the end of the 1980s with the collapse of the Eastern European governments and the widespread rejection of communism.

The African National Congress initially adopted a free market paradigm, but with considerable government input through the Reconstruction and Development Program. However, this policy was jettisoned for the Growth, Economic and Redistribution Program (GEAR), one more attractive and more 'market-friendly' to local and foreign investors. South Africans under GEAR are made to believe that this global economic paradigm embracing free markets and privatization is geared to accommodating the free flow of capital and to making South Africa more attractive to foreign investors. But the cumulative consequences for workers and economically marginalized groups are quite deleterious.[16]

In a context in which respect for human rights has historically been an alien tradition, as it was during the apartheid years, to be cavalier about the significance of the codification of rights may appear somewhat misguided. But the formal edifice of law often obscures the underlying structural dimensions which law cannot cure. For example, in the United States, where civil and political rights enjoy constitutional primacy (now being sorely tested by the new war on terrorism), the right to vote remains hollow. A huge proportion of the population, disproportionately people of color, have effectively disregarded the formal electoral process, which is seen as having no relevance to their lives (Bell, 1990). The challenge, therefore, is marrying substance and symbolism.

Extra-Legal Strategies for Reducing Poverty

> While economic growth contributes to poverty reduction, it may not necessarily reduce inequality. Further, there is evidence that countries starting off with significant inequality experience lower growth rates than others because lack of access to physical, financial and human assets constrains poor people from participating effectively and efficiently in the economy.[17]

A vast body of literature continues to illustrate and analyze the structural patterns or practices that result in economically marginalized people being trapped in a spiral of poverty (see, for example, Bhalla, 2002; Taylor, 2000). These patterns include the lack of access to education, health, and other resources that create the possibility of basic subsistence and upward mobility. In addition, the condition of poverty often precludes poor people from access to information about pursuing legal and other rights, and information about credit and access to government services, particularly social services. Another profound pattern is the legacy of internalized inferiority, resulting in, for example, diminished expectations and aspirations.

Despite heated controversies about the structure, role, and consequences of globalization, it is clear that globalization in the form of structural adjustment programs and the primacy of the market has generated inequalities and poverty on a global scale (Stiglitz, 2002; Friedman, 2000).

The post-apartheid democracy in South Africa emerged from a history of extreme economic inequality, one of the highest in the world. Despite South Africa's categorization in the UNDP's *Human Development Report* as a middle-income country, most South Africans can be classified as poor by all economic indicators, and many straddle the fine line between subsistence and vulnerability to poverty. Rural poverty is particularly pronounced in South Africa, and since the majority of residents in rural areas are women, poverty in South Africa has a particularly gendered flavour.[18] The challenge for South African democracy is therefore to reduce poverty by promoting opportunity, income and wealth and, at the same time, reduce economic inequality.

When faced with this challenge of Sisyphean proportions, constitutional imperatives appear somewhat ineffective. But the reality in South Africa is that the embrace and enforcement of social and economic rights through the Constitution are part of an overall package of transformation in the country. South Africa, through the constitutionalizing of social and economic rights, effectively chose a particular model of democracy unique not only just in the African continent but also globally. This stands in stark contrast to the prevailing orthodoxy in Africa at the time of independence as demonstrated by the late President Kwame Nkrumah's oft-cited aphorism: 'Seek ye first the political kingdom and all else will follow.'[19] South Africans could benefit from the lessons learned from the experience of successive forms of government adopted in post-colonial Africa, almost all of which failed to improve the economic lot of their citizenry. The lessons from these societies teach that the political kingdom must be predicated on changing both the political and economic realities of the citizenry.

In the absence of a redistributive economic paradigm, constitutionalizing social and economic rights creates the possibilities for holding governments accountable and imposing duties on them to provide for life's basic necessities. The South African Constitutional Court has demonstrated its willingness to do exactly that.[20] But as is the case with all rights enshrined in a constitution, their enforcement is limited by the ability and willingness of civil society to pursue the implementation of these rights and by the government's willingness to give effect to the orders of the Constitutional Court.

South Africa boasts an energetic civil society as evidenced by the large number of non-governmental organizations in the country. Arguably the innovation and determination of the vast range of NGOs contributed substantially to the demise of apartheid. Many of the tactics utilized during the struggle against apartheid are now being used by NGOs to pursue rights in this new constitutional era. The national and provincial governments have inherited an enormous backlog of economic needs and inequalities; they have an unenviable task in addressing these needs and redressing the inequalities. Addressing these problems will require fortitude, foresight, good planning, effective administration and a clear commitment to success. Even with strong commitment and planning, ultimately it is the organ of civil society that will ensure that the socio-economic rights in the Constitution remain more than symbolic.

Notes

1 Constitution of Republic of South Africa Act 108 of 1996 (hereinafter 'Constitution'); *see also* Dugard (1996: 13).
2 *Government of the Republic of South Africa and Others v. Grootboom and Others* 2000 (II) BCLR 1169 (CC).
3 *Minister of Health and others v. Treatment Action Campaign and Others* 2002 (5) SA. 721 (CC).
4 Section 38 of the Constitution provides as follows: Anyone listed in this section has the right to approach a competent court alleging that a right in the Bill of Rights has been

infringed or threatened, and the court may grant appropriate relief, including a declaration of rights. The persons who may approach a court are –
(a) anyone acting in their own interest;
(b) anyone acting on behalf of another person who cannot act in their own name;
(c) anyone acting as a member of, or in the interest of, a group or class of persons;
(d) anyone acting in the public interest; and
(e) an association acting in the interest or its members.
[5] The state must take reasonable legislative and other measures, within its available resources, to achieve the progressive realization of these rights. *Ibid.*
[6] *Ibid.* Indeed the Constitutional Court has noted that equality is 'premised on a recognition that the ideal of equality will not be achieved if the consequences of those inequalities and disparities caused by discriminatory laws and practices in the past are not recognised and dealt with'. *Pretoria City Council v. Walker* (1998) 2 (SA) 363 (CC).
[7] Albie Sachs, (2000a) The late Justice Ismail Mahomed set out clearly the transformative goals of the Constitution, and by implication the role of the Constitutional Court, in giving effect to those rights. In *S v. Makwanyane* 1995 (3) SA 391 (CC) he noted:
> In some countries the Constitution only formalises, in a legal instrument, a historical consensus of values and aspirations evolved incrementally from a stable and unbroken past to accommodate the needs of the future. The South African Constitution is different: it retains from the past only what is defensible and represents a decisive break from, and a ringing rejection of, that part of the past which is disgracefully racist, authoritarian, insular and repressive, and a vigorous identification of and commitment to a democratic, universalistic, caring and aspirationally egalitarian ethos expressly articulated in the Constitution...
[8] There has not been much litigation on socio-economic rights in constitutional democracies. India provides an exception. See Seth (1995, 97). The Court has also drawn from the constitutional jurisprudence of Germany and Canada, particularly with respect to the notion of dignity.
[9] This was not the first time that the Court had to consider the interpretation of social and economic rights in the Constitution. In 1998 the Court had occasion to consider the issue of the right to health brought by a man who had suffered kidney failure and who sought an order compelling the Kwa-Zulu Natal Health Department to provide him access to expensive dialasyis treatment. The Court found against the applicant, stating that it would be 'slow to interfere with rational decisions taken in good faith by the political organs and medical authorities'. *Soobramoney v. Minister of Health, Kwa-Zulu Natal* 1998 (1) SA 765 (CC).
[10] Section 28 provides in part as follows: (1) Every child has the right –
   a. to a name and a nationality from birth;
   b. to family care or parental care, or to appropriate alternative care when removed from the family environment;
   c. to basic nutrition, shelter, basic health care services and social services;
   d. to be protected from maltreatment, neglect, abuse or degradation;
   e. to be protected from exploitative labour practices .....
[11] When I visited South Africa in September 2002 I was informed by community activists in Cape Town that many of the *Grootboom* applicants had still not obtained the relief promised them by the Western Cape and national governments.
[12] The Western Cape government had not been brought in as a party because it had in place a program at public hospitals to distribute nevirapine to HIV-positive pregnant women.
[13] This duty is articulated in Sections 7 (2) and 8 (1) of the Constitution respectively:
7 (2): The state must respect, protect, promote and fulfil the rights in the Bill of Rights;
8 (1): The Bill of Rights applies to all law, and binds the legislature, the executive, the judiciary and all organs of state.
[14] Section 27 of the Constitution provides that everyone has the right to have access to health care services, including reproductive health care, Section 27 (1) (a). Section 27 (2) provides that the state must take reasonable legislative and other measures, within its

available resources, to achieve the progressive realisation of each of these rights.
[15] Section 28 (1) states that every child has the right to basic nutrition, shelter, basic health care services and social services. See note 10 above.
[16] For a detailed and passionate description of the negative impact of the post-apartheid economic paradigm on marginalized groups, see Desai (2002).
[17] 'Poverty and Inequality in South Africa', Report Prepared for the Office of the Executive Deputy President and the Inter-Ministerial Committee for Poverty and Inequality, 13 May 1998.
[18] This situation reflects the patterns of rural poverty in much of the rest of Africa. See Armstrong (1987). What is different about South Africa has been the migrant labor system which existed for several decades and which prohibited African women from gainful employment in the cities, thereby cementing the unequal economic status of African women. See Andrews (2001:326).
[19] For a thoughtful exploration of the ideology espoused by Kwame Nkrumah, see Williams (1984).
[20] The Constitutional Court is not the only body empowered to enforce the rights out-lined in the Bill of Rights. The Constitution empowers both the Human Rights Commission and the Gender Commission to pursue the implementation of these rights. Specifically Section 184 (3) provides as follows:

> Each year, the South African Human Rights Commission must require relevant organs of state to provide the Commission with information on the measures that they have taken towards the realisation of the rights in the Bill of Rights concerning housing, health care, food, water, social security, education and the environment.

The obligation imposed on the Gender Commission is less specific, but the Constitution states in Section 187 (2) that:

> The Commission for Gender Equality has the power, as regulated by national legisla-tion, necessary to perform its functions, including the power to monitor, investigate, research, educate, lobby, advise and report on issues concerning gender equality.

6

PETER N. TAKIRAMBUDDE & KATE K. FLETCHER
Civil Society in Governance & Poverty Alleviation: A Human Rights Perspective

Introduction

POVERTY alleviation efforts cannot be successful in the long term without respect for human rights. Poverty will continue so long as governments lack accountability to their citizenry and so long as the voices of large portions of populations, especially among the impoverished and socially isolated, remain weak. In the words of Kofi Annan, 'good governance is perhaps the single most important factor in eradicating poverty and promoting development' (UNDP Bureau for Development Policy, 2002: 1). Poor governance as well as the lack of transparency and accountability enable widespread poverty to exist in a nation. As Amartya Sen argues, 'no substantial famine has ever occurred in a democratic country because a government which has to deal with opposition parties, to answer unfriendly questions in parliament, to face condemnation from the public media, to go to the polls on a regular basis, simply cannot afford not to take prompt action to avert threatening famine' (Sen, 1999b: 3). Without transparent and fully participatory elections, without freedom of the press and freedom of speech, and without free association, governments will be unaccountable. And with unaccountable governments, poverty will continue.

The development community has increasingly come to recognize the links between civil and political rights, good governance, and economic development. Traditionally, scholars understood poverty in purely economic terms, referring primarily to income levels. After evaluating the many failed structural adjustment programs (SAPs) of the 1980s, the World Bank and the International Monetary Fund, as well as bilateral donors, have come to understand and define poverty more broadly: '[T]he goals of development have come to embrace the elimination of poverty in all its dimensions – income poverty, illiteracy, poor health, insecurity of income and powerlessness' (Goldin *et al.*, 2002: 5).

By recognizing the substantial role of the powerlessness and the lack of participation in perpetuating poverty, corruption, and overall poor governance, the international financial institutions concede to the link between sustainable development and human rights. In fact, the United Nations Development Program explicitly embraces a 'human rights approach to poverty alleviation [that] will emphasize empowerment, participation and nondiscrimination and address vulnerability, marginalization and exclusion' (UNDP, 1998: 11).

While the UNDP's declared intention to adopt a human rights approach carries real promise, one must not forget that the dominant development paradigm continues to understand economic growth as a priority over, and a precondition for, political reform and human rights advancement. How the international community defines poverty and the degree to which it acknowledges the necessity of political reform for economic development are particularly important at this moment, as the international development agenda of the United Nations and virtually all major donor nations are focusing on the Millennium Goals, which include reducing poverty by half by 2015. To realize and sustain this goal, the first discussion must be about governance, as well as about civil and political rights. Without the essential components of participatory governance and basic civil rights, development programs will continue to yield unsatisfactory results.

Accountability: Human Rights, Poverty, and Civil Society

The primary role of civil society with respect to poverty alleviation is to force accountability and transparency upon the government. Civil society organizations (CSOs) often work in conjunction with the media, acting as a thorn in the side of government and constantly prodding the government to account for its actions and expenditures. These activities require the political environment in which they operate to allow CSOs sufficient space to function. Specifically, certain human rights – freedom of association, freedom of expression, and freedom of the press – must be sufficiently strong to allow civil society actors to form organizations and to disseminate criticism of the government. Internally, CSOs require sufficient capacity to provide real pressure for accountability and transparency within the government. Without access to information, analytical expertise, and advocacy capabilities, CSOs are ill equipped to make an impact on government operations and conduct.

Putting Governance on the Development Agenda

The international community, including many African leaders, continues, explicitly or implicitly, to be guided by the 'full belly' thesis: the view that civil and political rights are secondary to economic advancement; that a government's first priority should be providing the essentials to the population; and that the agitation over civil and political rights must not hinder this priority as the government pursues the necessary economic development of the nation. Our position at Human Rights Watch has been and continues to be that civil and political rights are not luxuries that governments can set aside until the economy reaches a certain degree of success. Civil and political rights are the foundation upon which a country will build lasting economic success.

Human Rights Watch advocates the principle that meaningful exercise of economic and social rights requires principled protection of civil and political rights. It is all too common for the political elite to pass off these rights as necessary steps on the road to development. Experience increasingly demonstrates that when civil and political rights are lacking, economic and social rights are lacking as well. Without the check that civil and political rights provide on the government, citizens lack a means for redress when the government fails to deliver economic and social rights. In order to distribute economic resources effectively, the recipient communities must be able to communicate their needs to the leadership. 'Simply assuming or appealing to government commitment to poverty reduction may be both unrealistic and insufficient... The challenge is therefore not only to address poverty reduction and governance together but also to design and operate the governance mechanisms in ways which muster societal dynamics for the benefit of poverty reduction, in other words, to make governance participatory' (UNDP, 1998: 11).

Even if a government had the self-motivation to devote significant resources to poverty alleviation, there is no reason to believe that its successor would do the same. Sustainable poverty alleviation is created when domestic pressures and institutions force the government to respond to the needs of its citizenry, and when the masses are able to exert political influence: 'accountability has political, administrative, legal and moral dimensions which form a rather complex web relying on clear rules of transparency, and on the threat of sanctions in case of non-compliance' (Schneider, 1999: 8).

Lack of accountability and transparency also contributes directly to poverty and economic stagnation or recession by facilitating corruption. It is not uncommon to find poverty running rampant in countries with rampant government corruption. Corruption directly contributes to poverty by diverting resources away from programs and services meant to ameliorate the plight of the poor, such as education, health care, and even infrastructure expansion. Widespread corruption also undermines the rule of law and the justice system: endemic and ubiquitous corruption threatens personal security and individual rights and freedoms, because those who are sufficiently well connected and/or wealthy can circumvent justice. Corruption creates instability and unpredictability in governance, undermining a nation's overall economic health because individuals and corporations are hesitant to invest under such conditions. This kind of private investment is essential for sustainable economic growth. Today, the instability and lack of transparency that corruption fosters not only deter foreign investors, but also prompt domestic investors to put their capital into foreign economies.

'Rich poor nations'(countries that possess significant wealth in the form of natural resources) underscore the degree that the lack of accountability and transparency contributes to poverty, as their governments claim to suffer severe budget constraints and large portions of the population are impoverished. However, natural resources fund these states. The resources are a type of 'unearned income', which Mick Moore of the Institute of Development Studies defines as: 'income that derives from a few sources, requires little organizational and political effort to collect, and involves little interaction between the state (civilian) apparatus and the mass of citizens' (Moore, 2000: 17). Accountability requires that in some very tangible sense the government is politically and financially beholden to its people. Governments funded by natural resources are essentially independent of their citizenry, and face no adverse repercussions for failing to respond to the needs or to respect the rights of their citizens. Consequently, such nations are often 'undemocratic, despotic, politically unstable, vulnerable to coup and insurrection, and often plain ineffective' (ibid.: 14).

The 'Full Belly' Fails in Practice

A mounting body of evidence refutes the efficacy of development initiatives based on the 'full belly' thesis. In Asia, the economic crisis of the late 1990s severely undermined the notion that economic growth should precede democratization and broad political reform. The World Bank stated in its September 1998 report, *East Asia: the Road to Recovery*, that poor governance – lack of transparency and accountability – exacerbated the region's economic problems. Furthermore, it became clear that nations like South Korea and Thailand, which have begun to implement systems of protection for basic civil and political rights and have made significant reforms in their electoral systems, were in a better position to weather the downturn and to begin to recover.

ASIA

In both Thailand and South Korea, voters expressed their anger and frustration with the government's corruption and failures by electing a new leadership. The change to a large extent allayed public dissatisfaction, and the new government in each country was able to address the economic ills and associated crises without having to contend with widespread hostility. In contrast, dictatorial rule in Indonesia left no outlet for the public outcry that accompanied the economic meltdown. When President Soeharto was 'unanimously re-elected' in March 1998, chaos erupted as masses of dissatisfied Indonesians took to the streets. Over one thousand people were killed before Soeharto was forced to step down two months later. While South Korea and Thailand are recovering from the economic crisis, Indonesia's political and economic recovery remains highly uncertain. Responsive regimes prove better able to ride the ups and downs of economic cycles. Furthermore, people who lack peaceful means of expressing discontent and effecting change often see violence as the only alternative.

AFRICA

Experience in Africa also undermines the 'full belly' thesis. In several African countries, political and structural controls limit reform efforts by preventing effective querying of government policy and operations. Even those who gain office through institutional reforms within the government demonstrate reluctance to reform further to a fully developed democratic political system and the total realization of civil rights.

In Uganda, despite generous poverty alleviation funding from the World Bank, the IMF, and other international donors, President Yoweri Museveni's government remains an authoritarian regime hiding under a façade of inclusion. The so-called no-party 'movement' severely restricts any political or social opposition, while claiming to increase political participation and inclusion. Without an effective means to voice dissent, disenchanted groups appear to turn to violence. Rebel forces continue to operate in different parts of Uganda. The rebel activity in turn leads to counter-insurgency operations, which have depopulated huge areas of northern Uganda. The ongoing violence has caused increasing instability in the investment climate and has hampered the distribution of resources, making growth, let alone poverty reduction, difficult to sustain.

In Zimbabwe, President Robert Mugabe has created a *de facto* one-party system with highly centralized authority. Corruption is widespread in the government and the government severely restricts basic civil liberties. Critically, the lack of democratic accountability, respect for human rights, and the rule of law has damaged Zimbabwe's once excellent economic prospects. Violent intimidation of the opposition and vote rigging marked the 2002 presidential elections, which the international community outside Africa denounced almost universally. Several bilateral donors withdrew their aid. Adding to the precarious economic situation, President Mugabe carried out his land-redistribution plan, which forced white commercial farmers to halt farming even before their land was seized for redistribution. Once taken, the land was given to influential politicians and military officers. Agricultural production has been severely hit and large numbers of farm workers thrown out of work. The country now teeters on the brink of famine and total economic collapse, and inflation approaches 600 per cent.

Similarly, poor governance caused economic stagnation and a real drop in living standards in Kenya. In the 1970s and '80s, the West touted Kenya as the prime African investment target. Once in power, President Daniel Arap Moi increased restrictions on civil and political rights to reinforce his control, which caused widespread violence and intimidation to dominate Kenya for over two decades. The economic situation, like the political climate, declined under Moi; the infrastructure deteriorated, the budget deficit escalated, and inflation climbed steadily.

However, unlike in other similar situations, the international community took a stand on human rights abuses and corruption by limiting funding to the government while simultaneously increasing funding to CSOs. By investing significantly in Kenya's CSOs, donor nations enabled substantial capacity-building and helped establish one of Africa's most vibrant civil societies. The outcome of the 2002 presidential elections in Kenya indicates that the investment in civil society has paid off. It is readily apparent that civil society was a key force behind the successful democratic election and was instrumental in creating the political climate that prompted Moi to step down. His successor, President Kibaki, pledges to end corruption and cronyism.

Understanding Civil Society

Before delving into the myriad forms of civil society actions that contribute to participatory governance and ultimately to poverty reduction, it is worth briefly considering what *civil society* means. Civil society is a notoriously ambiguous term and its place in society is equally unclear. A civil society organization is any association of citizens who have come together, independent of government and political parties, to pursue a given social or political agenda. Such a definition includes associations of academics, NGOs, trade unions, and women's groups. Some debate exists as to whether the private sector is part of civil society, or whether it is a third sector operating independently of civil society and the government.

The role that civil society can or should play depends to some degree on how it is defined, as clearly some activity acceptable for corporations is not acceptable for NGOs and vice versa. Theoretically, one can understand civil society as occupying a space between the government and society at large, acting as a bulwark of participatory governance and democracy by bridging the gap between government and society. In reality, however, this 'middle-space' does not exist.

In reality, 'civil society' is a category of highly disparate and politicized elements of society. It is inevitable that the varied associations and organizations included under the 'civil society' umbrella will have different interests and will pursue agendas that are in tension with one another and, in some circumstances, in direct opposition: '[C]ivil society organizations are not used to acting together and often don't have the same views and positions. In some countries civil society is very fragmented; each section only considers its own sector' (Warnock and van der Gaag, 2002: 26). Any discussion concerning civil society must take this fact into consideration, otherwise whatever conclusions are drawn are likely to be fundamentally limited in their applicability.

GOVERNMENT REGULATION

Government policies also limit the degree to which civil society accurately represents the interests of the poor and other marginalized sectors of society. '[T]he nature of interaction between the state and civil society depends on the prevailing system of governance – of rights to information, accountability and transparency – and respect for democratic practice' (SGTS & Associates, 2000: 39). In several countries, the government places significant controls on civil society through licensing requirements and substantial fines for failure to follow the rules controlling civil society's conduct. In such countries, civil society is not necessarily a good proxy for the politically weak; it is likely that the government will license a limited number of organizations that lobby against its interests. Those that the government does allow are likely to be vigilantly monitored and perhaps harassed by the authorities. As a result, whole sectors of society may lack a voice in the civil society community because their interests run contrary to those of the government.

Across Africa, civil society activists are subject to intimidation, harassment, imprisonment, and torture. A small number of countries allow CSOs to operate with relative freedom, among them Botswana, Kenya, Mauritius, Mali, Nigeria, Senegal, Sierra Leone, South Africa and Tanzania. But in many more instances, the government heavily censors or entirely silences the press, and civil society activists work in rigorously limited political environments and face serious security risks. Many countries, including Cameroon, Côte d'Ivoire, the DRC, Ethiopia, Liberia, Mauritania, Sudan and Togo, restrict or entirely shut down research and advocacy efforts.

Swaziland and Rwanda provide two illustrative examples of the differing forms and degrees of government regulation that adversely affect CSO operations. In Swaziland, civil liberties are basically non-existent. The Swazi monarchy tightly controls the media and civil society. After the threat of an end to US trade relations, the Swazi monarchy allowed labor unions. No other CSO is allowed. Rwanda requires all local and international NGOs to register under a law passed in 2001. Thus far, the government appears to have granted registration to the majority of applicants, though the law gives the authorities broad power to interfere with CSOs. In February 2002, a new law took effect in Rwanda that punishes any speech or action considered as promoting discrimination or sectarianism. While, on the surface this law appears to be a positive measure, it provides a method for the government to repress opposition. Under the law, courts can dissolve political parties or NGOs found guilty of sectarianism and can annul election results if it is found that a candidate employed discrimination or sectarianism during the campaign. Under another new law, private radio and television stations can now be licensed. But the law also creates a national press council operating under presidential authority, which can accredit or ban publication and close down radio and television stations. It can also impose heavy sentences on journalists, publishers, or even street vendors for broadly defined infractions such as endangering law and order, defaming the authorities, or undermining army morale.

LIMITED CSO CAPACITY

One must also consider that an organization with significantly limited capacities can find its activities and effectiveness constrained. Capacity constraints affect the type and scope of CSO work as well as their ability to represent the poor:

> Civil society capacity for participation is limited, and organizations do not have the necessary analytical, advocacy and research capacities. Therefore, their ability to provide meaningful input is limited. Translating the perspective of the poor into a complex policy arena is a difficult task, and calls for greater 'economic literacy' skills in the community... [The] issue of how well these groups represent the needs of the poor needs to be addressed... (SGTS & Associates, 2000: 49)

National CSOs operate on excessively low budgets and are often highly understaffed. Under such circumstances, it is difficult to acquire the multi-disciplinary expertise that development activities often require. Similarly, CSOs are unlikely to have the resources to devote to extensive research, data collection, and information gathering, which often forces them to rely on secondary sources. Beyond this, unlike donor governments or international organizations such as the World Bank and the IMF, CSOs essentially lack leverage over government actors. Rather, they depend upon the government for information and for maintaining a political environment that enables civil society, and, in some cases for funding, a branch of government hires a CSO as an outside consultant. It is important to take these constraints into consideration when determining the role of civil society.

PRSP: Not Participatory Governance

In 1999, the World Bank and the IMF introduced a new tool in international development programming, the Poverty Reduction Strategy Paper (PRSP). The PRSP arose in response to widespread criticism of structural adjustment programs and strong advocacy for debt relief in developing nations. Formulating an approved PRSP is now a condition for debt relief. The World Bank and the IMF intended the PRSP to embody a broader approach to poverty alleviation that would include efforts to address good governance. In an attempt to tailor development programs to local needs and to facilitate participation in governance, which is a key aspect of good governance, the PRSP requires governments to undertake a process of consultation with civil society. The World Bank asserts that this consultation enables the PRSP to identify 'in a participatory manner the poverty reduction outcomes a country wishes to achieve and the key public actions – policy changes, institutional reforms, programs, and projects...which are needed to achieve the desired outcomes'. It has been observed that 'this new approach ... offers an unprecedented opportunity for development efforts to re-focus on poverty reduction, and for civil society organizations to influence anti-poverty policy' (ibid.).

However, as discussed earlier, it is risky to consider civil society participation as a substitute for popular participation. The Panos Institute, in addressing the PRSP, argues that 'many civil society organizations are not participatory, do not represent the poor or exclude certain social groups such as ethnic minorities, and have little legitimacy. Most of those involved have been urban based. It's not clear whether poor people themselves have been involved in most countries, and whether they have directly or indirectly had an impact' (Warnock and van der Gaag, 2002: 26). In Uganda, the vast majority of leaders of national-level development-focused CSOs come from western Uganda, the region where Museveni and the nation's political elite originate. This raises significant questions about the degree to which these organizations can speak for or represent the politically marginalized in a country where ethnicity is a significant component of political and social life (Brock et al., 2002: 20). In fact, some Ugandans view NGOs as illegitimate actors whose influence is eclipsing that of 'legitimately elected local politicians' (ibid.: 19).

The World Bank intended the PRSP to be a partnership between the government and actors in civil society, the private sector, and the donor community. The PRSP framework for this partnership is, however, incomplete. The PRSP requires national governments to describe their methods of consultation with civil society, but establishes no criteria for the depth of participation that the consultations should reflect. Consequently, governments can exercise immense control over the degree to which civil society can affect PRSP design and implementation. For example, convening consultations with civil society after the PRSP has gone through several drafts and is near its final form prevents civil society from making a meaningful impact. In contrast, consultations begun at the outset of the drafting process with opportunities for iterative feedback facilitate the influence of civil society. Fundamentally, the government controls the policy-making processes (even those prompted by the World Bank and the IMF) and the degree that civil society is enabled to affect these processes.

Furthermore, it is not entirely clear that information-sharing and consultation, the levels at which most governments involve civil society in the PRSP, can be considered participatory processes that facilitate government accountability (McGee and Norton, 2000: 63–5). Information-sharing and consultation with civil society can potentially make policies more sensitive to the needs of the poor, but this process is not binding on governments. The obvious potential for governments to comply with the consultation requirement while subverting substantive participation has raised doubts about the World Bank's commitment to participatory programming and partnership. In Uganda, CSOs suggest that the PRSP actually exploits civil society's claim to political legitimacy in order to facilitate World Bank programming: 'there is growing concern that perhaps [CSO] participation in the endeavor has amounted to little more than a way for the World Bank and IMF to co-opt the activist community and civil society in

Uganda into supporting the same traditional policies ... to create a perception that the NGO community has given its blessing to a strategy' that it opposes (Warnock and van der Gaag, 2002; 24)

Creating Change

It is important to recognize that procedural participation will not translate into accountability in a political environment that does not broadly embrace civil and political rights; elections can be manipulated to undermine accountability and participation. Participatory governance requires an open environment that enables the free flow of information and collective action. As Hartmut Schneider of the OECD Development Centre states, 'a climate of civil liberties is necessary both to perceive a variety of claims as legitimate and to encourage an active role of the poor in putting forward claims and getting involved in activities and organizations oriented towards satisfying those claims' (Schneider, 1999: 14). Yet, in many nations a 'climate of civil liberties' does not exist. While some threshold level of liberties is necessary, civil society can operate even under constraints to promote human rights and good governance.

Civil society is a highly diverse entity that incorporates divergent sectors of society. Circumstances such as geographical isolation, lack of information, and poor political education often marginalize civil society. However, affecting government policies and actions requires more force than any single sector can create on its own. It is therefore imperative for civil society organizations to develop shared goals and strategies and to co-ordinate action through broad coalitions along lines of shared interest: 'Since the poor are normally not a homogenous group, possibly located in different geographic areas and facing different types of deprivation, a variety of claims and configurations of actors can be envisaged' (ibid.: 13).

The primary weapon of the poor is their numbers. By networking and co-ordinating their efforts, CSOs can erect an 'infrastructure for empowerment' that exploits this strength and organizes the poor as 'stake holders and actors in their own right' (ibid.). CSOs can work to make poor populations aware of their rights and entitlements under the law. They can inform citizens of voting registrations and procedures. By acting as liaisons between the urban and rural poor, they can help to establish bridges of understanding for collective action. CSO networks create the potential for the 'voiceless' to be heard through working with the media to accurately represent the conditions of poverty, raising awareness among the larger public, and perhaps motivating international pressure for government action. Such undertakings begin to create accountability by revealing government neglect and/or abuse, thereby activating pressure points to take advantage of achieving government reforms.

Raising international awareness of corruption and human rights abuse can spur change, especially when a government depends on foreign aid. Ultimately, international pressure is a stopgap form of accountability that can lead to some degree of better governance. But one must not consider international pressure to be a replacement for government institutions that are answerable to the citizenry. Countries must create good governance, like poverty alleviation, from within. That is not to say that international pressure and accountability are not worth pursuing as an interim goal to open up space for developing greater local accountability.

Local CSOs can work with international NGOs to pressure donor nations to include audit requirements when they give loans or grants. By lobbying governments to release budget information and by bringing pressure to bear on governments to account for their funding, civil society makes it more difficult for corruption to continue. Of course, this approach is only applicable when a government depends on foreign aid. Accountability of any kind is far more difficult to achieve when natural resources such as oil fund governments which are therefore beholden to no one.

Angola, where oil generates roughly 90 per cent of government funds, illustrates the difficulty in achieving accountability in an 'oil state' (Human Rights Watch, 2001: 1). Angola's government finances are currently highly opaque, making it 'impossible for the Angolan public and media to hold the government accountable for its use of public funds... The government has responded to public and press criticism of its use of the country's oil revenues by clamping down on journalists and restricting freedom of expression...fiscal transparency, political accountability, and human rights are inextricably intertwined' (ibid.: 2). In April 2000, the IMF instituted the Oil Diagnostic to facilitate transparency and good governance by determining the amount of revenue to be deposited in Angola's central bank so that the executive branch could not divert oil revenues to secret projects. The Oil Diagnostic was part of a larger agreement that promised aid in return for reform. The Oil Diagnostic program hired an independent auditor, KPMG, to monitor the inflow of oil revenue into the central bank for two years. However, the findings are the property of the Angolan government, which has neither released the findings nor authorized the IMF to make the findings public. If the Angolan government does not make the KPMG report public, the increase in transparency and accountability from the Oil Diagnostic will be minimal.

The Oil Diagnostic illustrates the immense challenges there are in establishing accountability when the government is not dependent on its citizenry. It is a highly limited program between the IMF (a powerful international organization) and the Angolan government. Civil society will face even greater challenges than the IMF in attempting to create fiscal accountability. Yet, as mentioned in the Human Rights Watch 2001 report, the Angolan government has responded defensively to public criticism by seeking to limit freedom of expression.

Conclusion

Civil society organizations can contribute substantially to poverty alleviation. There are innumerable examples of highly successful programs implemented by CSOs that improve the well-being of the impoverished in real terms. However, organizations often develop these programs in isolation and consequently they do not affect poverty alleviation on a national scale. Nevertheless, civil society organizations do have a role to play on the national level.

Civil society has a role to play in publicly challenging the government and in demanding accountability. Since civil society was first recognized as a significant actor in African politics, its primary role has been democratic consolidation.

Civil society works to achieve this by altering the balance of power between the state and society; improving the accountability of politicians and administrators; and acting as an intermediary between state and society to legitimize the system by promoting liberal democratic values (Hearn, 1999: 14–15).

7

MUNA NDULO

Decentralization:
Challenges of Inclusion & Equity in Governance

Introduction

THERE are typically three levels of government: national, sub-national (regional) and local. Decentralization stresses the delegation of central government functions to lower levels of government (regional or local) to which may then be granted a sphere of autonomy protected from the supremacy of national government. In response to the demands for greater self-determination, influence in decision-making and efficiency in the delivery of services and goods, many countries are devolving political, fiscal, and administrative powers to sub-national tiers of government. This trend can be seen in countries with a long tradition of centralized government as well as in federalist systems, and in developing as well as industrialized countries.[1] Yet, the issue of the devolution of power is one that many African states have yet to address or provide for adequately. The African independence constitutions did not provide for elected governments accessible to the people at the local level. The local government systems that were established were centrally controlled through the Ministry of Local Government and power remained consolidated in the central government.[2] Typically local government was organized around provincial and local administration composed of urban and rural councils. Local authorities exercised only powers delegated to them by the central government. They have little autonomy vis-à-vis central authority.[3]

In this chapter we examine the arguments for devolution: the powers sub-national tiers of government should enjoy, the relationship between sub-national and central government, and the critical elements that must be addressed if devolution is to succeed. Since devolution seeks to transfer political, administrative and economic authority from the center to local communities, promote popular participation, empower local people to make decisions, enhance accountability and responsibility, and aims to introduce efficiency and effectiveness in the generation and management of resources – goals sometimes in tension with one another – the means adopted to devolve power must be skillfully tailored to the specific context in order to have a realistic possibility of achieving the objectives of devolution. Its success depends on its design and on the institutional arrangements governing its implementation (World Bank, 2001). This chapter will highlight the key issues relevant to the process of devolution of power to local communities. In this discussion, concepts like 'federalism' are avoided as not being conducive to productive analysis.[4] What form the devolution of power takes in an individual state should depend on the political and economic conditions that prevail in that country.

The shift toward devolution reflects the political evolution towards more democratic and participatory forms of government that seek to improve the responsiveness and accountability of political leaders to their electorates. It is premised on the fundamental belief that human beings can govern themselves in peace and dignity in pursuit of their collective well-being, once they are entrusted with control of their own destiny through the medium of popular local democratic institutions. The general arguments to support devolution are therefore clear. It is only through participatory and representative democracy that any form of government can legitimately formulate its priorities and programs. In economic terms, devolution permits governments to match the provision of local public goods and services with the preferences of recipients. Competition between sub-national governments can also lead to the introduction of innovative social and regulatory policies that can then be adopted nationwide. It also may enable people to vote with their feet as they move to regions that are better managed and are more prosperous. In political terms, devolution provides local minorities with greater opportunities to preserve their distinctive cultural and linguistic identities. As Ortega and Gasset observed:

> Devolution of power to regions will serve not only to satisfy historical, cultural and linguistic aspirations, but also, and above all, will draw the average citizen closer to the centers of power and increase his [or her] capacity to control and participate in the decisions of government (Rodden and Rose-Ackerman, 1997: 1580).

Devolution can further be justified on the grounds that, throughout history, it has developed as societies respond through government to reconcile diverse cultures, religions and languages, particularly in large countries where unitary and central administration is difficult. Yet, even in smaller nations, where such an administration might be feasible, devolution has proven attractive because it permits the accommodation of local interests within the framework of a stable, central authority. Not surprisingly, then, history shows that the balance of power between central and sub-national authorities tends to flow back and forth in response to changing conditions and leadership. Devolution of power to local communities is, therefore, a critical element of good governance, since it provides additional checks and balances on central government and a degree of security for constitutional order and social stability that is vital for economic order and development and thereby contributes to the reduction of poverty.[5]

Good Governance and the Devolution of Power

The development of a government's popular legitimacy and credibility correlates closely with its conduct and its establishment of institutions that allow for popular participation at all levels. This requires the effective devolution of government (Consultative Business Movement, 1993: 2). Before discussing some of the elements required for effective devolution, it is important to understand the case for devolution itself. It is equally important to be clear about the potential dangers inherent in the establishment of a sub-national system of government. Devolution does not automatically ensure good governance. Care must be taken to structure devolution in a way which ensures that its positive contributions are maximized and its negative potential minimized.

THE POLITICAL BENEFITS

One positive political contribution is that a well-constructed sub-national system can enhance good governance. As a South African study (ibid.: 11) has observed, devolution can deepen democracy by bringing government closer to the people. By creating a number of governments below the national level, it multiplies the opportunities for political participation and thus contributes to the creation of a democratic culture. The right to participation is an important opportunity embedded within the framework of decentralization. Participation as a human right is an essential aspect in determining the democratic content of any political system. The multiple layers of activity at various levels of local councils that result from devolution engender enormous community participation. Since locally-elected leaders know their constituents better than authorities at the national level, they are better positioned to provide the public services that local communities need. When things go wrong, physical proximity also makes it easier for citizens to hold local officials accountable for their performance. Furthermore, when a country finds itself deeply divided, especially along geographic or ethnic lines, which is the case in most African countries, devolution provides an institutional mechanism for bringing opposition groups into a formal, rule-bound bargaining process.

For example, in Uganda and South Africa devolution has served as a path to national unity (World Bank, 2000a: 109). In Uganda, the task Museveni faced when he assumed power in 1985 was to reunite a country that had splintered into hostile factions during years of turmoil. The broad-based politics of 'Resistance Councils' and committees that had developed during the years of civil war helped pacify most of the country (Museveni, 1992: 48). In South Africa, the adoption of a political system that gave substantial powers to the provinces was crucial to bringing the Inkatha Freedom Party into the 1994 electoral process that ushered in a democratic South Africa (UNOMSA, 1994). In both countries political participation at the local level laid a stronger foundation for stable national governance.

Another important political advantage of devolution is that sub-national authorities reduce the concentration of power at the center and thus hinder its arbitrary exercise. In other words, they form an additional accountability mechanism that helps to prevent the 'tyranny of the majority or authoritarian rule.' Furthermore, a devolved system can provide channels for the expression of regional sentiments, encourage national policies to become more sensitive to regional variations, and provide minority parties, which might otherwise be excluded from political power, with the opportunity to exercise policy influence.[6] It is also observed that corruption occurs less often at local than at national levels. In such a situation, decentralization may increase productive efficiency by limiting the leakage of funds and other resources.[7] In short, a regional system of government can be more, rather than less, 'inclusive' than a purely central government system.

THE ECONOMIC BENEFITS

A devolved system allows the opportunity to formulate and implement regional or sub-regional economic development plans within the context of national goals, thus enabling development strategists to more accurately target the specific needs of particular communities and areas of the economy. Regional plans also permit and encourage a greater sense of popular involvement in the work of economic development by bringing that work closer to the people. Furthermore, devolution can play a vital role in creating the conditions for balanced growth within the different areas of the country. It improves productive efficiency through the greater accountability of local governments, fewer levels of bureaucracy, and better knowledge of local costs. Regional formations can help maximize the benefits to be derived from intra-national comparative advantages, backward and forward linkages, and economies of agglomeration and enhance the optimal utilization of resources. Inequalities between regions can be counteracted by a deliberate national policy of interregional transfers. For example, in Uganda, the Constitution provides for an 'equalization grant', payable from the Consolidated Revenue Fund. The amount of the grant is based on the level of development of the sub-national region and the degree to which it is 'lagging behind the national average standard' for a particular service (Constitution of Uganda, 1995: art. 193(4)). Finally, regional formations provide an institutional framework for coherent balanced development, and for targeted interventions where needed.

DRAWBACKS TO DEVOLUTION

There are, however, political dangers in the devolution of power to sub-national units. For example, wrongly structured sub-national entities – such as regions – can provide an opportunity for political mobilization on the divisive basis of ethnicity or religion, with potential consequences of political oppression, intolerance and, at the extreme, secessionist movements. A related danger is that a regional system might frustrate the task of 'nation-building'. For instance, a study on Uganda showed that the power of the districts to employ staff led to a tendency by districts to employ people regarded as native to the district (Ahikire, 2002). Sentiments such as these find expression in the craving for new districts or transfer to preferred neighboring districts. The creation of a district has a multiplier effect; each district created results in new demands from local communities who feel marginalized. It is observed that in Uganda the notion of territoriality and homogeneity embedded within the logic of decentralization has tended to create an unending chain of marginalization and quest for autonomy (ibid.). Furthermore, regions have the potential to undermine democracy by inappropriately segmenting or compartmentalizing political functions at levels where there is no financial responsibility or policy-making power. Two additional dangers exist. First, regional systems may make government less transparent and accountable by creating a mass of interlocking bureaucracies or 'intergovernmental organizations'. Second, devolution can create a mushrooming bureaucracy or set of bureaucracies. Government departments can be multiplied unnecessarily, potentially further fragmenting government functions and services. Where this happens, devolution can, in fact, impede development.

There are also some potential negative economic considerations to the creation or demarcation of a country into a system of sub-national entities. One danger is that such an arrangement can create an exorbitantly expensive government. By unnecessarily multiplying government departments, regions can become costly and inefficient. Second, a devolved system might tend to preserve or shore up the existing economic inequalities between regions, and frustrate the redistribution of wealth that is needed to create a balanced and united nation.

Third, devolution can frustrate the implementation of a coherent national economic development program by creating a host of competing economic policies. Finally, different regional incentives relating to investments can create undesirable distortions in the economy.

Decentralization can also entail significant costs in terms of distributional equity and macroeconomic management. This can be especially important in large countries where the economic differences among regions are substantial and can lead to undesirable internal migration, as well as social and political pressures. Inequalities in capacity to govern among the sub-national entities created may further increase costs if they result in the substandard provision of certain public goods, such as primary education or basic health care, by impairing productivity and the long-term growth prospects of the economy.

Accordingly, for devolution to be successful, it must address or achieve several key goals. The devolved system must institutionalize the balance of power between the national government and the newly created sub-national governments. This requires clear rules on devolution, particularly concerning the distribution of political and economic power. A second goal is to develop rules dealing with the way sub-national governments are structured, what they do at each level, and how they are funded. These rules need to be determined as a system, taking into account the interaction between fiscal, political and administrative institutions. This leads to perhaps the most difficult and controversial issue of all: deciding which tier of government controls which resources. The ability of sub-national authorities to act independently of the center depends on whether they have access to independent tax bases and sources of credit. The third key goal is the development of rules governing relations between local officials and their constituents. The degree to which local officials become accountable to their constituents particularly determines whether devolution produces the intended benefits.

The task of constitution-makers is to ensure that all of the above goals are adequately addressed, and that different levels of government do not compete with but complement one another and further the process of good governance and development. In planning and execution, the positive sides of devolution must be encouraged and the negative sides minimized.

The Colonial and Post-Colonial Legacy

Traditional African society had its own highly devolved system of social and political organization (Colson, 1957; Gluckman, 1965; Dore, 1997). A World Bank report has noted the present-day contradiction that in over-centralized African regimes there are some of the world's strongest communities, yet services are usually provided through weak, centralized institutions that are seen as remote and inefficient by those they are supposed to serve (World Bank, 2000b). Gluckman, for instance, writing about the Lozi of Zambia, observed that in their complex economy which required many people to co-operate in various productive activities, the village was the basic unit of organization, the center from which they exploited gardens and parcels of land. Villages ran their own affairs, had their own judicial systems, conducted their own external relations with other villages, and ran their day-to-day affairs without any interference from the chief. The village was headed by a headman who was responsible for the village to the King in Council and represented the village at the council. The chief headed the council and governed with the assistance of councilors (Gluckman, 1967: 7; Mainga, 1973).

With the advent of colonialism, African societies experienced protracted economic and social changes. Colonial rule was philosophically and organizationally elitist, centrist and absolute. Colonial rulers distorted or destroyed pre-colonial governance systems by creating or encouraging arrangements such as indirect rule, which made local chiefs more despotic and created new warrant chiefs where none existed before. Culturally, colonialism divided states into two societies: the traditional culture found in the rural areas where the great majority of the people lived, which was largely outside the influence of colonial elitism, and the 'modern' culture found in the urban areas. The result was that the colonial state became characterized by a huge gap in the standard and quality of life between the rural and the urban areas. In the colonial period power was centralized in the governor. The governor, however, had an elaborate system of provincial and district commissioners, all appointed by the governor, that gave a lot of discretion to the officers mostly in the field of law and order and the adjudication of local disputes.[8] The colonial legacy has endured long after independence (Nwabueze, 1989; Seidman, 1987).

After independence, the degree of centralization in many African states increased, especially with the establishment of one-party systems of government. This trend was accompanied by attempts to transfer influence away from the civil service towards ruling parties. In 1975, the Zambian President, Kenneth Kaunda, in his address to the National Council of the United National Independence Party (UNIP) stated:

> UNIP is supreme over all institutions in our land. Its supremacy must not be theoretical nor is it enough to merely reduce it to a constitutional provision. More than ever before, our task now is to translate party supremacy into something much more meaningful in the life of our beloved nation. (Chikulo, 1985: 341).

Zolberg has observed a similar trend in West Africa. He notes that the cumulative effect has been to concentrate and personalize power at the center, i.e., in the office of the President, and adds that:

> The major trend suggested a steady drive to achieve greater centralization of authority in the hands of a very small number of men who occupy top offices in the party and the government, and even more in the hands of a single man at the apex of both institutions. (ibid.: 348)

These moves were primarily concerned with political consolidation and integration. It was often argued that a strong central government was necessary to advance integration and economic development. Kaunda himself argued that:

> In formulating proposals for decentralizing action in Zambia we need to bear in mind that Zambia is still a very young state – less than a single decade in age – so that we must be conscious of the dangers of learning to run before we can walk by putting burdens on the relationships within our infant state which may prove too much for our capacity to carry. (ibid.: 350)

In the name of nation-building, reversing the colonial structure and bringing about more relevant structures, many African governments destroyed the little decentralization that existed under the colonial system of provincial and district administration. This was seen as necessary since it was at the provincial and district levels that the extraordinarily autocratic powers of the colonial government were most visible. It was therefore decided that the local administration system should lose its power and its distinctive autocratic identity, which had so alienated the population. As a result, most of the the power was stripped from local authorities and transferred to newly created central government departments and ministries. As Chikulo has observed, the primary issue which concerned the political leadership at this stage was one of establishing political control over the public service and the country as a whole (ibid.: 341).

Predictably, political monopolies led to corruption, nepotism, and abuse of power. Presidents replaced the colonial governor. Like the colonial governor, post-colonial governors became the sole embodiment of the social will and purpose of the countries they ruled. This led to the increased dominance of the repressive one-party system of government (Gertzel et al., 1984: 9–10; Yusuf, 1994: 2–8; Zimba, 1984: 113), which ensured that power not only became centralized but also came to be concentrated in the person of the President. Dissent, for which there had always been a secure and honored place in traditional African society, came to be viewed with ill-concealed hostility, almost as if it was treason. Multiple parties, even if originally formed around national agendas, generally tended to become ethnically based parties that made African states ungovernable.[9] Single-party or military rule was often regarded as a viable and sometimes desirable solution to the ethnically based parties in Africa's new modern states (Mubako, 1973: Republic of Zambia, 1972). Ultimately, the party supplanted the machinery of the state and the differences between the two became blurred (Gerzel et al., 1984; Mwanakatwe, 1994: 101).

This centralization produced a growing list of failed states that litter the African continent. Typically, they are characterized by multiple complications: highly centralized systems of governance; excessive state control coupled with limited capacity to govern; arbitrary policy-making and abuse of executive power; erosion of the boundaries between the state and civil society; weak institutions of both state and civil society with few countervailing forces to the executive branch of authority; unaccountable bureaucracies; widespread corruption; limited participation in governance by the general citizenry; and preferential access to power and resources often determined by religious, ethnic or geographical considerations. Such political rigidity shut off the springs of activity in the people. As Obasanjo observed, 'the men and women of spirit who are the leaven of every society either began to go into exile in foreign countries or withdrew into stultifying private life; to their loss yes, but to the even greater loss of society at large' (Obasanjo, 1998). The result was unprecedented economic decline and mismanagement, resulting in unimaginable poverty and a growing economic divide between the urban and rural areas. The dreams of prosperity following independence and self-rule became the nightmare of insecurity and poverty (Shaw, 1982: 93).

Challenges to Providing Effective Devolution to Local Communities

The rural/urban divide inherited from the colonial period continues today and, in fact, has grown. The rural areas continue to be largely neglected, marginalized and impoverished, with an extremely weak state presence almost completely irrelevant as a provider of services. A large percentage of the people, many of whom live in the rural areas, remain outside the formal structures of the state and rely on self-help and self-reliance for their survival. There is also mounting evidence that the International Monetary Fund/World Bank stabilization and economic structural adjustment programs that are in place in many African countries have worsened the situation (Mkandawire and Soludo, 1999: xi). These programs have, for example, undermined the position of poor rural farmers because the high interest rates resulting from them have restricted the farmers' access to credit for production and marketing. Withdrawal of state marketing agencies has also exposed these farmers to exploitation by large city traders. The duality of the rural/traditional and the modern/urban sectors finds its legal underpinning in the dualism of European-inspired law and customary law (See generally Seidman and Seidman, 1984; Palmer and Ponlter, 1972; Ndulo, 1982: 121; Allot, 1970). It is further reinforced by the lack of popular participation in governance, and exacerbated by the lack of effective devolution of power to local communities.

There is thus a critical need for devolution to be undertaken in a manner that will not only improve governance and enhance the accountability of leaders but also make the state a positive force in people's lives. In the institutional sense, this means addressing the issue of the over-centralization of power, namely the concentration of power in the hands of a few executive offices, and therefore a few people, that undermines the constitutional importance of courts, legislatures and sub-regional governments. This is usually reinforced by the tendency of governments to concentrate the most critical human and financial resources at headquarters, leaving rural administration with a lean structure lacking adequate resources or discretionary authority. A further major feature of any centralized state is a preoccupation with bureaucracy and planning and, hence, the preference for concentrated structures rather than diversified and devolved institutions that emphasize the grassroots empowerment of the people. Another feature is financial centralization. The central state collects all of the most important and buoyant tax resources and makes scarce funds available to sub-national authorities. Compounding this problem is the fact that financial transfers to sub-national authorities are often done via grants, which are awarded on a sporadic, rather than a regular, systematic basis.

Effective devolution of power should result in the delivery of most government services by the local level, be it a regional or sub-regional government, thus alleviating the burden from already over-extended central governments (Stoddard, 1997: 85). It entails the existence of local communities endowed with democratically constituted decision-making bodies and possessing a wide degree of autonomy with regard to their responsibilities, the ways and means by which those responsibilities are exercised, and the financial resources required for their fulfillment. Citizens participate in the conduct of public affairs more directly at the local level. The existence of devolved authorities that are given real responsibilities can provide an administration that is both effective and close to the citizen. Unlike more centralized systems, this provides for more flexible responses attuned to local needs. It opens up opportunities for innovation and experimentation in policy formulation and delivery. It can alleviate the workload of an over-stretched central government, something that is especially important to African States in view of the numerous tasks of development and transformation with which they are typically faced (Simeon, 1995).

Even after the wave of democratization which swept African states in the 1990s, very few have made any serious efforts to decentralize power. Even among those that profess commitment to decentralization, there is often a wide gap between political rhetoric and reality (Chikulo, 1985; 340). There has been little devolution of power on substantive matters, policy and development programs, or administrative matters, budget and personnel, to enable sub-national governments to undertake their functions effectively. The current arrangements not only waste resources but also encourage corruption in central institutions and decrease the ability of lower-level institutions to expand or even maintain existing infrastructures. In addition, because power is not devolved, the struggle to control the central government becomes a matter of life (and sometimes death) among the political leadership. As a result, states tend to be strong in those areas in which they ought to be weak (repressive power) and weak where they ought to be strong (popular mobilization and responsiveness) (Paul, 1988: 5).

The process of democratization must therefore go hand in hand with that of the devolution of power to local communities. It is not enough to have democracy at the national level; it must be complemented at the sub-national and community levels. Societal and state institutions must exist as partners in social engineering and must seek to empower ordinary people in matters of governance. Democracy itself implies self-governance; local community-based social and political institutions ought to be the building blocks of a new and effective polity. South Africa and Uganda are the only two African states that have made serious efforts to decentralize power.

South Africa is divided into nine provinces. The legislative authority of a province is vested in its provincial legislature (Constitution, art. 104(1)). A provincial legislature is bound only by the national constitution and if it has passed a constitution for its province, by that constitution, and must act in accordance with, and within the limits of, the two (arts. 103, 104(2)(3)). In addition to the provincial system, there is a local government level consisting of municipalities, which must be established for the whole of South Africa (art. 159(1). The executive and legislative authority of a municipality is vested in its municipal council (art. 151(2) and (3). The Municipal Structures Act of 1998 calls for three main types of municipal councils: metropolitan, local and district. In the period 1999–2000 there were six metropolitan councils (Pretoria, Johannesburg, East Rand, Cape Town, Durban and Port Elizabeth), 41 district councils, 5 cross-border municipalities and 232 local councils. The councils are determined by the Municipal Demarcation Board on the following criteria: financial sustainability, local economic development and the interdependence of communities, existing managerial capacities and effective service delivery. The provinces and municipalities have the right to govern the affairs of their communities, subject to any national legislation (Constitution s.115, 151), whilst the central government retains primary fiscal responsibility for expenditure that has a major redistributive impact, such as on health and education.[10] The South African Constitution provides considerable space for local communities to play a part in the national development process.

The Ugandan system confers, on the people within a village, the power to freely elect their representatives to the district councils. The country, below the level of central government, is divided into 46 districts, which are subdivided into smaller units down to the village level which, like the districts, hold substantial responsibilities for education, health and local infrastructures.[11] Local governments are legally vested with planning and legislative functions. The District Council, as the supreme organ in local government, has powers to enact district laws as long as they are not inconsistent with the national constitution or any other law made by the national legislature. The 1997 Local Government Act permits local governments to budget and make development plans, and allows local government to levy, charge and collect fees and taxes, including rates, royalties, stamp duties, personal graduated tax, and registration and licensing fees.

Other African constitutions typically limit local governments' powers and functions. In Namibia, the Constitution provides for regions whose power and duties may be assigned to them by acts of parliament and as may be delegated to them by the president (art. 108). A similar provision exists in Zambia (art. 109). Similarly, the Malawi Constitution (s. 146) establishes local government authorities whose powers include the promotion of economic development, the presentation to central government authorities of local development plans and the consolidation of local democratic institutions and democratic participation. The powers do not include the capacity to enact legislation. In fact there is no transfer of political power in the arrangement.[12] When it comes to financial matters, the local authorities completely depend on the central government. Section 150 of the Malawi Constitution provides that government shall be under a duty to ensure that there is adequate provision of resources necessary for the proper exercise of local government functions. The budget for local government authorities is prepared by the National Local Government Finance Committee, which prepares a consolidated budget for all local government authorities and presents it to the National Assembly through the Minister of Local Government (s. 149 (d)). The Tanzanian Constitution in article 145 provides for the establishment of local government authorities and states that their purpose is to transfer authority to the people and to consolidate legislative powers and democracy at the local level (arts 145(1), 146(1)). Here again, the authorities are not provided with adequate powers to raise revenue.[13]

In a decentralized system, for the transfer of power to be meaningful subnational governments have to share in political power and be empowered to raise funds and draw up their own budgets, which the governing councils or parliaments of the regions or sub-regions must be empowered to approve. Taxpayers, either through their representatives or through interest groups, should be able to express their views at various levels of local government and influence public decisions. This in turn should increase the accountability of government. The empowerment of local authorities to raise revenue creates many possibilities for the generation of local economic initiatives. For this to be real, however, central government must not keep the major sources of revenue to itself and leave minimal sources which do not generate substantial revenue, such as graduated taxes and trade licensing, to local governments. In the case of Uganda, Ahikire observes that the graduated tax has proved costly in terms of assessment and collection and that performance indicators have declined as the number of defaulters has increased (Ahikire, 2002). Much more importantly, the tax base is narrow, in view of the fact that the majority of the population depend on agricultural production. As a result, local governments have tended to rely more on central government transfers rather than on internally generated revenue.

CONSTITUTIONALIZING DEVOLUTION

In order to achieve effective devolution of power from the central government to sub-national governments, the national constitution should recognize and provide for the principle of local governance.[14] For one thing, recognition of the principle in the constitution ensures legitimacy for the process. A regime finds it difficult to violate provisions of a constitution that its citizens consider to be legitimate. And as Weingast has observed in connection with federalism, '[F]ederal systems are not generally sustainable if they depend solely on the discretion of the highest political authority, because such delegation of power can always be reversed' (Weingast, 1995: 3). A central problem for local authorities is that the central authority may overawe the lower units. Constitutionalizing the devolution of power curtails the central government's ability to do so. The advantage of this approach is that, where the national constitution confers these powers, they may not be removed, except by the procedure described for constitutional amendments, whereas if they are conferred by an ordinary statute passed by parliament, they may be removed by parliament by a simple amendment or repeal. Thus there is greater protection of lower levels of government if their powers are conferred by or entrenched in the national constitution.

It should clearly be provided and explained that local governance denotes the right and ability of local institutions, within the limits of the law, to regulate and manage a substantial share of public affairs under their own responsibility and in the interests of the local population. The right should be exercised by sub-national assemblies composed of members freely elected on the basis of direct, equal and universal suffrage and, where they are relevant, for example in rural areas, should allow the participation of traditional leaders. Powers given to sub-national governments should generally be full, exclusive and clearly defined.[15] They should not be undermined or limited by the central government except as provided by law. To enable sub-national governments to function effectively, the national economic policy should allocate to them adequate financial resources, which they should dispose of freely within the framework of their powers. Sub-national governments should also have the power to levy local taxes and charges.[16] The need to protect financially weaker sub-national entities calls for the implementation of financial equalization procedures or equivalent measures that are designed to correct the effects of the unequal distribution of potential sources of finance.

In demarcating regional or sub-regional units that are to form the basis of sub-national governments, great care is needed to ensure that the resulting units are viable and do not lead to divisiveness. As ethnicity is one of the potential causes of instability, it would be unfortunate if the process of devolution were to have the effect of promoting ethnic divisions and of heightening the potential for conflict. The overriding goal in the demarcation of regions, therefore, must be to avoid the creation of exclusive ethnically homogeneous units. There are a number of criteria to consider when demarcating regions. Boundaries should be drawn in such a way that the requirements for effective development can be met. The logistics of transport, labor flows, goods and services, as well as planning and administration need to be consistent with both the shape and size of the regions created. This includes consideration of the need for inclusion of one or more modes of administration in each region, such as the identification of regional centers, as well as centers for sub-regional administration. It is important that regions or sub-regions be compact and not fragmented. In terms of administrative coherence, regions should not be so large as to be unmanageable, or so small as to lead to their excessive proliferation. Institutional capacity within regions or sub-regions will be crucial to effective planning and development. Regions or sub-regions which lack the necessary institutional capacity will be at a serious disadvantage in relation to those regions which are well endowed with this capacity. Improving local services requires effective local administration. Even a well-meaning political team cannot overcome incompetent administration.

THE ROLE OF TRADITIONAL INSTITUTIONS

Any examination of the modalities affecting the devolution of power in African states must address the issue of the future of traditional institutions of governance in modern political systems (Nana Wereko Ampem, 1995). There is a general consensus that traditional leaders, such as chiefs, should have a role in the governance of the state. Yet their exact role is a source of ongoing disagreement and, as a result, it remains largely undefined. In the South African constitutional negotiations, the question of what to do with traditional institutions was a major source of discussion. In the end, the South African Constitution states that national legislation may provide for the role of traditional leaders as an institution at the local level on matters relating to traditional leadership, the role of traditional leaders, customary law and the customs of communities observing a system of customary law.[17] Even so, this does not really integrate them into the mainstream post-apartheid political system. They are not, for instance, integrated into the provincial or local government structures. The Ugandan Constitution adopts the same approach, merely providing: 'Subject to the provisions of this Constitution, the institution of traditional leader or cultural leader may exist in any area of Uganda in accordance with the culture, customs and traditions or wishes and aspirations of the people to whom it applies' (art. 246(1)). Hence, neither South Africa nor Uganda integrates the traditional rulers into the sub-national government system. Several countries provide for a House of Chiefs with no substantive jurisdiction (Constitution of Zambia).

Constitutional arrangements need to accommodate traditional leaders or at least acknowledge their existence. Their incorporation into any decentralized government system could, quite conceivably, enhance its legitimacy in the rural areas where traditional leaders provide the link between the people and the external world – the government. Effectively reaching those communities requires us to confront this reality. If the colonial powers were shrewd enough to use traditional institutions in administering the colonial state (Lugard, 1905: 149–50), why should modern African political systems not make use of them in an effort to reach out to small communities and to help build national consensus and cohesion? (Nhlapo, 1995). In any event, it makes sense to find a place in the national political system for structures and institutions that cannot be wished away. Since democracy means involving the various communities in a country in the governance of their affairs, it is imperative that rural communities should not be ignored in any democratic arrangement. Every effort should be made to integrate traditional institutions into the modern political structures so that all institutions are made accountable and responsive to the people. The state's vital interests in public order and stability, it would seem, are enhanced, rather than diminished, by the accommodation of traditional governance within modem political systems.

In advocating this, we should not ignore the fact that aspects of these institutions are often oppressive, exploitative, discriminatory and intolerant, especially to women and children (Ndulo, 1981; Nhlapo, 1991). The argument, however, is not that traditional institutions are perfect; rather that it is more effective to build democracy and effective governance through the process of devolution using familiar institutions. Since the goal is to establish a democratic order, the need to incorporate traditional institutions into the modern system cannot take precedence over the needs of a democratic society.[18] With regard to objections that these institutions are gender-discriminatory, governments and the courts must address the areas that need reform and discard the discriminatory aspects of traditional institutions, and even further confront the traditional values that underpin gender discrimination and authoritarianism. Much of this discrimination is underpinned by customary law norms. South Africa, Namibia and Uganda have constitutional provisions that render invalid customary law norms which are in conflict with the constitution and give the courts the power to declare gender discriminatory customs and practices illegal and unenforceable. This practice should be emulated elsewhere.[19]

An example of a country that has adapted its traditional institutions to its modern political system is India. From ancient times, India had developed a number of systems of community-based management of local affairs. In most of the country these institutions were known as 'panchayats', which literally means a council of five persons. Their functions bordered on a local governance model akin to that which was prevalent in pre-colonial Africa. The local government system in India is now part of the constitution. The structures established under the system are termed 'panchyats', but are now democratic institutions with new content.[20]

Devolution and Its Relationship to the Center

A major question that arises in any discussion on the devolution of power is how to design the institutions to manage the intergovernmental institutions. Although there are many different approaches to devolution in place in different parts of the world, two broad models can be identified: of shared, or integrated governance and of divided governance (Simeon, 1995: 7; Johnson, 1995: 2). In the shared governance model a vast range of power is shared or concurrent. This model stresses not so much the autonomy and freedom of action of the individual devolved sub-national entities, but rather their collective influence over decisions made at the center. The chief advantages of the shared model are maximum uniformity and application of national norms and standards and maximum collective influence of devolved entities. Its chief challenges are gaining some local autonomy for the sub-national entities, achieving the flexibility for sub-national governments to meet local needs, and determining how to make clear decisions when most responsibilities are shared.

In the divided governance model, powers are allocated among devolved sub-national governments that have relative autonomy. The divided model maximizes the autonomy of each sub-national government, and so provides the widest room for variations in provincial policy, for experimentation and innovation. It increases the provinces' ability to set their own priorities. To the extent that responsibilities are clear, the model may also facilitate accountability and transparency for citizens. However, the divided model makes it more difficult to ensure common standards, common policies and harmonization in such areas as taxation or social policy. Another issue to resolve is where devolved government will fit into the intergovernmental picture. In most African countries local government is provided for in the Constitution, but little autonomy is given to the local authorities.[21] The exceptions, as noted above, are South Africa (Constitution s.151) and Uganda (Constitution, arts 117, 127) whose constitutions provide substantial powers to local authorities.

The division of power between the sub-national governments and the centre needs to be spelled out clearly, and mechanisms for the resolution of conflicts in the exercise of such power must be established. There are three common types of arrangements regarding the division of power: exclusive, concurrent and overriding powers.[22] Exclusive powers are those reserved for the sub-national entities and in these areas the center has no power. For example, under the South African Constitution, the provinces have exclusive legislative competence in provincial planning, veterinary services excluding regulation of the profession, provincial spots, cultural matters, and licensing matters relating to such things as parks and markets (Constitution, schedule 5). Concurrent powers exist where different responsibilities with regard to one function are allocated to different levels of government. In the South African Constitution provinces have concurrent powers in agriculture, airports, animal control, health services, housing, transport, consumer protection, education, language policy, media, police matters, and population control (Constitution, schedule 4). The modern growth of government functions and the complex linkages and interdependence that have developed, particularly in the economic and social spheres, have made it unrealistic to think of allocating all, or even most, functions exclusively. In certain circumstances, the central government is given overriding powers. This is its right to act as the higher legislative authority in an area allocated to a region or sub-region where the national interest demands such action.

A problem that often arises is what to do with residual powers, powers not specifically designated in the constitution as being either the exclusive or concurrent preserve of the various levels of government. What powers remain unallocated in a given jurisdiction depends on what the national constitution leaves unregulated. Approaches to this vary. One approach provides that any powers not expressly assumed by the autonomous communities in their statutes will continue to be exercised by the central government. This is just the opposite of the case in the United States where the powers of the federal government are only those specifically outlined in the US Constitution. Another approach is that if the government to which the subject has been entrusted does not act, the subject goes unregulated. In the United States, by contrast, the norm is that the non-exercise of federal power to regulate increases the area for state regulation; there are few if any separate spheres in which it is constitutionally permissible only for states to regulate.[23]

Several principles need to be taken into account when deciding the allocation of legislative powers (see Simeon, 1995). First, there is the imperative of the national government's responsibility for nation-building, including the promotion of national well-being and the celebration of the nation's diversity. Second, there is the imperative of regional or sub-regional responsibility and autonomy for the development and differentiation of regional public services to suit the particularities, needs and cultural identities of the different regions or sub-regions created. Third, there is the imperative of recognizing that there are 'national aspects' of many of the matters that are assigned to regions or sub-regions which must be taken into account in devising constitutional competences and arrangements, and in recognizing equally that there are regional or sub-regional interests in many of the matters where national legislation and/or financing is needed. The constitution should provide for a system in which central and sub-national governments complement each other. The objective should be to develop a 'co-operative model' of government that will enable greater co-operation between various tiers of government.

Fiscal Arrangements and Revenue-Sharing Measures

Perhaps the most important and controversial matter in the division of powers relates to revenue collection and other fiscal matters that impact on the ability of the sub-national governments to function effectively. At present, in most African states local governments are funded by direct grants from the central government. The Malawi Constitution, for example, provides that the central government is under a duty to ensure that there is adequate provision of resources necessary for the proper exercise of local government functions. This approach is unsuitable where it is intended to achieve effective devolution of power to local communities. One approach is to authorize sub-national governments to raise funds by a variety of taxes. Thus, for example, provinces in South Africa are allowed to impose taxes, levies, duties other than income tax, value added tax, general sales tax, or customs duties (art. 228).

Rye (1995) discusses three key questions concerning the allocation of fiscal measures. The first concerns what is the best allocation, between levels of government, of revenue-raising powers and expenditure responsibilities. He suggests a number of relevant considerations. First, is the geographical incidence of each service or tax. Thus, the benefits of defense against external threats accrue to the nation as a whole, and it is hard to see how this could be other than a national responsibility. At the other extreme, garbage collection and waste disposal is usually a local matter. There are, of course, many public services, such as education and health, where the answer is not so clear. On the tax side, the incidence of company tax is likely to fall well outside its notional geographic source, so this tax may properly be collected by central government. Property taxes, by contrast, seem to lie naturally at the local level. A second consideration is the need for the national government to be able to run an effective fiscal policy. One implication of this is that the national government might wish to retain a high degree of control over taxation. A third consideration is the need to provide financial resources for ironing out horizontal imbalances between the various regions that are created pursuant to decentralization.[24] Typically, arrangements are made to provide assistance to regions or sub-regions that lag economically behind others.

The second question concerns the best way of structuring fiscal transfers from the central to sub-national governments. This is a question of whether such transfers should be through tied grants (specific purpose payments) or untied (general) grants. As Rye points out, sometimes the objective of the 'specific purpose payment' is to provide a mechanism whereby the central government may achieve national objectives in particular areas. For example, if there are perceived problems in education provision by the regions, the central government may provide grants on condition that they are used to tackle these problems. However, in any transfer system designed to provide a measure of equalization, some general revenue grants are likely to be needed. In particular, it does not seem that specific purpose payments can effectively compensate for inequalities in revenue-raising capacity.

The third question concerns the extent to which grants from the central government to the provinces are untied and intended for equalization purposes. This raises issues as to what is the best mechanism, and the best institutional framework, for deciding on the allocations.[25] It is probably best to allocate such responsibility to an independent commission charged with this responsibility. It is important that such a commission should function in a transparent manner in order to instill confidence that political considerations are not paramount in decisions relating to the allocation of funds to sub-national governments. For example, under the South African Constitution a statute must provide for the equitable division of revenue raised nationally among the national, provincial and local spheres of government, and that a Financial and Fiscal Commission must be consulted on the division of revenue.[26] The division of the revenue should take into account the population, income per capita, indicators of backwardness, and the local authorities' own tax effort.

Resolving Disputes Between Sub-National Governments and the Center

Clearly sharp differences of opinion, and sometimes conflicts, are going to arise as to whether or not certain powers are vested in the central or the sub-national governments. Typically, disputes arise over conflicts between national and sub-national legislation or between national legislation and a provision of a sub-national government constitution. In addition, the organs of the central bureaucracy may resist relinquishing their powers to the sub-national governments. This results in continuous conflicts which weaken the efficiency of the intergovernmental arrangements. Articulating the division of roles as unambiguously as possible minimizes this conflict and makes adjudication correspondingly easier. However, no matter how much care is taken to demarcate power, there are bound to be numerous difficulties, given the complex apportionment of powers that exists in a state based on the devolution of powers to the sub-national governments. Typically, these difficulties will include long lists of competences attributed to the state or to the autonomous sub-national governments, which often affect both legislative and executive powers and frequently seem to belong to both the central and the sub-national governments.

Clearly there is a need for dispute-resolution mechanisms.

The courts could play an important role in arbitrating and resolving differences. Resolution before a court would mean that conflicts between the central and the sub-national governments are resolved in legal and judicial rather than in political terms. For example, as we have seen in the South African arrangement, a provincial legislature is bound only by the constitution, and, if it has passed a constitution for its province, also by the provincial constitution, and must act in accordance with, and within the limits of, the constitution and that provincial constitution.[27] Disputes are to be resolved by the courts (Constitution s.146(4)), although if a dispute cannot be resolved by a court, national legislation prevails over the provincial legislation or provincial constitution. But other supervisory bodies can be established to resolve disputes. For instance, national forums, committees or commissions could be used to bring together the different levels of government in relation to specific fields of shared competence (e.g. education and health) where collisions and conflicts could be forestalled and/or arbitrated. To resolve differences of gray areas which inevitably arise in the field of concurrent powers, it is not necessary to have constant recourse to the courts. In fact, the South African Constitution (art. 41(3)) requires an organ of state involved in an intergovernmental dispute to make every reasonable effort to settle it by means of mechanisms and procedures provided for that purpose and to exhaust all other remedies before it approaches a court to resolve the dispute. At the same time, care must be taken to ensure that the organs established to co-ordinate the two levels of government do not proliferate, and do not escape accountability.

Conclusion

Devolution can raise levels of popular participation and involvement and can provide people with an increased opportunity to shape the context of their lives. This can then result in more responsive and efficient local governance. The ultimate purpose of devolution is to place decision-making in the hands of the people through representation which is closer and more directly accountable, thereby promoting democracy and good governance. Devolution enhances equitable development through the mobilization of local resources, and increased efficiency and effectiveness in the delivery of public goods. It can also strengthen local ownership. However, when poorly designed, devolution can result in overburdened local governments without resources or the capacity to fulfill their basic responsibilities of providing local infrastructure and services. The objective should be to ensure policy development that addresses the political will to decentralize and delineate the types of devolution suitable to a country's circumstances. Such policy should specify the financial, legal, institutional and organizational changes necessary to effectuate devolution. It should also restructure the relative responsibility and authority between the central and sub-national governments. For decentralization to succeed it requires strong institutions and trained personnel to run local government. Capacity constraints can severely limit the effectiveness of local authorities and undermine the process of devolution. This means that there must be a deliberate policy to provide local authorities with the equipment they need to run their affairs and a policy to train skilled personnel.

Notes

[1] Agranoff (1994: 61), for instance, describes the situation in Spain where, after a history of dictatorship, the Constitution provides for a three-tiered system of national, autonomous-community and local government, a structure that, while not organizationally designed to be federal, in fact is moving Spain into the orbit of federal nations.

[2] Many of the African constitutions make no mention of local government. See Constitution of Zimbabwe, 1996, Constitution of Zambia, 1991.

[3] Nzuwah (1995). A constitutional review commission in Zambia reviewing the status of local government concluded: 'Petitioners felt that the present system alienated the ordinary people from their government, thereby creating as it were a perspective of powerlessness, marginalization, neglect and inequitable treatment by the center', see *Report of the Constitutional Review Commission* (1995: 46).

[4] For a discussion on federalism, see Weingast (1995: 1).

[5] See Preamble, *European Charter of Local Government*, Council of European Treaties ETS No. 122 (1985).

[6] A nationwide survey on decentralization in the Philippines found that citizens are more satisfied with their local government than with the national government. They felt that they were more able to influence the former than the latter. There were also more candidates than before – especially from a larger middle class – for positions in local government. These factors become more meaningful in terms of responsibility, powers and resources, see Santos (2001).

[7] In both Uganda and the Philippines studies on decentralization found that corruption was less pronounced at local than at higher levels. See Santos (2001); Ahikire (2002).

[8] See Zambian Cabinet Office Circular No. 13 of 1969, 1 February 1969 (on file). The circular was an attempt to reorganize the colonial system by the Kaunda government.

[9] Museveni's main justification for his movement system in Uganda is that political parties form on the basis of ethnicity. See Museveni (1992: 42). He observes that one of the biggest factors weakening Africa is tribalism and other forms of sectarianism and that in African politics tribalism is always emphasized. The UN Secretary-General has also observed that this is compounded by the fact that the framework of colonial laws and institutions which most states inherited had been designed to exploit local divisions, not to overcome them (see UN Secretary-General, 1998).

[10] Constitution ss.213–14. The relationship between national and provincial governments, the competence of provincial legislatures in respect of regional planning, local government and development, and local government registration of land tenure rights were considered by the South African Constitutional Court in *DVB Behuising (pty) Limited v North Western Provincial Government and another*, CCT 22/99/ (2 March 2000).

[11] See Constitution of Uganda, chap. 11. See art. 176 of the 1995 Constitution which enunciates the principles of District Councils as follows: the system shall be such as to ensure that the functions, powers and responsibilities are devolved and transferred from central government to local government units; decentralization shall be a principle applying to all levels of local government and in particular from higher to lower government units to ensure people's participation and democratic control in decision-making; the system shall be such as to ensure the full realization of democratic governance at local government levels; and appropriate measures shall be taken to enable local government units to plan, initiate and execute policies in respect of all matters affecting people within their jurisdiction. Furthermore art. 176 (3) states that: The system of local government shall be based on democratically elected councils on the basis of universal adult suffrage in accordance with clause (4) of Article 181 of the constitution.

[12] S.146 (3) makes it clear that: 'parliament shall, where possible, provide that issues of local policy and administration be decided on at local levels under the supervision of local government authorities.'

[13] Article 145(21) provides that Parliament shall enact a law providing for the establishment of local government authorities, their structure and composition, sources of revenue and procedure for the conduct of their business.

[14] In Uganda, the 1995 Constitution and 1997 Local Government Act specify five levels of government. The 1987 Philippines Constitution contains a state policy that 'shall ensure the autonomy of local government,' as well as a whole article on local government. In 1992 the Indian Constitution was amended. The 73rd Constitutional Amendment for rural local bodies (panchayats) and 74th Constitutional Amendment for urban local bodies (municipalities) made them 'institutions of self government'. The South African Constitution provides for provincial and local government structures.

[15] A good example is the South African approach where the Constitution provides for provinces and a system of local government created with their own legislatures and clearly defined powers: see Constitution ss.103–150.

[16] In both Uganda and South Africa, local authority structures enjoy revenue-raising powers: see Constitution of Uganda, art.191 and Constitution of South Africa, ss.228–9.

[17] See Constitution of South Africa, s.211(1)–(3) and 212 (1) (2). Even this has proved controversial, with ongoing conflict being reported between elected local structures and traditional leaders, with some local structures refusing to recognize traditional leaders. Botswana, on the other hand, is considered one of the few countries that has made use of its traditional leaders. See Dia (1996: 105–9). Zambia, for example, provides for a House of Chiefs without clearly defined powers. The constitution provides that the House of Chiefs shall be an advisory body to the government on traditional, customary and any other matters referred to it by the President.

[18] See the views of Thabo Mbeki, *Debates of the Constitutional Assembly* No. 1, 11, 24 January 1995.

[19] See Constitution of South Africa, s.211(3); Constitution of Namibia, art.66(1).

[20] For a discussion of the Indian system see: Mathew and Raj (2002).

[21] In Namibia Regional Councils have power within the regions as may be assigned to them by Act of Parliament and may be delegated to them by the President. See Constitution of the Republic of Namibia, art. 108.

[22] The Canadian Constitution, for instance, allocates each power exclusively to the federal or provincial level of government. Section 91 of the Constitution Act 1867 sets out the federal government's exclusive powers, and section 92 the exclusive powers of the provinces. In theory, these powers do not overlap. Sometimes, however, one aspect of a particular activity may come within a head of federal power, while another aspect of the same activity comes within a head of provincial power. In the case of direct conflict or pre-emption, the exercise of federal power prevails, but ordinarily either the federal or provincial legislature has exclusive power over a particular activity. Because of the exclusive allocation of power in Canada, a law or governmental action is always open to constitutional challenge on *ultra vires* grounds. See Sedler (1984: 1196–7).

[23] See Field (1992: 108). Field points out further that 'even if in both the USA and Canada the constitutions were written to give the central government more power, the interpretation of the powers of the central government has been different under both systems.' For example, in relation to the 'power to regulate commerce', in the US 'the clause has been read to allow Congress to regulate any activity that could have any impact at all on interstate commerce, leaving Congress free to regulate any economic activity it wishes and displacing any separate sphere for state legislative control of the economy. In Canada, by contrast, the clause giving the central government control over trade and commerce has been interpreted to allow regulation of only international or inter-provincial trade. The narrow interpretation of the commerce power is part of a more general cutback on the powers of the central government', see pp.109–10.

[24] See with respect to Canada, Federal Provincial Fiscal Arrangements and Federal Post Secondary Education and Health Act, 1976–7. Section 3 authorizes the federal Minister of Finance to pay fiscal equalization funds to provinces.

[25] The 1999 Constitution of Nigeria in section 162 (2) provides that 'The President, upon the receipt of advice from the revenue Mobilization Allocation and Fiscal Commission, shall table before the National Assembly proposals for revenue allocation from the federation account and in determining the formula, the National Assembly shall take into account the allocation principles especially those of population, equality of

States, internal revenue generation, land mass, terrain as well as population density.'
[26] Constitution of South Africa, s.214(1) and (2). See also *Uthekela District Municipality and Others v. President of the Republic of South Africa and others*, Constitutional Court-CCT7/02, 12 June 2002.
[27] Constitution of South Africa s.104(3). Article 104 provides: 'The legislative authority of the province is vested in its provincial legislature, and confers on the provincial legislature the power to(a) pass a constitution in and for its province or to amend any constitution passed by it in terms of sections 142 and 143.' Most of the provinces are still working on their constitutions.

8

TSATSU TSIKATA
Challenges of Economic Reform & Democratization: Some Lessons From Ghana

THIS chapter proposes to draw some lessons from the experiences of Ghana over the last two decades for a consideration of (i) the relationship between economic reform and democratization, (ii) the interaction between national authorities and the IMF and the World Bank, and by extension, other external agencies, in both economic reform and governance issues in Africa, and (iii) the significance of decentralization and grassroots participation for both democratic and economic reforms.

Economic Recovery Program

For a considerable period in the 1980s and early 1990s, Ghana's economic recovery was often touted as resulting from its being a star pupil of the IMF and the World Bank, dutifully carrying out the structural adjustment policies prescribed by these institutions and thereby being an IMF/World Bank 'success story'. The reality was considerably different; an examination of the actual experience of the period yields a rather more complex picture in which, in many respects, the real pupils were the IMF and the World Bank. The strong local and national outlooks in the initiation and early years of the Economic Recovery Program were the driving factors of success. The key elements of the ERP (Government of Ghana, 1983a), initiated by the Rawlings regime from 1982, were expressed, perhaps unusually for a government that came to power through a military coup, in terms of an aspiration towards attaining 'true democracy' both through the economic empowerment of producers, mainly rural-based, as opposed to rent-seekers, mainly urban-based, and through the participation of the grassroots in political decision-making. Democracy was seen by the regime as involving not only political processes such as elections, but, more importantly, implementing economic policies that gave increasing recognition to the real producers of the nation's wealth.[1] For instance, the devaluation of the local currency was explicitly regarded as arising from the need for fairer remuneration to the cocoa farmer who was responsible for earning most of the country's foreign-exchange resources.

The previous decade had seen a dramatic decline in cocoa production in Ghana as a result of the lack of incentives for the producer. While world market prices for cocoa were reaching their peak in the late 1970s, production in Ghana reached less than half of its historical peak. The share of the farmer in the revenues from cocoa exports was as low as 26 per cent and producer prices in real terms amounted to about 15 per cent (World Bank, 1984: 4, 11–12). The rationale expressed by the new economic managers for exchange-rate adjustment was to avoid foreign exchange earned from exports simply going into imports, particularly oil imports,

which would mainly benefit a 'parasitic urban minority' and not the rural producers generating the revenue. (Government of Ghana, 1987: 22, para. 76; World
Bank, 2000b: 175). Devaluing the local currency and increasing the farmer's share
of export revenues were thus conceived as a commitment to economic democracy,
a revolutionary overturning of the ways. Those ways had undermined the role of
the rural producers and given control of the scarce foreign exchange earned from
their hard work to an urban-oriented central government-controlled process of
administering scarce resources which encouraged rent-seeking and corruption
rather than production (Government of Ghana, 1987: 10, para. 28).

Multiple Exchange-Rate Regime

In the implementation of the exchange-rate reforms, some basic prescriptions of
the IMF – notably unified exchange-rate requirements – had to be sacrificed, if
only temporarily. In the pragmatic assessment of the Ghanaian authorities, tack-
ling the previous over-valuation of the currency required (a) close attention to
the consequences in each sector of adjustment of the exchange rate so as to tailor
remedies to specific sectoral requirements, (b) the recognition, therefore, that
imports and exports did not require the same rate, and (c) careful judgments
about the social and political acceptability of the impact of economic reform
measures. Thus, instead of devaluation requiring, for instance, immediate dramatic increases in petroleum product prices, considerations about cost-push
effects in an economy that had been experiencing high rates of inflation, as well
as political assessments of public acceptance of the reforms, led to a phased
approach to the petroleum product price increases and a program of extensive
public education to ensure understanding and acceptance of the new policies.

A system of providing bonuses to foreign-exchange-earning sectors and sur-
charging users of foreign exchange at rates that took into account the importance of various imports for the economy and the likely impact of a hike in oil
prices, was designed (Government of Ghana, 1983b). This was a home-grown
attempt to stimulate key sectors of the economy and their foreign-exchange generation capacity, and discourage unproductive uses of foreign exchange. It was
initiated before agreement was reached with the IMF in 1983 on a short-term
stabilization program (World Bank, 1987: xvi, para. 6). The government
program sought to reverse the disincentives to the productive sector that the
overvaluation of the local currency had brought about and to discourage the distortions and negative tendencies which had led to a downward spiral of the
economy. Though multiple exchange-rate practices are frowned on by the IMF,
its acceptance in early 1983 of this approach to economic reform began a
process of engagement between Ghana and the IMF and the World Bank that
had significant impacts for Ghana economically as well as politically. For the
cocoa farmer, these reforms led to a major transformation in economic fortunes
such that by the end of the millennium his share in cocoa export revenues had
steadily climbed closer to 60 per cent from 26 per cent (Government of Ghana,
1999). This meant significant resource transfers to the rural population over the
period. Representatives of cocoa farmers were also by now participants in the
setting of the producer price, being part of the membership of the Cocoa Price
Review Committee established by the government.

Terms of Trade

Unfortunately, however, by the time Ghana was beginning to restore cocoa production to its previous heights, world market prices of cocoa had crashed. The world market price of Ghana's other main export, gold, similarly plunged after Ghana had again succeeded in significantly increasing production over almost two decades through new investments. Such impacts undoubtedly call into question the legitimacy of the structural adjustment paradigms of the IMF and World Bank and undermine the political will to maintain the economic reform agenda. The limits of internal policy-making in the context of the global terms of trade also become evident. However, by evaluating the reform initiatives in terms of the pre-reform domestic reality of a collapsed economy (World Bank, 1987: 1), and appreciating the rationale and effectiveness of the reform initiatives within the limits of global trade realities, it is possible both to recognize the logic of the reforms and, at the same time, underscore the need for addressing the unfairness in the world trading system. The tendency to view such reforms as simply external prescriptions not only runs counter to the facts but may, in fact, also prevent a deeper analysis that unveils the real significance of external factors and the appropriate remedies for addressing these factors (World Bank, 2000b: 21).[2]

IMF/World Bank Role

The perception of the regime, in its early period, as a radical, anti-Western one did not exactly send the IMF and the World Bank rushing to the aid of Ghana. Over time, however, Ghana engaged more and more with the IMF and the World Bank, seeking resources to offset terms-of-trade losses and to achieve ambitious developmental goals during a period that has been dubbed 'Africa's lost decade'. It would, therefore, be unrealistic to over-state the homegrown nature of the economic reform policies of the Rawlings' regime. Even with the exchange-rate reform, it was agreed by the government that the multiple exchange-rate practice would, over a period, give way to a unified exchange rate. At the same time, it cannot be denied that the thrust of the initial reform effort owed more to internal judgments than to external prescription. Increasingly, then, the internal logic of economic reform gave way to external conditionality not only because of the resources provided by the Bretton Woods institutions themselves but also because their 'stamp of approval' was necessary for other official bilateral flows as well as for foreign private investors. The limited room of maneuver for a developing country economy that has experienced severe decline, as in the case of Ghana, cannot be gainsaid.

The engagement initiated with the IMF and the World Bank in 1983 grew into a wide-ranging relationship. Such engagement in a multiplicity of programs became virtually a full-time business, overwhelming the limited human resources available at the national level and increasingly diminishing the scope for independent initiatives. As policy-making and program implementation required a constant engagement between the government and the multilaterals, the earlier more independent internal perspectives gave way to an externally set agenda, often by sheer default having regard to the limited capacity in the national institutions' interaction with the external institutions.[3] Stanley Fischer, formerly Deputy Managing Director of the IMF, has observed in a recent reflection that: 'Another lesson we have learnt in the developing countries is that economic reform works best if the country is in the driver's seat...The role of the international institutions should be to support and advise and not to hector and impose. To that end, financial support should not have too many strings attached' (Fischer, 2000).[4]

These lessons have come twenty years too late as far as Ghana is concerned. A less prescriptive approach from the IMF in the 1980s might have encouraged a sustained home-grown approach to reform. Whilst the initial thrust of economic reform was rooted in a local context in which a new government sought to make its mark, the increasing hold of IMF and World Bank conditionalities, sometimes even pulling in different directions as these institutions also each sought to make their mark and carve out territory, was a major part of the framework that Ghana's economic managers had to deal with, and the reality has remained with Ghana ever since.[5] Indeed, the experiences of countries like Ghana have no doubt contributed to the realizations that Stanley Fischer now articulates.

Lessons – PAMSCAD

There are important lessons from Ghana's experiences which can inform the current outlook espoused by Mr Fischer. Very early on in their reform program, the Ghanaian authorities expressed a determination to factor social dimensions into the economic policy framework. A Program of Action to Mitigate the Social Costs of Adjustment (PAMSCAD) was developed, with significant support from UNICEF whose orientation was distinctly outside the IMF macroeconomic paradigm. PAMSCAD contained important poverty alleviation objectives, which were not then a typical part of structural adjustment programming. Little wonder that this aspect of the recovery program became somewhat sidelined in the preoccupation with macroeconomic conditionalities. Remarkably, poverty alleviation has now become the central tenet of the IMF in Africa, again twenty years too late for Ghana. As Fischer strikingly affirms: 'we need to ensure that the policies we recommend to boost growth are as pro-poor as possible'.

The problem with this current official stance of the IMF is not its legitimacy, but rather the capacity of the institution, given its history and how steeped its staff are in the pre-existing paradigm, to adapt their practice and meaningfully address poverty alleviation as a central goal. Fischer illustrates this starkly as he himself, having announced the good intentions and insisted on the need for less conditionality, very quickly backslides: 'For the IMF, this means confining conditions to what is necessary to get the economy back on an even keel and to get financial and other key markets working properly' (Fischer, 2002). Macroeconomic stabilization is effortlessly reinstated to pride of place even as the IMF battles with its failures of the past and announces its option for the poor. The traditional paradigm of the Fund regarding 'what is necessary to get the economy back on an even keel' did not typically address poverty alleviation, and it cannot be assumed that the announcement of such a goal will, by itself, change the practice of Fund staff in their conduct of country programs. Very clear direction would need to be given by management to how the new goal is to re-shape the existing orthodoxy.

Establishing policies in favor of the poor cannot be derived automatically from macroeconomic stabilization, even if such stabilization will often be an important element of pro-poor policies, as I suggest happened in the economic reform outlook of Ghana in the early 1980s. Pro-poor policy-making requires detailed attention to local conditions in a manner often missed in macroeconomic aggregates (Narayan-Parker, 2002: 10). Countries themselves must identify the elements of such a priority and negotiate their incorporation into reform programs. This is not, of course, an easy task, but I would suggest that the experience of Ghana shows the possibilities of some success in having such priorities progressively reflected even in the paradigm that has dominated the interaction with the international financial institutions. The current stance of the IMF appears to present further opportunities for extending the boundaries in this regard.

Political Reform

The economic reforms in Ghana were soon paralleled by political reforms that initially highlighted the importance of grassroots participation in government with the introduction of District Assemblies throughout the country, elections to which were on a non-party basis. The relatively long period of successful economic recovery in Ghana from the early 1980s to the 1990s and the stable political environment that resulted did provide the platform for the subsequent introduction of multi-party democracy, with elections at the national level under a new constitution. It is again necessary to note that the initiation of these political reforms actually pre-dated the period of such governance issues being elements of external resource conditionality. The steps that were taken reflected internal political perspectives, notably the government's outlook on strengthening grassroots participation as the basis of national-level democratic institutions. The first steps were therefore the holding of novel district-level elections well ahead of the multi-party national-level elections. Thereupon District Assemblies were established throughout the country as part of decentralizing local government and administration. These assemblies have created a framework for local leadership and initiative in development.

The 1992 Constitution went on to spell out the features of the decentralization program, requiring Parliament to make laws to institute these features. According to Article 240(2) of the Constitution:

(a) Parliament shall enact appropriate laws to ensure that functions, powers, responsibilities and resources are at all times transferred from the Central Government to local government units in a co-ordinated manner;

(b) Parliament shall by law provide for the taking of such measures as are necessary to enhance the capacity of local government authorities to plan, initiate, co-ordinate, manage and execute policies in respect of all matters affecting people within their areas, with a view to ultimately achieving localization of those activities;

(c) there shall be established for each local government unit a sound financial base with adequate and reliable sources of revenue; ...

The elections to the assemblies were conducted before the re-establishment of political parties in Ghana, but whether this attempt at non-partisan, local-level political institutions can survive the dominance of political parties at the national level remains to be seen.

The NPP, whilst in opposition, expressed its intention to seek a constitutional amendment that would make district-level elections also party-based. In a crucial acknowledgment of the important role that the district level has attained in Ghana's evolving democracy, the sponsorship by political parties of candidates during the district-level elections of 2002 was barely veiled, despite the clear terms of Article 248 of the Constitution:

248 (1) A candidate seeking election to a District Assembly or any lower local government unit shall present himself to the electorate as an individual, and shall not use any symbol associated with any political party.
(2) A political party shall not endorse, sponsor, offer a platform to or in anyway campaign for or against a candidate seeking election to a District Assembly or any lower local government unit.

Funding the District Level

The process of consolidation of the district level, however, involves the assemblies gaining assured access to a defined share of national revenues and their exercising real control over this share. This will require enforcement of the provision in Article 252(2) of the Constitution on the allocation of a specific portion of national revenues – 'not less than five per cent of the total revenues of Ghana' – to the assemblies 'for development'. The allocated amount is to 'be paid into the District Assemblies Common Fund in quarterly installments'. The distribution to District Assemblies is to be on 'the basis of a formula approved by Parliament' (art. 252(3). This allocation of revenue to the District Assemblies is to enable them to play a role in the economic development of their various areas as anticipated in the constitutional description of their function: 'the formulation and execution of plans, programs and strategies for the effective mobilization of the resources necessary for the overall development of the district' (art. 245(a)).

While in recent times the central government has sought to manifest the success of its decision to opt for Highly Indebted Poor Country (HIPC) status by announcing allocations of funds accruing from this to districts for development projects, these discretionary allocations outside the framework of the District Assemblies Common Fund are thus not a part of the anticipated constitutional process of transferring a definite share of revenue to the districts. The constant failure by the Ministry of Finance to comply with the Constitution, acknowledged by the Minister of Finance in the 2001 Budget Statement, despite the recognition of the existence of the provisions on allocations to the districts, has been unfortunate. To allow the continued disregard of these important provisions in Chapter 20 of the Constitution is to risk marginalization of the district-level institutions and disempowering the grassroots whilst maintaining the dependency relationship between districts and central government.

DISTRICT-LEVEL INSTITUTION BUILDING
There are clear signs, however, of the growing importance of decentralization to

democratic development in Ghana. The fact that political parties took such a keen interest in the district-level elections in 2002, as mentioned earlier, is an expression of the awareness of their political significance. The participation in the district assemblies of articulate local leaders, some of whom have subsequently stood for election to the national Parliament, as well as the participation also of retired civil servants, knowledgeable in national affairs and now committed to their locality, are manifestations of the increasing significance being attached to the district assemblies.

Their political clout is also attested to by occasions of their rejecting nominations by the President to the position of District Chief Executive. Subjecting the nomination of the President to approval by the district assembly is an attempt to reflect the local government character of the role of District Chief Executive. While recognizing the importance of development co-ordination at the level of central government, the importance the Constitution attached to transferring 'functions, powers, responsibilities and resources... from the Central Government to local government units' (art. 240(2)(a)) and making 'persons in the service of local government subject to the effective control of local authorities' (art. 240(2)(d)) manifests the intention to establish independent local power that would not simply be an arm of the national executive. Yet the fact that the District Chief Executive is appointed and removed by the President and is thus subjected to control from the centre does detract from the local character intended for this position.

Another important emerging issue has to do with the need to insulate the appointment and functioning of the administrator of the District Assemblies Common Fund from central government and party political control, so as to give full rein to the considerations about district-level initiative in development and equity in distribution to districts that are stated as being paramount. Here again, the fact that the administrator controls significant resources will likely generate party political interest in the position, to the detriment of the constitutional mandate.

Indeed, a serious danger to the sustenance of democracy in Ghana, as elsewhere in Africa, is the misuse of central government incumbency and the corrupt means resorted to by incumbents to raise funds for electoral campaigning and to maintain the dependency of the district level. Building capacity in economic management at district level, especially in respect of budget development and resource mobilization (external as well as internal), investment promotion and enforcement of environmental regulations (especially for mining projects) will be crucial to the effectiveness of district-level institutions. The local empowerment and initiative-taking for development that decentralization aims at are important aspects of democracy as well as national economic development. Decentralization will be severely undermined by a preoccupation with the national-level contests for power through elections that tend to be perceived, especially by foreign observers, as the main measure of 'democracy and good governance'. The undermining of district-level authority in favor of the power of central government is, in fact, both a negation of democracy and a fetter on the potential for economic development through mobilizing internal resources. The failure of internal resource mobilization inevitably subjects the economy, and hence the polity, to more external donor control, thus endangering not only democracy but national sovereignty as well.

Deepening Democracy

Since the promulgation of the 1992 Constitution, Ghana has successfully gone through four democratic elections at the national level, the elections in December 2000 leading to the party previously in opposition taking over the reins of power, something that some thought inconceivable in Africa. Even more remarkably, the presidential candidate of the party then in power conceded defeat in the run-off election before the Electoral Commission officially announced the results – and he did not call again to recall his concession![6] There is no question about the deepening of democracy in the Ghanaian polity. The explosion of local and national media, particularly radio stations and newspapers, and the vibrancy (even stridency) of political debate through these channels testify to this reality. Perhaps an even more significant expression of the deepening democratic experience is the evolution of district assemblies as organs of grassroots participation in government and rallying points of local development.

Amidst all this remains the stark reality that, after two decades of structural adjustment policies supported by the IMF and the World Bank, the aspirations of the majority of the population to better conditions of life and relief from grinding poverty are far from being realized. The challenge of national development remains for each government as daunting as ever, especially in the light of the global economic context. Clearly, such development is less likely to be attained if the preoccupation of national leadership is to satisfy external conditionalities for aid rather than empowering their population and increasing productivity. The institutions that consolidate local participation and power in a decentralized governmental framework are key elements of such national mobilization.

Conclusion

Ghana's first President famously said, 'Seek ye first the political kingdom and all other things shall be added'. Rather than being a misguided statist approach to development, this statement simply highlighted the fundamental importance of national empowerment, which in Nkumah's day signaled national independence and African liberation. The formulation of national strategies for economic survival and development after the attainment of independence was, and still is, a key element of the 'political kingdom'. The 'polis', or 'polity' is not just about decision-making processes, democratic or otherwise, but also about the way of survival and the well-being of the society. Evolving political institutions as manifested in the history of the Ghanaian Constitution, for instance, reflect the ongoing struggles in nation-building.

The dialectical relationship between political and economic realities was profoundly analyzed by Marx in terms which clarify the limits of national political power in the quest for developmentof a country like Ghana (Tsikata, 1977: 165; 1978: 113). The significance of ongoing deliberation, reflection, and interaction amongst the populace at all levels about their conditions of life is not only important politically but economically as well. They can ensure the rallying of the capacity of the population at large and the mobilization of internal resources to addressing the survival and development of a people. The economic reforms in Ghana in the early 1980s, which required the grassroots mobilization of natural resources, paved the way for the democratic reforms of the 1990s. Democracy reflects both economic and political aspirations and the ongoing challenge of economic development and democratic governance requires the mobilization of natural resources and the empowerment of the grassroots as envisaged through decentralization.

Fundamentally, then, the future prospects for the Ghanaian people lie less in the adoption of the changing paradigms of institutions like the IMF and the World Bank and compliance with the resulting conditionalities for development assistance, and more in the mobilization of national resources, human and material, to confront the challenges of nationhood. Sustaining reforms, whether economic or political, in Ghana as elsewhere in Africa, lies in increasing the effectiveness of local management both at the national and sub-national level and not in being, for however long a time, a success story of external donors.

Notes

[1] The recognition now given to the farmer was also manifested in the mobilization of the nation as a whole, particularly university students, to evacuate cocoa locked up in the hinterland because of broke-down infrastructure. The institution of more effective payments systems for cocoa farmers was also a major government initiative.

[2] Remarkably, in the case of Ghana, the pre-reform internal distortions prevented the country from benefiting from the favourable terms of trade in the late 1970s. Ghana subsequently experienced the bust in cocoa prices after it had increased production levels.

[3] 'Adjustment programmes have undermined local capacities and have tended to divert national capacities away from national projects towards donor-driven ones... Rather than focusing on enhancing the impact of local development efforts, the preponderance of aid interests ties up large amounts of scarce resources to enhance the effectiveness of aid, even when it is recognized that aid is not the catalyst, let alone the only development initiative taking place in the country. As a consequence, local administrators are left with little time for their own problems and initiatives.'(Mkandawire, 2002: 160–1).

[4] Whilst still Deputy Managing Director, Fischer had characterized the ambivalence in the role of the IMF as follows: '... it is essential to recognize the tension between two key roles that the Fund is expected to play in the international economic system... As a sympathetic social worker, the Fund provides friendly advice to its members about their economic policies and provides financial assistance in times of actual or potential difficulties... On the other hand, as the tough cop of the international financial system, the Fund is expected to point out explicitly (and, in the new age of transparency, also publicly) key deficiencies in the economic policies of its members. Its financial assistance to members is supposed to be limited to the "catalytic role" of filling in modest financing gaps that might remain after account is taken of the effect of a member's adjustment program in restoring market confidence. For this purpose Fund financial support should be tightly conditioned on a rigorous program of adjustment measures, with vigorous actions required to correct any deficiencies in meeting program objectives.' ('Lessons for the Fund', see http://www.iie.com, Fischer-Lessons 5iie 339x. pp. 67–8).

[5] For example, Road Fund and other sectoral funds were created in World Bank project agreements but the IMF opposed such sectoral arrangements as creating distortions in annual budgets. The much-vaunted improvements in the collaboration between Fund and Bank are also coming twenty years too late for Ghana!

[6] As happened in the US presidential election in 2000 between Al Gore and George W. Bush.

9

JOHN HATCHARD

Legal Techniques & Agencies of Accountability: Human Rights Commissions in Commonwealth Africa

I N the Harare Commonwealth Declaration of 1991, Commonwealth heads of government recognized that developing appropriate 'institutional structures which reflect national circumstances' is a key element for promoting and protecting human rights, just and honest government, and the rule of law (Commonwealth Secretariat, 1993). This reflects Nwabueze's warning that a major cause of the failure of Africa's constitutional government is the lack of understanding and acceptance of its principles and institutions by the populace (Nwabueze, 1989). Institutions do not have an independent existence, and survive only if they are capable of serving their society in a meaningful fashion. States, therefore, must develop their own oversight bodies that provide in practice meaningful protection to those seeking administrative justice and/or the enjoyment of their constitutional rights.

The 1960s and 1970s saw the development of ombudsman offices throughout Africa; the offices continue to operate. The 1990s saw the development of a new and potentially more significant institution, the Human Rights Commission (HRC). Today, HRCs operate in eight of the 18 Commonwealth states: Cameroon, Ghana, Malawi, Mauritius, Nigeria, South Africa, Uganda, and Zambia. Indeed, countries now widely accept a human rights commission as an essential building block in any new constitutional dispensation.[1] In addition, quasi-human rights commissions operate in Namibia and Zimbabwe, as the ombudsman is empowered to investigate allegations of human rights violations as well as maladministration.[2]

This chapter intends to assess the contribution of HRCs in Commonwealth Africa in supporting just and honest government and in promoting and protecting human rights. In addition, it examines some of the new challenges facing such commissions. The Commonwealth's *Best Practice Guidelines for National Human Rights Institutions* is the basis for the discussion.[3] Part I looks at why HRCs are currently an 'in vogue' institution. Part II discusses how states can develop effective HRCs, which is done through the Paris Principles and the *Best Practice Guidelines*. Part III looks at the new challenges that HRCs face in order to continue being an effective institution and to meet future needs. The two main challenges deal with promoting human rights, and transnational and cross-border co-operation between states. Part IV is an overview of the role of HRCs.

I: The 'In Vogue' Institution

A constitution or statute establishes a human rights commission as a multi-member body to promote and protect human rights. HRCs have extensive

108

investigative powers and enjoy a range of remedial powers. The reason why HRCs are 'in vogue' has much to do with the emphasis of international donors, if not individual African states themselves, on just and honest government and the rule of law as essential to development. This was evident in the 1991 Harare Commonwealth Declaration, in which Commonwealth heads of government pledged themselves and their countries to work for:

> The protection and promotion of the fundamental political values of the Commonwealth: democracy, democratic processes and institutions which reflect national circumstances, the rule of law and independence of the judiciary, just and honest government... (Commonwealth Secretariat, 1993)

Human rights commissions are attractive as they are often in a better position to protect and promote human rights than other institutions, as the following comparisons demonstrate.

OFFICES OF THE OMBUDSMAN AND HUMAN RIGHTS COMMISSIONS
The aim of the Office of the Ombudsman is the pursuit of administrative justice for all citizens in a manner which is confidential, flexible and inexpensive. Thus any person who claims to have suffered injustice at the hands of a government official may complain to the ombudsman and ask for an investigation into the matter. As a permanent (and often a constitutionally established) institution, the office is potentially a very effective investigatory body operating within, although not being a part of, government. This is because wide-ranging investigative powers give it unique access to government documents and officials, including the right to compel officials to testify before it and to produce relevant documentation. In addition, the development of personal contacts with high-ranking officials can often swiftly resolve a complaint, whilst officials are frequently extremely co-operative once they realize that the office is also an important protection for them against unfounded malicious or unfair attacks. Furthermore, the office enables members of the public to identify with a known individual who (it is hoped) retains their confidence, is impartial and is able to investigate their complaints fully (Hatchard, 1992: 215–16).

In many respects, HRCs have evolved from the ombudsman model, but the differences demonstrate why HRCs are potentially a more effective accountability mechanism. First, they are multi-member bodies, while a single member heads the traditional ombudsman office. More variation among those in control encourages the development of a more representative body as well as providing a greater range of expertise and experience within the institution.

Second, while an ombudsman's prime concern is investigating complaints of administrative injustice or maladministration, HRCs base their jurisdiction specifically on human rights norms. Third, an office of the ombudsman can only investigate complaints against public officials, while the jurisdiction of a human rights commission extends to the private sector. Fourth, unlike an office of the ombudsman, HRCs have a specific mandate to promote human rights. As the Commonwealth *Practice Guidelines* state:

> National human rights institutions should have the power to provide information, education, strategic advice and training on human rights issues including training for government and other public officials about applicable norms and human rights standards. Specific training should be designed for members of the police, military

forces, judiciary, legal profession and other members of society that have particular powers or responsibility relevant to human rights.[4]

Fifth, only HRCs have the power to undertake a variety of other human rights-related functions, such as reviewing proposed legislation for compliance with the state's international human rights obligations. Finally, while an ombudsman is traditionally restricted to making recommendations to resolve a complaint, HRCs often enjoy a wider range of remedial powers.[5]

COURTS AND HUMAN RIGHTS COMMISSIONS

The introduction of constitutions that provide a wide range of justiciable rights in many Commonwealth African countries during the 1990s has enhanced the courts' power to develop a human rights jurisprudence.[6] But courts do not and cannot provide a complete solution to resolve human rights issues for several reasons. It is here that human rights commissions can assist.

First, courts are essentially reactive in the sense that they must wait for parties to bring the cases to them.[7] HRCs not only investigate complaints received from the public, but governments specifically empower them to act on their own initiative in order to protect human rights. Second, while a judicial decision may itself have wide implications, a court cannot look beyond the issues before it. In other words, a court cannot deal with systemic human rights problems or look at wider issues of social policy. This is precisely what HRCs do.

Another problem limitation on courts providing a solution is that procedural complexities, restrictive rules on state privilege, and strict rules of evidence often hamper those seeking to bring human rights issues before a court. The wide investigative powers of HRCs, including the power to order the production of documents and the attendance of witnesses, can overcome many limitations of courts.[8] HRCs are also more accessible and offer a more cost-effective and less formal means of conflict resolution. Of course, human rights commissions are not and should not be seen as being rival bodies to the courts. But they can provide invaluable assistance in circumstances where enforcement of rights is not readily available through the courts.[9]

II: Developing Effective Institutions

Despite the considerable optimism generated by the introduction of HRCs, the reality is that they are very new institutions that are still 'finding their feet'. This has led to efforts to establish some basic ground-rules for their operation. This section briefly examines the role of the United Nations, and then focuses on the work of Commonwealth African Human Rights Commissions (CAHRCs).

THE PARIS PRINCIPLES

Establishing a human rights commission is not enough to ensure that a country respects human rights. To be effective, HRCs have to 'work' in the sense that the institution has widespread support from the public, civil society, the public service, and the government. A 'model' HRC does not exist, and commissions within Commonwealth Africa vary considerably in terms of their structures and powers. Yet, some basic principles for their organization and operation are vital.

The international community made an effort in 1993 to lay down some such principles in the *United Nations Principles Relating to the Status of National Institutions* (the Paris Principles).[10] The key Paris Principles are that HRCs (national institutions) should:

* be established in the constitution or by legislation;
* have as broad a mandate as possible;
* have a membership that represents civilian society;
* enjoy adequate funding; and
* have wide investigative powers.

Underlying the Paris Principles is the recognition that the guarantees of independence and pluralism lie at the heart of an effective commission.

The 1993 World Conference on Human Rights encouraged establishing and strengthening HRCs and endorsed the Paris Principles. It reaffirmed the HRCs' role in promoting and protecting human rights, in particular in advising governments on remedying human rights violations, disseminating human rights information, and educating the public about human rights.

BUILDING ON THE PARIS PRINCIPLES:
DEVELOPMENTS IN THE COMMONWEALTH

Representatives from a range of different institutions and legal traditions attended the Paris Conference, which the principles reflect by covering multiple factors in an attempt to cover as wide a field as possible. That the Paris Principles lack specificity is in part due to the variety of institutions that call themselves 'Human Rights Commissions'. The challenge, therefore, is to develop more meaningful guidelines that go beyond generalizations.

The Commonwealth has been particularly active in developing more specific guidelines. At a Commonwealth conference at Cambridge University, UK in 2000 participants from human rights commissions and offices of the ombudsman recognized that HRCs 'play a critical role in the entrenchment of the universality, interdependence and indivisibility of human rights and the maintenance of good government'. They further recognized that 'the common legal and governance traditions and values of the Commonwealth provided an opportunity to build on the Paris Principles to reflect more clearly the Commonwealth's fundamental values as enshrined in the Harare Commonwealth Declaration' (Commonwealth Secretariat, 2000: 6).

This led, in the following year, to the Commonwealth Secretariat developing the *Best Practice Guidelines,* which provide a recommended framework for the organization and powers of HRCs. Even then, the countries rightly recognized that much still depends upon the range and content of the human rights provisions enshrined in the constitution of an individual state (and, in some cases, on its international and regional obligations), as well as the state's size, structure, and history. The *Guidelines* also recognize that establishing HRCs is merely the first step. Making them effective requires Commonwealth states to apply both the Paris Principles and the *Best Practice Guidelines.* Some examples from CAHRCs' *Best Practice Guidelines* are given below.

APPLYING THE *BEST PRACTICE GUIDELINES*

Guideline 1.2 Legal foundation

* The legal provisions that established the National Human Rights Institution
  (NHRI) guarantee that its independence and funding should be entrenched
  in the constitution or clearly stipulated in the enabling legislation.
* The preferred method of establishing a NHRI is through incorporation in the
  constitution of a state.
* Establishment other than by the constitution or an act of parliament, e.g. by
  a presidential decree, is undesirable.

The above best practices reflect the fact that 'the most certain way of preserving
the independence of a human rights commission is to incorporate its establishment and vested powers into the national constitution'.[11] Virtually all African
Commonwealth countries comply with this guideline. The two exceptions are
Cameroon and Nigeria. A Cameroon presidential decree established the
National Commission on Human Rights and Freedoms in 1990. Its method of
establishment and composition reflects the position in other francophone African
states, where the Commission's membership is a personal 'gift' of the President
from among his officials.[12] Indeed, it is not unusual for a serving government
official to also hold a Commissioner appointment.[13] In 1995, a military decree
established the Nigerian Human Rights commission.[14] In Cameroon and
Nigeria, the legal foundation for such commissions remains unacceptable, as it
does not provide a guarantee for either the continued existence or independence
of the commissions/commissioners.

Guideline 4.1 Accountability to the public

* A NHRI should actively evaluate the effectiveness of its activities, including
  through the engagement of independent consultants, and it should incorporate the results of such evaluations in its annual reports.
* Evaluations should examine the quality of the NHRI's programs and the
  extent to which existing programs sufficiently address the human rights issues
  in the country. The evaluations should include both qualitative and quantitative analysis.
* NHRIs should undertake an annual strategic planning exercise to establish
  programmatic targets and goals. Some targets and goals should be measura-
  ble, for example, by the number of complaints resolved, number of detention
  centers visited, etc. The strategic plan should be included in the annual
  report.
  The Commentary to this Guideline then states:
* NHRIs exist to serve the public, and accordingly, the public should have a
  mechanism for assessing how effectively a NHRI is performing its mandate.
  Public assessment requires that NHRIs evaluate their own programs regularly and include the results of such evaluations in their annual reports.

Several CAHRCs have not only failed to develop effective evaluation mechanisms, but remain unable to produce their annual reports on time. For
example, a statute does not oblige the Permanent Human Rights Commission
in Zambia to produce an annual report. By 2002, its latest report was for

1998.[15] But the excellent Annual Reports and other materials from the Uganda Human Rights Commission, the Ghanaian Commission on Human Rights and Administrative Justice, and the South African Human Rights Commission (together with their useful web sites)[16] demonstrate that, with the appropriate organization and training, HRCs can develop effective accountability mechanisms.[17]

Guideline 4.5 Relations with the international treaty machinery

- CHRCs should co-operate with the efforts of international treaty bodies to monitor states' compliance with their international human rights treaty obligations.
- CHRCs should make recommendations to the executive and the parliament regarding efforts needed to achieve compliance with international human rights treaty obligations.
- CHRCs should contribute as appropriate to the preparation of government reports regarding state responses to the recommendations of treaty bodies.

One significant recent development is the growing acceptance that HRCs merit a separate presence at UN Human Rights Commission meetings and at meetings of regional human rights bodies. The acceptance is in recognition of the fact that they are neither government bodies nor non-governmental organizations, but a separate category of institutions that merit a separate status. This is an area that deserves further attention.[18]

Guideline 5. Accessibility

- NHRIs must proactively reach out to vulnerable and disadvantaged persons
- NHRIs should be geographically and physically accessible by constituents
- The offices of a NHRI should be, whenever possible, located away from other government and military offices.

The issue of accessibility is epitomized in Ghana, where the Constitution *obliges* the Commission on Human Rights and Administrative Justice to establish regional and district branches. This has enabled the Ghana Commission to lobby successfully for increased government funding to establish a nationwide presence.[19] The location of offices is another challenge. While Guideline 5 recognizes that CAHRC must emphasize their independence by being physically separate from government offices, the practice, cost, and availability of suitable premises may make this impossible.[20]

Accessibility is inevitably tied to resources. The continuing economic constraints in African states make the ability and willingness of governments to provide adequate funding increasingly uncertain. The fact that funding is only normally provided on an annual basis is also potentially problematic, as HRCs may require medium- and long-term financial support for projects such as decentralization. External funding from both civil society and international aid agencies is an obvious way to alleviate the problem, and some make good use of these funding sources.[21] While such funding may raise concerns, particularly by the government, over its possible effect on the recipient institution's independence, funding can only help facilitate a HRC's effectiveness, and evidence does not support a lack of independence.[22] Therefore, the question of whether or not to accept outside funding is entirely a matter for the institution itself and any requirement for ministerial approval is both unnecessary and unacceptable.[23] Perhaps the one caveat to external funding is the practical point that 'secure' government funding should cover recurrent expenditure, in case of the withdrawal, non-renewal, or non-availability of donor funds.

Guideline 6.1 Role of NHRIs in conflict situations (including war and civil strife)

• NHRIs should continue to work in conflict situations to protect and promote human rights and the peace process.
• A NHRI should do whatever lies within its powers to assist particularly vulnerable groups.
• A NHRI should work with other organizations, i.e. UNHRC, NGOs and other relief organizations, to address the needs of internally displaced persons.

The Commentary on Guideline 6.1 states that:

> In time of war or civil strife, the functions performed by NHRIs become even more necessary. Commissions find it extremely difficult to protect human rights in conflict situations and thus should work in co-operation with other actors, for example, NGOs and other relief organizations, to fortify their position as a protector of human rights.

Dealing with conflict situations is likely to be one of the most challenging issues for CAHRCs. Their record to date is a matter of concern. For example, while not a full-blown HRC, the Office of the Ombudsman is charged by the Zimbabwe government with protecting and promoting human rights. Zimbabwe's human rights position needs no highlighting. But it appears that the Ombudsman has made no public statement nor taken any action in an effort to protect the millions of Zimbabweans who continue to suffer at the hands of the government and its supporters.

III: New Challenges

The work of national institutions must evolve to take on new roles and new challenges. As the *Best Practice Guidelines* (Chapter VII) puts it: 'NHRIs should proactively and reactively respond to new challenges as and when they arise, e.g. the human rights implications of the AIDS pandemic, scientific and technological advances, and privacy considerations' (Commonwealth Secretariat, 2001). This section discusses two challenges: first, promoting human rights, and second, the issue of developing transnational and cross-border co-operation.

PROMOTING HUMAN RIGHTS
HRCs have the task of promoting respect for and observance of human rights. This is a heavy responsibility as it involves developing a culture of understanding human rights issues that extends to people at work and at school, in families and in public life, including government officials, parliamentarians, and security forces members. The findings of the Ugandan Commission of Inquiry into the Violation of Human Rights (also known as the Oder Commission) that a key factor in the perpetuation of the cycle of violence in Uganda before 1987 was

lack of knowledge about human rights by both law enforcement officers and their victims emphasizes the importance of culture. Consequently, 'officers and agents of the state regularly abused the rights of those who fell into their hands and the victims and the public often aided the process by being passive'. Further, the Commission remarked that all Ugandan institutions, including the family, had a pervasive lack of 'internal democracy'. In its view, this 'breeds people, who from childhood, are nurtured to violently repress other people's rights' (Oder Commission Report, 1994: 10).

Guideline 3.4 of the *Best Practice Guidelines* sets out well the scope of the role of CAHRCs in the promotion of human rights. The *Guidelines* state that NHRIs should have the power to provide information, education, strategic advice, and training on human rights issues including:

- training for government and other public officials about applicable norms and human rights standards. Specific training should be designed for members of the police, military forces, judiciary, the legal profession and other members of society who have particular powers or responsibility relevant to human rights;
- targeted education for vulnerable groups;
- building the capacity of human rights advocates and NGOs to perform their work;
- training NHRI staff to build the capacity of the NHRI to perform its work;
- public awareness campaigns; and
- developing and supporting human rights clubs – particularly in schools and other formal educational institutions.

Further, the *Guidelines* state that

- NHRIs should widely disseminate information on their complaint process, the remedies available, and the contact details of the NHRI.
- NHRIs should have the power to use mass media as appropriate and available to communicate with the public. For example, in developing countries, radio may be very effective. In other countries, toll-free phone systems and web sites may be useful.
- NHRIs should collaborate with other public and private institutions to maximize the provision of human rights education.

Yet, promoting human rights is not just about education and three related issues require separate discussion.

Taking a position on national human rights issues
International practice widely accepts that HRCs should be free to comment on national human rights issues,[24] and must do so if they encounter evidence of human rights violations.[25] How they should respond to national debates on controversial human rights issues is more problematic. For example, in a debate on the death penalty, abortion, or euthanasia, should a commission merely provide information and facilitate public discussion, or should it seek to lead public opinion by taking a specific position? The Commission on Human Rights and Administrative Justice in Ghana faced this dilemma on the death penalty issue. Commissioners found it extremely difficult to adopt a detached attitude, particularly because the media were continually seeking their views, and (somewhat

encouragingly) regarding the Commission as the 'conscience of the nation'.[26] National circumstances limit the possibility of adopting a hard and fast rule, although the prime role of the HRC in such matters is to facilitate debate, provide information, and ensure that all views on the topic are widely disseminated. In addition, taking sides may adversely affect the Commission's independence, but, as a multi-member body, it may be impossible for commissioners to reach a consensus.

Overseeing a state's compliance with international human rights obligations
With many African states failing to fulfil their obligations under international and regional human rights instruments, national institutions should have a role in overseeing their compliance with these obligations. The Uganda Human Rights Commission has this specific task, although it is arguably included in the promotion of human rights mandate of other commissions by implication.[27] Such a power has the potential to be extremely significant, as a broad interpretation of 'monitoring' would require a government to report to a commission on the steps it took to comply with its international human rights obligations.[28] A monitoring role could also extend to overseeing the preparation of national reports required under regional and international human rights instruments and, where necessary, providing appropriate training in their preparation for government officials. The importance of retaining independence means that a commission should not take responsibility for compiling such reports. Indeed, a commission should be free to provide a separate 'alternative' report if necessary.

Reporting on a state's human rights
The Uganda HRC provides a useful model on national reporting of the state of human rights. In line with the Paris Principles, the government requires the Uganda HRC to prepare reports both on the state of human rights and on specific issues when necessary.[29] Civil society can also play a key role by following up the commission's reports and endeavoring to ensure that the government duly implements any recommendations for action. Preparing such reports is a potentially valuable 'stock-taking' exercise and, if widely disseminated, could be an effective means of promoting and strengthening human rights.

The Ugandan HRC mandate also requires it to submit an annual report to Parliament on the state of human rights and freedoms in the country. This requirement is unusual for an annual report, which normally provides an overview of the commission's work. The obligation is significant as it emphasizes the importance of providing Parliament with an objective, reliable, properly structured, and 'user-friendly' assessment of the country's human rights situation.[30] Parliaments do not have a statutory duty to debate such reports, which is a major oversight since a danger remains that the report will otherwise have little impact. However, wide media publicity of the reports may persuade parliamentarians of the importance of debating them.[31]

TRANSNATIONAL AND CROSS-BORDER CO-OPERATION
Increasingly, CAHRCs are facing matters that include a transnational or cross-border dimension, such as matters relating to refugees, asylum cases, and the investigation of corrupt practices in international business transactions.

However, at present, they are generally ill-equipped to deal with such issues, as the region regards them as *national* bodies whose task is to tackle *national* issues.[32] They can no longer afford to retain this limited focus. Some institutions have developed 'networking' capacities with similar bodies elsewhere, and the recent establishment of a pan-African national human rights institutions body is a welcome development. But little work has been done on the development of mutual co-operation and assistance regimes *inter se* to facilitate cross-border and transnational investigations.[33] A useful starting point is the signing of a Memorandum of Understanding by such institutions. An example of this kind of arrangement is the 1995 Memorandum of Understanding between the Canadian Human Rights Commission and the National Human Rights Commission in India, which provides for sharing information and documentation, staff exchanges between the two commissions, and developing stronger links between human rights centres in universities in their respective countries aimed at enhancing the quality of information available to them.

A Memorandum of Understanding is a useful device already used by other investigative agencies, such as the police and customs authorities in dealing with cross-border crime. For oversight bodies, a Memorandum might include an agreement that the HRC in Country A will investigate complaints originating in Country B that have a transnational element and *vice versa*. Furthermore, a Memorandum might provide for staff exchanges, leading to closer professional ties between staff from different institutions. This type of partnership facilitates co-operation and trust, clarifies knowledge of the transnational aspect of the problem, and enhances efficiency. The use of universities and other institutions of higher learning in a research role is also attractive, especially as time and staffing constraints often make this almost impossible for the institutions themselves.

A Memorandum of Understanding is not the sole mechanism for developing transnational and cross-border co-operation between oversight bodies, but it does illustrate a potentially effective method. It also highlights the crucial fact that national institutions must respond to new challenges in a positive and effective manner.

IV: Overview

When critically examining Commonwealth HRCs, we need to remember that they are new institutions; all are creatures of the 1990s or the present century. Their tasks are in some of the most sensitive areas of public and private life, and it is little wonder that some are still seeking to establish themselves. Thus, any effective analysis of their work must be based on the recognition that they are still evolving, and that it takes time for both the governors and the governed to understand and accept their work and their powers.

Certainly the HRCs in Africa merit much of their criticism, and the 2001 Human Rights Watch Report *Protectors or Pretenders: Government Human Rights Commissions in Africa* is particularly scathing in this regard.[34] But several points must be made. First, CAHRCs represent an important new and different type of accountability institution that enjoys significant advantages over existing mechanisms. Second, their jurisdiction and powers mean that they hold out the promise of being able to make an effective contribution towards a just and honest government, as well as providing effective protection and promotion of human rights.

Another aspect is that the international community should be aware of unrealistically raising public expectations about HRCs. This is critical. Staffing and financial constraints inevitably mean that HRCs have to make choices as to what human rights issues will be given priority. A consensus on the priorities will be rare, but they should be spared criticism so long as they make a rational and informed choice. Promoting public inquiries to examine areas of major systemic human rights problems might assist here. Also, states need to identify and address the weakness of HRCs in order for them to be effective. An ineffective body is likely to raise false hopes among the people and prejudice the promotion and protection of human rights. In such cases, it may be desirable to simply scrap the body.

Fifth, the highest echelons of government must support the commissions. Action is necessary to refute the criticism of Human Rights Watch (2001b) that, in some countries, 'The creation of the commission seemed to be motivated more by a desire to deflect criticism of the government's recalcitrance to political liberalization'. Finally, establishing and maintaining effective HRCs throughout Africa, not just in Commonwealth Africa, must be given the highest priority.

The task, then, is to seek to strengthen CAHRCs. Several mechanisms should be explored, including:

- Fully implementing the Commonwealth Best Practice Guidelines.
- Developing links between CAHRCs. This is currently being done, but these links need to cover a number of areas: (i) exchange of information on best practice; (ii) mutual support mechanisms (for example, publicly supporting the work of another HRC when it faces attack from the government); (iii) exchanges of staff between institutions; and (iv) providing technical assistance (a human rights commission might assist with the establishment and maintenance of a web site for another commission).
- Providing training for key commission personnel. The staff of HRCs are relatively new and inexperienced. Training in areas such as record-keeping, case management techniques, and report writing would make a difference in many commissions.

Overall, it is worth reiterating the views of the participants in the Cambridge national institutions conference in 2000, since these underline the importance of human rights commissions in Africa (Commonwealth Secretariat, 2000: 6):

> One of the recurring themes was the recognition that national institutions play a critical role in the entrenchment of the universality, interdependence and indivisibility of human rights and the maintenance of good governance... However, described, national institutions that work to protect and promote human rights ought to form a fundamental part of a society in all Commonwealth countries.

ANNEX 9.1

**Principles Relating to the Status of National Institutions
(Paris Principles)**
Competence and responsibilities

1. A national institution shall be vested with competence to promote and protect human rights.
2. A national institution shall be given as broad a mandate as possible, which shall be clearly set forth in a constitutional or legislative text, specifying its composition and its sphere of competence.
3. A national institution shall, *inter alia*, have the following responsibilities:
   (a) To submit to the Government, Parliament and any other competent body, on an advisory basis either at the request of the authorities concerned or through the exercise of its power to hear a matter without higher referral, opinions, recommendations, proposals and reports on any matters concerning the promotion and protection of human rights; the national institution may decide to publicize them; these opinions, recommendations, proposals and reports, as well as any prerogative of the national institution, shall relate to the following areas:
      (i) Any legislative or administrative provisions, as well as provisions relating to judicial organization, intended to preserve and extend the protection of human rights; in that connection, the national institution shall examine the legislation and administrative provisions in force, as well as bills and proposals, and shall make such recommendations as it deems appropriate in order to ensure that these provisions conform to the fundamental principles of human rights; it shall, if necessary, recommend the adoption of new legislation, the amendment of legislation in force and the adoption or amendment of administrative measures;
      (ii) Any situation of violation of human rights which it decides to take up;
      (iii) The preparation of reports on the national situation with regard to human rights in general, and on more specific matters; and
      (iv) Drawing the attention of the Government to situations in any part of the country where human rights are violated and making proposals to it for initiatives to put an end to such situations and, where necessary, expressing an opinion on the positions and reactions of the Government.
   (b) To promote and ensure the harmonization of national legislation, regulations and practices with the international human rights instruments to which the State is a party, and their effective implementation;
   (c) To encourage ratification of the above-mentioned instruments or accession to those instruments, and to ensure their implementation;
   (d) To contribute to the reports which States are required to submit to United Nations bodies and committees, and to regional institutions, pursuant to their treaty obligations and, where necessary, to express an opinion on the subject, with due respect for their independence;
   (e) To co-operate with the United Nations and any other organization in the United Nations system, the regional institutions and the national institu-

tions of other countries that are competent in the areas of the promotion and protection of human rights;

(f) To assist in the formulation of programmes for the teaching of, and research into, human rights and to take part in their execution in schools, universities and professional circles; and

(g) To publicize human rights and efforts to combat all forms of discrimination, in particular racial discrimination, by increasing public awareness; especially through information and education and by making use of all press organs.

Composition and guarantees of independence and pluralism

1. The composition of the national institution and the appointment of its members, whether by means of an election or otherwise, shall be established in accordance with a procedure which affords all necessary guarantees to ensure the pluralist representation of the social forces (of civilian society) involved in the promotion and protection of human rights, particularly by powers which will enable effective co-operation to be established with, or through the presence of, representatives of:

   (a) Non-governmental organizations responsible for human rights and efforts to combat racial discrimination, trade unions, and concerned social and professional organisations, for example, associations of lawyers, doctors, journalists and eminent scientists;

   (b) Trends in philosophical or religious thought;

   (c) Universities and qualified experts;

   (d) Parliament; and

   (e) Governmental departments (if they are included, these representatives should participate in the deliberations only in an advisory capacity).

2. The national institution shall have an infrastructure which is suited to the smooth conduct of its activities, in particular, adequate funding. The purpose of this funding should be to enable it to have its own staff and premises, in order to be independent of the Government and not be subject to financial control which might affect its independence.

3. In order to ensure a stable mandate for the members of the institution, without which there can be no real independence, their appointment shall be effected by an official act which shall establish the specific duration of the mandate. This mandate may be renewable, provided that the pluralism of the institution's membership is ensured.

Methods of operation

Within the framework of its operation, the national institution shall:

   (a) Freely consider any questions falling within its competence, whether they are submitted by the Government or taken up by it without referral to a higher authority, on the proposal of its members or of any petitioner;

   (b) Hear any person and obtain any information and/or any documents necessary for assessing situations falling within its competence;

   (c) Address public opinion directly or through any press organ, particularly in order to publicize its opinions and recommendations;

   (d) Meet on a regular basis and whenever necessary in the presence of all its members after they have been duly convened;

(e) Establish working groups from among its members as necessary, and set up local or regional sections to assist it in discharging its functions;

(f) Maintain consultation with the other bodies, whether jurisdictions or otherwise, responsible for the promotion and protection of human rights (in particular, ombudsmen, mediators and similar institutions); and

(g) In view of the fundamental role played by non-governmental organizations in expanding the work of national institutions, develop relations with non-governmental organizations devoted to promoting and protecting human rights, to economic and social development, to combating racism, to protecting particularly vulnerable groups (especially children, migrant workers, refugees, physically and mentally disabled persons) or to specialized areas.

Additional principles concerning the status of commissions with quasi-jurisdictional competence

A national institution may be authorized to hear and consider complaints and petitions concerning individual situations. Individuals, their representatives, third parties, non-governmental organizations, associations of trade unions, or any other representative organizations may bring cases before it. In such circumstances, and without prejudice to the principles stated above concerning the other powers of the commissions, the functions entrusted to them may be based on the following principles:

- Seeking an amicable settlement through conciliation or, within the limits prescribed by the law, through binding decisions or, where necessary, on the basis of confidentiality;
- Informing the party who filed the petition of his or her rights, in particular the remedies available to him or her, and promoting his or her access to them;
- Hearing any complaints or petitions or transmitting them to any other competent authority within the limits prescribed by the law; and
- Making recommendations to the competent authorities, especially by proposing amendments or reforms of the laws, regulations and administrative practices, especially if they have created the difficulties encountered by the persons filing the petitions in order to assert their rights.

ANNEX 9.2

Extracts from the Commonwealth *Best Practice Guidelines*
Chapter III: Mandate and powers

3.1 Overview
- An NHRI should have a broad mandate covering the full range of human rights issues and recognizing the universality, interdependence, interrelatedness, and indivisibility of human rights.
- 'Human rights' should be defined not only by reference to domestic law, but also by reference to all international human rights instruments whether or not acceded to by the relevant State.
- The mandate of an NHRI should, in addition to providing for the protection

and promotion of human rights:
  • cover both the private and the public sector; and
  • cover the promotion of accession to international human rights instruments and the harmonization of domestic law with international human rights instruments.
• The legislative base of NHRIs should confer a power to take such action as is necessary and convenient to enable the institution to discharge its mandate. The specific powers of NHRIs should be clearly and expressly prescribed in the legislation governing the institution and should include the power to:
  • independently initiate investigations of individual and systemic human rights violations and other related issues;
  • encourage and promote human rights through education;
  • advise government and legislators on draft and existing legislation and submit recommendations to the Parliament to resolve human rights violations resulting from legislation, regulations or any other cause;
  • work with and consult appropriate persons, governmental organizations, international organizations and NGOs;
  • monitor government compliance with human rights treaty obligations and promote the ratification of human rights treaties;
  • establish advisory committees to advise the NHRI in relation to the performance of its functions;
  • submit recommendations to the Executive for the resolution of human rights violations relating to administrative action or inaction or any other cause;
  • provide remedies for human rights violations and, when relevant, seek and facilitate the provision of remedies by the courts;
  • conduct quasi-judicial hearings. These hearings should generally be held in public. However, an NHRI should have the power to determine that hearings be held in private in appropriate circumstances;
  • compel attendance of witnesses before it, order production of documents and secure access to locations;
  • require co-operation from other government agencies and public actors; administer an oath or affirmation;
  • inspect custodial facilities and places of detention;
  • co-operate as appropriate with NHRIs in other countries, the UN and other relevant international organizations and
  • do all things that are necessary or convenient to be done in connection with the performance of its function.
• Where in a particular country it is considered necessary and desirable that an NHRI should have search and seizure powers, then these should only be exercised by obtaining a judicially approved warrant and implemented in co-operation with law enforcement authorities.

4.4 Relations with the courts
• NHRIs should play a role complementary to that of the courts.
• There should be an expressly established mechanism for the enforcement of appropriate NHRI decisions by the courts.
• Individuals should be able to access the court system directly to seek a remedy for a human rights violation and should not be required to first file a com-

plaint with the NHRI.
- NHRIs should be more accessible and offer a more cost-effective and less formal means of conflict resolution than the courts.
- NHRI staff and members should try to establish a co-operative working relationship with the courts.
- NHRIs should refer matters for prosecution before the courts when appropriate.
- NHRIs should not commence investigations into matters already pending before the courts unless required as part of the duty of NHRIs to investigate systemic issues relating to equal protection under the law and access to justice.
- Courts should permit NHRIs to provide assistance to individuals seeking to redress grievances through the courts.
- NHRIs should be accorded standing to bring complaints to court in their own right.
- Courts should accord NHRIs official status as a friend of the court.
- Courts should grant NHRIs the rights to join as a party in relevant cases.
- The decisions of NHRIs should be subject to judicial review.

Notes

[1] A point epitomized by the Report of the Kenya Constitutional Review Commission in 2001 that recommended establishing a Commission for Human Rights and Administrative Justice along the lines of the Ghana model.

[2] From a practical point of view, this type of body is probably less effective than a full-blown HRC since the lack of a collegiate body can negatively affect the independence of the institution and may lead to an excessive workload.

[3] These were drawn up in 2001 by an expert group convened by the Commonwealth Secretariat and comprising members from Commonwealth HRCs and offices of the ombudsman, and designed to represent all regions of the Commonwealth. The *Guidelines* refer throughout to 'National Human Rights Institutions', thus intending to refer to both human rights commissions and offices of the ombudsman. In practice, they relate almost entirely to HRCs.

[4] Guideline 3.4. The point is further discussed below.

[5] For example, those of the Commission on Human Rights and Administrative Justice in Ghana and the Uganda Human Rights Commission.

[6] Much of the impetus for this derives from the 1989 Bangalore Principles that encourage courts around the Commonwealth to apply international human rights norms and to utilize comparative Commonwealth jurisprudence. In practice, the Constitutional Court in South Africa and the pre-2001 Supreme Court of Zimbabwe have led the way. Courts throughout the common law world (except the USA) have widely accepted the Principles and have helped develop significant new jurisprudence enhancing the enjoyment of human rights.

[7] Of course, this does not preclude them from encouraging the bringing of test cases.

[8] See further, *Best Practice Guidelines*, 3.1 'Mandate and Powers', set out in Annex 2.

[9] For further issues relating to this relationship and manner in which the courts can assist a HRC, see Best Practice Guideline 4.4 set out in Annex 2.

[10] Adopted by the United Nations as an Annex to General Assembly resolution 48/134 of 20 December 1993. Annex 1 sets out the principles in full.

[11] Commentary on Guideline 1.2.

[12] Cameroon did not join the Commonwealth until 1995.

[13] Indeed, at some UN meetings, government delegates have been known to speak on behalf of the government and then speak separately in their role as a Human Rights Commissioner.

[14] National Human Rights Decree 1995. The Preamble states, amongst other things, 'AND WHEREAS the Federal Military Government is desirous of creating an enabling environment for extra-judicial recognition, promotion and enforcement of all rights recognised and enshrined in the Constitution of the Federal Republic of Nigeria, 1979, as amended, and under other laws of the land'. Given the human rights position in Nigeria at the time, the reasons behind establishing a HRC are certainly questionable. Remarkably, the Commission still operates under the decree (now styled on 'Act').

[15] Staff shortages and illness were given as the reasons for this situation. Private communication to the author, March 2002.

[16] The best web sites are those of the South African Human Rights Commission (www.sahrc.org.za) and the Uganda Human Rights Commission (www.uhrc.org).

[17] A particularly useful recent publication comes from the CHRAJ in Ghana, which published its decisions reached following a formal hearing for the years 1994–2000. The decisions provide a fascinating insight into the workings of the institution. See *Decisions of the Commission on Human Rights and Administrative Justice (Ghana) 1994–2000*, CHRAJ, Ghana, no date.

[18] In recognition of this, in October 2002, a British Council-sponsored workshop for Commonwealth HRCs held in Belfast, Northern Ireland, specifically examined the manner in which HRCs can make use of the UN human rights machinery.

[19] Constitution of Ghana art. 220. By the end of 2002, the Commission had established ten regional offices. It was also well on its way to establishing a full complement of 110

district offices. See Short (1997: 5).

[20] This remains a problem for the Zambian Permanent Human Rights Commission, whose accommodation is hidden away in the midst of government offices in Lusaka. As the author discovered when visiting the Commission in 2002, it takes an enterprising individual to locate the office.

[21] For example, the Uganda HRC received a sizeable grant from a Canadian donor to expand its office complex in Kampala. External funding has also proved invaluable in the development of human rights promotional programmes by the Commission on Human Rights and Administrative Justice (CHRAJ) in Ghana. See Short (1997: 21) and the 1997 Annual Report of CHRAJ, pp.3–4.

[22] Certainly the Ghanaian Human Rights Commissioner and Chair of the Uganda HRC have both publicly stated that such funding has in no way compromised the operations of their commissions. See Short (1997: 21).

[23] Compare the position in Uganda where the Minister responsible for justice acting in consultation with the Minister responsible for finance must approve any external funding offered to the Uganda HRC.

[24] See Paris Principles, para 3(a)(iv).

[25] But see the earlier discussion on the Zimbabwean Ombudsman.

[26] For example, the Commissioners regularly appeared in televised debates on capital punishment. The Commission eventually publicly proclaimed its support for the abolition of the death penalty.

[27] See Constitution of Uganda art. 52(1)(h). This led to the setting up of a Monitoring and Treaties Department tasked with monitoring government's compliance with its international treaty obligations.

[28] Presumably, a commission could then recommend, or take, action to remedy any shortcomings. This is an area that requires specialist knowledge and one where input from organs of civil society, such as human rights NGOs, could prove invaluable.

[29] Para 3(iv) of the *Paris Principles* states that HRCs have the responsibility for drawing the government's attention to human rights violations in any part of the country and to propose initiatives to remedy the violations.

[30] The development of model guidelines on reporting by national institutions should be considered, along similar lines to those adopted by UN human rights agencies.

[31] A duty to provide copies of all annual and other reports to the appropriate minister(s) and requiring a public response thereto within a specific time would also be useful.

[32] Conference on African National Institutions for the Promotion and Protection of Human Rights, Durban, 1–3 July 1998 made no mention of either any transnational aspect of the work of the ombudsman or the impact of privatization and non-state actors.

[33] For example, exchanges of information between institutions in different countries to facilitate investigations into allegations of the systematic bribery of public officials by a multi-national corporation based elsewhere. Other examples include addressing the problem of refugees, migrant workers, or the trafficking in women and children as well as environmental issues.

[34] The well-researched Report contains a wealth of information about African HRCs. It is of interest to note that virtually all the criticism is directed at commissions in the francophone countries. As noted earlier, these have a very different structure from the CAHRCs and probably merit the criticism. The full Report is available on www.hrw.org/reports.

10

BRIAN LEVY

Are Africa's Economic Reforms Sustainable? Bringing Governance Back In

CONTROVERSY over the course and impact of economic reform has been a staple of the development discourse in Africa for the past 20 years. In the past decade, a discourse on the challenges of deepening democracy and improving governance across the continent has paralleled the economic discourse. This chapter aims to integrate these two discourses by analyzing interactions over the past quarter-century between economic reform, economic performance, and changes in governance. The data are from interactions of 21 countries across Africa.[1] The countries are Benin, Burkina Faso, Cameroon, Chad, Côte d'Ivoire, Ghana, Guinea, Kenya, Madagascar, Malawi, Mali, Mauritania, Mozambique, Niger, Nigeria, Senegal, Tanzania, Toga, Uganda, Zambia and Zimbabwe.

Two conclusions emerge from the analysis. First, the evidence seems unambiguous that the reform process has helped to improve the performance of many African economies. For a large majority of the selected countries, their post-reform economic growth is more rapid, the productive sectors appear more competitive, and business-government relations are on a more constructive footing. But, second, while economic reform appears to have helped reverse a downward spiral of dysfunctional governance, the sustainability of the new arrangements seems very uncertain. Unless gains in fragile governance become better consolidated with a more unambiguous commitment to workable pluralism, the rule of law, and a developmentally oriented bureaucracy, the gains achieved over the past decade risk reversal.

This chapter presents its analysis in four sections. Section I sets out the framework used to analyze governance-economy interactions. Providing an historical backdrop for the subsequent discussion, Section II reviews how a dysfunctional, 'neopatrimonial' dynamic took hold across Africa, to varying degrees, in the decades following independence. Section II also looks at the associated economic policies and the extent the policies were unwound during structural adjustment. Section III empirically examines the impact of reform by focusing on the subsequent patterns of growth, structural change, and changes in business-government relations in the sample countries. Section IV probes the sustainability of the governance underpinnings in the reforming economies.

Before proceeding, a prefatory comment on the selection of countries is necessary. The intention is to survey broadly in a way that is unbiased with respect to the impact of adjustment, but excludes idiosyncratic experiences. Thus, beginning with the full set of the 47 sub-Saharan African countries, three sets of 'outlier' countries were excluded – very small countries, countries affected by profound internal conflict, and the current middle-income countries, as they show consistent high performance. Furthermore, to facilitate comparison with

126

earlier analysis, the selection of countries was limited to those in the 1994 World Bank study, *Adjustment in Africa*. Taken together, these criteria generate a set of 21 countries that provide the empirical backdrop for the discussion.[2]

I: Governance-Economy Interactions: A Framework for Analysis

Figure 10.1 depicts a 'governance diamond' (developed by Michael Porter),[3] which highlights seven sets of interactions (causal relations) among four variables:

- *Political interests*, which is the social and class structure of civil society;
- *Formal institutions*, which includes the constitutional structure of the state (legislative structure and oversight, judicial independence, the structure of decentralized, intergovernmental relations, and the rules governing political representation) and the formal, representative political leadership;[4]
- *Bureaucracy*, consisting of public employees who formulate policy, regulate economic activity, and deliver services;
- *Economy*, defined as a society's productive factors and the associated levels of economic activity.

As the figure highlights, these four variables comprise an interdependent system, which together shapes the economic, public sector, and, more broadly, performance trajectories.

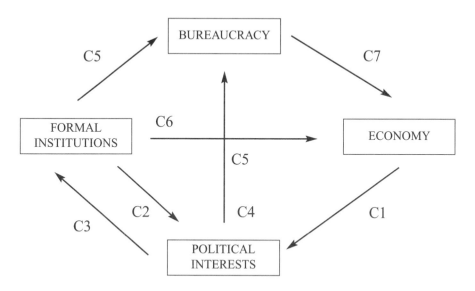

Figure 10.1 Africa's Governance Diamond

This chapter aims to describe how the interactions among these four variables play out over time, and the consequences of their performance. Logically, sixteen sets of causal relations interact among the four variables. The focus here is on the seven sets of interactions that appear to be the most dominant:

Causal Relation C1: Economy ⇒ Political Interests. This relation analyzes how the structure and competitiveness of economic production helps shape the patterns of political interests in society.

Causal Relations C2 and C3: Political Interests ⇔ Formal Political Institutions. One facet of this interdependent relationship (C2) is the way formal institutions provide a 'container' for political activity by structuring the legitimate channels of influence-seeking (including contestation for political leadership). The second facet of the relationship (C3) is the way powerful political interests seek to influence formal institutions – legitimately as well as efforts to reshape the structure of formal institutions to their advantage.

Causal Relation C4: Political Interests ⇒ Bureaucracy. This relation highlights efforts on the part of political interests in civil society to influence bureaucratic behavior directly, unmediated by formal institutional structures. The stronger these formal institutions are in providing the 'container' for politics, the less likely it is that this causal chain will be important.

Causal Relation C5: Formal Political Institutions ⇒ Bureaucracy. This is the agency relation that exists between political 'principals' and their bureaucratic 'agents' – with politicians having the authority to set the policy, regulatory, and service delivery goals of bureaucratic actors and to monitor their performance vis-à-vis these goals.

Causal Relation C6: Formal Political Institutions ⇒ Economy. This relation looks at the extent that formal institutions provide stability and predictability to the economic environment, with associated influence on the levels of private investment and economic activity.

Causal Relation C7: Bureaucracy ⇒ Economy. This relation highlights the economic effects of bureaucratic decisions and actions through policies, regulation, and service delivery.

To give life to these causal relations, and to set the stage for the analysis of African countries that follows, consider Figure 10.2a, which depicts how these cause-effect relations generally play out in well-functioning mature democracies. Two features in Figure 10.2 are noteworthy for the subsequent analysis. First, the presumption (which is presumed to apply universally) that political interests engage in self-interested lobbying – potentially to the point of bypassing both the formal institutional arrangements that are intended to structure this lobbying and the agency relationships that are intended to insulate bureaucracies from informal lobbying. But, second, note that in well-functioning, mature democracies, the five remaining causal relations work to counteract the potentially corrosive effects of this lobbying:

• Strong formal institutions provide a check on extra-legal activities by political interests; govern bureaucracies in ways that hold them accountable for achieving public ends; and provide credible signals of stability to private investors.
• Accountable bureaucracies make policy, as well as regulate and deliver services in ways that support private economic activity.
• A diversified economy creates a multiplicity of sufficiently different business activities that putative lobbying efforts by the dispersed interests are likely to offset.

The net result is a virtuous spiral (or, alternatively, a stable equilibrium) that supports openness, strong public sector performance, and a productive private economy. As this chapter will argue, Africa's development dilemma is that one cannot take a virtuous spiral for granted.

Figure 10.2 Cause-Effect Relationships in the Governance Diamond in Four Settings

Figure 10.2a: Well-functioning, mature democracy

	Political interests	Formal institutions	Bureaucracy	Economy
Political interests		★	★	
Formal Institutions	+++		++	++
Bureaucracy				++
Economy	+			

Figure 10.2b: Africa, circa 1965

	Political interests	Formal institutions	Bureaucracy	Economy
Political interests		★★	★★	
Institutional	+		++	++
Bureaucracy				+
Economy	★			

Figure 10.2c: Africa, circa 1980

	Political interests	Formal institutions	Bureaucracy	Economy
Political interests		★★★	★★★	
Formal Institutions	0		★	★★
Bureaucracy				★★
Economy	★★			

Figure 10.2d: Africa, circa 2000

	Political interests	Formal institutions	Bureaucracy	Economy
Political interests		★	★	
Formal Institutions	+		★	★
Bureaucracy				★
Economy	0			

Legend: +++= strongly positive, ++ = positive, + = weakly positive, 0 = neutral
★ = weakly negative, ★★ = negative, ★★★ = strongly negative

II: From Neopatrimonialism to Structural Adjustment: A Review

This section provides a historical backdrop by reviewing earlier analyses of Africa's neopatrimonial experience and episodes of policy reform. The aim is to set the stage for subsequent analysis in Sections III and IV, which look at the post-adjustment period interactions between economic performance and governance trends.

THE 'NEOPATRIMONIAL' DOWNWARD SPIRAL
Upon independence, many African governance structures had a strong shell of
formal institutions, both political and bureaucratic. Often, however, the shell of
richly articulated formal institutions turned out to reflect a combination of colonial legacy and high-minded aspirations at independence more than it reflected
the reality of a state with the ability to structure (beyond a narrow urban
segment) state-society relations in a way that supported a 'developmental
project'. The short-run consequence, similar to Joel Migdal's (1988) comparative and theoretical exploration, was that the mode of governance shifted rapidly
from a formal system of checks and balances to a *de facto* (and in many countries a partly *de jure*) system of rule that African scholars describe as 'neopatrimonial'.[5] The medium-run consequence was an accelerating downward spiral of
deteriorating institutional and economic performance, to the point of state collapse in some countries. Figures 10.2b and c summarize this process through the
governance diamond framework.

In neopatrimonial settings, though the outward features of formal institutions
are in place, the constraining capacity of C2 radically diminishes how a country
exercises political power. A country exercises power through informal channels
built around relationships of patronage, not through governance systems that
are both formal and credible. In the 1970s and 1980s, neopatrimonialism
seemed to provide a stable, if not especially dynamic, form of rule. In practice,
as the governance diamond implies, and as the subsequent unfolding of events
in country after country confirms, slow-moving but inexorable forces of decay
underlay the neopatrimonial model.

Consider the neopatrimonialism pressures on bureaucracy – C4 and C5 in the
governance diamond. As noted earlier, organizational discipline is the key to a
well-functioning bureaucracy, as well as the presence of well-defined, specialized
roles for each bureaucratic agent, clear mechanisms for monitoring behavior,
rewarding performance within these roles, and punishing behavior that is inconsistent with the assigned agency role. With the rise of neopatrimonial rule, the
mode of governing the bureaucracy shifted from the clarification, monitoring,
and enforcement of formal rules, to informal rules that a country's political leadership set non-transparently and sometimes capriciously. The inevitable consequence was a decline in bureaucratic performance.

Now consider C6 and C7, which are the relations from the impact of governance on economic performance. In C6, the decline of bureaucracy affects economic performance via policy-making, regulation, and service delivery.
Neopatrimonial rule generally operates by conferring discretionary rents on
favored allies, with little attention to the impact of rentier policies on economic
growth, the efficiency of public services, or the quality of business regulation.
The classic consequences, evident in country after country, include the disruption of markets, rising costs of doing business, urban bias, and rising protec-
tionism. Perhaps as damaging to growth, are the C7 consequences – a rise in
actual and perceived arbitrariness in economic policy leads to a decline in
investor confidence and investment rates. The consequence is progressive economic slowdown.

Completing the circle, the intensification of a rentier relationship between
business and government progressively transforms the structure of the business
class through the progressive rise of a politically dependent business class. To

put the point differently, the C1 relation shifts over time from a (modest) check on dysfunctional (from the perspective of efficient economic growth) political influence to a source of further intensification of the dysfunctional political dynamic. The difference between Figures 10.2b and 10.2c in the developmental impact of each respective causal relationship in the governance diamond as of circa 1965 and as of circa 1980 respectively is one way of summarizing the dysfunctional developmental impact of neopatrimonialism. Though the underlying logic of the neopatrimonial downward spiral appears similar across countries, important cross-country differences influence its intensity and degree of reversibility. In some countries, for example Sierra Leone, it proceeded to the point of state collapse. In others countries, like Benin or Ghana, domestic political intervention pre-empted the cycle of decline.[6] This chapter examines the impact of adjustment only for a subset of this broader experience, specifically the countries that retain (or reconstruct) functioning states.

STRUCTURAL ADJUSTMENT

This sub-section provides a selective overview of economic reform among the selected countries, which is a springboard analyzing the impact and sustainability of reform in subsequent sections. Tables 10.1 and 10.2 summarize the extent of reform between the early 1980s and early 1990s for the selected countries. Viewed as a whole, two conclusions are evident. First, the data serve as a stark reminder of how extreme economic policy distortions were in many African countries in the early 1980s.

Second, the extent of reform was far-reaching across almost all the countries. Consider the reforms to liberalize markets. After more than a decade from the collapse of the Soviet empire, the idea of putting major impediments in the way of the purchase, sale, or pricing of basic commodities seems almost anachronistic. Yet, as Table 10.1 startlingly reminds us, this was hardly the case in the early 1980s: 19 of the 21 countries had extensive price controls; 12 had major restrictions on the purchase and sale of food crops. Perhaps almost as startling is the uniformity with which countries rolled back these policies. By 1992, only four countries in the sample – Kenya, Zimbabwe, Burkina Faso, and Mozambique – still had major controls in one of these domains, with three of them increasing these controls. The fourth country, Zimbabwe, also rolled back controls after 1992, only to re-impose them in the face of its recent political and economic turmoil.

The overall direction of change is similar for the exchange-rate and fiscal reforms highlighted in Table 10.2, although the record is not as uniform. Consider the management of foreign-exchange markets. While disagreements remain as to the optimal degree of liberalization of exchange controls, there is no disputing that controls, which result in the emergence of a parallel market and offer significant premia on the official rate, can generate widespread corruption and wreak havoc on economic incentives. Certainly, there would today be little dispute that a parallel market premium above 50 per cent of the official rate is economically destructive. Yet, as Part A of Table 10.2 highlights, as of the early 1980s, 9 of the 12 countries for which the *Adjustment in Africa* study provides data, had premia above 50 per cent, with the premia in 5 countries above 200 per cent. As Table 10.2 shows, by the early 1990s, countries had rolled back the extreme distortions: only in 4 of the 12 countries did the

Table 10.1 Adjustment I – Extent of Market Reforms in the Selected 21 African Countries*

	Number of countries (before reform)	Number of countries (late 1992)	Specific countries (before reform)	Specific countries (late 1992)
A: Government Intervention in Marketing of Food Crops				
Major restrictions on purchases and sales	12	2	All others in sample	Kenya, Zimbabwe
Limited intervention by government buying agency	4	3	Cameroon, Mauritania, Senegal, Togo	Malawi, Mauritania, Zambia
No intervention except in food security stocks	4	15	Chad, Cote d'Ivoire, Ghana, Nigeria	All others in sample
B: Price Controls on Goods				
Extensive controls (on 26 goods or more)	19	2	All others in sample	Burkina Faso, Mozambique
Limited controls (on 10–25 goods)	1	4	Malawi	Cameroon, Côte d'Ivoire, Kenya, Madagascar
Few controls (on fewer than 10 goods)	1	10	Chad	All others in sample
No controls	0	5		Ghana, Mali, Mauritania, Uganda, Zambia

*The table excludes Uganda from the food-crop marketing sample.
Source: World Bank (1994b)

parallel market premium remain above 50 per cent, and none were above 200 per cent.

One can make a similar argument for budget deficits, highlighted in Part B of Table 10.2. While disagreement remains as to the (un)desirability of relatively modest deficits, there is little dispute that those deficits including grants above 5 per cent (and *a fortiori* above 7.5 per cent) of GDP signal severe, unsustainable economic imbalances. Yet, as of the early 1980s, 8 of a sample of 19 countries had budget deficits above 7.5 per cent of GDP and only 5 had deficits below 5 per cent. Countries had reversed these proportions a decade later, as 9 countries had deficits below 5 per cent of GDP and only 5 countries had deficits above 7.5 per cent.

Some countries experienced changes between the early 1980s and early 1990s in their destabilizing fiscal policies. By the 1990s, Benin, Burkina Faso, Malawi, Mali, and Tanzania successfully reduced their budget deficits to below 7.5 per cent. Indeed, during the 1990s, 4 of these 5 countries, with Malawi the sole exception, continued to tighten their budget discipline. By contrast, Mozambique, Zambia, and Zimbabwe had deficits above 7.5 per cent in both periods (although Mozambique's had declined from 14 per cent of GDP in the early 1980s and has consistently been below 4 per cent since 1994). Meanwhile, two new countries, Cameroon and Côte d'Ivoire, had out-of-control macro-policies.

Table 10.2 Adjustment II – Extent of Macroeconomic Reform

	Number of countries (1981–86)	Number of countries (1990–91)	Specific countries (1981–86)	Specific co intries (1990–91)
A: Parallel Market Exchange-Rate Premium				
500% or more	3	0	Ghana, Guinea, Mozambique	
200–499%	2	0	Nigeria, Tanzania	
100–199%	2	2	Mauritania, Uganda	Mauritania, Zambia
50 – 99%	2	2	Malawi, Zimbabwe	Mozambique, Tanzania
20 – 49%	2	4	Madagascar, Zambia	Malawi, Nigeria, Uganda, Zimbabwe
Under 20%	1	4	Kenya	Ghana, Guinea, Kenya, Madagascar
B: Fiscal Deficit, Including Grants (% of GDP)				
7.5% or more	8	5	Benin, Burkina Faso, Malawi, Mali, Mozambique, Tanzania, Zambia, Zimbabwe	Cameroon, Côte d'Ivoire, Mozambique, Zambia, Zimbabwe
5 – 7.4%	6	5	Côte d'Ivoire, Kenya, Madagascar, Nigeria, Senegal, Uganda	Benin, Kenya, Madagascar, Mali, Niger
Under 5%	5	9	Cameroon, Ghana, Mauritania, Niger, Togo	All others in sample

Source: World Bank (1994b: 222–3, 228).

III: The Impact of Reform: An Empirical Overview

Though almost all African countries have undertaken some adjustment reforms, the degree of systematic and sustained process varies. It follows that, in evaluating the impact of economic reform (the subject of this section), it is necessary to organize the 21 countries according to the degree that the reform has been sustained and longstanding. This chapter divides the 21 countries into three groups:

- *Sustained Adjusters*. This group is the eight countries that a 1998 OED review of the Special Program for Africa identified as the only ones which consistently remained 'on-track' in their reform programs throughout the 1988–96 SPA 1–3 programs. These countries are Benin, Burkina Faso, Ghana, Malawi, Mali, Mozambique, Uganda, and Zambia.
- *Later Adjusters*. The eight countries in this second group initiated strong policy reforms in the 1990s, and continued to sustain their reforms through the end of 2001. These countries are Cameroon, Chad, Guinea, Madagascar, Mauritania, Niger, Senegal, and Tanzania.
- *Governance Polarized*. The five countries in this group comprise Côte d'Ivoire, Kenya, Nigeria, Togo, and Zimbabwe. Though these countries initiated some policy reforms during the 1990s, in all cases some kind of a domestic political disruption ended up overshadowing the efforts of economic policy reform.

The remainder of this section examines patterns of growth, changes in economic structure, and changes in business-government relations for each of these three groups.

PATTERNS OF GDP GROWTH

Table 10.3 reports the average annual real GDP growth rates for each of the three groups over four distinct periods.[7] (Annex A10.1 provides country-specific data.) The data strongly suggest that adjustment contributes to an acceleration of aggregate economic growth.

For the Sustained Adjusters, the sustained commitment to policy reform since the latter 1980s appears to have paid off, with growth accelerating in each of these countries. But the average pattern conceals some disaggregated variation. First, Zambia's economy failed to rebound; over the 1990s, its GDP growth averaged less than 1 per cent per annum. Also, the disaggregated data suggest a possible leveling off of growth rates as economies stabilize to the new policy equilibrium: in Ghana, Malawi, and Uganda, growth was somewhat slower for 1996–2000 than for 1991–6. Furthermore, (though perhaps reflecting global stimuli) six of the eight countries grew more slowly in 2000 than they did in 1999. But the overall trend makes it clear that growth has occurred.

Table 10.3 Average Annual Growth in Real GDP for 21 African Countries, 1975–2000

% of Growth

	1975–84	1985–89	1991–96	1996–2000
Group 1: Sustained Adjusters	1.7	3.2	3.7	4.7
Group 2: Later Adjusters	2.4	2.7	1.9	4.2
Group 3: Governance Polarized	2.3	4.1	2.3	1.4

Source: World Bank (2002a: 15)

For the Later Adjusters, the overall pattern of growth prior to policy reform with subsequent acceleration is consistent across these countries, though some qualifiers exist. Note that seven of the eight countries in the group are fran-cophone, that the 1994 Franc Zone devaluation was a signal event of the 1990s, and that the acceleration of growth in 1996–2000 is consistent with the impact of that devaluation. Second, three countries, Guinea, Mauritania, and Senegal, though not included in the SPA-8, have had relatively stable and reform-oriented economic policy regimes since the 1980s. Their growth trajectories resemble those of the Sustained Adjusters, steady since the latter 1980s, with some acceleration in the 1990s. Tanzania, the eighth country in the group, has also seen a steady acceleration of growth over the 1990s.

As for the Governance Polarized countries, the contrast with the others is clear, given the absence of any evidence of accelerating growth, and possibly a declining trend. The average, as Annex 10.A1 details, disguises especially sharp period-by-period discontinuities in individual countries, reflecting in part the governance-related instabilities to which these countries have been subject.[8]

TRENDS IN AGRICULTURAL VALUE ADDED

As has long been understood (Chambers, 1978; Lipton, 1978), the combination of overvalued exchange rates, import controls, and price controls on basic commodities imparts a powerful urban bias to a country's economic incentives and structure. Thus, trends in agricultural growth provide a useful measure of the extent that adjustment reforms have achieved their intended effect of reversing this urban bias.

Table 10.4 summarizes the trends in agricultural value added, organized along the same lines as Table 10.3. The observed pattern is remarkably consistent across all groups – a shift in the mid-1980s in the trend rate of growth from under 1.5 per cent to above 3.0 per cent. This shift occurred at a similar period for all three groups of countries, reflecting (as suggested by Table 10.1 and Table 10.2 earlier) a broad, early recognition of the need to correct egregious anti-agricultural policy biases; and at least part of the reform agenda was readily achievable domestically. The gains in agricultural growth were on average some-

Table 10.4 Average Annual Growth in Agricultural Value Added for 21 African Countries, 1975–2000

% of Growth

	1975–84	1985–89	1991–96	1996–2000
Group 1: Sustained Adjusters	1.4	4.7	4.1	4.1
Group 2: Later Adjusters	1.4	3.1	3.2	3.3
Group 3: Governance Polarized	1.3	3.4	3.0	3.1

Source: World Bank (2002a: 16)

what larger among the Sustained Adjusters. At the individual country level, as Annex A10.2 details, for all but two countries, the data point to an unambiguous acceleration in agricultural growth at some point subsequent to the 1975–84 period, with the shift clearly dated at 1985–9 for at least ten countries.

TRENDS IN INDUSTRIAL VALUE ADDED

This chapter defines industrial value added broadly, following the UNSITC categories, to include not only 'narrow manufacturing' but also natural resource processing and mining. Table 10.5 presents the growth trends for this variable, along lines corresponding to Table 10.3 and Table 10.4. Especially for industrial value added, it is important in interpreting the trends to complement the averages with more country-specific information, which Table 10.6 provides. Four general patterns emerge from scrutinizing the two tables together.

First, as Table 10.4 highlights and as Annex A10.3 details, the country-by-country variations within each subcategory are very substantial. Only seven of the selected countries have had positive, substantial growth in industrial value added since at least the mid-1980s (since the mid-1970s for four of the seven – Burkina Faso, Mali, Côte d'Ivoire, and Senegal). Furthermore, eight countries experienced cycles of boom-and-bust in the 1970s and 1980s, before settling into a path of seemingly sustainable recovery in the 1990s. For six countries, the experience of industrial development over the last quarter-century has been less happy.

Second, the data suggest that policy reform contributes to an eventual acceleration of industrial growth. As Table 10.3 suggests, consistent with a positive impact of reform, industrial recovery came earlier among the Sustained Adjusters than the Later Adjusters. The former group, Burkina, Ghana, Malawi, and Uganda, had embarked on industrial recovery by the late 1980s, while industrial activity picked up in the early 1990s in Benin, Mali, and Mozambique. Among the latter group, in five of the eight countries – Cameroon, Chad, Madagascar, Niger and Tanzania – only in the latter 1990s did sustained industrial recovery get under way. Also, alone among the subgroups, the Governance Polarized countries failed to see any acceleration of industrial growth during the course of the 1990s, which is consistent with the proposition that sustained industrial expansion requires a foundation of sustainable (and hence outward-oriented) policies.

Third, following from the above, but worth noting explicitly, the country evidence shows no systematic pattern of reform contributing to de-industrialization. Only one of the 21 countries, Zambia, had a lower level of industrial value added in 2000 than in 1980. The remaining 20 countries all experienced positive industrial growth over the two decades, but a more rapid growth in agriculture than industry in six countries (Madagascar, Malawi, Niger, Nigeria, Togo, and Zimbabwe) implies a *relative* secular decline of industry.[9]

Finally, when the reforms summarized in Section II are considered together, the patterns suggest that across the vast majority of the 21 countries, the underlying competitiveness of African industry is substantially stronger in the first decade of the twenty-first century than in 1980. In 1980, much of African industry grew behind high walls of protection against imports. Without exception, these walls have come down. For many of these countries, the transition was a wrenching one, as evidenced by cycles of bust subsequent to earlier booms. But, with only one clear exception, the countries are now at the other side of this transition, with industrial sectors which are both more internationally competitive and substantially larger than at the outset of the period.

Table 10.5 Average Annual Growth in Industrial Value Added for the 21 African Countries, 1975–2000

% of Growth

	1975–84	1985–89	1991–96	1996–2000
Group 1: Sustained Adjusters	0.6	2.7	3.6	7.4
Group 2: Later Adjusters	4.7	2.3	1.2	5.0
Group 3: Governance Polarized	2.3	5.1	1.7	0.8

Source: World Bank (2002a: 17)

Table 10.6 Some Cross-Country Variations in Industrial Growth

	Structural stagnation	Very slow, continuing expansion	Decline 1975–84, subsequent recovery	Boom 1975–84, Subsequent bust, then recovery	Sustained expansion
Group 1: Sustained Adjusters	Zambia (since 1975)	Malawi	Ghana	Benin (Mozambique)	Burkina Faso Mali Uganda
Group 2: Later Adjusters			Chad Madagascar	Cameroon Niger (Tanzania)	Guinea Mauritania Senegal
Group 3: Governance Polarized	Kenya (since 1990) Zimbabwe (since 1990)	Nigeria Togo			Côte d'Ivoire

Source: World Bank (2002a: 17).

CHANGES IN BUSINESS-GOVERNMENT RELATIONS

Causal relations 6 and 7 in the governance diamond highlight two distinct ways in which governance can directly affect economic performance – through a bureaucratic channel (quality of policy-making, service delivery, and business regulation) and a credibility channel (stability imparted by formal institutions to the business environment as a whole). A survey conducted for the 1997 *World Development Report, The State in a Changing World*, generates data to use in identifying changes in the way private firms perceive the impact of adjustment on these two channels. The data, summarized in Tables 10.7, 10.8 and 10.9, point to an association between economic reform and governance gains, both across countries and across the averages for the three country sub-groups.

The *World Development Report* survey explores the perceptions of over 3,600 entrepreneurs as to the character and quality of the public institutions that underpin market transactions in each of 69 countries, including 22 in Africa (18 of which are included in the sample used in this chapter). Of particular relevance to the present chapter[10] are three survey items that explored changes in the quality of governance between 1986 and 1996.[11]

The first item in the 1997 survey and ten years previously was the following:

• Please rate your overall perception of the relation between government and/or bureaucracy and private firms.

Each firm scored its perceptions as to the relation on a 1 to 6 scale, with a score of 1 signaling the perception of government as a helping hand and 6 signaling the perception of government as an opponent. The difference between the proportion of respondents who picked relation 1 or 2 and the proportion that picked relation 5 or 6 provides one simple way of summarizing the extent to which the respondent perceived the government as a net helping hand (or, conversely, an opponent). Table 10.7 summarizes the results for 18 countries, organized into the three sub-groups used in the present chapter.

Table 10.7 Trends in Relations between Private Firms and Government in 18 African Countries, 1986–96

Country	Net Helping Hand (+ve) or Opponent(-ve)		
	1996	1986	Net Change
Benin	−23	−43	+20
Ghana	+39	−48	+87
Malawi	+17	−29	+46
Mali	+11	−29	+40
Mozambique	−19	−55	+36
Uganda	+37	−38	+75
Zambia	+19	−56	+75
Average for Group 1	+11	−43	+54
Sustained Adjusters			
Cameroon	−24	+7	−31
Chad	−31	0	+31
Guinea	−10	−10	0
Madagascar	−42	−37	−5
Senegal	−20	−8	−12
Tanzania	−36	−51	+15
Average for Group 2	−27	−16	−11
Later Adjusters			
Côte d'Ivoire	−16	−2	−14
Kenya	−2	−13	−11
Nigeria	+6	+61	−55
Togo	−21	+10	−31
Zimbabwe	−36	−24	−12
Average for Group 3	−14	+6	−8
Governance Polarized			

Source: Survey conducted for World Bank (1997b)

The results point to a remarkable turnaround among the Sustained Adjusters between 1986 and 1996 in business-government relations – an average gain in the net helping hand ratio of 54 per cent. As of 1986, the ratio was negative among all seven countries; by 1996, the ratio had turned positive in five countries. Though the net ratio was still negative, relations improved by at least 20 per cent in the remaining two countries. For the other countries, the ratio grew worse in the five Governance Polarized countries, as well as in three of the six Later Adjusters for which data were available. Only Chad and, to a lesser extent, Tanzania enjoyed gains approximating those of the Sustained Adjusters.

While Table 10.7 somewhat blurs the distinction between credibility (see Causal relation 6) and bureaucratic quality (see Causal relation 7), the questions for which responses are summarized in Table 10.8 distinguish sharply between these two dimensions of governance. The two survey questions were:

- In the last 10 years, has predictability of laws and policies increased; remained the same; decreased?
- In the last 10 years, have difficulties in dealing with government officials increased; remained the same; decreased?

Table 10.8 Changes in Credibility and Bureaucratic Quality in 18 African Countries, 1986–96

Country	Change in predictability (+ve = improvement)	Changes in difficulties with officials (+ve = improvement)
Benin	+28	+9
Ghana	+35	+37
Malawi	+21	−4
Mali	+45	+25
Mozambique	+68	−4
Uganda	+33	+20
Zambia	+9	+31
Average for Group 1 *Sustained Adjusters*	+28	+16
Cameroon	−7	−79
Chad	−8	−38
Guinea	+25	+25
Madagascar	−26	−26
Senegal	+12	−12
Tanzania	−11	−43
Average for Group 2 *Later Adjusters*	−3	−29
Côte d'Ivoire	+22	+2
Kenya	+12	−3
Nigeria	−19	−21
Togo	−6	−28
Zimbabwe	−32	−8
Average for Group 3 *Governance Polarized*	−5	−16

Source: Ibid.

The former question probes credibility, while the latter probes bureaucratic quality. Table 10.8 reports net changes over the previous ten years (proportion reporting 'increased' less proportion reporting 'decreased') for the 18 countries.

Combining the results in Table 10.7 and Table 10.8 yields the country disaggregation of patterns of governance change highlighted in Table 10.9. The table shows that, in 7 of the 18 countries sampled, the most marked governance changes between 1986 and 1996 appear to be in the predictability of laws and policies; in 5 countries, the most marked changes appear to be in the quality of the bureaucracy; while in 6 countries, the changes appear to be spread evenly across the two variables. Clearly, while the association between improved governance, sustained adjustment, and improved economic performance is striking, no simple formula for improving governance is likely to fit all circumstances.

Table 10.9 Changes in Direction of Governance, 1986–1996

| | Overall Direction of Governance Change, 1986–96 | | | |
	Improvement	Worse	Little change	Unclear[a]
Relatively large change in credibility	Benin Malawi Mali Mozambique		Zimbabwe	Senegal Côte d'Ivoire
Relatively large change in Tanzania bureaucratic quality	Zambia	Cameroon Togo		Chad
Similar changes in both	Ghana Uganda Guinea	Madagascar	Kenya Nigeria	

[a] Countries designated 'unclear' are those where the overall direction of change as between Tables X and Y is inconsistent.
Source: Ibid.

IV: How Sustainable are the Recent Gains?
Bringing Governance Back In

As the previous section documents, for a large majority of the 21 countries surveyed, the performance record subsequent to economic reform is unambiguously positive. Reform appears to usher in a period characterized by both accelerated growth (though not at world-beating rates) and a more constructive business-government relationship. However, insofar as the reform impetus lay largely in some combination of short-term response to looming crisis and external pressure, the risks of reversal could be large. Crucial to sustainability is the extent to which the changes reflect a more profound transformation of Africa's institutional landscape.

As the governance diamond highlights, two sets of empirical relationships are key in answering questions on sustainability. A first key relationship is the extent to which economic change helps to transform the interests of key economic actors, and thereby alter the extent and type of pressure they place on political and bureaucratic institutions (C1 in the governance diamond). A second key set of relationships comprises the extent to which capacity gains across the continent in formal political and bureaucratic institutions improve their abilities to contain dysfunctional (from a development perspective) pressures from the political realm (C2, C5, and C6). Exploring these relationships requires a great deal of country-specific analysis, which is beyond the scope of this chapter. This final section, as a prelude to subsequent work, sets out some issues in an introductory method and considers each of the two sets of empirical relationships.

ECONOMIC CHANGE AND THE TRANSFORMATION OF POLITICAL INTERESTS
As noted earlier, a central presumption of this chapter is that a general tendency for influence-seeking by political interests exists to corrode both formal state institutions (C3) and bureaucratic performance (C4). The magnitude of this deleterious relationship depends in part on the degree of differentiation of private interests – with less differentiated relationships providing fewer internalized checks and balances, and hence being more damaging (C1). How Africa's recent economic reforms (and associated economic performance) transform the structure of business interests thus becomes a key issue for examining sustainability. Two propositions seem reasonable.

First, taken together, the data on changes in economic policy, governance, and economic performance suggest that a substantial majority of the sample countries have broken (at least for now) the dysfunctional neopatrimonial dynamic described earlier. Economic policies that place discretionary authority in the hands of public officials have been rolled back. The scope for arbitrary action by such officials has been correspondingly reduced. Economic competitiveness has improved. The structure of the economy no longer fuels a vicious downward spiral of rent-seeking between dependent economic agents and avaricious public officials.

But, second, the reversal of a dysfunctional dynamic does not appear to be sufficient on its own to transform Causal relation 1 into a constructive contributor to a virtuous spiral. For this to happen, the economies of the turnaround countries would need to be already sufficiently diverse in order to generate a multiplicity of distinctive private economic interests. And for two reasons, countries are unlikely to achieve this. First, the economies (and the absolute magnitudes of recent changes) remain quite small and are typically too small to support the kind of diversified economic base on which workable pluralism might comfortably rest. Second, and perhaps more fundamental, as comparative studies show (and as discussed earlier) (Moore Jr, 1966), an inclusive economy generally provides the strongest buttress for workable pluralism. For low- and middle-income countries, such inclusiveness will generally be associated with some combination of labor-intensive, export-oriented manufacture and smallholder cash-crop agriculture. Yet, in most African countries, neither of these appears to have an immediate prospect of becoming a major driver of economic expansion.[12] Nor, contrary to some more romantic suppositions of a few years back, does Africa's so-called informal/micro-enterprise sector appear likely to become a dynamic economic and political influence.

A prudent conclusion (reflected in Figure 10.2d) might thus be that across many African countries, while the private sector is no longer part of the problem of dysfunctional governance, it also is not yet part of the solution. At this stage in the continent's development, anchors of sustainability will need to be found elsewhere.

FORMAL POLITICAL INSTITUTIONS AS 'ANCHORS' OF SUSTAINABILITY
As detailed earlier in introducing the governance diamond, well-functioning formal political institutions can support sustained economic development in three distinct ways. First, they provide a container for channeling political influence in transparent and non-violent ways (C2). Second, they provide an oversight framework for policy-making and a service provision for functions of the bureaucracy (C5). Third, they provide a general underpinning of credibility for private economic activity more broadly (C6).

Many recent analysts have been preoccupied with the process of democratic transition and the quality of the resulting representative democracies in these institutions,[13] which certainly are a central part of the story. Looking beyond elections, five more micro-level transformations emerge as potentially influential in underpinning the capacity of public institutions to support sustainable development.

- *Reducing excessive centralization of state institutions*, through political reforms that foster the emergence of an elected tier of local government and assign expanded responsibility for services to this local tier; through fiscal reforms that both strengthen the autonomous tax base of local governments and transfer (preferably on a transparent, formula-driven basis) grant resources to the local tier; and through administrative reforms that deconcentrate central government, re-focus the center on oversight, regulatory and strategic functions, and build local government capacity.[14]
- *Strengthening judicial independence and performance* by strengthening insulation of the judiciary from political and executive pressure; building judicial capacity and nurturing impartial dispute resolution by judges; and improving the justice system's organizational efficiency.[15]
- *Improving accountability for the use of public resources* by building capacity that facilitates providing information on how the government uses public monies. The information is comprehensive (not excluding off-budget expenditures from scrutiny), accurate (via improvements in the quality of public accounting), timely (both timely monthly accounts as a real-time management tool for public financial control, and timely audit reports that facilitate meaningful independent scrutiny), and public (open to parliamentary oversight and scrutiny by civil society organizations).[16]
- *Translating political priorities into consistent and implementable policies* by fostering (and inter-linking) participatory mechanisms that identify social processes (most notably, in the past two years, the Poverty Reduction Strategy Paper process), plus coherent mechanisms that make explicit trade-offs at the highest levels of government, and embed the resultant decisions in a rolling, multi-year budget expenditure framework.[17]
- *Strengthening the administrative capacity of the public bureaucracy* by clarifying the roles of individual ministries and agencies, improving cross-cutting personnel and financial control systems, and organizing capacity-building and human resource development within the public bureaucracy.[18]

Table 10.10 summarizes how these five micro-level transformations can help strengthen each of the C2, C5, and C6 channels of Africa's governance diamond. Some common themes underlie the various entries in the table. At the most general level, the various interventions can help nurture the state's capacity for collective action by building up 'flexibility within restraint', which is the flexibility to pursue public ends in the context of mechanisms that restrain self-seeking action by public officials.[19] Within the general rubric of 'flexibility within restraint', three sub-themes are worth explicit mention:

- *Formal checks and balances mechanisms*, which impart stability and predictability by restraining arbitrary, discretionary action by political and bureaucratic actors. The first two sets of actions in the table – decentralization and judicial reform – directly aim to strengthen the checks and balances mechanisms. The remaining three do so indirectly, by strengthening transparency in policy formulation and execution, and by building coherent management controls into the public bureaucratic apparatus.
- *Legitimacy of state action in the eyes of citizens* emerges as an indispensable guarantor of the stability of formal institutions. As Weingast and other political scientists make clear, the stability of political systems depends ultimately on their self-enforcement – in the sense that the citizens are sufficiently committed to the constitutional order so that the likelihood of their opposition restrains political leaders who might otherwise try to bend the rules to their personal advantage (Weingast, 1983). The increases in transparency, participation, rule-boundedness, and bureaucratic responsiveness that follow from successful implementation of the actions highlighted in Table 10.10 help strengthen state legitimacy.
- *Checking corruption* is key both to strengthening legitimacy and, more broadly, to improving public performance. As Table 10.10 makes clear, an anti-corruption strategy is not an add-on to state reform but an integral part of the process – resulting in an increase in transparency, decentralization reforms which bring the state closer to its citizens, and an increased judicial independence and impartiality.

To be sure, the gap is vast between identifying a set of high-potential micro-level interventions with the potential to strengthen and the actual strengthening of political institutions. Nor is the challenge simply one of initiating the various reforms within individual African countries, as this already is very much under way. The World Bank (one of many development organizations active in this area) is working with over twenty African governments on at least some of the five micro-level interventions.

The deeper dilemma is that gains in governance require a transformation in the incentives that shape the behavior of political and bureaucratic leaders, a task that is at least as political as technocratic. In the early 1980s, given the political incentives prevailing at the time (described in Section II as the neopatrimonial downward spiral and summarized in Figure 10.2c), constructive governance reforms could hardly be contemplated. As the data in Tables 10.7, 10.8, and 10.9 in Section III suggest, one benefit of economic reform has been breaking the iron grip of these perverse political incentives, and their consequences for governance. Even so, the transformation does not appear to be so dramatic as to transform a vicious spiral into a virtuous one. As Figure 10.2d depicts, on balance, even subsequent to economic reform, formal political institutions and the public bureaucracy still seem to exert a downdraft on Africa's governance

Table 10.10 Strengthening Africa's Governance Diamond

Actions	Intended Effects		
	Formal institutions as container of politics (C2)	Governance of public bureaucracy (C5)	Stability and predictability of economic environment (C6)
Reducing excessive state centralization	Multiple centers of political competition → stronger checks and balances → multiple focal points for political competition	Enhanced opportunities for citizens to hold bureaucracy accountable for performance	Stronger checks and balances reduce scope for non-incremental, discretionary decision-making
Strengthening judicial independence and performance	Courts (and Constitution) as check on unconstrained executive action	Safeguards due process in executive action; checks against corruption	Helps protect rule of law, including contract enforcement
Enhancing public expenditure accountability	Increased transparency (and hence legitimacy) of public life	Transparent monitoring of how bureaucracy uses public resources; check against corruption	Reduce probability of unexpected fiscal shocks; check against corrupt, discretionary dealing between officials and firms
Improving policy formulation processes	Increase participation in decision-making and transparency (and hence legitimacy) of public life	More coherent and transparent goal setting for public bureaucracy	More coherent and inclusive policy processes to reduce the scope for non-incremental, discretionary decision-making
Strengthening public administration	Greater public sector responsiveness improves legitimacy of public/collective realm	Improved responsiveness of bureaucracy to public goals	Improved confidence in delivery capacity of public sector

diamond, rather than being the buttress of good governance as they become mature democracies (Figure 10.2a).

In sum, institutional reform appears to offer yet another example of economic development's cruel paradox of cumulative causation – 'to those that have will be given'. Technocratic institutional and organizational reforms that strengthen public performance are likely to be most effective in settings where the baseline performance is reasonably good, a starting point that prevails in only a few African countries.

Yet, while sobering, attention to the demand-side incentives for institutional change is not intended to be a counsel of despair. Rather, it offers a key pointer to how to prioritize institutional and organizational reform in settings where the governance starting point is weak: *focus first on initiatives that build demand for continuation and success into the reform itself.* Using this criterion, two initiatives with especially high potential are decentralizing reforms that rapidly provide resources to and empower local communities, and expenditure accountability reforms which subject the spending decisions of governments to public (domestic and international) scrutiny. Such reforms have the potential to alter quickly the character of interactions between governments and citizens. And the governance diamond suggests that success in these areas could plausibly help set a broader virtuous spiral of improving governance into motion.

Annex A10.1 Average Annual Growth in Real GDP for the 21 African
Countries, 1975–2000

% of Growth COUNTRY	1975–84	1985–89	1991–96	1996–2000	1999	2000
Group 1 Sustained Adjusters						
Benin	3.8	1.5	4.4	5.2	4.7	5.8
Burkina Faso	3.6	4.4	4.1	4.9	6.3	2.2
Ghana	−1.1	5.2	4.1	4.2	4.4	3.7
Malawi	3.2	1.9	2.7	3.2	4.0	1.7
Mali	2.3	0.8	3.2	5.2	6.1	4.5
Mozambique		6.0	3.7	8.1	7.5	1.6
Uganda		3.4	7.7	5.3	7.5	3.5
Zambia	0.2	2.3	−0.1	1.7	2.0	3.5
Group 2 Later Adjusters						
Cameroon	8.5	−0.1	−0.2	4.7	4.4	4.2
Chad	0.4	0.7	0.7	3.3	1.0	0.6
Guinea		4.7	4.5	3.7	3.6	2.0
Madagascar	−0.2	2.3	1.4	4.3	4.7	4.8
Mauritania	1.6	3.3	3.2	5.2	4.1	5.2
Niger	2	4.2	0.9	3.1	0.1	2.0
Senegal	2.1	3.5	2.6	5.4	5.1	5.6
Tanzania			2.3	4.0	3.6	5.1
Group 3 Governance Polarized						
Côte d'Ivoire	2.2	2.0	3.0	2.7	1.6	−2.3
Kenya	4.7	5.9	2.1	1.2	1.3	−0.2
Nigeria	−0.7	5	2.4	2.4	1.1	3.8
Togo	2.1	3.4	1.9	0.9	2.4	0.7
Zimbabwe	3.0	4.2	2.1	−0.1	−0.7	−4.9

Source: World Bank (2002a)

Annex A10.2 Average Annual Growth in Agricultural Value Added for the 21 African Countries, 1975–2000

% of Growth COUNTRY	1975–84	1985–89	1991–96	1996–2000
Group 1 *Sustained* *Adjusters*				
Benin	3.0	4.6	5.4	5.7
Burkina Faso	1.0	4.6	3.5	2.1
Ghana	0.2	2.3	2.4	3.8
Malawi	2.2	1.2	6.1	5.9
Mali	3.2	8.9	3.5	5.0
Mozambique		7.3	3.8	5.9
Uganda		2.7	4.0	3.5
Zambia	0.5	5.6	3.9	1.1
Group 2 *Later* *Adjusters*				
Cameroon	4.5	0.6	5.2	5.2
Chad	0.6	1.1	2.8	2.1
Guinea		3.1	4.3	3.2
Madagascar	0.2	2.8	1.7	1.0
Mauritania	2.9	4.5	4.3	5.8
Niger	1.1	5.4	0.8	3.0
Senegal	−1.2	4.5	2.7	2.8
Tanzania			3.2	3.0
Group 3 *Governance* *Polarized*				
Côte d'Ivoire	2.7	3	2.5	5.9
Kenya	4.1	4.4	1.1	0.4
Nigeria	−3	6.4	2.7	4.7
Togo	2.8	4.3	5.6	0.5
Zimbabwe	−0.1	1.2	3.0	3.9

Source: Ibid.

Annex A10.3 Average Annual Growth in Industrial Value Added for the 21 African Countries, 1975–2000

% of Growth COUNTRY	1975–84	1985–89	1991–96	1996–2000
Group 1 *Sustained* *Adjusters*				
Benin	5.4	–1.9	5.0	3.7
Burkina Faso	1.6	4.8	5.7	6.1
Ghana	–7.5	9.1	1.0	4.6
Malawi	2.7	3.7	0.1	3.2
Mali	1.6	1.4	3.6	9.4
Mozambique		–4.5	4.9	24.1
Uganda		6.4	13.2	9.7
Zambia	–0.4	2.7	–4.7	–1.3
Group 2 *Later* *Adjusters*				
Cameroon	18.2	0.7	–5.6	7.3
Chad	–2	2.5	–0.8	6.3
Guinea		3.1	5.0	4.4
Madagascar	–2.9	2.8	1.0	5.0
Mauritania	0.6	3.7	5.1	0.1
Niger	10.4	–4.1	1.1	2.8
Senegal	3.7	4.9	3.7	6.9
Tanzania			0.5	7.4
Group 3 *Governance* *Polarized*				
Côte d'Ivoire	6.5	6.5	4.3	3.0
Kenya	4.7	5.2	1.8	0.8
Nigeria	0	2.1	0.5	1.3
Togo	1.5	6.2	0.9	2.5
Zimbabwe	–1	5.4	1.1	–3.5

Source: Ibid.

Notes

[1] A large amount of the literature does explore governance-growth interactions – often via the use of large-scale data sets and multiple regression analysis.

[2] The 1994 study focused on 29 countries. The present discussion excludes eight of these from consideration: Burundi, Central African Republic, Congo-Brazzaville, Guinea Bissau, Rwanda, and Sierra Leone, as conflict subsequently affected them, plus Gabon and Gambia, as they are small country outliers.

[3] Michael Porter presented a 'competitiveness diamond' in Porter (1998).

[4] Note that the New Institutional Economics, which is an important source of inspiration for the present chapter, emphasizes that the 'rules of the game' comprise informal as well as formal institutions. Exploring the role of informal institutions is beyond the scope of the present chapter. But it is to be noted that social norms, specifically the relative salience of horizontal through vertical networks of obligation and accountability, are likely to be an important determinant of how some key interactions in the governance diamond operate in practice. See Levy (2002) for further discussion of this point.

[5] See Dia (1996) for a detailed discussion of the impact of 'neopatrimonialism' on African public management. See Lewis (1996) for a review of the burgeoning academic literature on neopatrimonialism in Africa.

[6] See Levy (2002) for a more detailed discussion of these diverse trajectories.

[7] World Bank (2002a) reports directly the growth rates for 1975–84, 1985–9, and 1990–2000, and annual data for 1991–2000. The present chapter used the 1991, 1996, and 2000 data to calculate growth rates for the sub-periods 1991–6 and 1996–2000. The gap in information between 1989 and 1991 is an artifact of the way the data were made available, with (based on inspection of the not-reported-here 1990–2000 growth rates) no implication on the patterns detailed in Table 10.1 and the text.

[8] Oil price shocks (combined with economic policies which accentuated rather than muted their impact) are, of course an important part of the Nigerian story.

[9] The measure of relative secular decline is the ratio of industrial to agricultural value added in 2000 relative to the ratio in 1980. A decline in this ratio implies relatively more rapid growth of agriculture. Only for the seven countries in the text (including Zambia) was the ratio below 0.9. Specific values were Zambia 0.50; Togo 0.59; Nigeria 0.61; Zimbabwe 0.66; Niger 0.71; Malawi 0.73; and Madagascar 0.77.

[10] For a more thoroughgoing analysis of the survey data for African countries, including details of the survey sample, see Levy (2002).

[11] This within-sample comparison over time eliminates an important part one of the key limitations – sample selection bias – that can limit the comparative potential of subjective surveys of governance.

[12] Note that Ghana is a possible exception.

[13] See Bratton and Van Der Walle (1997) for a comprehensive analysis of Africa's upsurge of democracy in the early 1990s.

[14] World Bank partnerships with government and other stakeholders to support decentralization include Ethiopia, Nigeria, South Africa, Uganda, Guinea, Mozambique, Chad, Madagascar and Zambia.

[15] African countries in which the World Bank is collaborating with government and other stakeholders to support judicial reform include Ethiopia, Tanzania, Madagascar, Nigeria and Cameroon.

[16] All of the 22–plus African countries participating in the expanded HIPC debt reduction initiative are working in close collaboration with the World Bank, the IMF, and other development partners to strengthen their systems of expenditure accountability. In many of these countries, this includes support for independent organs of oversight themselves (e.g. audit institutions, parliamentary accounts committees, and civil society watchdog organizations).

[17] All African countries participating in the expanded HIPC debt reduction initiatives have initiated the PRSP process. Since the World Bank intends to base its country strategies and allocations of concessional resources on country-level PRSPs, the expectation is that all significant recipients of such concessional support will incorporate participatory poverty strategy development into their planning processes.

[18] African countries in which the World Bank is creating partnerships with governments and other stakeholders to strengthen the administrative capacity of the public bureaucracy include Benin, Burkina Faso, Chad, Congo-Brazzaville, Ethiopia, Ghana, Guinea, Kenya, Malawi, Mozambique, Tanzania, Uganda, and Zambia.

[19] For a detailed exposition of 'flexibility within restraint' as a framework for building state capacity, see World Bank (1997b).

11

COLLEEN LOWE-MORNA
From Rhetoric to Reality: Governance & Gender Equity

Nowhere, is the gap between de jure *and* de facto *equality among men and women greater than in the area of decision-making.*

Without the active participation of women and the incorporation of women's perspectives in all levels of decision-making, the goals of equality, development and peace cannot be achieved. (United Nations Fourth World Conference on Women, 1995)[1]

Gender equality is not a bi-product of democracy and it does not derive only from the clauses of the constitution. Democratic constitutions deliver formal, but not substantive equality.... A conscious development of theory is critical to help us understand the workings of patriarchy, its character, and form in our countries as it exists in and interacts with other oppressive forms such as racism and capitalism. Indigenous approaches, informed by other experiences but based on our concrete situation should be applied. (Thenjiwe Mtintso, former Deputy Secretary General of ANC)[2]

I SHALL begin by making a somewhat controversial statement – no country in the world today, not even the Scandinavian countries where close to 40 per cent of parliamentarians are women, can claim to be a democracy, if we understand this term to mean representative government. No country has yet achieved an equal representation of men and women in the corridors of power. Indeed, on average, only 14.5 per cent of the world's legislators are women. With an average of 13.6 per cent of women in both lower and upper houses, Africa is slightly below the global average, although this figure is about two percentage points higher compared with two years ago. But Africa's average also masks significant regional differences. In Southern Africa, the average proportion of women legislators is about 18 per cent. This is three times higher than in Northern Africa.

Perhaps because it has become the experimental ground on the links between good governance, democracy, growth, and development, Africa enjoys a more lively dialogue compared with other parts of the world on how exactly gender fits into this intricate jigsaw puzzle. This chapter provides a brief overview of gender and governance in Africa. Part I examines the different arguments put forward for equal representation of women in decision-making. Part II, drawing on the conceptual framework created by Thenjiwe Mtintso, the chairperson of the Gender Links Board and a leading Southern African feminist, examines the links between access by women to decision-making and delivery on the ground. Part III examines some of the links between legislation and economic governance initiatives that have a strong representation of women in governance

150

structures. Finally, the chapter highlights the need for more research on the qualitative difference that women bring to decision-making.

I: Key Concepts and Issues

AFRICA AND GOVERNANCE

Over the last decade, Africa has been in the grip of major social, economic and political change. Following the 'lost decade' of the 1980s when a combination of stumbling commodity prices, conflict, war, political instability, and misman-agement led to major economic decline, the continent is slowly but surely on an upward swing. According to a concept paper of the African Governance Forum, led by the Economic Commission for Africa (ECA) and the United Nations Development Programme (UNDP), the end of the Cold War had three major impacts on Africa. First, it highlighted democracy as the preferred system of government, putting pressure on African one-party states and military regimes to commence democratization. Between 1989 and 1995, African countries held 35 presidential and parliamentary elections, prompting reference to Africa as 'the world's most democratically contested continent'. Although these elections seldom led to a change of government, the democratization wave opened the door to political dissent and debate, a mushrooming of civil society organiza-tions, and a new lease of life for the continent's beleaguered media.

Second, economic liberalization became the order of the day. The painful medicine of IMF- and World Bank-sponsored structural adjustment programs is paying dividends in more stable macroeconomic environments, investment, and growth. But this at the cost of harsh cuts in social spending.

Third, by promoting a link between democracy and economic and social progress, the end of the Cold War obliged Africa and the international commu-nity to focus on governance. As the African Governance Concept Paper puts it: 'The continent's economic crisis was seen not just as resulting from faulty eco-nomic strategies, but linked to more fundamental causes relating to peace, secu-rity and stability' (UNDP, 1997b: 13).

Defining governance

The political and economic reforms following the end of the Cold War led to an increased focus on governance as it became apparent that the crises in African countries was not just a result of faulty economic strategies but of more funda-mental problems relating to such issues as institutional and human capacity, security, and the rule of law. Narrow definitions focusing on economic and administrative governance have since broadened to include political and legal considerations as illustrated in the following selection of definitions by three prominent inter-governmental organizations (see Box 11.1).

Box 11.1: Definitions of Governance

World Bank: 'Good governance is epitomized by predictable, open and enlightened policy making (that is, transparent processes); a bureaucracy imbued by a professional ethos; an executive arm of government accountable for its actions; and a strong civil society participating in public affairs; and all behaving under the rule of law.[3]

United Nations Development Program: 'the exercise of economic, political and administrative authority to manage a country's affairs at all levels. It comprises the mechanisms, processes and institutions through which citizens and groups articulate their interests, exercise their legal rights, meet their obligations, and mediate their differences.'[4]

Organization for Economic Co-operation and Development: 'Governance denotes the use of political authority and exercise of control in a society in relation to the management of its resources for social and economic development. This broad definition encompasses the role of public authorities in establishing the environment in which economic operators function and in distribution of benefits as well as the relationship between the ruler and the ruled.'[5]

The definitions in Box 11.1 encompass the government's (the executive and administration) responsibility to manage; the role of the judiciary, statutory bodies, the media, and civil society in providing checks and balances; and the importance of private sector and civil society initiatives. Sally Baden of the Institute of Development Studies at the University of Sussex comments:

> A distinction is commonly made between narrow definitions of governance which center on economic and administrative governance (i.e. providing an enabling environment for private sector activity and reform of public administration); and broader definitions which encompass political governance, including the promotion of democratic political structures and human rights.... UNDP's definition incorporates economic, political and administrative aspects of governance (Baden, 1999).

Jo Beall of the London School of Economics and Political Science adds:

> Participation and civic engagement are critical determinants of good governance, a concept that addresses issues of social equity and political legitimacy and not merely the efficient management of infrastructure and services (Beall, 1996).

GLOBALIZATION AND GOVERNANCE
Globalization increases pressure on the 'good governance agenda'. The *ECA and Africa* report notes:

> It is increasingly evident that in a rapidly changing global environment, where efficiency and competitiveness are the hallmarks of success, African governments need effective institutions that will enable them to participate in, and benefit from, the increasing global economy. In this light, Africa's systems of governance hold the key to the continent's integration into world markets (Economic Commission for Africa, 1999).

The UNDP adds:

> Governance can no longer be considered a closed system. The state's task is to find a balance between taking advantage of globalisation and providing a secure and stable social and economic domestic environment, particularly for the most vulnerable (UNDP. 1997a: 3)

At a panel discussion on gender and governance during the UNDP conference on Governance for Sustainable Growth and Equity in 1997, participants warned of the danger of state power being eroded in the new era of globalization, and of its accountability shifting from national constituencies to actors in the global arena. The challenge for the women's movement would therefore be to 'get governments back on their side'.

STRUCTURES OF GOVERNANCE

Table 11.1 summarizes governance structures as now commonly defined and understood, with the addition of the family that, feminists argue, has to date been an important omission. In her paper 'Gender, Governance and the Feminisation of Poverty', Sally Baden notes that the UNDP describes governance as every institution from the family to the state (Baden, 1999). However, she argues that governance debates are not informed by a gendered understanding of family governance. She points out that, while governance and poverty debates have concentrated on government and market failure, they ignore such issues as men's reluctance to contribute to household and child maintenance, and the failure of institutional and welfare arrangements to give women an effective choice.

Table 11.1 Structures of Governance

	State	Private Sector	Civil Society	Family
Structures	• legislature • judiciary • executive • law enforcement agencies • statutory bodies • parastatals	• entrepreneurs (formal and informal sector) • employees	• NGOs • church groups • trade unions • media (1)	• different family forms
Key Functions	• make the laws • enforce the laws • deliver services	• create jobs • create goods and services	• watchdogs • deliver services at community level	• care • nurturing • social security

GENDER AND GOVERNANCE

According to the Inter Parliamentary Union (IPU), since the Fourth World Conference on Women in Beijing in 1995, the average representation of women in the world's parliaments has increased by a fraction – from 11.3 to 14.5 per cent. This is still below the 14.8 per cent achieved in 1988. The decline is largely due to the decreasing number of women in the parliaments of the former eastern bloc countries. As can be seen from Table 11.2, these figures have wide variations across the globe – from 39.7 per cent in the Nordic states, to 6.1 per cent in the Arab states.

Table 11.2 Women in the World's Parliaments by Region: October, 2002

	Lower House	Upper House	Both Combined
Nordic states	39.7%	–	39.7%
Europe, including Nordic countries	16.6%	14.8%	16.2%
Americas	16.2%	17.5%	16.4%
Asia	15.1%	13.0%	14.9%
Europe, excluding Nordic states	14.0%	14.8%	14.2%
Sub-Saharan Africa	13.6%	12.7%	13.5%
Pacific	13.7%	25.9%	15.2%
Arab states	6.1%	2.6%	5.7%

Source: IPU (1999)

Sub-Saharan Africa scores sixth out of seven in the world for women in politics. But, with an average of 18 per cent, Southern Africa is in the same league as the Americas and Europe including the Nordic states. Three African countries (Mozambique, South Africa, and Seychelles) are close to achieving 30 per cent, which the UN regards as the 'critical mass' for women to make a mark in decision-making. Globally, only the Nordic countries have achieved this target.

While stereotypes cut across all areas of governance, there are variations. Because of its very public nature, the political arena is more daunting for women than management. This explains why in developed countries, where women and men have equal access to education, women are rapidly entering into managerial positions, but are still under-represented in politics (for example, on average only 16 per cent of legislators in the US and Western Europe are women).

In developing countries, women's unequal access to education militates against their participation in both politics and management, whether in the private or public sector. Nevertheless, women's representation is more likely to be in management rather than in politics (in Botswana, for example, nearly half of all senior civil servants are women, yet women comprise only 18 per cent of members of parliament). In both developed and developing countries, women tend to be in middle management (the ultimate boss is still male).

The deeply ingrained stereotypes surrounding men as guardians and protectors explain the extremely low representation of women in diplomacy, security, and peacekeeping related fields, even in countries with high representations of women in politics. While Sweden is close to achieving gender parity in the political arena, women comprise only 4 per cent of its defense force.

The fact that there are only six women heads of state, and that the proportion of women cabinet ministers is usually lower than that of parliamentarians, further highlights male dominance of political, social, and economic space in the world (IPU, 1999). Africa has no women heads of state. There is also limited research on women in decision-making positions in civil society. Even in Sweden, which has high levels of women in parliament, women comprise only 20 per cent of executive posts in trade unions.

The percentage of women in the military of most countries is between zero and 5 per cent. With 12 per cent women in the military, the US and Canada have the highest such percentage. Israel is the only country with compulsory military service for women, but they cannot serve in combat positions and they serve for two years, as opposed to three years for men. Only Belgium, Denmark, Greece, Luxembourg, Norway, Portugal, Spain and Zambia admit women into all kinds of military activity, including combat positions. Perhaps most telling is the fact that, despite the high level of women representation in parliament in the Nordic countries, the percentage of women in the armed forces of these countries averages 4 per cent.

II: Why Should Women be Equally Represented in Governance?

Originally viewed primarily in economic management terms, there is a growing appreciation that 'good governance' can only prevail if citizens are able to elect and remove governments; if there is the rule of law; if the private sector and civil society have an enabling environment; and if a robust system of checks and balances prevails. With the growing shift in emphasizing development assistance from short-term economic stabilization to long-term sustainable development, a greater emphasis in recent years has been on strengthening governance institutions and boosting investment in human capital.

Simultaneously, and especially since the Fourth World Conference on Women in Beijing, women are demanding equality of outcomes, not just equality of opportunity. The mid-term review of the Beijing conference in June 2000 shows that, while there is increasing political commitment to, and a growing number of constitutional and legal reforms aimed at achieving, gender equality, major gender gaps still exist in every sphere of life and in every region of the world.

The gap between *de jure* and *de facto* equality has sharpened the focus on women's access to, and participation in, structures and processes of governance. The mere presence of women in structures of governance, which is justifiable in its own right in equity terms, does not guarantee mainstreaming gender considerations in laws, policies, and programs. But a growing body of literature suggests that, when women are present in critical numbers and are able to participate effectively, a more socially responsive governance results.

A growing body of research in the corporate sector points to the business advantages of increasing workplace diversity. Scandinavian studies show that the participation of women contributes to marked changes in legislative and policy agendas towards advancing equality between men and women.

The lively debates in Africa advance three broad arguments on the issue of equal representation of women in all structures of governance.

• **Efficiency:** An accepted premise of development is that participation by all parties is essential to the sound formulation of legislation and policies, as well as to responsive service delivery. Commenting on the participation of women in governance, Karl stresses the importance of diverse voices and experiences for effective governance:

> While bearing in mind that the question of whether or not women have distinct bio-logically or socially determined values is a controversial one, as well as the dangers of gender stereotyping, several studies of women in politics show that women's experiences, particularly as mothers and in their traditional roles in the home and family, make them more acutely aware than men of the needs of other people and thus more likely to take into account in their work the needs and rights of women, children, the elderly, the disabled, minorities and the disadvantaged. Women are also more likely to advocate measures in the areas of health and reproduction, child care, education, welfare and the environment, and are generally less militaristic and more supportive of non-violence and peace (Karl, 1995: 64).

The UNDP takes the view that 'the marginalisation of women in the political process and governance in general has been both a cause and effect of the slow progress made in the advancement of women.... It is precisely the participation of women at the highest decision making level in political and economic life that can drive the change for greater equality between men and women' (UNDP, 2000: 4).

• **Poverty reduction:** Recently, the broadening interpretation of governance to include political accountability and popular participation has increased the convergence in the discourse on governance and poverty reduction. Some development agencies, like those from the United Kingdom, have adopted rights-based approaches to poverty reduction. Current approaches to poverty reduction emphasize empowerment, particularly of women, as central to poverty reduction.

• **Equity:** This school of thought argues that equal participation by women is a fundamental right. A 1992 IPU resolution states 'The concept of democracy will only assume true and dynamic significance when political parties and national legislation are decided upon jointly by men and women with equi-table regard for the interests and aptitudes of both halves of the population' (IPU, 1992).

Globally, regionally and nationally it is now accepted that

• Access to, and participation by, women at all levels of decision-making is a fundamental right.
• For women to make an impact on decision-making, they must constitute a 'critical mass' of at least 30 per cent of such structures.

Box 11.2 National, International and Regional Obligations to Increase the Representation of Women in Politics

The 1997 Southern African Development Community (SADC) Declaration on Gender and Development commits member states to 'ensuring the equal representation of women and men in the decision making of member states and SADC structures at all levels, and the achievement of at least a thirty per cent target of women in political and decision making structures by the year 2005'.[6]

The UN Convention on the Elimination of All Forms of Discrimination Against Women states: 'parties shall take all appropriate measures to eliminate discrimination against women in political life and shall ensure to women, on equal terms with men, the right to participate in the formulation and implementation of government policy and to hold public office and perform all public functions at all levels of government.'[7]

The Beijing Declaration and Platform for Action calls on governments to take measures to ensure women's equal access to, and full participation in, power structures and decision-making by creating a gender balance in government and administration; integrating women into political parties; increasing women's capacity to participate in decision making and leadership and increasing women's participation in the electoral process and political activities. (United Nations, 1995)

MTINTSO'S CONCEPTUAL FRAMEWORK

To analyze the barriers to women's participation in governance and strategies to overcome them, the following sections draw on the conceptual framework developed by the former Deputy Secretary General of the African National Congress and former chair of the South African Commission on Gender Equality, Thenjiwe Mtintso (Mtintso, 1999). Mtintso argues that it is essential to understand the cultural, economic, and political constraints on women accessing structures of governance. Short-term strategies such as targets and quotas, as well as long-term strategies that aim to shift deep-seated attitudes and behaviors, can work to overcome these constraints. The sheer presence of women in the corridors of power leads to changes in institutional cultures and agendas, but Mtintso stresses that numbers are not enough. She quotes a South African woman parliamentarian: 'we have to go beyond making history to making policy' (ibid.).

Mtintso argues that states must address the institutional practices that inhibit the effective participation of women, for institutions that are not sensitive to gender needs are not likely to be able to deliver laws, policies, or programs that recognize and redress gender gaps. Women and men in these institutions need to be imbued with technical and analytical skills to understand what the gaps are. While Mtintso concedes that women are not homogenous and society should not automatically expect women to represent 'women's interests', she points to a growing body of evidence that the presence and effective participation of women are strong contributory factors in transforming the deliverables of governance from a gender perspective.

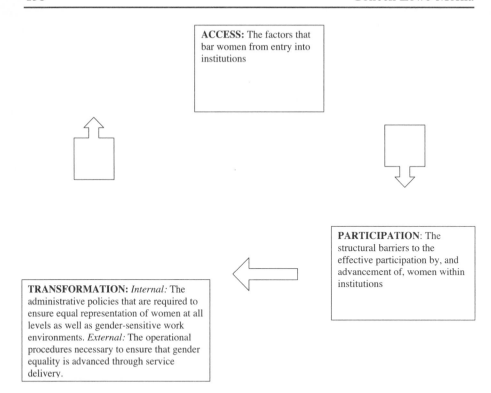

Figure 11.1 Mtintso's Access, Participation, and Transformation Framework

The central message of this analysis is that access, participation, and transformation are inextricably linked. As the UNDP puts it:

> There is a growing recognition that economic participation and political participation cannot be separated. Institutional transformations are needed to create the enabling environment for the economic and political empowerment of women...Transforming and increasing the accountability of institutions to women's interests, and especially the interests of poor women, is necessary for poverty reduction and good governance. (UNDP, 2000a: 4)

BOOSTING THE NUMBERS

To start at the beginning of the cycle, what is keeping African women out of decision-making, and how do we change that? A study on leadership in women's empowerment in Africa has two indicators (Longwe and Clarke, 1999):

* A **Women's Empowerment Index** (WEI), which provides a quantitative indicator of women's progress. WEI measures progress in terms of women's level of representation in leadership positions, including the executive, members of parliament, and managerial positions.
* A **Women's Self-Reliance Index** (WSI) to measure women's individual capacity to advance. The WSI looks at capacity in terms of education, training, and access to resources, including level of education, share of income and proportion of women in industry.

The report's main finding is that 'absolutely no correlation' exists between self-reliance and empowerment. This supports global trends that suggest a lack of correlation between women's education, affluence, and levels of representation in politics and decision-making. Put differently, Mozambique, one of the poorest countries in the world and with the highest illiteracy levels, has the highest representation of women in parliament. Yet, Mauritius, Africa's 'little tiger', is 36th in the same table! Similarly, sub-Saharan Africa, the world's least developed continent, is not far behind Europe and America when it comes to women in parliament. As Namibia's Minister for Women's Affairs Netumbo Nandi Ndaiwah commented wryly during the UNDP's 1997 Governance for Sustainable Growth and Equity conference: 'At least in one area (women and decision-making) developed and developing countries share a similar record!'

The survey concludes that: 'Gender gaps in empowerment are far more fundamental and intractable, by comparison with gender gaps in self reliance...women's occupation of top leadership positions poses a much greater threat to male interests and privileges, which therefore attracts greater resistance to women's advancement in these areas' (ibid.). In other words, even in the most conservative countries, men are not likely to object to women going to school or getting a job. But they will resist women being in positions of power over them. This is nothing new. At the root of all oppression are differences in power, both perceived and real. The moment such power is threatened, the party in the more powerful position recoils. At the heart of the under-representation of women in politics are age-old attitudes and stereotypes that assign women to the private and men to the public domain. Custom, culture, religion, and the media reinforce this assignment to varying degrees.

It is no coincidence that five of the bottom ten African countries in Table 11.3 are in North Africa, which is where custom and religion exercise a powerful influence. Mauritius, with one of the lowest levels of women in parliament in SADC, has strong religious influences. Swaziland, 36th on the list, is a monarchy with socially conservative traditions. Despite the fact that women in Lesotho, which has a high level of male migrant labor to the mines in South Africa, are the majority of heads of households, women are not allowed to participate in the traditional public decision-making meetings known in Sotho as the *pitso*. One of the reasons that women are in higher levels of national parliaments than at the local level in Southern Africa is because custom and tradition play an even stronger role at the local than at the national level.

The media feed into and reinforce gender stereotypes. In a review of gender, politics, and the media in South Africa just prior to the 1999 elections, the Media Monitoring Project noted:

> Women entering the political sphere provide the news media with a 'problem', They embody a challenge to masculine authority. They also defy easy categorization. The scrutiny of women's work in our society, therefore, is closely tied to their traditionally defined roles as 'women'. Their images fit in well with prevailing cultural perceptions of women. These images also help to maintain the patriarchal structure by inculcating restricted and limited images of women. (Media Monitoring Project, 1999)

Even in South Africa, with its laudable achievements, politics remains a man's world. The Media Monitoring Project found, for example, that 87 per cent of the news sources in the 1999 election were men.

Table 11.3 Women in Parliament in Africa as at 1 March 2000

Country and Rank	Region	Next Election	Total	Total Women	% Women
1. Mozambique	SA	2004	250	71	28.4
2. South Africa[a]	SA	2004	490	137	28.0
3. Seychelles	SA	2003	34	8	23.5
4. Botswana	SA	2004	44	8	18.0
5. Uganda	EA	2001	280	50	17.86
6. Rwanda	EA	?	70	12	17.14
7. Tanzania	EA	2000	275	45	16.36
8. Angola	SA	2000	220	34	15.45
9. Eritrea	EA	?	150	22	14.67
10. Namibia[a]	SA	2005	99	14	14.1
11. Senegal[a]	WA	2003	200	28	14.0
12. Zimbabwe	SA	2000	150	21	14.0
13. Mali	WA	2003	147	18	12.24
14. Congo	CA	2001	75	9	12.0
15. Tunisia	NA	2004	182	21	11.54
16. Cape Verde	WA	2000	72	8	11.11
17. Liberia[a]	WA	2003	90	10	11.1
18. Zambia	SA	2001	158	16	10.13
19. Lesotho[a]	SA	2003	112	12	10.7
20. Burkina Faso[a]	WA	2003	287	30	10.4
21. Ghana	WA	2000	200	18	9.00
22. Gabon[a]	WA	2001	211	20	9.5
23. São Tomé & Principe	WA	2002	55	5	9.09
24. Guinea	WA	2000	114	10	8.77
25. Sierra Leone	WA	2001	80	7	8.75
26. Malawi	SA	2004	193	16	8.29
27. Madagascar	EA	2003	150	12	8.00
28. Guinea Bissau	WA	2003	114	10	8.77
29. Mauritius	SA	2000	66	5	7.58
30. Central African Republic	CA	2003	109	8	7.34
31. Benin	WA	2003	83	5	6.02
32. Burundi	EA	?	117	7	5.98
33. Cameroon	WA	2002	180	10	5.56
34. Equatorial Guinea	CA	2004	80	4	5.00
35. Togo	WA	2004	81	4	4.94
36. Swaziland[a]	SA	2003	95	6	4.20
37. Algeria[a]	NA	2002	524	20	3.8
38. Kenya	EA	2002	224	8	3.57
39. Nigeria	WA	2003	468	15	3.2
40. Chad	WA	2001	125	3	2.4
41. Mauritania[a]	NA	2000	135	3	2.2
42. Gambia	WA	2003	49	1	2.04
43. Ethiopia[a]	EA	2000	654	11	1.7
44. Niger[a]	NA	2004	83	1	1.20
45. Morocco[a]	NA	2003	594	4	0.67
46. Egypt	NA	2000	454	9	1.98
47. Djibouti	EA	2003	65	0	0
48. Libya	NA	2000	760	0	0
TOTAL			8983	809	9.0

Source: IPU (1999) Note: a) Upper and Lower House. No data available for Comoros, Côte d'Ivoire, Somalia and the Sudan.

POLITICAL SYSTEMS, COMMITMENT AND PHILOSOPHY
Of the top ten African countries with regard to women in parliament, eight –
Angola, Mozambique, South Africa, Uganda, Rwanda, Eritrea, Seychelles,
Namibia – five of them from Southern Africa, have recently undergone social
revolutions or upheavals. This suggests that upheaval can create opportunities
for women to play non-traditional roles and opens the door a little wider for
women to participate in decision-making. Another feature is that eight of these
top ten countries, six from Southern Africa, have come from social democratic
or socialist roots – Mozambique, South Africa, Seychelles, Uganda, Tanzania,
Angola, Eritrea and Namibia. At the very least, this suggests that women's
involvement in politics and decision-making is not something to be left to
chance. Rather, involvement must be part of a deliberate strategy and must have
strong political backing. It is no coincidence that the ruling Frelimo in
Mozambique, the African National Congress in South Africa, Chama Cha
Mapinduzi in Tanzania, and the South West Africa Peoples Organization in
Namibia featured gender equality in their manifestos.

Southern Africa is unique, as many countries have relatively new constitutions, drafted at a time when issues of gender equality were the subject of lively
debate, lobbying, and advocacy. The constitutions of South Africa, Namibia and
Mozambique explicitly outlaw gender discrimination and provide for affirmative
action. In South Africa, the Women's National Coalition, an umbrella of NGOs
working in the gender area, conducted a participatory research campaign that
culminated in a 'Women's Charter', presented to the negotiators in Kempton
Park. Each three-person delegation to the negotiations had to have at least one
woman. The presence of women made a symbolic statement and led to a substantive difference in the outcome of the constitutional negotiations.

Constitutions are not static. Malawi and Tanzania incorporated gender considerations into their constitutions, including, in the case of Tanzania, a quota
for women. Several countries are undertaking or anticipating constitutional
reviews. Therefore, incorporating scope for strong gender provisions is within
the scope of the constitution in all SADC countries.

THE SOUTHERN AFRICAN REGIONAL CAMPAIGN
The SADC Declaration on Gender and Development, adopted by SADC
heads of state in 1997, committed all 14 members to achieve a 30 per cent
level of women in decision-making by 2005. SADC is the only regional group
in Africa with this position. Figure 11.2 illustrates where different countries
stand. A key function of the Declaration is routinely gathering and publicizing
statistics as a tactic for showing the countries that fall short of the agreed
target.

Table 11.4 shows that of the eight countries with elections since the
Declaration, two remained static and two experienced a minor decrease in the
representation of women. An interesting case in point is Botswana. Before 1994,
the maximum female representation in parliament was 5 per cent. Thanks
largely to NGO lobbying, the representation of women in parliament rose to 9.1
per cent in the 1994 elections. In May 1999, a few months before the Botswana
elections, SADC held a conference, 'Women in Politics and Decision Making in
SADC: Beyond 30 per cent in 2005' in Gaborone, at which Botswana President
Festus Mogae warned that the deadline of 2005 could not be extended. In the

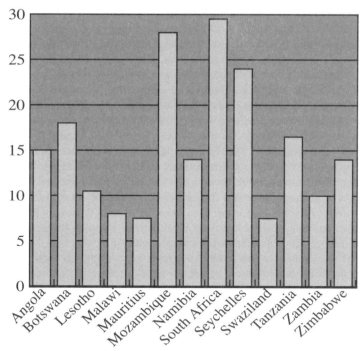

Figure 11.2 Women in Parliament in SADC Countries, 2002
Source: SADC Gender Unit (2002); IPU (2002)
Note: Madagascar joined SADC in 2005.

October elections, women's representation in parliament in Botswana doubled to 18 per cent. This shows that the requisite political will can dramatically increase the levels of women participation. However, the 30 per cent target or gender parity in politics is not likely to be achieved without taking specific affirmative actions.

Table 11.4 Women MPs in SADC Countries that Held Elections Post 1997

Country	Pre-Election		Post-Election		Increase
	No. of Women	Percentage	No. of Women	Percentage	Percentage
Botswana 1999	4/44	9	8/44	18	9
Malawi 1999	9/171	5.2	16/192	8.3	3.1
Mozambique 1999	71/250	28.4	71/250	28.4	0
Namibia[a] 1999	14/99	14.1	14/99	14.1	0
South Africa[a] 1999	128/490	26.1	137/490	28	1.9
Mauritius 2000	6/70	8	4/70	5.71	-3
Zambia	15/158	10.1	19/158	12	1.9
Zimbabwe	21/150	14	15/150	10	-4

[a] Upper and lower house
Sources: IPU (1999); SADC (1999)

ELECTORAL SYSTEMS, QUOTAS, AND SPECIAL MEASURES
Overwhelming evidence suggests that women stand a better chance of getting

elected under proportional representation, as opposed to a constituency-based electoral system, the reason being that candidates in the former system focus on the party and its policies, rather than on a particular individual. This works in favor of women, at least in getting their foot in the door, because of the built-in prejudices against women (Lowe-Morna, 1996). The chance of women getting elected is even higher when the proportional representation system works in concert with a party or legislated quota.

Table 11.5 Electoral Systems and Affirmative Action

Type of quota	Proportional Representation system	Constituency-based system
Voluntary party quota	The ANC in South Africa; Frelimo in Mozambique	The Labour Party in UK
Constitutional or legislated quota	In the local government elections in Namibia, which has a PR system, 33 per cent of all candidates had to be women. Overall, women constitute 41 per cent of local councilors	The Ugandan and Tanzanian constitutions reserve certain percentages of seats for women

Source: Lowe-Morna (1996)

As illustrated in Table 11.5, four different combinations of quotas and electoral systems exist:

- *The voluntary party quota, combined with the Proportional Representation (PR) system*, in South Africa and Mozambique. It is no coincidence that these two have the highest representation of women in parliament in SADC. The two ruling parties, the ANC and Frelimo, have their own voluntarily adopted 30 per cent quotas. Because of the PR or list system, every third person on their list was a woman. As the majority parties, this system ensures levels of female representation close to 30 per cent. The disadvantage is the ruling party's reliance on getting substantial majorities. In other words, unless every party contesting has a 30 per cent quota, obtaining the 'critical mass' of 30 per cent is not guaranteed. There are also strong arguments against the PR system because of the perceived lack of accountability to constituents in this system. South Africa's 1995 local government elections, which were held on the basis of a mixed system, did not engender much confidence. In the PR seats, women won 27.9 per cent of the seats, but only 10.4 per cent in the constituency-based seats. This gave an overall average of 19 per cent of the seats in local government being won by women, which is substantially below the 27 per cent at national level where elections were held entirely on the basis of PR.
- *The legislated quota, combined with the PR system*, which occurred in Namibia's local government elections. Because the quota was legislated as opposed to being voluntarily adopted by one party or other, the elections guaranteed an outcome of 30 per cent women. However, since some parties fielded even more women candidates, the overall outcome was 41 per cent. This suggests that combining a legislated quota and PR system is the most powerful

combination to achieve gender parity in politics, which is the ultimate objective. However, some parties strongly resist the idea of a legislated quota. In South Africa, for example, the opposition parties have made it clear that they oppose a legislated quota on the basis that it is contrary to freedom of association.

*   *The voluntary party quota, combined with the constituency-based system:* An example of this internationally is the Labour Party in the UK, which through its commitment to fielding women candidates, managed to increase the representation of women substantially. In Botswana, which has a constituency system, two opposition parties (the Botswana Congress Party and Botswana National Front) had a quota of 30 per cent women in the 1999 elections. All political parties contesting elections must have a 30 per cent quota to ensure that the target is met. Moreover, unlike the list system, women candidates have to be fielded in 'safe constituencies', where they are assured of winning, for the voluntary quota to increase the representation of women. Studies in Botswana and Mauritius show that women in constituency systems often get dropped at the party primaries, which are often secretive and dominated by intra-party intrigue. These factors explain why Southern African countries with the constituency-based system are further behind than those with a PR system when it comes to women in politics.

*   *Legislated or constitutional quotas in the constituency-based system:* The southern Africa example of this is Tanzania, where the constitution stipulates that at least 15 per cent of the 238 members of parliament must be women. In other words, the Constitution reserves 38 seats for women. With the eight seats that women contested directly and won, the overall representation of women is16.4 per cent in Tanzania's parliament. Clearly, the quota has boosted the level of representation by women. But, as the Minister for Community Development, Women's Affairs and Children, Mary Nangu, points out, having reserved seats for women 'perpetuates the stereotype that women are not capable of competing with men'.

In addition to quotas, electoral systems may allow the head of state to make some appointments to parliament (examples are Zimbabwe, Botswana and Swaziland). Indeed, of the eight women in the Swazi parliament, voters elected only two: the king appointed the other six. The SADC Plan of Action on Women in Politics and Decision-Making recognizes such appointments as another short-term measure at the disposal of countries to ensure that they meet the 30 per cent target.

The area where heads of state have complete discretion to make appointments is with regard to the cabinet. The fact that, with the exception of South Africa and Botswana, levels of women's representation in cabinets are far behind their representation in parliament calls into question the political commitment of heads of state to the SADC Declaration. The SADC Plan of Action also highlights this issue as a lobbying and rallying point.

Significantly, despite the inevitable charges of tokenism that accompany debates on quotas and discretionary appointments, there is very little evidence that women who enter politics in this way are incompetent. On the contrary, anecdotal evidence suggests that women members of parliament and cabinet ministers find themselves under pressure to be twice as good in order to be half as recognized as their male colleagues. Mtintso cites, as an example, the way many ANC women parliamentarians improved their position on the ANC list between the 1994 and 1999 elections (see Table 11.6) as evidence that, once in parliament, women gain acceptance and credibility.

Table 11.6 Position of Some Women in the ANC National List, 1994 and 1997

Name	Position in 1994	Position in 1999
Nkosazana Zuma	51	3
Geraldine Fraser-Moleketi	61	9
Winnie Madikizela-Mandela	31	10
Gill Marcus	47	12
Frene Ginwala	54	13
Stella Sigcau	26	28
Nosiviwe Mapisa-Nqakula	52	29
Baleka Kgositsile-Mbethe	34	33
Bridgette Mabandla	66	36
Melanie Verwoerd	83	64
Lindiwe Sisulu	93	27
Phumzile Mlambo-Ngcuka	90	35
Sanki Mthembi-Mahanyele	84	34
Thoko Msane-Didiza	108	42
Pregs Govender	85	50

Source: *Government Gazette*, 14 May 1994 and ANC list, March 1999.

Recognizing that the 30 per cent target will not be achieved without direct intervention, the SADC Plan of Action requires member states to adopt specific measures, including constitutional or legislated quotas and non-constituency seats over which heads of state have discretion to achieve this objective.

WOMEN IN POLITICAL PARTY STRUCTURES, SUPPORT FOR WOMEN
CANDIDATES AND WOMEN VOTERS
The location of women in political party structures is an area that requires further study. Available evidence suggests that, while espousing increasingly progressive rhetoric on gender equality on the outside, parties continue to marginalize women within. The ANC, for example, has not applied its 30 per cent quota to party leadership (one out of six of its top officials are women). This is a critical issue as leadership within the party is an important training ground for women in politics (Lowe-Morna, 1996).

A common feature of most parties in Africa is women's wings. As in other parts of the world, these structures have an ambivalent role, and often reflect the inferior status of women by serving as the hospitality wing of the party. In Botswana, the NGO Emang Basadi has taken the conscious policy decision to work with the women's wings of political parties because, despite their present overwhelming concern with the 'welfare' of the party, the group sees them as a potentially powerful tool for advancing the status of women (Machangana, 1999).

Aside from societal stereotypes and marginalization within political parties, women candidates are at a disadvantage because of their lower levels of education, limited access to funds, and dual responsibilities, which limit the time available for campaigning. NGOs like the Women's Development Fund in South Africa, Emang Basadi, and the Zambia National Women's Lobby Group offer training to women candidates in public speaking and campaign management. Research has yet to look at less formal programs, such as the mentorship of younger candidates by older ones, and the women's wings of political parties may usefully take these on. Given the intensely competitive nature of party politics, the most important source of support for women candidates should be from within the party.

African women have enjoyed universal suffrage since their country's independence. Voter turnout in African countries is generally higher than in the West, and the turnout of women voters is especially high. But the link to advancing gender equality is still weak. Emang Basadi has found that 'a lot of women lack the knowledge of what their vote is in a democracy as a voter and what obligations of those they vote for are towards them' (African American Institute, 1995).

In the 1999 South African elections, a million more women than men were registered voters. A survey carried out by the Commission on Gender Equality of the 1999 elections in South Africa noted:

> Women need to be aware of the huge power they wield as the majority of the supporters of the main political parties in the country. These parties have not yet made a clear link between the women's vote and the need for unequivocal policies and practices aimed at achieving gender equality. This is because women have not articulated either their needs or their collective political muscle strongly enough to influence party positions. The challenge is therefore both to the male dominated party hierarchies, and to women voters and party members, to reshape the agenda. (Motara, 1999: 12)

This is an area for further research, since establishing a link between women's votes and women's concerns would be a powerful impetus for political parties to take gender seriously, in fielding women candidates, and in formulating gender-sensitive campaigns and programs.

III: Effective Participation and Transforming the Agenda

Much remains to be done to ensure women's access to politics. Besides numbers, Africa must concern itself with the effective participation of women in politics.

THE LOCATION OF WOMEN IN DECISION-MAKING POSITIONS

Once women access parliament and cabinet, their location in the power structures and stereotypes limits their effective participation. With the exception of South Africa, where both the Speaker and Deputy Speaker in parliament are women, all the other leaders of the SADC upper and lower houses are men. Table 11.7 illustrates the pervading gender stereotypes: women, after South Africa's historic 1994 elements, were assigned to far more developmental and social clusters in parliamentary committees, compared with the security, internal and foreign affairs, and the economic and financial affairs clusters.

Table 11.7 Distribution of Women in the Parliamentary Committees of South Africa

Cluster	Women/Total	Percentage of Women
Developmental – land, agriculture, RDP, public works	42/121	34.7 %
Social – education, environment, health, housing, sport, welfare, arts	91/ 260	35 %
Security, internal and foreign affairs – Constitutional, communications, legislation, correctional, defense, foreign, home, justice, safety, security	72/358	20.1 %
Economic and financial affairs – finance, mining, public enterprise, public Service, trade, transport, labor	46/ 233	20.0 %

Source: Mtintso (1999)

Globally, according to the Inter Parliamentary Union, women comprise 24.7 per cent of the ministers of women's affairs and gender equality and 23.2 per cent of ministers of social affairs, but only 2.1 per cent of ministers of defense and 4.7 per cent of finance ministers (IPU, 1999). In SADC, women ministers predominate in the areas of gender and women's affairs, housing, and social welfare. But there are exceptions. Mozambique's Minister of Finance and Angola's Minister of Energy are women. South African President Thabo Mbeki made a powerful statement in the selection of his cabinet not just by upholding the one-third principle, but also by assigning women to non-traditional cabinet posts. Cabinet positions in South Africa held by women include vice president, foreign affairs, health, housing, minerals and energy, public service and administration, agriculture and land affairs, and public works. Deputy ministerial positions in South Africa held by women include those in the arts, culture, science and technology, defense, environmental affairs and tourism, home affairs, justice, minerals and energy affairs, public works, and trade and industry.

GENDER-UNFRIENDLY WORK ENVIRONMENTS

Parliaments are notorious for their family-unfriendly practices. When there is a critical mass of women in parliament, parliament challenges some of the norms. For example, in South Africa, thanks to the pressure exerted by the multi-party Parliamentary Women's Group, hours of sittings have been changed, dress codes reviewed (allowing women to wear trousers in parliament), women's showers installed in the gym, and a crèche established for members of parliament and parliamentary employees. Such changes, small as they may be, send out a powerful symbolic message. And both men and women benefit. Men, for example, can leave parliament earlier to spend time with their families and use the parliamentary crèche if they have young children.

Sexist attitudes and sexual harassment are rife in many parliaments.[9] Unfamiliar language and rules, lack of training and experience, lack of adequate support (such as research back-up for parliamentarians) also hamper effectiveness. Training and support – formal and informal – can assist men and women. Men have long developed and rely heavily on the 'old boys' network' for peer support and mentorship. Women are just beginning to do so with women caucuses in parliament, networks of women in business and the professions, and gender support structures in government.

According to a 1996 report, *What the South African Parliament Has Done to Improve the Quality of Life and Status of Women in South Africa*, which the Speaker commissioned,

> the cut-throat way in which proceedings were handled intimidated some women. Some women Parliamentarians struggle with the assumption within the institution that business should proceed as usual, believing instead that the culture of Parliament should be reassessed so as to accommodate differing values that women may bring to Parliament. An observation made from reading the debates seemed to indicate a reduced level of participation by women MPs in 1995 as compared to 1994. There exists a need for the transformation of Parliament not only in terms of the nature of issues debated but the ethics which are imbued in the style of debate.

The key is to learn the rules, use the rules, and, where necessary, change the rules of institutions to facilitate more effective participation by women (Karam, 1999).

Women, like male parliamentarians, suffer from capacity constraints that reduce their effectiveness as legislators. To the extent that women also suffer from a hostile environment and an inferiority complex, training that helps to strengthen their technical, conceptual, analytical, and communication skills can help women members of parliament and ministers overcome some of the structural barriers.

Mtintso points out: 'Differing views exist on whether or not women are a homogeneous group with common interests that can be represented in parliament'. She challenges the notion of 'sisterhood', which attributes particular qualities to women, and sees them as representing common and general 'women's interests'. She presents the persuasive view that women are not homogeneous, do not have universally shared interests and perspectives, and do not speak with one voice. But she notes that 'both the literature and international experience confirm the view that when women, who are perceived to belong to the private sphere, enter parliament, a public sphere perceived as a male domain, the two spheres begin to merge. Such a merger changes the attitudes of both women and men about their roles in society. This changes gender relations in parliament as well as in society's attitude, which is a prerequisite for gender equality' (Mtintso, 1999: 37).

LEGISLATIVE REFORM

Africa has too few cases of women constituting a critical mass in parliament or the cabinet. The instances of women's participation have been in existence for too short a time to judge what difference the presence of women makes to actual legislation. But anecdotal evidence suggests that women's presence, even in small numbers, introduces agendas and issues that a male-dominated chamber would not be likely to feature. The handful of women parliamentarians in Mauritius was instrumental in pushing through a far-reaching Domestic Violence Act, which is now a model for other countries in the region. In Tanzania, women were at the forefront of the passage of the 1998 Sexual Offences Act and the 1999 Land Village Act.

The 1996 report commissioned by the South African Speaker highlights the many achievements of women parliamentarians:

- South Africa's ratification of the Convention on the Elimination of All Forums of Discrimination Against Women (December, 1995), without reservations.
- Establishment of a Commission on Gender Equality, a body with few parallels internationally, which has widespread powers to ensure realization of constitutional provisions for gender equality.
- Recognition of 9 August, the anniversary of the historic women's march against the pass laws during the apartheid era, as a holiday. While South Africa celebrates international women's day on 8 March, the South African Women's Day on 9 August is one with which women around the country identify more closely. It has become an important occasion for reminding the government of its commitment to gender equality under the Constitution and CEDAW.
- Provisions for women's ownership in land and housing legislation, though this has not necessarily led to substantive gender equality.
- Passing the Choice of Termination of Pregnancy Act, the Domestic Violence Act, the Maintenance Act, and the Recognition of Customary Marriages Act.

While the South African government has removed much of the blatant discriminatory legislation, the major challenge is getting to the heart of structural or hidden discrimination. As the report to the Speaker puts it: 'Our study points to the need for a formal methodology to be adopted by Parliament for integrating gender issues into the legislative process' (Serote et al., 1996).

ECONOMIC GOVERNANCE: GENDER BUDGETING
The last few years have witnessed a plethora of 'gender budget' initiatives in different parts of the world, driven by state and non-state actors, with enthusiastic participation by African women parliamentarians and NGOs. These initiatives capture the imagination of those concerned with gender and governance for a number of reasons:

- Analyzing budgets from a gender perspective is integral to gender mainstreaming. If policies and project design build in gender considerations, they should be reflected in resource allocation. When the designs do not build in gender considerations, the outcomes are not likely to deliver substantive equality for women. Budgets are thus a critical tool for mainstreaming.
- Gender budgeting is a tangible way for women to engage in hard-core resource allocation debates that are likely to enhance empowerment rather than tinkering at the fringes of social welfare policies as has traditionally been the case.
- It increases the transparency of, and citizen participation in, economic governance.

The central plank of gender budgeting is that, because of the different locations of men and women in society and in the economy, no budget line is neutral. To take the latter example, by obtaining gender-disaggregated data on such issues as land tenure, credit, and agricultural extension, a picture emerges as to whether or not a budget line item on agriculture is actually addressing gender disparities in this sector, and by so doing contributing to the empowerment of women.

Gender budgeting involves an analysis of allocations both between sectors (such as defense versus social allocations) and within sectors to determine their impact. A commonly used model for distinguishing between the types of gender expenditure is that developed by the Australian economist, Rhonda Sharp. Sharp has played a leading role in gender budget initiatives in Australia, which is where the concept originated. She distinguishes different types of expenditures:

- *Specifically identified gender-based expenditures*, for example, women's health projects, which are typically less than 1 per cent of the overall budget.
- *Equal employment opportunity expenditure*, for example, writing job descriptions to reflect equal employment opportunity principles.
- *General or mainstream budget expenditure* by government departments and authorities to assess gender impact. For example, does the education budget, minus the above two considerations, reflect gender equity objectives? Are boys and girls equally represented in all categories of education? What proportion of the education budget goes towards education and adult literacy? Not surprisingly, this category of questions is most critical for policy reform because the 'mainstream' budget in Australia, as elsewhere, constitutes some 98 per cent of government expenditure.

Examples of gender budget initiatives in Africa include:

- The Tanzania Gender Networking Programme (TGNP), which reviews the budgets of the planning commission and specific ministries, as well as working with the government to implement recommendations.
- The Ugandan Gender Budget Initiative (GBI) is a joint undertaking of the Women's Caucus in parliament and the Forum for Women in Democracy (FOWODE), an NGO that provides training and research capacity for women members of parliament. After carrying out research on the national budgets for education, health, and agriculture, GBI is piloting research in these areas at the district level.
- The South African Women's Budget Initiative (WBI), which the Australian example inspired, has its roots in civil society and in parliament. The WBI did detailed research in all sectors and government departments, using a team of researchers in civil society, which worked closely with the Parliamentry Committee on the Quality of Life and Status of Women. WBI published the findings in four volumes of the *Women's Budget*, and in the simplified version, *Money Matters*. The WBI found an entry point into government when South Africa became one of two Commonwealth countries participating in a pilot study on integrating gender into macroeconomic policy, which was launched at the Fifth Meeting of Commonwealth Ministers Responsible for Women's Affairs in Trinidad and Tobago in 1995. The Central Statistical Services

worked with the Ministry of Finance to incorporate gender considerations into budget reviews that raised significant analysis and questions on the gender impact of specific expenditures.

Although still in their early stages, gender budget initiatives have scored important successes, ranging from actual expenditure re-allocations to opening traditionally secretive budget processes, to greater transparency and accountability.

- *Re-prioritization of expenditure:* A report from the South African Minister of Finance to the Committee on the Quality of Life and Status of Women in 1997 stated:

  > Following a cabinet meeting in February 1996, the Department of Finance committed itself to considering the reallocation of military expenditure to support women's economic advancement. The Department has reduced expenditure on defence from 9.1 per cent of total government spending in 1992/93 to 5.7 per cent in 1997/98. The priority has shifted instead to the social services, which benefit predominantly women and children. Spending on social services increased from 43.8 per cent of total spending in 1992/93 to 46.9 per cent in 1997/98.

- *Exposing general budgetary weaknesses:* Because of work on gender budgets, general budgetary problems have surfaced. For example, work at the local government level in Uganda demonstrates that payments to government officials consume a large portion of meager budgets, leaving little money for actual programs (Budlender, 2000). But the work also raises the specter of conflict that is bound to accompany any re-prioritization.

- *Sharpening approaches to gender mainstreaming:* As a result of TGNP research, the Tanzania Ministry of Finance issued general guidelines for mainstreaming gender in its 1998–9 budget. The government invited TGNP to work with six sectors in an initial gender budget mainstreaming exercise, especially in building the analytical capacity of technocrats. The TGNP also took part in Tanzania's Public Expenditure Review. In South Africa, the most visible outcome of the budget initiative in government has been a discussion of gender issues woven into budget documents tabled by the Minister of Finance. South Africa also has a requirement that departments disaggregate output indicators when preparing their submissions for the budget process.

- *Developing economic literacy and participation:* The Uganda Women's Caucus documents how the GBI helped demystify budget processes for new women legislators. This led to the discovery that only six to eight officials create the budgets, and that there was only a 5 per cent variation in allocations each year, which means that they perpetuate the biases and prejudices every year. The Caucus has since engaged in a campaign to make the budget more transparent and to reform budgetary processes. In South Africa, the simplified *Money Matters* has been converted into workshop materials that government and civil society audiences use for simple budgeting concepts. This year, a South African NGO, Women's Net, worked with the WBI in setting up a web site where women could make comments on the budget to be forwarded to the Minister of Finance. The TGNP produced a simplified version of its research findings as well as flyers in Kiswahili.

Conclusion

Far more research is needed about the links between gender and governance in Africa. We take inspiration from Swedish Speaker Birgitta Dahl:

> The most interesting aspect of the Swedish Parliament is not that we have 45 per cent representation of women, but that the majority of women and men bring relevant social experience to the business of parliament. This is what makes the difference. Men bring with them experience of real life issues, of raising children, of running a home...and women are allowed to be what we are, and to act according to our own unique personality. Neither men nor women have to conform to a traditional role. (Karam, 1999)

This would be a critical measure of whether we have succeeded in creating truly representative and responsive governance.

Notes

[1] Report of the United Nations to the Fourth World Conference on Women in Beijing in 1995.

[2] Thenjiwe Mtintso, former Deputy Secretary General of the African National Congress in *Women in Politics and Decision Making in SADC: Beyond 30% in 2005*. Report of the proceedings of a conference held in Gaborone, Botswana, March 28 to April 1. (SADC, 1999).

[3] http://www.worldbank.org/publicsector/overview.htm.

[4] http://magnet.undp.org/policy/default.htm.

[5] http://www.oecd.org/dac/.

[6] SADC Declaration on Gender and Development, Blantyre, 1997, September.

[7] Convention on Elimination of all Forms of Discrimination Against Women, 18 December 1979. G. A. Res. 34/180, 34 UNGADR, supp. (No. 46), art. 3.

[8] Thenjiwe Mtintso, in SADC (1999).

[9] In *Beyond Inequalities, Women in Namibia*, the author relays how, while sitting as a research adviser to a ministerial committee, one of the male members gave a long speech about how nice it was to have a 'flower' on that committee, since it demonstrated 'mothers' commitment to their children'.

12

DANIEL MANNING

Realizing Rights through Advocacy: The Role of Legal Services Organizations in Promoting Human Rights & Attacking Poverty

Good governance is perhaps the single most important factor in eradicating poverty and promoting development. (Kofi Annan quoted in UNDP, *Human Development Report*, 2002: 51)

WHILE good governance is the aspiration, bad governance is the reality for the majority of poor people throughout the world. They are victims of violence, corruption, and deadly neglect. Laws are often harmful, discriminatory, or simply irrelevant to the real needs of the poor. Lawmakers do not listen. Law enforcement is malicious or arbitrary. Courts are hostile, corrupt, indifferent, or inaccessible. Change, however, is taking place. Poor people are demanding that governments hear them, and NGOs are forcing governments to pay attention.

There appears to be general agreement among the international community that democracy and human rights are essential to development. The challenge is how to move from a world with massive numbers of people living in dire poverty to one where government is transparent, democratic, and participatory, and where poor people become progressively healthier, better educated, and wealthier by using their civil and political rights to promote their economic, social, and cultural rights.

This chapter argues that poor people are more likely to gain control over their lives if they have access to legal information, advice, and representation. Skilled, independent legal services NGOs are the best way to provide legal help for the poor. Legal services organizations can assist in building democracy and enforcing rights because:

- Poor people are their clients, and hence the poor give them directions, so that the organizations work on issues that are critical to the poor.
- They can educate and advise people about their rights.
- They provide support for people to advocate for themselves.
- They can work to enforce existing rights.
- They are able to advocate for the creation of new rights.
- They can create and improve democratic institutions.
- Their advocacy helps to reform the judiciary.
- They help to expose corruption.

Legal services organizations work on vitally important problems. They help women get protection from domestic violence. They work with people with HIV/AIDS, as well as working on employment, housing, land, and health care issues.

173

Commitment to Building Democracy and Promoting Human Rights is Necessary to Attacking Poverty

In the United Nations' 2000 Millennium Declaration, all 189 member states committed themselves to eradicate extreme poverty and hunger, achieve universal primary education, promote gender equality and the empowering of women, reduce child mortality, improve maternal health, combat diseases like HIV/AIDS and malaria, ensure environmental sustainability, and develop a global partnership for development by 2015. To accomplish this, the Declaration states that the member states 'will spare no effort to promote democracy and strengthen the rule of law, as well as respect for all internationally recognized human rights and fundamental freedoms, including the right to development' (para 24). Particular emphasis was placed on 'Meeting the special needs of Africa: We will support the consolidation of democracy in Africa and assist Africans in their struggle for lasting peace, poverty eradication and sustainable development, thereby bringing Africa into the mainstream of the world economy' (ibid.).

The United Nations Development Program's *Human Development Report 2002: Deepening Democracy in a Fragmented World* poses and answers the question: 'Good governance – for what?' From the human development perspective, good governance is democratic governance. Democratic governance means that:

- People's human rights and fundamental freedoms are respected, allowing them to live with dignity.
- People have a say in decisions that affect their lives.
- People can hold decision-makers accountable.
- Inclusive and fair rules, institutions and practices govern social interactions.
- Women are equal partners with men in private and public spheres of life and decision-making.
- People are free from discrimination based on race, ethnicity, class, gender or any other attribute.
- The needs of future generations are reflected in current policies.
- Economic and social policies are responsive to people's needs and aspirations.
- Economic and social policies aim at eradicating poverty and expanding the choices that all people have in their lives (UNDP, 2002: Box 2.1).

The 2002 *Human Development Report* is only one in a steady stream of reports, declarations, and papers to affirm the key role of democracy in development. The New Partnership for Africa's Development's (NEPAD) *Declaration on Democracy, Political, Economic and Corporate Governance* affirms the commitment of participating states to eradicate poverty, support human rights, uphold the rule of law, and promote good governance (NEPAD, 2002b: Preamble). The challenge, of course, is to translate the lofty abstractions of democracy and human rights into actions that change the lives of poor people. Accomplishing the goal of real change requires creating enforceable rights, building institutions that will enforce these rights, and enabling poor people to use the institutions.

HUMAN RIGHTS ARE ENFORCEABLE
Traditionally, the international community views human rights as having distinct components – with civil and political rights on the one hand, and

economic, social, and cultural rights on the other. Many governments, and even some human rights advocates, consider civil and political rights to be the primary human rights and treat economic, social, and cultural rights as worthy, but unenforceable, aspirations. 'It is not erroneous to describe economic, social, and cultural rights as the "ugly sister" to the more widely recognized civil and political rights. Not only is there a lackluster approach to their effective realization, but lingering questions exist about their conception. Some have even gone so far as to argue that economic and social rights are not rights; they are merely unenforceable individual or group entitlements' (Oloka-Onyango, 1995).

Treating human rights as divisible and, in part, inspirational undercuts all human rights. Rather, the international community should view all rights as mutually reinforcing one another. 'Political freedom empowers people to claim their economic and social rights, while education increases their ability to demand economic and social policies that respond to their priorities' (UNDP, 2002: 53). Political and civil rights provide the base on which to build democratic institutions. Economic, social, and cultural rights supply the values that guide the work of these institutions. The African [Banjul] Charter on Human and Peoples' Rights declares the inter-connectedness of all human rights:

> It is henceforth essential to pay particular attention to the right to development and that civil and political rights cannot be dissociated from economic, social and cultural rights in their conception as well as universality and that the satisfaction of economic, social and cultural rights is a guarantee for the enjoyment of civil and political rights.

It is 'futile to speak of the right of participation in conditions where basic necessities, such as food, shelter, and water are beyond the reach of the majority of the population' (Oloko-Onyango, 2000: 44). A person cannot exercise democratic rights when her very existence is threatened, while conversely, as Amartya Sen demonstrates, famines do not occur in democracies (Sen, 1999). The answer is 'for a human being to be considered whole, he or she must be able to enjoy both civil and political rights and economic, social and cultural rights as well...Conceived in this fashion, human rights then becomes the bedrock of a wholesome and integrated approach to sustainable human development' (Oloko-Onyango, 2000: 44).

The integrated approach to human rights can only work if people can realize all such rights in practice. People tend to view this issue as primarily a question of whether courts can enforce economic, social, and cultural rights. 'Frequent objection focuses on the issue of justiciability. The argument most often heard is that economic, social, and cultural rights are simply not justiciable. In other words, they cannot be enforced through litigation and judicial enforcement in the way that civil and political rights can' (Oloko-Onyango, 1995: 56–7). The question of whether courts can enforce these rights has two responses. First, a growing body of experience shows that courts can make a difference. Second, litigation, or at least litigation alone, is not always the most effective way to enforce rights. As to the justifiability issue, Indian and South African courts have disproved this objection. 'The experience of Social Action Litigation (SAL) in India dramatically radicalized human rights activism in that country, and, prompted by a sympathetic Judiciary, provided an exemplar of the use of law in the service of broadly-defined human freedoms' (ibid.). Sen supports this view by observing that public interest litigation and class actions can serve as 'catalysts for drawing neglected issues into the limelight of open scrutiny and social challenge' (Sen, 1999: 19). Justice Albie Sachs, of the South African Constitutional Court, makes the same point (Sachs, 2000b). The Constitutional Court has issued several decisions that demonstrate the significance and justifiability of incorporating economic rights into the South African Constitution. While courts cannot create resources, they can push for the effective use of available resources and can compel the legislature and executive to implement 'progressively' a priority to meet basic rights enshrined in the constitution.

Whatever the power of the courts, litigation is only a part of the answer to effective realization of rights. Muna Ndulo, in addressing the issue of promoting prosperity in Africa, comments:

> Democracy means the freedom of the people to determine their life-destinies such as the right to build their own organizations, residences, schools and cultural institutions... Largely, a democracy is less of a formalistic system than an attitude. It is a way of approaching the business of government, setting up rules for government, a way of creating enough checks and balances... (Ndulo, 1998: 87–8)

Rights come into being and are enforced in large measure because of people's attitudes and expectations.

The history of women's struggle to seek protection from domestic abuse is a compelling example of the grassroots creation of rights. Women all over the world have spoken up against permissive abuse. Through mutual support, education, and advocacy, women demand governments adopt laws to prohibit domestic violence. They insist that the police protect them, not look the other way, or, worse, support their abusers. They are teaching the health care profession to take the problem seriously. They are forcing courts to hear cases and grant remedies for what courts traditionally view as 'private matters'. Of course, protecting women from domestic abuses still has a huge distance to travel, but women have made considerable progress. While the international covenants such as CEDAW provide inspiration and a set of guiding principles, change has come from the ground level. The extent that women are gaining protection from violence has come about in part due to a change in expectations on the part of individual women and of the societies of which they are a part. Courts are an important part of the emerging protection systems, but their effectiveness depends on the attitudes of both the victims and the abusers.

Realization of Human Rights Requires a Fair and Accessible System of Justice

An effective justice system is an essential component of a developed democracy. Sen argues: 'The conceptual integrity of development requires that we value the emergence and consolidation of a successful legal and judicial system as a valuable part of the process of development itself' (Sen, 2000: 14). Legal development, Sen points out, is not just about what the law is, but rather about the enhancement of people's capabilities and their freedom to exercise rights and entitlements. The system of justice works for all members of society for a society to be truly developed.

A fair and accessible system of justice is essential to the realization of human rights. The justice system, however, is much more than the courts. The system of justice is a set of values and institutions committed to the rule of law and to the advancement of human rights.[1] A true system of justice requires a knowledgeable citizenry, a culture of rights, open government at all levels, democratic legislative bodies, fair laws, judicial review, and an independent, accessible judicial system.[2] At its core, the system of justice must embody fundamental human rights if it is to meet the needs of the poor. Largely, these rights exist only as goals in international human rights instruments. Even if incorporated into national constitutions, statutes or regulations do not always codify them, nor the executive apply them, nor does the judiciary enforce them. To the extent that institutions exist for enforcing rights, they are often inaccessible and/or biased. Serious as these deficiencies are, correcting them still leaves the larger question of whether the system of justice can address the core issues of poverty.

The challenge is to figure out how to make the justice system truly work to advance the critical interests of the poor. The basic answer is to make it possible for the government to hear the poor. The starting point is to educate people about their rights, but this is truly only the beginning. Rights do not mean anything in the abstract; the state must enforce them in practice. Enforcement requires advice, advocacy, and effective institutions. Ample experience demonstrates that the poor have a significantly greater chance of being heard and actually realizing their rights if they have access to independent, skilled legal advice and representation. Legal advocacy NGOs are the best means to provide the poor with effective legal assistance.

Legal Services Organizations: An Effective Means to Promote Good Government and Allow the Poor to be Heard

Legal services organizations operate throughout the world. Some are devoted exclusively to representing poor people in civil legal matters. Others provide a wide range of social services in addition to legal advocacy. Labor, human rights, women's rights, and government organizations provide legal representation. In some countries, several organizations collaborate on programs ranging from legal literacy and community legal education to public interest litigation, high court appeals, and legislative lobbying. Law schools frequently use clinical legal education programs both to train students and to advance the interests of disadvantaged groups. Funding comes from national governments, international development agencies, foundations, court user fees, law societies, and private contributions. Paid staff, volunteer attorneys, government attorneys, lawyers that the government reimburses for their services, paralegals, and community advocates provide services. There is no single model for providing legal assistance for poor people concerning civil law issues. This chapter focuses on the work of legal advocacy NGOs as a component of systems to meet the legal needs of the poor.

The day-to-day work of legal advocacy NGOs is quite basic. They keep people from being evicted. They protect workers from discrimination and enable pensioners to collect benefits. The NGOs help women with divorces, child custody, and claims for maintenance. They get court orders to protect women from domestic violence. Working with other groups, they prevent communities from being dispossessed. They help people get access to water, electricity, health care, education, and other basic services. More abstractly, they enable people to think differently about themselves in relation to their spouses, landlords, employers, and government agencies that have power over their lives. This helps to create a culture of rights. They also work to help change the rules, whether embodied in constitutions, statutes, regulations, municipal ordinances, leases, or the myriad of other codes that determine what happens to poor people. They change the way that judges, bureaucrats, and the police apply the rules. They work with and for their clients, and collaborate with other organizations to meet their clients' basic needs. In the long run, change is the essence of the work they do – from change for a particular individual on an immediate problem to, whenever possible, lasting change that empowers people to have control over their own lives. In order to be effective, a legal advocacy NGO must have certain core values and attributes: loyalty to clients, independence, skill, and the ability to offer a range of services.

CLIENT LOYALTY

Client loyalty is a relatively straightforward concept. It simply means that the lawyer is obligated to advocate zealously for the client. If the lawyer cannot do that, whether because of personal reasons or conflicting obligations to other clients, s/he must not take the case or must withdraw if such circumstances arise during the course of representation. It does not mean that the lawyer blindly does the client's bidding. The objectives and means of representation must be lawful.[3] The lawyer must not wrongfully use the legal system to the disadvantage of others. But within those limits, a lawyer's job is to advise the client conscientiously, present the client's case forcefully and effectively, and resolve the matter on the terms that the client sets. In providing representation, the profession obligates lawyers to maintain confidentiality regarding matters the client discloses. Proper legal advice depends on the client telling the lawyer everything without the fear of disclosure.

While the intent of ethical rules is to control the relationship between individual clients and lawyers, they must also represent organizational values. Poor people must be able to rely on the fact that they will get advice and representation that their interest guides when they seek help from a legal services organization. Without that assurance, people cannot bring real problems to the organization and real solutions cannot be developed.

INDEPENDENCE

Client loyalty in turn requires independence. People who can afford lawyers are in effect paying for loyalty. Poor people who cannot pay lawyers have a different dynamic. Inevitably, whoever pays for free legal assistance for the poor has influence over who the clients are and what is done for them. To the extent that the existing legal order is oppressive and must be challenged, there is an inherent contradiction in having the powers-that-be (the government) pay for legal services that enable the poor to change the rules.[4] This dilemma lacks an easy answer. Poor people themselves simply cannot pay. While some labor organizations are able to raise money for lawyers and communities can come up with money in isolated instances, money must come from outside in the overwhelming majority of cases.

This is not an argument against government funding of legal services. On the contrary, there is a strong case that government provision of legal services is one of the hallmarks of a mature democracy. In one form or another, the majority of developed countries provide civil legal assistance for the poor. The recent US experience notwithstanding, there are ways of having government funding without compromising client loyalty and organizational independence to any significant degree. Nevertheless, if stable democracies in developed countries cannot resist limiting the types of legal services, the problem is significantly worse in developing countries.[5] It is simply unrealistic to expect a government with very little money to pay for services that enable lawyers to sue the government. It is not, however, an all-or-nothing situation. A government-funded system can pay for basic legal services on routine matters, while NGOs with other funding can address more systemic issues. Whatever the arrangement, the lesson from experience is that truly independent advocacy is necessary for real change.

SKILL

Skill is the third necessary attribute of an effective legal services organization. It is not simply a question of legal expertise. Knowledge of the law and advocacy skills are, of course, necessary, but effective representation requires much more. Skill encompasses the ability to communicate effectively with clients and to have a deep understanding of the issues that they face. This requires language skills and the ability to understand a client's culture, religion, ethnic identity, and economic circumstances. Ideally, this means that the lawyers speak the language and come from the community. Though this is usually not the case, there are ways of compensating for the gaps between lawyers and clients by training community investigators, advocates and translators, and by the investment of time to learn about a client's background and circumstances. In addition, lawyers and other advocates from the legal services organization should be present in the communities where their clients live on a regular basis.

Skill also includes the ability to deal with the institutions and organizations that influence the lives of poor people and to advocate in the fora that can provide remedies. Thus, legal service organizations must understand who has power and who exercises it, whether it is government, employers, landlords, religious institutions, or the myriad of other powerful entities that determine the allocation of resources within the society. They must have a sophisticated understanding of how to get redress for their clients, whether through the courts, the media, legislative bodies, the administrative rule-making process, institution building, negotiations, or other means.

Beyond providing advice and representation, a legal services organization must have the skill to counsel and represent groups. While such work requires the same basic set of legal skills that go into effective individual work, it also requires more. It requires respect for poor people and their ability to act collectively in their own interests. It requires an understanding of group dynamics, as they are forming and as they take action. Furthermore, organizations need to understand that pursuing legal claims in certain ways – the pursuit of class action litigation is a typical example – can empower lawyers and disempower the group because it puts the lawyer and not the group in control of strategy.[6] While advocacy on behalf of an individual can produce fundamental systemic change, group work, for the most part, is what enables legal services organizations to make a difference.

RANGE OF SERVICES

No single legal strategy or form of assistance by itself can make a lasting difference. Legal literacy can inform people of their rights but offers no guarantee of protection or enforcement of those rights. At the other end of the spectrum, ringing pronouncements of constitutional courts will not change daily life for poor people without political and practical support for the enforcement of decisions. Individual cases can produce major changes for the immediate beneficiaries, but helping a thousand out of a million people does not necessarily alter the lives of the poor. Reformed courts cannot, in and of themselves, ensure that oppressed communities get sanitation, clean water, electricity, or jobs.

In order for legal advocacy to make a difference, the entire range of strategies must be available for use by poor people and their communities. The strategies build on one another. Literacy promotes access. People who pursue their cases with legal aid lawyers in reformed courts can educate judges and break new ground for the un-represented people who follow. Groups acting with legal advice change laws that have an impact on all poor people. Communities that win victories that ensure their survival go on to build schools, health centers, and businesses that create jobs. When advocacy resolves legitimate claims, they convert retribution into reconstruction. Collaboration between legal advocacy organizations and service providers enables people to survive while they vindicate their rights.

It is not necessary or often even feasible for a single organization to provide the entire range of legal services that are required to make a difference. However, it is critical that any system includes organizations that embody the core values of client loyalty, independence, and skill. NGOs are best situated to promote those values. With proper support, NGOs can develop the required expertise, adopt a philosophy that puts clients at the center of all work, and take measures to insulate the organization from undue influence by outside forces. Government-funded legal aid can serve these same purposes, but only with proper protection from political influence. Even without this protection, legal aid can provide useful services. Similarly, law school clinics, *pro bono* services, and public education campaigns can extend the reach of core legal services programs.

In the end, however, there is no substitute for organizations with a clear mission to represent the poor in whatever way is required, and that have the expertise to do so and the institutional credibility with the communities they serve, as well as the capacity to engage in sustained advocacy efforts and the ability to take on powerful foes. Legal advocacy NGOs with these attributes can make a lasting difference for their clients in the following ways:

- They help the poor speak for themselves on matters of critical importance by educating them about their rights and supporting them in the assertion of those rights.
- They represent poor people in courts, legislatures, and other government and private arenas that make significant decisions.
- They advance judicial reform by pushing to open courts to all members of society.

- They promote gender equity.
- They facilitate reconstruction and redevelopment following major conflicts.
- Overall, they advance the social and economic well-being of society generally and the poor in particular by addressing core issues of housing, income, family, health, and education.

Africa Legal Advocacy NGOs: Building Democracy and Helping the Poor Gain Control over their Lives

There are dozens, and by some measures hundreds, of legal advocacy NGOs in Africa that are dealing, on a daily basis, with some of the most serious problems facing the poor. These are problems such as HIV/AIDS, violence, the lack of health care, the lack of clean water and sanitation, the lack of education, gender discrimination, unemployment, landlessness, and homelessness. Some NGOs are large, national organizations with highly skilled, paid staff. Others are fledgling organizations relying on volunteers with great spirit but little training or experience. In some cases, they establish constitutional rights affecting entire countries; in most cases, they are solving immediate problems one person at a time. Collectively they make a huge difference. What follows are a few examples of the type of work that is going on across the continent. The examples are the FIDA and the Legal Resources Centre in Ghana, and the Legal Resources Centre in South Africa

FIDA – GHANA

UN Secretary General Kofi Annan stated, 'It can no longer come as a surprise to anyone, including the men of Africa, that gender equality is more than a goal in itself. It is the precondition for meeting the challenge of reducing poverty, promoting sustainable development and building good governance'.[7] Though Ghana has a comprehensive framework of laws that protect women's rights, the problem is the implementation and enforcement of the laws (Oye Lithur, 2000). Often women do not know, or have an effective means of asserting, their rights. Women in rural areas have an especially hard time in gaining access to justice. Institutions that states intend to protect women against violence do not do their job. 'There is a gap between policy and policy implementation. Institutions do not always or consistently put legislation into practice. Legislators who do nothing about this inactivity further compound this problem... By trivializing violence, State agencies, like the family, collude in perpetuating violence' (ibid. citing Cusack, 1999).

A group of dedicated female Ghanaian lawyers committed to improving the situation of women and children and to strengthening their position in the overall developmental process of Ghana set up the FIDA – Ghana[8] in 1974 as an affiliate of the International Federation of Women Lawyers.[9] The organization conducts seminars to educate women about their rights on topics including family law, inheritance rights, and domestic violence. FIDA – Ghana reviews laws and traditional practices to assess their impact on women. It also translates laws into simple English and some Ghanaian languages as part of its legal literacy program.

Since 1984, FIDA – Ghana has run legal aid clinics to provide advice and assistance to women unable to afford lawyers. The clinics provide assistance on matters such as divorce, child custody, inheritance, employment discrimination, and domestic violence. They offer counseling sessions and use various alternative dispute resolution methods like mediation, conciliation, and arbitration. The legal aid program uses paid staff and volunteer lawyers, social workers, and psychiatrists to provide services.

Over the years, the organization has undertaken a variety of projects. In 1993, it mounted an effort to eliminate the practice of *Trokosi*, which is 'where virgin young girls are given as sacrifices to the gods as compensation for crimes committed by their ancestors' (ibid.). Priests, who ultimately abuse them sexually and psychologically, keep these young girls in camps. FIDA – Ghana was instrumental in bringing to light the plight of these young girls, and played a crucial role in getting parliament to criminalize this practice. Because of this work, some of the young women were freed.

FIDA – Ghana also conducts campaigns to increase public awareness of domestic violence and to persuade parliament to establish criminal penalties, helps organize workshops for women candidates for public office, and provides gender sensitivity training to the police. It played a significant role in passing an intestate succession law, which marks a significant change from customary law. The law enables Ghanaian widows to inherit property. While much work is needed to implement this law, under the old regime a woman whose husband died without leaving a will was stripped of all her possessions and left with no means of support for either herself or her children (Fenrich and Higgins, 2001).

In making the case for the type of work done by FIDA – Ghana, Oye Lithur cites a World Bank study showing that women head 40 per cent of African households and supply 70 per cent of the labor for food production. 'In spite of this, in many societies in Sub-Saharan Africa, a wide range of laws and regulatory practices still prohibit and/or impede women to a greater extent than men. These distortions in resource allocations, which result from this discrimination, carry high development costs' (Oye Lithur, 2000: 00). FIDA –Ghana seeks to end this type of discrimination.

LEGAL RESOURCES CENTRE – GHANA
The Legal Resources Centre – Ghana was established in 1997.[10] Its initial objectives were to:

* promote human rights awareness;
* link victims of human rights violations with institutions established by the state to enforce the protection of human rights;
* provide through competent personnel other legal assistance as the Centre may deem necessary to victims of human rights violations; and to
* serve as a centre for legal research in human rights and development.

The LRC later expanded its objectives to include:

* governance issues, especially grassroots participatory governance;
* policy advocacy at the local and national levels; and
* promoting key economic and social rights.

The Centre is organized in three main departments: public education, legal aid, and research and advocacy. The public education department develops educational programs in response to community requests. The topics normally relate to inheritance laws, marriage and divorce laws, children's rights, women's rights, political rights, civic responsibilities, economic and social rights, and citizens-police relations. More in-depth seminars on topics of particular importance often follow the general community educational sessions.

The legal aid department provides advice and representation to indigent individuals. While litigation is undertaken when necessary, the emphasis is on alternative dispute resolution, both arbitration and mediation. The Centre recognizes that traditional social and political bonds are still strong in Ghana, as most members of the communities look to their elders and chiefs for dispute resolution and conflict management. The Centre conducts workshops to increase the capacities of local leaders and chiefs to resolve disputes efficiently and manage conflicts effectively. It set up a community Alternative Dispute Resolution Centre, which chiefs and community leaders control with support from the Centre. The Centre is also attempting to establish an arbitration center for more formal alternative dispute resolution.

The research and advocacy department conducts investigations and develops advocacy campaigns related to issues that the Centre's public education and legal aid work identifies. The Centre then sets up committees to address these issues, including committees for community and youth leaders and committees on topics like gender, health, education, and dispute resolution. The research unit provides support for the committees by obtaining the information needed to engage in advocacy. The department also includes a Parliamentary Advocacy Team, which collects and analyzes draft bills, provides information to interest groups, and assists them in preparing presentations for parliament. The Centre organizes workshops for interest groups and members of Parliament.

A legal team conducted a survey of households in one of the communities it serves and convened a series of grassroots workshops to develop an advocacy program for the Centre. The results identified two significant issues: (i) affordable health services, particularly through the full enforcement of statutory exemptions to health care user fees; and (ii) adequate sanitation services and infrastructure, including toilets, wastewater drainage, and garbage disposal. The Centre decided to take on projects in both of these areas. The projects combine a public awareness campaign with legislative and litigation strategies.

The goal of the sanitation part of the project is to create a healthy living environment. The basic goal of the affordable health care project is to implement properly the user fee exemption. The World Bank's structural adjustment program had initially imposed user fees as a means of improving health care quality. In practice, these fees have had several negative effects. While an exemption based on income exists in theory, the failure to enforce the exemption denies health care access to many poor people. Furthermore, the fees are a regressive form of taxation, and have not produced quality improvements. Both the Ghanaian government and the World Bank acknowledge that the government must enforce the fee exemptions to ensure the right to health for all Ghanaians.

The Centre has several larger goals for these projects as well. First, to raise consciousness among poor Ghanaians about human rights in general, as well as the right to health care and to participate in the democratic process. Another goal is to promote reform in the courts, the legislature, the executive agencies, and the human rights commission. The final larger goal is to build up the capacity of institutions and civil society to advance human rights. Each of the projects has a multi-stage process. On the health financing issue, the Centre undertook research and gathered evidence about widespread violations of the exemption law. In September 2001, it filed a law suit in the Ghana High Court contesting the government's failure to enforce the exemption law as a violation of the right to health. It also brought health care providers together to discuss steps that the health facilities could take to ensure enforcement of the exemption law. Based on these discussions, health care providers agreed on eight administrative practices for all health facilities to follow. The Centre then presented the practices at a public hearing and community workshops.

At the same time, it conducted an education campaign with community-based 'mother groups'. These groups monitored the government health clinics' compliance with the law. The Centre also engaged in advocacy with the World Bank to put additional pressure on the government to grant the required exemptions. Finally, discussions were held with members of the Ghanaian Parliament's standing Committee on Health about strategies for ensuring that the government fully fund and equitably administer the user-fee exemption statute.

The group gathered testimony on the sanitation issue from community residents about the multiple health impacts of living without an adequate toilet, garbage collection, or wastewater drainage, and held meetings with community opinion-leaders to devise strategies for addressing the local government's failure to meet its sanitation-related obligations. The legal team researched the local government's legal obligations surrounding sanitation and the framework for funding sanitation infrastructure. It then developed a potential litigation strategy.

Once the group had finished the background work, they mobilized community-based organizations to monitor the local government's compliance with its statutory duties to provide toilets, garbage collection, and sanitation services. Organizations made demands that the Accra Metropolitan Assembly comply with its statutory duties regarding environmental health and sanitation. Residents in large community meetings informed elected officials and donors about the serious health and sanitation problems and their campaign to deal with these problems.

The Centre conducted a comprehensive evaluation of the health and sanitation project, as of the end of 2002. A final report (Aryeetey et al., 2003) has been issued, concluding that 'the LRC's health campaign is an ongoing unique experience in how a developmental issue – health – can be cast in rights language and operationalized as such. It shows how human rights language and tactics can be used to mobilize ordinary citizens to identify, analyze, plan and execute activities around a developmental issue. The project also shows how human rights tools can be used to engage various institutions, local, national and international, in working to improve a developmental issue.' Clearly, the project has both mobilized members of the affected communities and captured the attention of officials. As just one example of this, the Parliamentary Select Committee on Local Government and Rural Development held a special public hearing on sanitation problems in August 2002 to make recommendations to Parliament. Confirming the significance of the problem, the Office of Parliament issued a statement that 'Parliament has been much concerned with the deterioration of the environmental and sanitation situation in many Ghanaian communities, particularly within the Accra Metropolitan Assembly Area. Almost on a daily basis, the media have reported bad sanitation and unacceptable environmental practices in various places in the Accra Metropolis, which carries negative implications for national development'.[11]

Even at this stage of the project it is fair to conclude that the Centre has not only made progress on the basic goals of improving health and sanitation, it has made a strong start towards the goals of raising awareness and engaging institutions in the process of advancing human rights.

LEGAL RESOURCES CENTRE – SOUTH AFRICA

The Legal Resources Centre (LRC) is a national organization[12] committed to serving the interests of the poor:

> The Legal Resources Centre is an independent, client-based, non-profit public interest law centre which uses law as an instrument of justice. It works for the development of a fully democratic society based on the principle of substantive equality, by providing legal services for the vulnerable and marginalized, including the poor, homeless and landless people and communities of South Africa who suffer discrimination by reason of race, class, gender, disability or by reason of social, economic and historical circumstances.

Inspired by our history, the Constitution, and international human rights standards, the Legal Resources Centre, for both itself and its work, is committed to:

- ensuring that the principles, rights and responsibilities enshrined in our National Constitution are respected, promoted, protected and fulfilled;
- building respect for the rule of law and constitutional democracy;
- enabling the vulnerable and marginalized to assert and develop their rights;
- promoting gender and racial equality and opposing all forms of unfair discrimination;
- contributing to the development of human rights jurisprudence;
- contributing to the social and economic transformation of society.

To achieve these aims the LRC seeks creative and effective solutions by using a range of strategies including impact litigation, law reform, participation in partnerships and development processes, education and networking within and outside South Africa (Legal Resources Centre, *Mission Statement*, 6 May 1998).

The LRC began operations in 1979 and has operated through three distinct phases over the past 20 or so years: the apartheid era (1979–90), the dismantling of apartheid and the transition to democracy (1990–94), and the era of constitutional democracy (1994–present). The LRC was one of many civil society organizations in South Africa that opposed apartheid. The LRC's unique contribution is that it took on the apartheid government by pointing out the contradictions and lunacy of its own legal edifice, and did so by using the law (Abel, 1995; see also Foreword by Nelson Mandela).

In some of its most successful early efforts, the LRC worked closely with residents of communities threatened with forced removals. For example, in the mid-1980s the 'disestablishment of the settlement and removal to a "homeland"' 20 kilometers away threatened thousands of residents of Oukasie, a black township on the border of a white community near Pretoria (ibid.). The community organized itself and began a concerted campaign to remain in and upgrade their homes. At several key stages of the struggle, the LRC obtained court orders invalidating actions by the local white government. The court orders themselves did not win the fight, but they did enable the community to continue its political campaign. However, throughout the long battle LRC lawyers consistently worked with the community members to develop a negotiation strategy and advise them of their legal claims and vulnerabilities (ibid.: Chap. 12).[13]

In the end the community of Oukasie not only survived, it thrived. In 1991, it established the Oukasie Development Trust, which included a LRC lawyer, to redevelop what had been a very dilapidated settlement. By 1997, the Trust had obtained funds to develop 2050 sites for housing and a clinic with a maternity wing, as well as obtaining electricity service, building two schools and a community hall, establishing a day care center, securing subsidies for 600 additional houses, constructing a road, and building a sports field. Programs for economic development are under way, including sand mining, the development of a plant to crush and utilize stone from a nearby mine, an eco-tourism project, and several ventures involving recycling and agriculture (Oukasie Development Trust, 1997; 1995).

The end of apartheid and the advent of democracy have, of course, brought profound changes to South African society. The government is no longer the enemy of the people. On the contrary, there is a massive effort under way to improve the lives of all South African citizens. The LRC has been very much a part of this change. Key staff members worked with the negotiating parties to formulate the new Constitution, which is the most progressive in the world in terms of protecting and promoting human rights. Some of the organization's most talented and experienced lawyers joined the new government in 1994 – as judges (Constitutional Court, High Court, Land Claims Court), top civil servants at all levels of government, and special change agents in entities like the world-renowned Truth and Reconciliation Commission.

In order to continue its vital role in building a new democratic society, the LRC reorganized itself to focus on two major areas: (i) constitutional law, and (ii) land, housing, and development. The new Constitution and Bill of Rights created significant opportunities for real change. As Justice Arthur Chaskalson, President of the Constitutional Court,[14] said, the role of the LRC is 'as important as it has ever been. Under the new constitutional order, it is able to function within a legal framework which enables it to do more for the poor and downtrodden people of our country, and ignorant of their rights, than ever before. It is able to apply its skills to give substance to the provisions of the Bill of Rights, and to the upholding of the rule of law, which is a foundational value of our new democracy'.[15]

Justice Chaskalson's prediction that the new constitutional order would enable the LRC to do more for the poor of South Africa came to fruition in the judgment by the Constitutional Court in *Government of the Republic of South Africa v. Grootboom*.[16] As described by Geoff Budlender, the lead LRC lawyer on the case, Irene Grootboom was one of about 900 people (adults and children) who

> lived in appalling conditions. They decided to move out, and occupied vacant privately owned land across the road. The owner, supported by the local council, obtained a

magistrate's court order for their eviction. Their homes were demolished. They were now truly homeless: they could not go back to where they had come from, because other people had occupied that land. They had literally nowhere they could live. While there is a very large government-housing programme, the waiting list is such that they would have to wait for many years, perhaps as many as twenty, for proper housing to be made available to them. Meanwhile they would have simply nowhere they could lawfully live. The government said that it could and would do nothing to assist them. They applied to court for an order to require the government to provide them with housing or shelter, and basic services.[17]

When the case reached the Constitutional Court, the issue was whether the Court could require the government to meet the immediate and short-term needs of people in a desperate situation. Section 26(2) of the South African Constitution provides: 'The state must take reasonable legislative and other measures, within its available resources, to achieve the progressive realisation of this right'. The government defended the case by arguing that it had adopted a carefully considered, comprehensive nationwide housing program that fully met the Constitution's requirements. The Court acknowledged that the program represented a 'major achievement' in which 'considerable thought, energy, resources and expertise have been and continue to be devoted to the process of effective housing delivery'. However, there was 'no express provision to facilitate access to temporary relief for people who have no access to land, no roof over their heads, for people who are living in intolerable conditions...'

Accepting the LRC's arguments and explicitly acknowledging the organization's role, the Court ruled that the government housing program did not meet the constitutional test of reasonableness. While the national program might have been reasonable if it produced housing for poor people in a reasonably short time, given the magnitude of the problem, this simply could not happen. Under the requirements of Section 26(2): 'The nationwide housing programme falls short of obligations imposed on national government to the extent that it fails to recognise that the state must provide for relief for those in desperate need'.[18] In reaching this conclusion, the Court clearly established the justiciability of social and economic rights.

In Budlender's opinion:

> The impact of the judgment has been varied. Government has started shifting its housing programme to have regard to the needs of people in intolerable conditions, or threatened with eviction – a process that a highly publicised land invasion has recently accelerated. When local councils seek to evict homeless people, they no longer obtain a court order for the asking – courts increasingly ask the councils what they have done, and what they are going to do, to meet their Grootboom obligations in respect of the people concerned. But the Grootboom community is still living under highly unsatisfactory circumstances. Further litigation may result. Many other people continue to live in desperate circumstances. The picture is generally uneven, but I think there is no doubt that we have taken a major step forward.

With regard to land, housing, and development work, the LRC has had years of experience from the apartheid era learning about land dispossession, forced housing removals, and the devastating effects of apartheid planning on rural and urban development. Under the new order, the LRC has converted that knowledge into specialized areas of work focusing on rural and urban restitution of land rights, tenure security, housing, land law reform, and urban and rural land development. Once the LRC has helped people obtain land, it does not abandon its clients. It continues to work for the provision of basic services such as water, electricity, housing, sewerage, schools, and clinics. Legal services are sometimes required to establish frameworks for communal access to land and natural resources. Years of effort are often required.

For example, the LRC has worked with the Port Elizabeth Land and Community Restoration Association (PELCRA) since 1993, when citizens established the group to seek restitution for loss of their homes under apartheid-forced 'removal'. LRC attorneys worked closely with the group, helping them decide whether to pursue individual claims or a group restitution initiative. Having made the hard decision to seek group relief, the PELCRA reached an agreement on behalf of the 840 families with respect to 1286 urban residential sites. The national government paid R42 million for the claims, and the provincial government provided prime residential land and high-value commercial land at a discounted price. Income from the commercial property will subsidize the development of housing and community facilities. Arrangements have been made for substantial government involvement through the development process. Implementation is moving ahead and it is anticipated that people will soon be able to move into their new homes, some on land taken from them years ago.

According to PELCRA's chairperson, people must give credit for the success so far to the LRC. 'The Legal Resources Centre is the only legal agency in the country with sufficient knowledge and expertise to deal with land issues in an innovative manner. They have worked with land issues since the 1980s, they are closely involved with drawing up land legislation, I just cannot possibly conceive of any other group of lawyers being able to deal effectively with land issues of this nature in this country' (Palmer, 2001). *Grootboom* and the PELCRA case are just two examples of major work by the LRC. Equally effective advocacy has been done on issues such as the right to water, the right not to be evicted without a court order, and the right not to be discriminated against based on HIV status. Through the LRC, the country has heard the voices of the poorest South Africans as it goes about building a true democracy.

Conclusion

The work of the three organizations, the FIDA and the Legal Resources Centre in Ghana, and the LRC in South Africa, illustrates the range of legal services NGOs in activities in legal education, counseling, and advocacy in many places throughout Africa. NGOs are doing work at the individual, community, and national policy level. Unless individuals understand their rights and have the means to enforce them, progress cannot occur. Effective enforcement often requires mobilizing entire communities and changes in basic laws, policies, and institutions. Legal services NGOs have a vital role to play in working with poor people to achieve the goal of the UN Millennium Declaration of peace, poverty eradication, and sustainable development in Africa.

Notes

[1] The rule of law is often discussed as if was synonymous with democracy, but apartheid South Africa was very committed to the rule of law. Likewise, the American Constitution recognized slavery and the United States Supreme Court enforced laws that deemed slaves to be 'property.'

[2] See Ndulo (1998: 79) for a comprehensive description of the elements of a constitutional democracy.

[3] The concept of lawfulness in this context does not simply mean in compliance with existing law. It encompasses the idea of challenges to existing law based on higher law, including fundamental human rights principles.

[4] An epic struggle, which this chapter will not describe in any detail, has been going on in the US over the last 20 years. Originally funded as part of Lyndon Johnson's War on Poverty, the government explicitly designed legal services to take on state and local powers. From the Reagan Administration (1991) to the Gingrich Congress (1994), there were relentless efforts to stop legal services lawyers from challenging the existing order. Ultimately, Congress succeeded in severely limiting whom the federally funded organizations could represent and what they could do. Organizations in wealthier communities such as Boston withdrew from the federal program to avoid these restrictions.

[5] The Legal Resources Centre in South Africa (described below) has about as much political support as an advocacy organization could expect. The LRC features Nelson Mandela in the annual report and he attends key organizational events. Nonetheless, the LRC does not currently accept any significant government funds out of a concern that they would compromise its independence. (Interview with Bongani Majola, Executive Director of the LRC, 21 January 1999.)

[6] Much has been written on this topic in the US. The essential point is that lawyers sometimes have a tendency to take over when working with poor people's groups in ways that stifle the development of the group. This is not, however, an argument against doing class actions for groups, only that the lawyer must carefully advise the group of the possible downsides of such a strategy.

[7] Speech at UN Economic Commission for Africa Conference May 1998 cited in Ayisi Agyei (2000).

[8] FIDA is the Spanish acronym for the International Federation of Women Lawyers. (Federacion International d'abogadas).

[9] FIDA Ghana website, http://www2.h-net.msu.edu/~deitutu/fida/

[10] For information about the Legal Resources Centre – Ghana, see: http://www.lrc-ghana.org/

[11] 'Ghana Home Page – General News', of Thursday, 29 August 2002. http://www.ghanaweb.com/GhanaHomePage/NewsArchive/artikel.php?ID=26875

[12] The LRC is the largest and oldest non-profit public interest law organization in South Africa, with regional offices in Cape Town, Durban, Grahamstown, Pretoria, and Johannesburg.

[13] For an analysis of the role played by LRC lawyers in working with communities opposing forced removals see White (1988).

[14] Also an LRC founder and former National Director.

[15] *Legal Resources Centre Document*, April 1999 (On file with author).

[16] Constitutional Court of South Africa, 2001 (4) SA 46 (CC).

[17] Budlender, 'Justiciability of the Right to Housing – The South African Experience' www.lrc.org.za.

[18] *The Government of the Republic of South Africa v. Grootboom*, Constitutional Court of South Africa, Case CCT 11/00: 39, 45.

13

THOMAS R. LANSNER
The Media
& Information for Democracy

DOES increased access to information foster democratic development? This is certainly the received wisdom. The notion has been enshrined in Western liberal tradition by thinkers, theorists, and politicians, including Milton, Mill, Madison, Jefferson and Carlyle. It is supported more recently as crucial to human development by Amartya Sen, and broadly by democracy advocates around the world.

Anecdotally and instinctively, this sounds and feels right. Without access to information, how can a citizenry reach reasoned choices that make democratic participation meaningful?[1] And the 'sunlight' of accessible information makes operations of governmental and societal institutions more transparent, a prerequisite for the accountability that is the foundation of representative rule. Western governments, international organizations, and private donors have committed tens of millions of dollars over the last few decades to promoting open media systems and alternative media outlets they believe will promote understanding and respect for fundamental freedoms, demands for their realization, and transitions to democracy.

Systematic analysis that backs this belief, however, is largely lacking, and issues of causality and unique factors contributing to democratic transitions make statistical correlations difficult to prove convincingly.[2] Even more problematical is the role of emerging information and communications technologies in challenging authoritarian regimes and fostering democratic development. A new set of case studies suggests that the Internet can be a powerful tool for dissidents and civil society, but it is also used by repressive regimes to reinforce their rule (Kalathil and Boas, 2003).[3]

It is no mystery that media as new as instant messaging or as old as theses tacked to a door can be used for good or ill. This chapter offers an overview of how the mass media are viewed as a crucial positive component of democratic development, citizen participation and conflict resolution. It surveys efforts to assist media in countries under authoritarian rule or those undergoing democratic transitions to become an intrinsic part of these processes for democracy, and assesses the greatest challenges to their success.

'Active Open Media'

The pluralist view of the media describes a 'fourth estate' watchdog that exercises 'eternal vigilance' over societal actors to serve as a counterweight to powerful interests.[4] The muckraking tradition of crusading and investigative journalists taking on corporations, governments, religious groups, and other

190

entrenched interests is indeed alive and thriving in many parts of the world. To fulfill this role meaningfully and on a long-term basis, the media must be free, independent, diverse, and professional. A benchmark definition regarding the roles of media in democratic systems is the 1991 Windhoek Declaration on free, independent and pluralistic media.[5] These conditions are rarely fully realized and too often remain notable by their absence in developing countries.

Complementing the watchdog function is the media's 'public interest' role. The media's ability to set agendas and to provide civic forums to debate issues can be influential. German political theorist Jürgen Habermas describes the historical development of a 'public sphere' in Europe as crucial to freeing the market from the state, even if that public sphere (with media as an important element) is now seen as largely subservient to vested interests rather than a mediator between state and society (Habermas, 1984). Publicly owned media may rightly be envisioned as directly serving citizens' interests. Proponents of 'public' or 'civic' journalism argue that even private media should take up similar roles of identifying societal problems and encouraging debate about their solution.[6] The watchdog, civic forum, and public interest roles, pursued vigorously, produce the ideal of what is here described as 'active open media'.

How and when people receive information can significantly affect how they view their societies and themselves. Mass media's potential to educate, to inform – and to misinform – is immense. The content of media messages clearly influences society's perceptions and expectations, helping to shape public opinion and set public agendas. It can stir (or shame) authorities and other societal actors to action, and evoke – or perhaps inflame or incite – popular reaction.

In addressing issues around the media's role in transitional or emerging democracies, with special reference to Africa, this chapter presumes that democratic governance under the rule of law, and the broadest possible public participation therein, is desirable. Those who dispute this basic assumption will of course hold very different views on the media's importance as a tool for transparency, accountability, and engagement. Some of these arguments are referred to below, but mostly to frame problems facing the media.

Any polity that aspires to democratic structures, or at least participatory governance, is best served by active open media. Active open media must be, at least in some combination, free, independent and pluralistic, must pursue a watchdog role over the broadest array of societal institutions, and provide a public sphere of civic forums and citizen debates. Government, business, religious groups, civil society organizations, and even the press itself are subject to scrutiny by active open media. Such media are essential to provide transparency, accountability, and voice across a society.

Access, Content, and Emerging ICTs

Access to information offered by active open media is also a crucial issue. The impact of even the most vibrant mass media is intrinsically limited to those who can see or hear their messages. Without broad access, the media's power to inform, to shape agendas, and to provide a civic forum, may be severely limited. Issues of distribution, literacy, vernacular media, and consumer costs all affect access. Emerging information and communications technologies (ICTs), including the Internet and satellite broadcasting, are reaching new and diverse audiences, enabling 'many-to-many' communications, and redrawing established hierarchies of communications. Localized community media serve small areas with information needed to improve daily lives, and can be connections to the wider world. In significant areas, national sovereignty is challenged as transnational communication and coalition-building become easier.

Audience reception of information is also of central importance. Even well conceived and polished messages may not be received in the manner intended. Social, cultural, economic, ethnic, geographic, and other identity issues can cause even the most accurate information to be peremptorily rejected. Here, some may see cultural authenticity or resistance to external manipulation, and others, false consciousness. In either case, even the most powerful media inundation carrying undeniably accurate information can be dashed against powerfully held stereotypes or other social constructs.

The content of messages is also important to any analysis of media roles in promoting rights and democracy. Far more research has been performed on shaping development information, a usually politically 'safer' topic that also receives far greater funding than democracy information. The suitability of messages is frequently culturally bound, and they are often better received when embedded as part of soap operas or in other popular culture forms, a strategy that can be described as 'devetainment'.

The manifold challenges to imparting information that promotes democratic development have been taken up by numerous official and non-governmental donors and organizations. Those engaged in such activities typically subscribe to the idea that an active open media itself is not only desirable, but that committing resources to media infrastructure, improved legal and regulatory enabling environments, training, content development, and/or diversification of media control and access enhances prospects for democratic transitions and consolidation, and perhaps for social justice. The voices of Mill et al. may be heard in the background here: the fourth estate as the eternally vigilant watchdog guarding against tyranny, and as a vehicle for citizens' voices to be heard.

Yet it is not certain that free media produce a more democratic society or are one of its products. And what qualifies as open media is debatable. Even many moderate critiques of existing media structures in the most democratic societies urge a much greater popular participation in generating media content and decentralizing its means of dissemination.[7] The political economy view of media largely dismisses the possibilities of genuine public journalism or civic forums in private media. It sees the production and dissemination of media content as largely controlled by and intended to serve the class-based status quo. Chomsky's propaganda model (Chomsky and Herman, 1988) and Schiller's work (1992) back this supposition with case studies and anecdotal evidence drawn principally from American media, politics, and international policy. It can be argued that in many developing countries domestic media are usually even more demonstrably beholden to the state or elite interests through official control or the narrow economic base of most private media enterprises. In many cases, mass media consent is merely mandated rather than manufactured.

While blatant biases can often be detected in state media, with regime preservation too often masquerading as 'nation building', much information in private media is also less than balanced and fair, sometimes by partisan design, and sometimes because of poor reporting standards. The ostensible wall dividing news and editorial comment in the American media is rarely given lip service in most other countries. In many instances private media are utilized as just one means to pursue the grand prize of power.

It also must not be forgotten that if the media can be utilized to promote peace and respect for rights, they can and have been used to evoke ethnic hatred, incite violence, and manipulate people with half-truths and outright lies. How to respond to the dangers that such media present is a difficult and contentious issue.

New ICTs can be double-edged. Community radio that serves a small area or a group can help to provide important local information that may promote better health and development practices, and build solidarity and civic participation. But it may at the same time reinforce the insularity of a particular identity that resists change or co-operation. Skewed distribution of advanced ICTs may also increase gaps in local empowerment, as networked groups gain greater access to information and perhaps international resources.

There is no doubt that the media are utilized to advance parochial interests, and like other tools may be used for evil ends, as well as good. Yet this chapter proceeds from the premise that, however imperfect and far from fully realized, an active open media may be defined, as was democracy by Churchill, as the worst possible system except for all the others.

BASIC STANDARDS: OFT DENIED

The most basic international standard for media protection is clear. Article 19 of the 1948 Universal Declaration of Human Rights states succinctly that 'freedom of expression' includes the right 'to seek, receive, and impart information and ideas of all kinds, regardless of frontiers, either orally, in writing, or in print, in the form of art, or through any other media'.

This right is far from universally honored. The Freedom House Press Freedom Survey for 2002 describes 75 of 187 countries or territories assessed as 'free'. Fifty-one are rated as partly free, and 61 as not free, which includes 24 sub-Saharan African nations.[8] It is little surprise to note that the 17 countries with top scores of less than 15 on a 1 to 100 scale, with 1 being most free, are mostly developed democracies. It is an equally small shock to find among the two dozen worst scoring nations in the Press Freedom Survey most of the world's worst abusers of human rights and fundamental freedoms.

In transitional or emerging democracies, issues surrounding media freedom often involve physical safety and even the survival of journalists and their 'means of production'. They also include gross censorship and myriad forms of intimidation. Journalists and media outlets may suffer legal assault through the use of criminal defamation, sedition, and libel prosecutions that are often politically motivated and pursued under broad statutes that seem tailor-made for abuse. Protecting journalists should be an important policy aim of democratic governments and civil society groups. Without physical safety for journalists and the legal 'right to work' for media practitioners, most of the rest of this discussion is, in fact, moot.

Encouraging the legal and regulatory environments that permit open media to take root must also continue to be an important priority ('Media Law Reform', 1998). The economics of publishing or broadcasting is an area where the state can also have great influence. Restrictive licensing, selective placement of government tender advertisements, and control over permits to import equipment, papers and inks can compromise or subsidize commercial viability.

Watchdog Role: No Less and Much More

Even in more mature democratic states, which may enjoy broad prosperity and strong traditions of the rule of law, the media's watchdog role is crucial to balancing the tremendous power inherent in government, amassed by business, and sometimes accorded to other societal actors. Presenting the views and concerns of the public is another central role. Active open media serve to inform, articulate and report public opinion, to the edification of policy-makers, opinion leaders, and the public itself.

To many advocates of media freedom, especially in the United States, these are the only roles media should be expected to play: the nominally objective 'reporter' of events and the provider of 'disinterested' analysis upon which an engaged citizenry can base its informed participation in the political process. This idealistic (and certainly self-interested, sometimes illusory, and often entirely disingenuous) approach reflects the traditional US 'Journalism School 101' dictum that the media somehow stand apart from the society in which they are embedded. An ongoing argument over the merits of more admittedly conscious agenda setting, usually described as 'public' or 'civic' journalism, divides the American media community. Proponents of public journalism point out that putting something on the public record does not equal raising it to the public agenda. Acknowledging that deciding what and how events and issues are reported is intrinsically value-laden, they argue that it should be done consciously with a clear notion of the public interest as a prime consideration.

In emerging or transitional democracies, the media's role is in some ways more demanding and more difficult. Local adaptations and cultural context may produce media with distinctive characteristics. Yet the watchdog role is essential everywhere, and made more possible and powerful through international linkages facilitated by new ICTs. Who is corrupt? Are the public trust or basic rights being honored, circumvented, or trampled? And active open media can provide early warning of conflicts or other threats, and sometimes help prevent calamities. Nobel laureate Amartya Sen assigns India's free press the credit for helping that country avoid major famines since independence because its reporting stirred elected governments – concerned at the minimum about their public standing and future electoral prospects – to action when hunger reached life-threatening levels. Sen compares this to massive but largely unreported famines in China, during which that country's unaccountable authoritarian regime faced neither domestic or international pressures to save its own citizens (Sen, 1999).

In Africa, an instructive comparison is between the two oil-rich countries of Nigeria and Gabon. The former is often described as the epitome of governmental corruption. Yet this perception is at least partly due to the assiduous and sometimes dangerous and costly efforts by Nigeria's civil society and media to expose malfeasance.[9] Gabon, where President Omar Bongo and a small clique of cronies have ruled with close French support for over three decades, is today perhaps the world's most venal kleptocracy. The country's stunted civil society and weak media sector allow gross corruption to continue virtually unchallenged, as well as almost unremarked in the wider world.

An open society and free media live in a sometimes tense symbiosis. Respect for fundamental freedoms allows free media to exercise the 'eternal vigilance' necessary to preserve those freedoms, even if the media face many pressures, and are occasionally reviled as the bearers of bad news. The ills of countries with active and open media will always be more apparent to their own peoples and to the wider world – recognition essential to the possibility of their amelioration.

Media Roles in Promoting Democracy and Human Rights

An essential element of democratization is the ability of peoples around the world to understand the fundamental freedoms that are their irrevocable birthright. These rights are recognized in international human rights instruments to which most states are signatories, and are often enshrined in national constitutions. Yet citizens in many emerging democracies or countries struggling to escape autocratic rule often have little awareness or only limited understanding of their rights and their government's responsibilities to protect and promote them.

The media can play crucial roles in developing this awareness. Freedom of expression – if respected as guaranteed by Article 19 of the Universal Declaration of Human Rights – opens the way for the spread of information, education and debate. Even in transition situations where full freedom of expression is tenuous, the media can supply important information regarding citizens' rights and means of redress if they are violated. Quick advantage should be taken of any window of opportunity to explain and encourage responsible citizen participation in the democratization process. Once people learn of their rights, renewed repression can never be as effective.

However, most media practitioners in emerging democracies lack sufficient educational background or life experience to relate this information to their audiences directly or as an important component shaping their reporting. Seminars on the reporting of human rights, the rule of law and electoral processes can help bridge this gap between the *de jure* existence of these rights and the media's ability to communicate their meaning to the public. The exposition of basic civil and political rights is central to any such civic education program. But beyond describing the very existence of such rights – a surprise in itself to many people – information regarding the means of implementing and protecting them under the rule of law is necessary. The notion of accountability must be assiduously cultivated even where its proper practice is not yet realized.

Offering primers in fundamental freedoms is thus important, but certainly not enough. Journalists, editors, publishers, and other media practitioners must be encouraged and assisted in developing strategies to disseminate this information and incorporate it into their overall reporting on events in their countries and elsewhere. This is clearly not an overnight task. In the long process of democratic consolidation, the ongoing work of the media is of cardinal importance to the evolution of a new political culture that protects and promotes fundamental freedoms under the rule of law.

Global networking and support should be emphasized to help dispel the isolation that advocates of fundamental freedoms, including media practitioners, often suffer in less than free societies. Contact and co-operation with international governmental organizations and NGOs on the national, regional and international level should be encouraged and assisted.

Another key area for countries in transition is the understanding and reporting of electoral processes. Media practitioners are very often left with an intellectually paralytic hangover from decades of electoral charades, reported by a tightly controlled press, which presented only the façade of democracy. The need to assess the entire electoral landscape, including the electoral law, election commissions, voters' lists, opposition and non-partisan participation, as well as the more obvious questions of freedom of expression and association, is often little appreciated.

The most basic civic and voter education campaigns should begin early with training for media practitioners in analyzing and reporting these fundamental questions. The need for such information is clear in countries undergoing democratic transition or those with little experience of electoral processes, where governments are willing to at least tolerate human rights activities and open media. Providing guidelines on these issues, explaining the role of national and international vote-monitoring organizations, and suggesting ways to cooperate with such groups, is important.

FADING SOVEREIGNTY

The concept of open media is one that has been traditionally applied within individual nations, usually in reference to its press. However, the notion of national 'sovereignty' over any communications or cultural production is fast fading. Historically, sovereignty was defined as an area over which a particular group could exercise physical control. This usually extended no further than did the command over lines of physical communication by land or water. Sovereignty also presumed the power of exclusion – of people, of goods, of information. This last power of sovereignty has eroded at a quickening pace since the development of long-distance telecommunications, beginning with the telegraph in the mid-nineteenth century.

Today, new ICTs are rapidly changing how people, cultures, and countries access and exchange information.[10] Satellite broadcasting, internet access, and other new or expanding ICTs reduce the power of single sources of information. Hierarchical forms of information distribution are being supplemented, if not supplanted. This 'disintermediation' of data flows expands access, but raises questions of the integrity and reliability of information. Cheaper and faster communications allow much greater contact, networking and dissemination of information even among civil society groups with scant resources. Thousands of African and Africa-related NGOs and institutions are now web-enabled or exist only as virtual entities (see 'Africa on the Internet'). Most African governments are now online, and some are making efforts to develop 'e-government' capacities to deliver information and services to citizens.[11]

'Digital divide' concerns address important matters of access and useful content, but there is no doubt that, however uneven the distribution is to date, new ICTs are broadening debate and building new communities around the world. Except in a few of the world's most reclusive and repressive lands, exercising sovereignty to exclude information is becoming nearly impossible. Open access to information is now the prerequisite and not a perquisite of modern economies. High levels of information access are the oxygen of economic growth for countries that wish to join the global knowledge-based economy. Without it, inbound investment is inhibited and domestic innovation stifled. But increasing information that open and accessible media provide inevitably spurs political debate as well as economic development. Restrictions on media and other information flows by regimes seeking to suppress political discussion, 'ideological impurity' or 'cultural contamination' are not only increasingly ineffective, but also negatively impact economic prospects.

PUBLIC SERVICE, PUBLIC GOOD?
The notion of the media as the providers of a public service is sometimes offered as an excuse to control them. African and other developing or authoritarian countries cite the requirements of 'nation-building' or similar pre-emptive priorities to justify media controls. Even in the most democratic countries, security and public order concerns during war or conflict have evoked severe media restrictions and sometimes significant self-censorship.

The US government has regulated broadcast media almost since their inception because they occupy a finite public resource – the airwaves – to distribute their product. For many years, American broadcasters were required to make airtime available for 'public service announcements', and needed to provide time for the 'right of reply' on political coverage.

These requirements have been eliminated. Yet the broadcast media are still widely viewed as a 'public good'. Many countries regulate content on prevailing moral standards. Political controls are most evident during election periods. Some countries restrict political advertising and offer parties and/or candidates air time in an effort to assure equitable access to competing voices in electoral contests. Even the most ardent defenders of press freedoms have little argument that, if applied fairly, this is seriously inimical to the functioning of open media.

A succinct formulation of the role of public broadcast media is offered by British sociologist Graham Murdock, who suggests that the media can promote democratic culture by fulfilling four basic conditions:

- establishing space for free expression beyond commercial and government influence
- offering free public accessibility
- maintaining an arena that exposes and negotiates differences and provides the possibility of achieving consensus on the common good through exposition of diverse and inclusive programs and perspectives
- providing communications aimed at the audience's role as citizens rather than consumers (Murdock, 1997).

Murdock's criteria, if realized, would certainly help empower active, open media. The focus is on encouraging popular participation by providing space for diverse sectors of civil society to engage in public policy debate. The criteria demand that state-controlled or public media be balanced and representative of all citizen stakeholders, and serve as 'democracy-building' institutions that promote representative and participatory governance.

State-controlled media often take on new roles during democratic transitions.

It is important to encourage positive transformations of publicly owned media resources. Means used to accomplish such transformations may include introducing maximum autonomy for, and professionalizing personnel in, media that will remain in the custody of the state, and by privatizing some assets where that may introduce competition in the media market.

It is also important not to lose sight of the need for all sectors of society to gain skills in presenting information to the media. Efforts to help NGOs, social justice advocates, parliamentarians, political parties, and even governments to become more effective communicators will help broaden the voices heard in the mass media. This can also help build constituencies for media freedom by persuading more groups that open media are useful for them. Training on media strategies, message formulation, interviewing, spokesperson's roles, and advice in using new ICTs are among the areas that can help societal actors understand how the media work, and how to present useful information to them. Some training material in this area is available on the Internet.[12]

Accepting the media potential in an important pro-democracy political role does not demand that all media be non-partisan. Private media, beyond the boundaries of reasonable laws of incitement and libel in the context of guarantees of free expression, should bear no such responsibility. Political parties, advocacy groups, religious organizations, and purely commercial interests operate media for what may be their own very parochial purposes. And programming decisions driven by self-censorship, and even free editorial choices, may produce information no less skewed than official propaganda. For-profit media worldwide largely operate on the lowest common denominator principle, seeking broad commercial appeal to maximize profit. The trend towards sensationalism and exploitive coverage is clear. It is essential to acknowledge that the marketplace's demands may in effect be no less insidious than a government's dictates. Bottom-line considerations, especially in an era of rapid concentration of media ownership, can reduce the pluralism that is a key to an open media by making content no more than a servant to ratings.[13]

MEDIA'S POSITIVE ROLE?

Governments can encourage 'public service' media content by buying advertising space, or by mandating a certain amount of public service announcements for which it can also offer (but not impose) appropriate content. Democracy-building activities must not be equated with 'nation-building' formulas that demand only 'positive' news that bolsters the image of certain politicians or parties.

This chapter does not revisit past battles over the New World Information and Communications Order (NWICO). There is no argument here for the official imposition of media 'responsibilities'. There is no case for mandating coverage of certain areas or issues. In the long run, far worse than open but sometimes irresponsible media are media controlled by or compliant to the powers that be. Improved media training and media self-discipline through press councils and strong ethics codes are among the viable means to encourage stronger and more responsible media. The International Federation of Journalists has launched 'media observatories' in four African countries, 'which are aimed to create well-respected, independent, and efficient systems of media accountability while promoting freedom of information and conditions for ethical journalism'.[14]

The media's informational role in developing democracies is more complex than in mature democracies. The structures and processes of new or newly empowered institutions, of the roles of the judiciary, of legislatures and of governmental bodies require explanation. Awareness of rights must be widespread for rights to be asserted and respected. Very basic health, literacy, and other social services information may also be an important part of effective and useful media in developing democracies. The West Africa Non-Governmental Organization Network[15] is among the newest of Africa-based web portals dedicated to imparting such information, while seeking to evoke local participation.[16] Success stories of new information and communications technologies in realizing development goals are increasing, and groups working in the field have documented some of the most promising stories.[17]

Many African countries have undertaken civic and voter education campaigns which utilize various media, including song, live performance and radio and television dramas or soap operas. For example, the media played a crucial role in a civic and voter education campaign that is credited with helping to avoid violence during the run-up to Benin's 1996 presidential election. Targeted radio and television programming produced with external aid played an enormous role in explaining the electoral process through skits and songs. A song entitled 'Nous Sommes la Même' ('We Are One') encouraged a peaceful election and received extensive radio coverage reaching people throughout the country. A German foundation funded production of the song and an accompanying video, which also sponsored 'Entre Nous' ('Between Us'), a widely popular twice-monthly television show broadcast on state television that presented skits and panel discussions on governance and democratization topics.[18] Radio soap operas have also been widely used in disseminating health information, and were identified as among the most popular offerings on externally funded 'peace radio' in Burundi.

Media, Crisis and Conflict

Mass media can be crucial in shaping public opinion about conflict.[19] Even in the most established democracies, independent media often demonstrate chauvinistic and jingoistic tendencies in wartime, as even a cursory viewing of America's CNN or Fox News Networks reveals. During internal strife, the media can serve to dampen or fan incendiary situations. Rwanda's *Radio Télévision Libre des Mille Collines* (RTLM) actively promoted genocide by broadcasting calls for the extermination of Tutsi citizens. Successful prosecutions for inciting crimes against humanity through broadcast media have been brought by the United Nations International Criminal Tribunal for Rwanda.[20] In March 2002, the popular Rwandan singer Simon Bikindi was extradited from the Netherlands to face trial in Arusha for composing and performing songs demonizing Rwandan Tutsi and urging that they be murdered, a profoundly negative example of a misuse of popular culture to deliver a policy message, in this case allegedly to incite genocide.[21]

When media clearly incite conflict and local authorities do not intervene, external actors need to make very difficult decisions on whether and how they should seek to block mass media dissemination of incitement messages. UN administrators in the Balkans closed down radio stations and newspapers judged to be dangerous to civic peace. Electronic jamming of broadcasts is sometimes possible. Attacking broadcast facilities (as US forces did, to harsh criticism in Belgrade, during the Kosovo conflict) should be a final and desperate option. Such violence against the media must be reserved only for the most extreme cases in which it will prevent media incitement of serious and perhaps widespread crimes.

Information interdiction, however, is only an ephemeral and superficial solution. Providing alternative information is probably more productive, especially in the long term. The idea that peace-building information is effective in reducing conflict is the foundation for many such efforts. The philosophical underpinning to this approach is encapsulated in the preamble to the 1945 UNESCO Constitution, which states 'Since wars begin in the minds of men, it is in the minds of men that the defences of peace must be constructed', adding 'Ignorance of each other's ways and lives has been a common cause, throughout the history of mankind, of that suspicion and mistrust between the peoples of the world through which their differences have all too often broken into war'.[22]

Various governments, UN agencies, and NGOs have all funded peace-building media. In Africa, 'peace media' broadcasting has over recent years been supported in Angola, Burundi, the Central African Republic, Democratic Republic of the Congo (DRC), Ethiopia, Liberia, Rwanda, Sierra Leone, Somalia, Tanzania, and Zimbabwe.[23] The largest alternative radio operation currently being undertaken is *Radio Okapi*, a joint project in the DRC of the United Nations and the Swiss Hirondelle Foundation, which has performed similar work in other African countries, including a radio project in the Central African Republic. *Radio Okapi* broadcasts from Kinshasa and regional studios in French, Lingala, and local languages.[24]

Burundi's *Studio Ijambo* radio station is viewed as one of the more successful examples of peace-building media. *Studio Ijambo* ('wise words' in the local Kirundi language) was launched in 1995 expressly to counter virulent media programming that was applauding and encouraging some of the worst violence in Burundi's long-running civil war. The US-based NGO Search for Common Ground, which has extensive experience in conflict-resolution education and media, received US government funding to help create the station. Radio Netherlands' website, which includes an extensive section on 'hate radio' and 'peace radio' describes the story of the station's beginnings, growth, and impact.[25]

An evaluation of the station's development and impact was conducted for the US Agency for International Development in 2001 (*Media Intervention in Peace Building in Burundi*). Its introduction relates that in 1995 the extant Burundian media 'not only reflected the country's deep ethnic divide, but actively promoted it', and its members 'tried to rival each other over calls to kill, or in advancing their mutually macabre ideologies generating mutual terror and distrust based on historical fears'. In five 'interrelated areas of peace building in Burundi' that the report identifies (inter-group relations, social and political mobilization, political elite negotiations, public institutions and processes, and mass or elite conflict behavior), it found that *Studio Ijambo* had produced positive effects. The station's long-running soap opera, which incorporated peace-building themes and a newsmagazine format program that highlighted individual experiences, was most effective in changing behaviors, as reported by 270 interviewees in Burundi. This certainly corresponds to experience in Africa and elsewhere that democracy or development messages embedded in other programs are often better received than those delivered directly in civic education formats.

The report also states that it is 'more definitive and visible' that the project's media training, which has helped produce the station's high-quality independent journalism, has also positively influenced overall media culture in Burundi. This is a welcome result, and one that may offer lasting impact in a country that remains mired in civil strife. Highlighting the results of journalism training as the project's most verifiable outcome also reflects the extreme difficultly of gauging the 'preventive impact' of media or other interventions in conflicts.

Community radio in some other parts of Africa is thriving, helping to deliver development information and often becoming a focus for local mobilization and participation in political and resource decision-making.[26] New technologies increase the capacity and utility of such local broadcasting. Community radio stations across Africa receive content for rebroadcast via the Internet or on cassette tapes. The Africa Learning Channel, sponsored by the WorldSpace Foundation, provides content to 51 African countries.[27] Direct satellite radio receivers are becoming small and cheap enough for widespread use. The British Freeplay Foundation distributes wind-up radios and supports content development for community radio.[28]

Getting the message right in local terms is an important challenge, even when the means of delivery are available. The South Africa AIDS awareness soap opera 'Soul City' is a highly popular example of health information delivered in an entertaining format. In Uganda, the Straight Talk Foundation was a pioneer in using radio drama and comic books to promote AIDS and health issues.[29] The UN has launched a new multi-country radio and television series for Africa, 'Heart and Soul', which will focus on five themes: HIV/AIDS, environmental protection, gender, governance, and human rights. Inclusion of the last two topics is a welcome departure from most development media programming, especially that funded by intergovernmental organizations, which typically avoids directly addressing such issues.[30]

The American NGO Internews is one of the best-funded media support groups, working in about 30 countries worldwide on a variety of health, media support, conflict resolution, and democratization promotion activities. One of its projects in Africa, called *Local Voices*, aims to promote the broadest possible media engagement in disseminating HIV/AIDS information, emphasizing radio as the most effective mode of transmission in the African context. Describing the project, Internews explains, 'By interweaving AIDS messages into a variety of popular programs – from music programs with young audiences to political talk shows that reach policy makers – *Local Voices* will have cross-cutting impact that significantly improves public awareness and dialogue'.[31] A similar approach is used for conflict resolution and pro-democratization activities. Other NGOs, such as the US-based Street Law Foundation, use comic book formats to introduce concepts of rights and the rule of law and practical information on how to seek redress if rights are violated.[32]

In countries that have not yet begun democratic transitions, or those with limited or restricted media, surrogate external media can be important sources of more balanced or accurate reporting. During the Cold War, Radio Free Europe, Radio Liberty, and other outlets often broadcasting in the vernacular, were enormously popular among peoples in Eastern Europe and the Soviet Union whose domestic media were tightly controlled. Radio Free Asia, an autonomous US-funded service launched in 1995, draws large audiences in Burma, China, and elsewhere. A proposal to create a parallel US-funded 'Africa Democracy Radio' stalled in Congress. However, the BBC, VOA, and other external broadcasters remain widely popular in Africa, especially in authoritarian states or where local media are simply not trusted. These services also have a long record of providing development and rights information, as well as news and other feature programs.

Ongoing Media Support

Supporters of sustainable democratic development must not presume that the existence of apparently open media indicates that continued engagement and support to the media sector is not required. Media in developing countries often struggle for their commercial survival. Furthermore, in societies without established traditions of press freedom, uneven or irresponsible reporting standards cast doubt on media credibility and erode public trust. Opportunities to encourage the dissemination of information on human rights, democracy-building, and political participation should be an important part of any program supporting emerging democracies. Some groups have detailed their strategies and approaches.

The Open Society Initiative for Southern Africa's (OSISA) vision of how media can support an open society is laid out in its guidelines for media-related grants. The OSISA emphasizes assistance that improves access to and control over the means of communication for 'marginalized' groups. The 'guiding principles' are to support local initiatives that:

• promote the right of all people to communicate
• play a role in holding those in authority and power accountable to those they are supposed to serve
• encourage the free flow of diverse and relevant information through mass media
• support the development of mass media that are accessible to and/or controlled by the people these media seek to serve
• enhance the long-term sustainability of non-governmental mass media.[33]

The guidelines reflect the perspective of those who seek to promote more open, responsive, and participatory media as a tool for social change. They also reflect the guiding assumption of OSISA's parent organization, the Open Society Institute, that information access is a key element in democratic empowerment. Other bilateral, multilateral, and NGO efforts are under way to help make the media more effective in specialized areas. The World Bank sponsors research and training for the media in reporting on corruption and other economic issues.[34] The International Federation of Journalists (IFJ) sponsors a special project on 'Promoting Accountability' that offers numerous tools and resources to help media investigate, illuminate the operation of societal institutions, and perhaps expose malfeasance.[35]

The IFJ's Media for Democracy Africa Program issued a 'Media in Africa Strategy' in 1999. It identifies three principal objectives that, as befits a journalist organization, are more directly aimed at the roles and operations of the press than the OSISA initiative. These are:

- identifying and removing practical obstacles to press freedom and independent journalism
- building awareness of human rights issues among journalists and policy-makers and strengthening public confidence in the role of media in democracy
- improving conditions for independence and professionalism in African journalism.

The report includes a very useful list of methods to pursue these objectives, and both short- and long-term indicators to measure their realization. Importantly, the proposals call for enduring partnerships between the media and civil society groups, and for the media to take the leading role in strengthening their own capacities and in self-regulation. The Media for Democracy Africa Program web page offers a rich set of resources and links.[36]

The US Agency for International Developments identifies the media as a crucial component in democratization assistance and made it a key area for democratic transition assistance. The USAID Center for Democracy and Governance 1999 report, 'The Role of Media in Democracy: A Strategic Approach', looks at the media's roles in supporting democratic development and at avenues for external assistance.[37] The report offers a list of goals encompassing a broad range of activities that underscore 'why the reform of the media sector necessitates a web of mutually reinforcing activities, the lack of any one of which can endanger any others'. One of the report's primary conclusions is that 'media activities should not be viewed in isolation from other areas of democracy and governance', and that 'greater impact may be achieved by integrating' media support into a broad range of democratization activities.

The report outlines five programmatic approaches, as well as listing some 'best practices' and 'lessons learned' regarding each that can help build the 'web of mutually reinforcing activities' needed for media reform: shaping the legal enabling environment, strengthening constituencies for reform, removing barriers to access, supporting the capitalization of the media, and training media personnel. The interrelation and interaction of these approaches are important points for any long-term media strategy, although, as the report argues, this might justifiably be postponed during crises or transition situations where the most pressing priority is to offer alternative voices or information in a restricted media environment.

The report also recognizes that entry points and funding to support a wide range of activities might not be available. How to make best use of even limited 'democratic space' is a challenge in many situations. In extreme circumstances where severe media repression is imposed, Internet technologies and surrogate radio services that bypass state control may be supported as alternatives to domestic media.

The report also warns of 'the need for clear distinctions between media assistance programs and public information campaigns that promote US policies and viewpoints'. This caveat should be kept in mind by all donors. Media that do not exhibit a healthy skepticism to all societal actors cannot be truly independent.

Since 1997, other official American media aid has come from the US State Department's Office of Transition Initiatives (OTI), which funds media assistance in Angola, Liberia, Nigeria, Rwanda, and Sierra Leone, and helps promote democratic transitions in Africa. OTI describes its objectives as:

- to help the public make more informed decisions
- to expand public support for reconciliation and democratic values
- to counter extremist propaganda and encourage public debate and discussion on critical issues
- to support the independence and professionalism of the media, and
- to multiply the effect of other transition programs.

Some of these efforts have focused on specific issues, for example, landmines awareness in Angola and reporting on the International Criminal Tribunal for Rwanda. Among the lessons OTI lists from its experience is the importance of helping to develop appropriate media content, as well as funding alternative media channels to 'encourage challenging and political content'. The OTI also notes that, in transition situations, state-run media might accept such content, which could be 'a significant gesture in a post-authoritarian society'.

OTI reinforces the notion that if funding for alternative media outlets continues for over two years, sustainability issues must be considered. This is an important point for external funding sources, as well as for long-term domestic media landscapes. Efforts in countries in crisis or during the early stages of a democratic transition may correctly emphasize the need to supply alternative media outlets that counteract inflammatory or simply highly biased media. Even in this context, training and equipment supplied may form a basis for launching more enduring local media outlets once external funding sources reduce their aid or depart entirely. Yet media commercial viability in countries with weak economies is problematical, and radio holds a distinct cost advantage here over both print and television.

Other programs have focused heavily on more traditional journalism skills training, an area that certainly should not be neglected.[38] If professional and credible media are absent, the value of community access and pluralism in communications will be diminished. Some funders clearly feel more comfortable in supporting formal journalism training rather than 'media development' that may include community participation, increased media access, and broader media ownership as important goals.

More specific information and recommendations are found in reports that focus on media in one country. *Media Pluralism Landscape: An Overview of the Media Sector in Mozambique* is a 1999 study prepared by the Nordic-Southern Africa Development Community Journalism Center for the UNESCO/UNDP Media Development Project in Mozambique. The array of materials describing UNESCO/UNDP-supported assistance in developing Mozambique's media since 1998 is an excellent case study in international assistance. Its scope, focus, and clarity are a highly useful example for future analyses of media capacities and needs in the context of support for development and democratization.[39]

Local capacity-building should promote professional media. However, the wider constellation of constituencies that help to develop and sustain active open media, from freedom of expression organizations to think-tanks that analyze public policy, should also be considered when reviewing the media landscape. Just as the media should be viewed as an organic part of efforts to promote civil society and the rule of law, the strength of other sectors – exemplified by the two groups described very briefly below – increases the likelihood that active open media will survive and perhaps prosper.

- The Namibia-based Media Institute of Southern Africa (MISA) carries out roles including research, training, and advocacy that support and complement open media. For example, in 2002, MISA helped lead publicity and lobbying efforts that persuaded South African legislators to amend new broadcasting regulations that would have increased direct government influence over the state-owned South African Broadcasting Corporation.[40]
- In South Africa, the Institute for a Democrative Alternative in South Africa (IDASA) is a think-tank that provides a forum for public debate, and helps inform the public and media about governmental actions and policy options. The IDASA's Political Information and Monitoring Service is a rich source of current political information and analysis tapped by South African media. The group has also made direct forays into mass communications by producing weekly commentaries for broadcast on community radio stations around South Africa through its 'Democracy Radio' project.[41]

Media Monitoring

Civil society has an important role in promoting active open media by pressing for a conducive legal and regulatory environment, and by providing content to the media. Ongoing scrutiny of the mass media reporting and structures also encourages increased accountability and better performance. Monitoring can provide both quantitative and qualitative evaluation of media coverage on specific issues or events. Formal media monitoring structures have appeared as a regular election feature in many emerging democracies. Statistical reporting on quantitative coverage can identify and perhaps confirm or dispel allegations of media bias. Qualitative analysis of media reports, if prepared in a balanced manner, can evoke even more compelling conclusions. Assessment of private media coverage may reveal biases and distortions that can alert the public to dangers of media manipulation. Analysis of public media's reporting sometimes shows how state resources are being used to support certain parties or candidates, and can encourage fairer use.

The Washington, DC-based National Democratic Institute for International Affairs (NDI) released a very useful guide to election media monitoring in 2002 (Norris and Merloe, 2002). In 1998, NDI helped launch MEMO98, a Slovakia-based media monitoring group backed by leading Slovak civil society groups that has grown to provide advice on similar projects in several other countries.[42] The European Institute for the Media monitors the press during elections, mostly in Europe. The institute collaborated with a Zambian NGO to assess media coverage of Zambia's 2001 presidential and parliamentary polls.[43]

Media monitoring on an ongoing basis outside of election periods can also provide an important source of early warning of incipient conflict. The International Crisis Group, for instance, reported on rising vitriol in both the Serbian and Albanian language media in Yugoslavia well before the outbreak of large-scale hostilities in Kosovo. Monitoring of African media could provide similar signs of incipient strife.

Active Open Media for Sustainable Democratic Development

This chapter began by posing the question, 'Does increased access to information foster democratic development?' Limited research indicates positive correlations between media freedom and access to open media, with improvements in governance and democratic development. But the intertwining of basic liberties makes the identification of direct causation problematical. The assertion that greater access to information is a predictor of better democratic performance cannot yet be made with statistical assurance. Relationships among factors including information access, media freedom and pluralism, and message formulation, are important areas for further research. How they each, and in combination, contribute to democratic development is still, as mentioned at the start of this chapter, largely described in anecdote informed by conventional wisdom. Formal assessments of the impact of the media and the information they convey on democratization may usefully produce broad lessons and useful pointers for practitioners, but it already seems evident that messages and their format must remain firmly grounded in local realities to be effective.

The existence of active open media does not guarantee that rights will be respected and that democratic development will be sustained. It is certain, however, that societies with a restricted or docile media are more susceptible to bad governance and rights abuses, simply because leaders need not account for their actions. Unless ruled by the most benevolent of despots, societies lacking active open media will likely display lower and less informed levels of citizen participation in public decision-making.

Poverty reduction and other development programs and projects that value input from their target beneficiaries and other stakeholders – from grassroots to policy-makers – in shaping priorities will find greater success in situations where the media are open and accessible. Several reports on the media in developing countries flag gender imbalance in media ownership, employment and reporting, and suggest increasing support for women's participation in each area. It is also widely argued that an increasing concentration of media ownership in developed and developing countries can threaten pluralism, as well as editorial independence.

Efforts to allow people to readily comprehend and relate to development and democracy information are essential. A central consideration must be how messages are presented to specific audiences. People are storytellers, and especially in less literate societies which may still rely on oral transmission as an important conduit for exchanging information. Anyone seeking to import pro-democratization information should consider the long experience of groups engaged in 'social marketing' – of condoms, for example, in the effort to reduce the prevalence of HIV/AIDS. Embedding messages about health, development, democracy, rights, and reconciliation in popular formats such as soap operas often proves more effective than more direct, and usually far drier, efforts to convey such information.

Even in crisis or transitional situations where alternative media outlets are anecdotally reported to be effective in changing people's attitudes towards conflict and its resolution, the conundrum of disproving the negative prevails: would the strife be worse without alternative media? Yet even if it is impossible to know, efforts to support alternative media voices must not be abandoned. Especially when strife is driven by stereotypical group perceptions that feed on (and are all too easily manipulable on the basis of) historical fears or prejudices, alternative media can challenge both fixed beliefs and rumors that may spark or sustain cycles of violence.

Most media assistance programs include training elements, and these can be very important in helping to create professional media cultures that value honesty, accuracy and balance in reporting. Helping media practitioners gain technical expertise to understand, investigate and report on development, business and finance, rights, elections, and the functioning of government under a system of the rule of law is essential to any credible journalistic enterprise. As emphasized earlier, however, skilled reporting can thrive only within a system that sustains free, independent and pluralistic media that will challenge any societal actor. The complex web of requirements to promote active, open media includes respect for basic freedoms of expression, a conducive legal and regulatory environment, financial viability, and means of access for broad audiences to media output. Boosting the capacities of civil society groups to produce media content and promulgate their messages through mass media is a complementary but crucial media development strategy.

An appended list summarizes actions cited in this chapter that can help promote the growth and sustainability of active, open media, and often the democratic development and pursuit of social justice. As previously discussed, many public and private groups are already engaged in supporting such activities.

Promoting active, open media must be understood as both a means and a goal for supporters of democratic development. Short interventions can promote alternative voices and help prompt positive change. Overcoming the many challenges to firmly root a professional media culture that serves society as a whole rather than special interests requires long-term assistance. It is imperative that those committed to democratic transitions and consolidations maintain a lively awareness of the media's importance to the success of their work.

APPENDIX

Summary of International Actions Promoting Active Open Media

1. Support for freedom of expression, media rights, and protection of journalists through local, regional, and international groups.

2. Advice on media law and regulatory regimes conducive to active, open media.

3. Support for media training, including:
   - basic journalism techniques aimed at developing professional and credible media that are honest, accurate, and balanced
   - specialized training on development, rights, corruption, election coverage, governance, economics, finance and other areas
   - media management and finance
   - adapting and utilizing new information and communications technologies
   - media accountability systems such as ethics codes and councils
   - media skills for NGOs, parliamentarians, and other societal actors.

4 Communications infrastructure development, including community media that promote media access and popular participation.

5. Financial assistance to open media outlets and assistance in helping transform state media into public service media.

6. Content development and provision on issues related to rights, rule of law, democracy, governance, and development by media and by specialized groups, including embedding such information in a wide variety of programming.

7. Support for media monitoring efforts during elections and as early warning.

8. Support for surrogate media services for countries without viable domestic open media.

9. Response to media incitement through alternative information, or interdiction as an emergency measure.

10. Capacity-building support for local and regional groups to carry out the above efforts.

Notes

[1] Article 19 of the Universal Declaration of Human Rights guarantees freedom of expression and rights to information. European Courts have gone much further, arguing in several cases that governments in fact have an affirmative duty to encourage pluralism in media coverage, and describing the citizen's right to be informed through 'impartial', 'independent', 'accurate' and 'full' information.

[2] A useful recent overview on this issue is offered by Harvard professor Pippa Norris's paper, 'Giving Voice to the Voiceless: Good Governance, Human Development and Mass Communication'. Norris creates a communications index based on various press freedoms scores, and measures this against human development indicators and, importantly, levels of media access. She finds positive correlations, but warns that the 'causal interpretation of these relationships is not unambiguous'. http://ksghome.harvard.edu/~.pnorris.shorenstein.ksg/ACROBAT/Voice.pdf.

[3] For two earlier studies, *see* Ott (1998) which finds little correlation between internet access and degree of democratization, and Kedzie (1997) which reaches an opposite conclusion.

[4] 'Eternal vigilance is the price of liberty' is a popular slogan that adorns the masthead of several newspapers around the world. The quote is often wrongly attributed to Thomas Jefferson. It is a paraphrase of words by John Philpot Curran in Dublin in 1790, regarding the right to elect the city's lord mayor: 'It is the common fate of the indolent to see their rights become a prey to the active. The condition upon which God hath given

liberty to man is eternal vigilance; which condition if he break, servitude is at once the consequence of his crime and the punishment of his guilt.'

[5] See at: www.unesco.org/webworld/com_media/communication_democracy/windhoek.htm. In a similar vein, a US government report on media and democracy states, 'A media sector supportive of democracy would be one that has a degree of editorial independence, is financially viable, has diverse and plural voices, and serves the public interest.' The definitions of 'a degree of editorial independence', and of financial viability, diversity, and the public interest make this more limited description malleable and subject to interpretation and debate. Its requirements are those that an 'active open media' would almost certainly exceed. See USAID Center for Democracy and Governance, 'Role of Media', p. 4.

[6] The role of 'public' or 'civic' journalism is still contentious, especially in the United States. The International Media and Democracy Project website offers discussion and 'how-to' guides regarding the practice of public journalism: www.imdp.org.

[7] An April 2001 conference on 'Democratisation and the Mass Media' sponsored by the World Association of Christian Communications and the Rockefeller Foundation held in Bellagio, Italy offered many interesting perspectives on this issue. For an overview of the meeting, see www.wacc.org.uk/publications/md/md2002-1/sparks.html#top. Another interesting perspective is O'Siochru (1997).

[8] For the full report, see: http://www.freedomhouse.org/research/pressurvey.htm.

[9] The Nigerian NGO Media Rights Agenda publishes a monthly newsletter, www.internews.org/mra/mrm/newsletters.htm. See also 'Media for Democracy in Nigeria', which describes a European Union-funded collaboration between Nigerian groups and Article 19, the International Federation of Journalists, and Reporters Sans Frontières 'aimed at providing comprehensive support for defence of press freedom, reform of media legislation, structural assistance to media and strengthening of independent and professional journalism'. www.ifj.org/regions/africa/mdnigeria.html. The Media for Democracy program is also operating in several other African countries: www.ifj.org/regions/africa/mfdabk.html.

[10] The very nature of how communications are transmitted can determine how they are perceived. The impact of broadcast media differs from that of print media. How people engage with interactive media is a moving target today, subject to lively debate. That there is much discussion regarding how the medium shapes a message may merely be noted here.

[11] For a list of African governments on the web, see: http://www.uneca.org/aisi/nici/africagovinternet.htm.

[12] See http://forefrontleaders.org/resources/advocacy/lansner.htm, the author's paper offering practical media advice to human rights advocates published on the web in four languages. The Institute for War and Peace Reporting offers extensive and excellent media training and development information on its website, but has little activity in Africa: http://www.iwpr.net/index.pl?training_index.html.

[13] For an interesting overview of media concentration issues, see World Association of Christian Communications. Also, particularly, 'Seminar on Media Ownership in Central and West Africa' pp. 35–37, and 'Seminar on the Political Economy of Media Ownership in Southern Africa', pp. 38–44.

[14] See: www.ifj.org/regions/africa/mfdabk.html. French Professor Claude-Jean Bertrand discusses options for encouraging media accountability in his book, *An Arsenal For Democracy:* (Bertrand, 2001). A compendium of codes of ethics may be found at http://www.uta.fi/ethicnet/. The Media Institute of Southern Africa has published a *Handbook on Journalism Ethics – African Case Studies*, www.misanet.org/publications.html.

[15] www.wangonet.org

[16] A plethora of websites exists in related fields. A reasonable compendium may be viewed at: http://www.usaid.gov/democracy/demlinks.html.

[17] The Institute for International Communication and Development www.iicd.org/, and the World Bank's Information for Development, or 'infoDev' program www.infodev.org/

co-operate to produce a series of ICT/Development success stories that are found at: http://www.iicd.org/base/story_home?sc=86.

[18] The author's observations during democratization assessment consultancy performed for the National Democratic Institute for International Affairs in Benin and Cote d'Ivoire, June 1996.

[19] The broader issues of how media report on civil wars and humanitarian disasters in the developing world is addressed in Minear et al., (1995).

[20] Radio Netherlands offers a history of RTML and the prosecution of some of its staff: www.rnw.nl/realradio/dossiers/html/rwanda-h.html.

[21] See: www.diplomatiejudiciaire.com/UK/Tpiruk/BikindiUK.htm.

[22] http://unesdoc.unesco.org/images/0012/001255/125590e.pdf#constitution.

[23] Radio Netherlands offers extensive coverage of hate media/peace media issues, with particular emphasis on radio. See www.rnw.nl/realradio/dossiers/html/hateintro.html. A leading NGO involved in peace broadcasting is Search for Common Ground, www.sfcg.org. See also a very useful short article by experienced BBC broadcaster Alster (1995).

[24] See: http://www.hirondelle.org/hirondelle.nsf/caefd9edd48f5826c12564cf004f793d/8603a2d41fc59612c1256b3c004bb371?OpenDocument.

[25] http://www.rnw.nl/realradio/community/html/ijambo120299.html. Studio Ijambo information is also available on the Search for Common Ground website: http://www.sfcg.org/locdetail.cfm?locus=Burundi&name=programs&programid=424&CFID=15669&CFTOKEN=dbee33b393b26d99–8634B323–032E–6692–D3DC9B673F7C627F.

[26] The World Association for Community Broadcasting, www.amarc.org/ promotes and supports community radio worldwide. For a description of the impact of one community radio station, see Thurow (2002).

[27] www.worldspace.org/alc.html.

[28] www.freeplayfoundation.org/.

[29] The Straight Talk Foundation, www.straight-talk.or.ug.

[30] 'Heart and Soul', http://www.heartandsoulafrica.org/site/unspons.html. Health Unlimited, http://www.healthunlimited.org/greatlakes/index.htm, a British-based NGO, works in several African countries to produce health-related radio and other media programming. The Johns Hopkins University Center for Communications Program offers an impressive array of health-related media materials, http://www.jhuccp.org/africa/index.htm.

[31] See: www.internews.org.

[32] www.streetlaw.org/world.html. An example of a South African Street Law manual may be viewed at http://www.csls.org.za/slmanual1.html.

[33] The Open Society Initiative for Southern Africa Media Programme guidelines: http://www.osiafrica.org/eng_osisa-2_3.php. Also see the Soros Foundation's Network Media Program (NMP) http://www.osi.hu/nmp/.

[34] See Stapenhurst (2000) http://www.worldbank.org/wbi/governance/pubs/mediacurb.htm. The World Bank Institute also offers training in economics and business journalism, and has conducted several seminars in Africa, http://www.worldbank.org/wbi/ebj/index.htm. In July 2002, it published *The Right to Tell: The Role of Mass Media in Economic Development*.

[35] See: www.ifj-pa.org.

[36] See: www.ifj.org/regions/africa/mfdabk.html.

[37] USAID Center for Democracy and Governance (1999) http://www.usaid.gov/pubs/ads/200/200sbc.pdf; *Program Options in Conflict Prone Areas*. USAID Office of Transition Initiatives, pp. 39–41, http://www.dec.org/pdf_docs/pnacm211.pdf; USAID Office of Transition Initiatives media examples, http://www.usaid.gov/hum_response/oti/focus/media.html.

[38] A survey of American support for journalism training internationally is offered in Hume (2002).

[39] http://mediamoz.tripod.com/.

[40] See: www.misanet.org.

[41] See: www.idasa.org.za/.

[42] MEMO98's experience is an example of strong internal coalition formation, and of local capacity building. The author helped organize MEMO98's first media monitoring efforts in 1998. See http://www.memo98.sk/.

[43] See: http://www.eueu-zambia.org/. The European Institute for the Media's 'Media and Democracy' page may be viewed at: http://www.eim.org/MaDP.htm.

14

REGINALD AUSTIN
Constitution-Making, Peace Building & National Reconciliation: Zimbabwe

Introduction

THIS chapter focuses on the extent to which the process of constitution-making can become a vehicle for national dialogue and the consolidation of peace, allowing competing perspectives and claims within society to be aired and incorporated. There is a motley of issues involved in the drafting of a country's constitution. Nevertheless, most scholars would agree that one issue that continues to bedevil many African countries is how to establish national states with institutions that promote economic development and good governance, facilitate political harmony and stability, manage diversity and serve as a vehicle for the processing of disputes between state and citizen and between citizens, and avoid conflicts through enfranchisement of their people. This chapter seeks to outline the unique experience of Zimbabwe in its efforts to develop a constitution that consolidates democratic rule and good governance and enjoys the allegiance and support of all Zimbabweans. It will examine broadly the constitutional history of Zimbabwe and detail the efforts that have been made towards developing an enduring constitution, the structure of the processes that have been employed and the nature and effectiveness of public participation in them. While recognizing the uniqueness of Zimbabwe, it is hoped that an examination of its experience will provide best practices and pitfalls to be avoided in the development of national constitutions that are legitimate and provide stability and good governance.

Zimbabwe's history provides important examples of a number of phenomena, including: the imperial injection of 'modern state' governance into Africa, via the private sector; the fate of 'shared responsibility' between a settler state and its imperial authority; the central place of expropriation and exploitation of land in colonial and post-colonial situations; the tension between an authoritarian and a constitutionally limited government, as well as the resilience of inherited authoritarianism; the influence of the United Nations and decolonization and the democratizing role of the Commonwealth Secretariat; the effect of the Cold War's military and ideological influence; the complications arising from ethnic divisions; the positive and negative creative roles of the judiciary and judicial interpretation; the significance of civil society, and the critical effect of the economy on governance, especially on constitutionalism in transition.

Like South Africa almost two decades later, the Zimbabwe independence Constitution marked the beginning of majority rule and the hope of transition to democracy, which the international community hailed as a miracle. Twenty-five years later, some regard Zimbabwe as a democratic disaster. The ZANU(PF) government asks, 'Why are our necessarily radical changes to governance, our search for economic democratization and actions on the constitution so misunderstood, our need to defend ourselves and the programme of the ruling party so distorted and the party so vilified, hated and sanctioned?' The Zimbabwean opposition were as surprised by the government's resistance to change as the government was by the demand for it. The legal and physical repression unleashed upon the opposition appals them. Repression includes the overt denial of state protection to their persons and property (especially if they are white farmers) and the government's blatant refusal to respect the rule of law. Significant sections of the international community share this sense of shock, and seek to penalize the government leadership into reversing its practices and policies. Zimbabwe's neighbouring states indicate varying degrees of 'concern' at the radical developments, but are generally muted in criticizing the government. The country's economy is in tatters, famine is threatening, and the miracle of 1980 has turned into a nightmare.

Why has the miracle gone wrong? Why has the constitution, made and re-made over the past decades, not enabled the obvious conflicts of interest in Zimbabwean society to be constructively mediated and reconciled so that stability and prosperity can grow within a maturing democracy? In particular, can the situation in part be explained by the 'process' of making the constitution in the broadest sense rather than looking exclusively at its substance? In this context, there is an important relationship between these two aspects. First, the desire to deal with specific substantial issues, including such significant matters as land ownership and the state's authoritarian tendencies, has consistently driven the process of constitutional formation. Second, the persistent feature of the process has been, and remains, essentially top-down in nature. These aspects combine with a consistent readiness on the part of the 'managers' of the process, from the Imperial 'chartered' occupying authority, the British South Africa Company, to those currently in power, to use their authority, dominance, and even deceit to create a constitution to do primarily what they want. Judicial oversight or forms of popular consultation have occasionally mitigated or cosmetically concealed to varying degrees this control of the constitution.

Conquest and Constitution-Making

The pre-colonial government in what is now Zimbabwe had a complex constitutional basis (see for example, Mudenge, 1988; d'Elgelbronner-Kolff et al., 1998). However, this chapter focuses on the more recent colonial and post-colonial history of the processes associated with and following the conquest of the traditional political authorities. This began in 1890, when the Company, avoiding Matabeleland, settled its Pioneer Column at Fort Salisbury, now Harare, and granted each settler a 1500 morgen (3175 acres) farm and 15 prospecting claims.

The British South Africa Company (BSAC) asserted its initial bases of governmental authority through a Royal Charter granted by the British Crown to carry out 'the avowedly commercial aims of the Company's promoters. The charter attempted to reconcile the treasury's desire to avoid calls for imperial funds with the need to control the Company so as to protect British foreign relations and to preclude disputes with…chiefs that might lead to military involvement' (Palley, 1966: 32). This early example of privatized government was not a total success. The Crown granted the charter on the basis of a concession agreed in 1888 between the Company and King Lobengula, which allowed the Crown, in essence, to prospect for and mine minerals within the Kingdom but not to settle or purport to govern it (Lippert, 1960: 15). In 1891, Britain unilaterally declared a Protectorate over Mashonaland, the area the Company continued to administer, in order to exclude possible claims on it by the South African Republic. By 1893, Lobengula's insistence on maintaining Ndebele hegemony in Mashonaland, and his dispute in the taking and alienating of the land, proved a fatal combination, as the Company's disappointment over the lack of gold in Mashonaland and its interest in Ndebele land and cattle provided a *casus belli*. The Matebele War followed, resulting in the overthrow of Lobengula and the Ndebele state. The Matebele Order in Council of 1894 constitutionalized the conquest by extending the Company's administration to Matabeleland under Imperial protection, and creating radical changes based upon the conquest in the pre-existing regime governing land (Tshuma, 2001: 15). Dramatic changes in economic relationships between the white and black populations arose from the new legal order, which included the introduction of taxation (a hut tax) on black adult males to bring them into the colonial economy and the expropriation of their property and traditional livelihoods. As put by Phimister (1988: 16), 'both Company and the settlers turned to looting the Shona and Ndebele economies'. Ranger et al. (2000) describing the situation in Matabeleland, observed: 'After 1893, the Ndebele were treated as a conquered people. The entire Ndebele heartland on the highveld around Bulawayo was alienated to white settlers; Ndebele cattle were looted on a grand scale'. He points out that by far the most dramatic immediate effect was the removal of the cattle. By mid-1894, an estimated 100,000 cattle were taken, a loss that an outbreak of Rinderpest in early 1896 further exacerbated.

All these fundamental changes to the lives of the people under the new governance were the result of autocratic acts of either the Imperial authorities or the Company as their 'agent'. It was not an unusual process at the time, but it was an unfortunate model for the future. The tendency has been to seek constitutional 'solutions' by sadly similar processes.

The outcome of this belligerent foundation stage of what has become the Zimbabwean state was, not surprisingly, further violent conflict rather than conflict management. Violence emerged surprisingly soon, given the apparently complete defeat of the Ndebele Kingdom and the initial quiescence of the Shona people to the occupation. The 1893 war had ended with a 'peace agreement' achieved by Rhodes, whose name was now 'given' to Southern Rhodesia. At a much-vaunted 'Indaba' (an early example of 'Dominant Third Party Mediation'), Rhodes presented himself to the Ndebele military leaders as a 'Father Figure', rather than the CEO of the Company. The promises made, especially regarding Ndebele land, resurfaced as a cause of disaffection and complaint in very much the same way as have similar 'promises' made over 80 years later in the context of the Lancaster House Constitutional Conference and cease-fire agreement. Rather than a basis for reconciliation, they became the source of continued conflict.[1] In 1896, seeking to take advantage of the Company's temporary and disastrous preoccupation with the South African Republic, the Ndebele and Shona leadership (including the traditional spirit mediums) combined to make a serious and almost successful effort to end European occupation. Imperial forces were required to overcome the two-year-long resistance. The war was carried out with considerable ruthlessness and ended with the execution and imprisonment of the Ndebele and Shona leaders. Though the war underlined the dangerous inequity of the land distribution, it did not lead to effective intervention by Britain.

British/White Settler Constitutions

In 1898, the British set up the first elements of representative government, confirming the Company Administrator and a five-man Executive Council (including the British-appointed Resident Commissioner and four Company-appointed members). A nine-person Legislative Council, five nominated by the Company and four elected representatives of the white settlers, was established to legislate for the peace, order and good governance of Southern Rhodesia. Like the legislatures under subsequent Rhodesian constitutions up to 1965, a right to veto and disallow this legislative power was retained by the British government. The creative tensions, first, those between the settlers and the Company and, second, those between the settlers and the Imperial government, dominated the evolving constitutional processes of these decades. But, as with the process at all stages, other voices and pressures were influencing and shaping the emerging constitutions. A constant feature in the process is the predominant role of those with political and economic power, and, at especially critical moments, those enjoying the support and control of the security arms of the state.

In 1903 and again in 1911, pressure from the settlers resulted in British Orders in Council, which provided the first equal and then majority settler representation in the Legislative Council. In the wake of World War I, the settlers pressed for the end of the Company's economic and political dominance. An important landmark in the process was the settlers' claims to the land that the Company had been administering but which had remained un-alienated. In 1914, the British referred the case to the Privy Council, which, delayed by war, handed down its decision in 1919. *In re Southern Rhodesia* is another important indicator of the central place of land in the search for an appropriate legal order, balancing the competing interests of the country's peoples (Tshuma, 2001: 17). The parties in the case represent the main historic actors: the Company, the British Crown, the settlers, and the African people. The court held that the Company could not have acquired title by the 1893 conquest, this being a prerogative of the Crown. The settlers' argument that the Crown had given up its right to govern to the new local order was held unproven. The fundamental argument on the part of the African claimants, that their rights to the land were of such a nature that it could not legally have been ceded, and thus the conquering power would protect this right like other non-public property rights, was rejected. The court's opinion was that 'the notion of separate ownership in land was foreign to the ideas of the Africans ... and ... that the Africans of Southern Rhodesia were on the lower end of the scale of social organisation such that their conceptions of right could not be reconciled with the institutions of civilized society' (1919 A.C. 211). Accordingly, the Crown owned the un-alienated land of Southern Rhodesia. In the circumstances the Company, which had never been a commercial success, sought to rid itself of its administrative obligations, leaving the settlers the choice of self-government or to join South Africa.

In 1920, the settler-controlled Legislative Council called on the British to grant a 'responsible government'. Winston Churchill, then Colonial Secretary, set up the Buxton Commission to examine the issue, and in 1921, it recommended limited self-government. The Commission's process was in essence a consideration of the settlers' views. The possibility of asserting greater imperial control, which might have been considered in view of the conflicts since 1890, was not contemplated. The Commission did, however, recommend that the British government retain its reserved powers. Churchill sought to persuade the Rhodesians that amalgamation with South Africa was the best option, and was prepared to offer Northern Rhodesia (now Zambia) to Jan Smuts. In October 1922, Rhodesia held a referendum to choose between responsible government or union with South Africa. Since 1919, Charles Coghlan, the leader of the Legislative Council, had supported the responsible government option. In the event, partly because of strong anti-Afrikaans language sentiment among the Anglophone settlers, and despite mining capital's support for union, 8,774 votes to 5,989 white votes, including women, approved the responsible government. The process involved almost no organized involvement of the black population, though an estimated maximum of 60,000 were qualified to vote at the time (Chikuwa, 1988: 73).

Based on Constitutional Letters Patent, Britain annexed Southern Rhodesia as a British Crown Colony with responsible government, and retaining its extensive reserved and disallowance powers that enabled it to prevent discriminatory legislation (Palley, 1966: 216). Section 48 required the settler government to pay Britain £2 million for the un-alienated land belonging to the Crown. At this stage, settlers could freely purchase land outside the Native Reserves, and they immediately pressed for legislation to segregate the land and to control black agriculture. This led, in 1925, to the Morris Charter Commission, which recommended the territorial segregation of the black and white populations. The 1930 Land Apportionment Act set aside 51 per cent of the land for exclusive ownership by European settlers, including, until 1941, all the urban areas. The Act established the essential framework for land ownership and agricultural activity and production up to 1977; it also provided the backbone of racial and agrarian policy throughout the era of minority rule and shaped the national political economy. The Liberation War contested this central feature, which dominated the independence constitutional debate and has remained a major issue of both substance and emotion. The Land Tenure Amendment Act of 1969 abolished the racial restrictions on land ownership. In 1977, in a desperate search for an accommodation between the minority regime and its subject majority, the Land Tenure Amendment Act abolished the racial restrictions on land ownership.

From then on, landowners would rely, in their relations with the state and public authority, upon the legal protection of property within the sphere of private law. The very special 'constitutional' regime of the colonial era thus shaped and characterized the distribution of land at independence. Much of what one can regard as the country's constitution was, as it still is, in the laws and conventions outside the formal Constitution. Thus, the legislation relating to land, racial discrimination, and political freedom consisted of the Land

Apportionment Act, the Masters and Servants Act, and the Law and Order (Maintenance) Act, all of which might have been disallowed had Britain used its reserved powers. The imperial contribution to this process and to the shape of the constitution was (at the very least) its persistent inaction (Palley, 1966: 230; Linington, 2001: 6). It was this 'shape' that the Lancaster House Constitution of 1980 ultimately designed, through agonizing negotiation and extremely fragile compromises, to preserve and perpetuate the Zimbabwean democracy of the future.

The long and carefully constructed socio-economic feature, the land, retained its historically central place in the constitutional structure. It is also vital to understanding and seeking effective means of managing the conflicts in Zimbabwe. But before examining the Lancaster House process, it is necessary to return to the processes associated with the country's other British-White settler constitutions.

Southern Rhodesia enjoyed a special status between a colony and a dominion. There was no direct colonial administration from London and a new surge for full settler autonomy emerged after World War II. After 1949, its Prime Minister attended Commonwealth Prime Ministers' meetings and the government created its own citizenship. It is useful to note the psychological importance of Rhodesians 'rallying to the flag' in both World Wars. They exploited this to the full in their efforts to distance themselves from Britain's post-1945 hesitant, but worrying, non-racial rhetoric and growing anti-colonial sentiment suggesting limitations on unfettered minority settler control. The tactic, which worked particularly well in 1965 during the critical days surrounding Ian Smith's Unilateral Declaration of Independence (UDI), was to rekindle the 'comradely' loyalty of Britons to an earlier, more basic cause – survival against the Fascist Axis, now replaced by black proto-Communists.

THE FEDERAL CONSTITUTION OF RHODESIA AND NYASALAND

The first of these constitutional processes involved the Federation of Rhodesia and Nyasaland, established in 1953. The Central African Federation, as it was also known, emerged for several reasons. One was the earlier idea of the amalgamation of the two Rhodesias; another was enthusiasm for federations (beyond the metropolis) among British constitution-makers at the time. Strengthening capital interests, especially in Southern Rhodesia, favoured the economic arguments. White leaders in both Rhodesias, Sir Godfrey Huggins and Roy Welensky, were in favor of the proposal. Black organizations in both Nyasaland and Northern Rhodesia tended to oppose the idea along with those in the South who joined in the All African Convention in opposition.

The image of the Federation was of 'partnership', the meaning of which was sharpened by Huggins' vision of a horse and rider, the rider being the whites. Britain forged ahead with the idea, and Westminster approved the Federal Constitution in March 1953. In an April referendum, Southern Rhodesian settlers approved the Federation by 25,580 to 14,929 votes. Only a few hundred blacks were qualified to vote at the time.

The opposition to the Federation in Southern Rhodesia came primarily from whites who found the Huggins' formulation of partnership a threat to their segregationist ideals. This concern was to result, as the Federal multiracial policies and the growing articulation of Black Nationalist ambitions became clearer, in the formulation of the Dominion Party in 1956 by a split from the United Federal Party. The key word here is 'Dominion', signaling a desire for a return to white autonomy (or independence) and a separation from the growing non-racial liberalism. The scene was being set for the confrontation that was to dominate Rhodesian/Zimbabwean politics for the decades to come, including the militarized conflicts that began in the 1960s, dominated the 1970s, and fundamentally shaped political life thereafter. In August 1955, the Youth League was founded in Salisbury, led by James Chikerema. On 12 September 1957, Nkomo formed a new African political party known as the African National Congress (ANC) and dedicated to constitutional action to achieve universal adult suffrage and an end to discriminatory laws, including the Pass Law from 1892. The ANC proclaimed a non-racial approach and attracted a small white membership.

Notwithstanding its multiracial program, political repression increased as racial equality and majority rule forced themselves to the top of the political agenda in the federal period. Both Federal and Rhodesian authorities resorted to emergency powers, detention, and the wholesale banning of Black Nationalist parties. This led to the formation of new parties. In January 1960, the National Democratic Party (NDP) replaced the banned ANC with an augmented leadership including Nkomo (elected President *in absentia*), Robert Mugabe, Dr. Parirenyatwa, and Advocate Herbert Chitepo. Black opposition to the federation was becoming more organized and strident. At the same time, a new Industrial Conciliation Act enabled the formation of African trade unions. Arrests were followed by demonstrations, and the Law and Order (Maintenance) Act of 1960 criminalized almost any political activity critical of government practice or policy. The Federal Chief Justice, Sir Robert Tredgold, criticized the Act on the ground that it would make the courts a party to widespread injustice; his criticism was ignored and he resigned in protest.

The courts' role in the constitutional process in Rhodesia and then Zimbabwe has been significant. Judges, by actions like the resignation of Justice Fieldsend when the Rhodesian High Court majority endorsed the legality of UDI, as well as through legal interpretations, have promoted and supported both the liberal democratic and the autocratic repressive modes of the legislature and executive over the decades (Hatchard, 1993). In 1953, the first black members participated in the Federal Legislature. Their views frequently contrasted with the nationalist extra-parliamentary demands, including their increasing insistence on ending the Federation. Britain's role was central in this process. The banning and resort to emergency powers ultimately made it necessary for Britain to examine and decide the issue. In 1963, the Federation was dissolved.

The British decision implied the imminent grant of independence and majority rule to Nyasaland (as Malawi), followed by Northern Rhodesia. Welensky threatened, as Ian Smith did in Rhodesia a couple of years later, the unilateral seizure of independence by the Federation. The reaction of Ian Macleod, the Conservative Colonial Secretary at the time, was restrained but effective; he moved a RAF Canberra squadron from the Middle East to Kenya, which was within easy striking distance of the Federation. It is also clear that the military containment of black opposition in the three populous and politically complex Federal territories would have made such a unilateral coup more difficult. Furthermore, Rhodesia, with Britain's agreement, inherited the most important elements of the Federal military hardware on the break-up of the Federation.

THE BRITISH–SETTLER 1961 CONSTITUTION

In 1958, Sir Edgard Whitehead, then Prime Minister of Southern Rhodesia, began negotiations to 'transfer to Southern Rhodesia the powers reserved to the United Kingdom government' (Palley, 1966: 312). The process went ahead in 1960 and constitutional negotiations continued into 1961. The political changes noted above, as well as the decolonizing process in other parts of the Commonwealth, explain the unambiguous demand by Duncan Sandys, the British Secretary of State for Commonwealth Affairs, that a new constitution must make provisions to advance the political rights of Africans. The Constitution extended Rhodesia's competence in external affairs and internal control, but retained residual reserve and disallowance powers to Britain, including the ultimate sovereign authority of Westminster. Two other elements were the justiciable Declaration of Rights and a 'watchdog' Constitutional Council to advise on Bills inconsistent with the Declaration. A new system of representation was attached to a franchise providing differing qualifications for an 'A' Roll, electing 50 members, and a 'B' Roll, electing 15 non-white members. The qualifications were not overtly racial, but maintained white dominance in the legislature. A degree of cross-voting between Rolls was also intended to encourage candidates to appeal to both constituencies and reduce racial polarization.

Palley has explained that though this was 'a constitution couched in largely non-racial terms which could eventually lead to majority rule…in practice (it) meant that European control was to continue for a lengthy period' (ibid.). Nkomo originally accepted the constitution, but the party would not support this, calling for a boycott of the elections and organizing its own 'referendum' on the constitution, which confirmed popular black support for its rejection. Undoubtedly, the atmosphere in which the process took place, the use of emergency powers, the introduction of draconian security laws, and the overwhelming unpopularity and distrust of the purportedly liberal Federation encouraged radical rather than compromise attitudes.

The regional and international contexts were also confrontational. In South Africa, the apartheid regime rejected the Commonwealth's non-racial agenda. While Britain preached the advancement of the interests of black Rhodesians, it was conducting a fierce rearguard action against UN efforts to put Southern Rhodesia on the Non-Governing Territories agenda. Black Nationalist leadership saw this as the preface to yet another deal with Rhodesian kith and kin. Confidence building was generally lacking on all sides, and the timing of the constitution's introduction was as unfortunate as the determination to force it through.

The NDP had by this time hardened its insistence on majority rule and found the 1961 Constitution unacceptable. In a sense, this meant that the die was cast and violent confrontation was made more probable. Consequently, black voter registration was low, which made cross-voting ineffective. As a result, instead of moderate candidates winning 'A' Roll seats in what was an almost entirely white-dominated election, the segregationist radicals won. Whitehead, who had led the whites into accepting the new constitution, lost his seat. The Rhodesia

Front (RF), which had succeeded the Dominion Party, won the election. Ian Smith soon replaced Winston Field as the RF's leader. Thus the processes surrounding this stage of Zimbabwe's constitution-making, even if now purely historical, are important.

The 'liberal' constitution with its justiciable Declaration of Rights found itself in the hands of a radical right-wing government dedicated to achieving its fundamentally racially discriminatory goals by whatever means were necessary and regardless of world opinion. As a result, the courts conducted an important part of the country's politics over the next four years. This intensified tensions between the executive and the judiciary, which had begun to emerge over the emergency powers and 'security' legislation introduced to suppress Black Nationalist opposition. They came to a head with the UDI and the threat of a major confrontation in the courts in *Madzimbamuto v. Lardner-Burke* (1968(2) S.A.284). The fact that, by this stage, the majority of the Rhodesian bench were acclimatized to the dominant mood favoring independence and used their forensic skills to confirm its legality, limited the confrontation. It was thus resolved by a combination of the abolition of the justiciability of the Declaration, which excluded judges from their 'political' role as protectors of human and political rights; the resignation or voluntary retirement of some judges in the face of the executive's resolute illegality; and the more subtle self-selection of a UDI-serving bench.

THE SETTLER CONSTITUTIONS: 1965 AND 1969

The 1965 UDI Constitution is described as a 'settler' constitution because it was, for the first time, not the combined product of the British and Rhodesians. But its making did, like all the others, involve other parties and actors. The British by now had established Five Principles that they regarded as pre-requisites for the grant of independence. These principles, referred to as NIBMAR, were:

- unimpeded progress to majority rule,
- guarantees against retrogressive amendments of the constitution,
- an immediate improvement in the political status of Africans,
- progress towards ending racial discrimination, and
- the acceptability of any independence proposal to the people as a whole.

In Rhodesia, the RF under Smith had won all the 50 'A' Roll seats in the May 1965 election under the 1961 Constitution. The black MPs in the previous Parliament formed the United People's Party (UPP), and were all returned as the official opposition. In preparation for his negotiations to demand independence from Britain, Smith detained Nkomo, Sithole, and other black nationalists. He held a referendum on the independence issue, without mention of unilateral action, and received 58,091 Yes to 6,906 No votes. Harking back to Rhodes's methods, he also organized the 'Domboshawa Indaba' with black chiefs who he claimed approved his approach.

On 11 November, timed to coincide with Armistice Memorial Day, they declared independence and amended the 1961 Constitution. Britain responded by passing the Southern Rhodesia Act and the Southern Rhodesia Constitution Order, reaffirming that Southern Rhodesia remained under the jurisdiction of the British government, and declared void any action to facilitate the 'Rhodesian

Constitution'. UDI provided an opportunity for UN involvement in the process. Britain did not veto a UN resolution that gave broad authority for economic sanctions, and which the UN later used for authority to impose a partial naval blockade on oil supplies to Rhodesia through Mozambique. The Security Council reinforced UN involvement in December 1966, with its decision that 'the present situation in … Rhodesia constitutes a threat to international peace and security' (SC Resolution 232). Following the involvement of Rhodesian courts in the constitutional process, the *Madzimbamuto* case came to the Privy Council, in spite of the government's purported abolition of such appeals. The Privy Council confirmed Britain's constitutional authority over Southern Rhodesia, despite the *de facto* control exercised by the Rhodesians. Soon after this decision in 1968, which the Rhodesian authorities ignored, the Appellate Division in Salisbury held, in *R. v. Ndlovu*, that Rhodesia was now in full and probably continued control of the country and declared it the *de jure* government (Judgement A.D. 138/68).

The 'Battle of Chinhoy' on 28 April 1966 is generally acknowledged as the first significant engagement of the guerrilla war which continued until 1979. The government did not re-enter discussion on constitution-making until the mid-1970s, though there were sporadic negotiations on board British naval vessels, *HMS Tiger* in 1966 and *HMS Fearless* in 1967. In 1969 Smith introduced a new constitution, severing the link, preserved in 1965, between the Crown and Rhodesia, which was now declared a republic. The constitution provided for a non-executive president and a bi-cameral parliament. Voters elected 50 of the 60 seats in the House of Assembly on the unambiguously racial 'European Roll'. The 'African Roll', four from both Mashonaland and Matabeleland, together with the four electoral colleges of Chiefs, Headmen and Councillors in Mashonaland and Matabeleland, elected the remaining 16 MPs. The Declaration of Rights remained non-justiciable, but the Senate Legal Committee continued to provide non-binding advice on the constitutionality of Bills. As Linington states (2001: 30) in his recent work on the Zimbabwean Constitution, 'In essence the 1969 Constitution entrenched white supremacy and racial discrimination in Rhodesia'.

The British Conservative government again made quite elaborate proposals in 1971 to find a constitutional settlement acceptable to the Rhodesians. Palley estimated that under these proposals majority rule could be achieved in 2035 at the earliest (Palley in Meredith, 1979: 80). Having achieved agreement with Smith, the Fifth Principle required the people as a whole to accept this proposal and the Pearce Commission was sent to Rhodesia to examine this estimate. The real concern among the black nationalist leaders in prison and in exile was that this exercise – which would not be a secret vote referendum, but an elaborate 'consultation' – would be manipulated to allow Britain an easy escape from its responsibilities. As a result, a temporary 'diplomatic alliance' brought individuals from ZANU and ZAPU, together with two essentially non-partisan clergymen: Bishop Abel Muzorewa and the Reverend Canaan Banana, to lead the campaign against the proposal's acceptance and to organize within Rhodesia, to ensure that the response was an overwhelming NO. For this purpose, the African National Council was formed in December 1971. The nationalist strategy was effective in marshalling the rejection of a constitution that excluded the participation of the Liberation Movement, as ZANU and ZAPU and their military wings, ZANLA and ZIPRA, were now generally called. However, the introduction of Bishop Muzorewa, who had no previous political base or clear relationship with the movement, created complexities for the future constitutional process and a golden opportunity for the Rhodesians to confuse the issue.

Eventually the so-called Internal Settlement of 1978 and the Zimbabwe-Rhodesia Constitution of 1979 were achieved. A fresh enthusiasm to find peace and an agreed framework for future government dominated the mid-1970s constitution-making process. This was of concern to apartheid South Africa and the US, as the independence of Mozambique in 1975 under a Communist bloc-supported government brought the possibility of an enhanced base area for the Zimbabwean liberation forces. Smith had sought to develop an alliance with Muzorewa as early as 1972. The ANC was committed to non-violent change and at one stage, in December 1974, announced that it had merged the military parties under its umbrella. In the same month, the government released the main nationalist leaders from detention and launched a variety of tentative negotiations, which coincided with dramatic military-related events, such as the assassination in March 1975 of Herbert Chitepo, a central planner and organizer of ZANLA's military strategy, in Lusaka. In August, South Africa's Prime Minister Vorster and Zambia's President Kaunda sponsored a meeting of Nkomo, Sithole, Muzorewa, and Chikerema with Smith, in a railway carriage on the Victoria Falls. The talks broke down almost immediately because of Smith's refusal to contemplate the participation of wanted 'terrorists' in constitutional talks. In December 1975, Nkomo continued discussions in Salisbury with Smith, which in turn came to nothing and ended in March 1976.

On the military front, a restructuring and amalgamation of certain ZIPRA and ZANLA units based in Tanzania led to a new formation, the Zimbabwe People's Army (ZIPA) at the end of 1975. This was seen as a powerful regrouping, and continued during the first attempted Peace/Constitutional Conference in Geneva in late 1976, but broke down after conflicts between units of the two forces and the purging of ZANLA's commanders in September 1977. Despite this, recruitment to the two liberation armies continued during this period and the war intensified, making its own contribution to the process of constitution making.

In 1974, Sithole had been removed from the leadership of ZANU by his fellow detainees. Nevertheless, he was able to rely on his formal status, the party's geographically disconnected leadership and the willingness of the Rhodesians to recognise him for the purposes of their talks, to continue to claim the position. The situation clarified in 1976 when Robert Mugabe left Rhodesia for exile and the leadership of ZANU in Mozambique. It was from this situation that a new alliance was forged on 9 October 1976 with the formation of the Patriotic Front (PF) between ZANU under Mugabe and ZAPU under Nkomo. Over the next three years this grouping took the peace-making and constitution-making process forward on behalf of the militarily effective liberation movement, excluding both Muzorewa and Sithole. It gained the recognition of the Liberation Committee of the OAU and the Presidents of the Front Line States, which constituted yet another group of actors in the constitution-making process. Some, especially Mozambique, Tanzania, and Zambia, played critical roles in the final complex negotiations, which resulted in the 1979 Lancaster House Conference and the independence Constitution of Zimbabwe in 1980.

The war was a major factor during these final years. In April 1976, Secretary of State Kissinger visited Zimbabwe to put proposals to Smith to enable him to accept majority rule in the country within two years rather than the 1000 years that Smith insisted it would take. Though the Front Line States rejected the Anglo-American proposal, it was to be discussed at a constitutional conference of all the parties: British, Rhodesian Front, internal nationalists, and the PF convened in Geneva in October and chaired by the British. An element of the proposal was the establishment of a large Zimbabwe Development Fund, one possible use of which was to support a substantial land reform program. The Geneva conference became deadlocked by December and was postponed *sine die*. In 1977, the Anglo-American proposal was expanded and discussed further; the Fund was considered in terms of a $1.5 billion figure. A Bill of Rights was added, which included protection of private property from confiscation, except on stipulated grounds of public interest, with prompt and adequate compensation to be freely remitted abroad. For various reasons, the plan was not accepted and was the subject of further discussions in Dar es Salaam in 1978.

The PF was greatly concerned about the constitutional arrangements in the transitional period. These contemplated a UN peacekeeping force and a transitional Advisory Council, on which the PF would be in the minority. Once again, the talks led to nothing. A negotiated solution to the problem appeared impossible. The scale of death and destruction in the country as well as in Mozambique and Zambia continued to grow.

The Internal Settlement of March 1978 brought Smith together with Muzorewa's UANC (United African National Council), Sithole's ZANU, and Senator Chirau's ZUPO (Zimbabwe United Peoples Organization). The parties agreed on a new constitution, which ensured a majority of black MPs and an effective veto for the minority of white representatives. A Security Council Resolution, from which five major Western states abstained, condemned the settlement. Based on the new constitution, elections were held in April 1979, which the PF condemned but was unable to disrupt. In June, the Muzorewa government was installed and the war intensified. International recognition of the new non-racial regime and the ending of UN sanctions became a serious possibility. The Conservative Party had sent observers led by Lord Boyd to the elections, and he had concluded that 'Though the election may not have been fully fair because of the war conditions it was at least as fair and free as possible... [and] it could be taken as "a kind of referendum" on the constitution' (Palley, cited in Meredith, 1979: 80). In relation to the Five Principles, Boyd stated that 'the result represented the wish of the majority of the electorate of the country however calculated' (ibid.). Was this a satisfaction of the Fifth Principle, which would enable Britain to end its role in this 'long-standing source of grief?' (Renwick, 1997: 17). The election of Margaret Thatcher in May 1979 made this scenario more feasible. Other international actors were still part of the process, including the UN, the Commonwealth, and the Carter administration.

The Commonwealth Summit meeting in August 1979 restrained the new British government's temptation to grant immediate independence. Combined with the views of African political leaders, it was of the opinion that a new constitution and free elections must precede such a move. This was the background to the Constitutional Conference at Lancaster House, convened on 10 September 1979, the management of which by the new Foreign Secretary, Lord

Carrington, was the subject of much discussion and analysis (Renwick, 1997; Davidow, 1984). Davidow saw it as a particularly good example of what he described as 'Dominant Third Party Mediation', in that it achieved an apparent agreement between parties whose interests, ambitions, and policies were so far apart that decades of discussion had only increased their differences. It 'must', in his view, 'be regarded one of the United Kingdom's few recent diplomatic triumphs' (Davidow, 1984: 16). Robin Renwick, who played a major role in the Lancaster House process, was acutely conscious of the strategic position Britain enjoyed by insisting that it was the 'arbitrator' rather than a negotiating party in the process (Renwick, 1997: 34). This certainly worked in both the historical and the immediate context of the conference. But from a broader perspective, this self-effacing position has not been sustainable. Indeed, it may have made things more difficult in the long run. Britain, as has been shown, has always been a major player with significant interests in the governance and prosperity of Rhodesia and then Zimbabwe. It has emphasized, ever since 1890, that it was in the 'unfortunate' position of 'being required to exercise responsibility without power' (ibid.). But this position was the result of the particular form of colonialism the imperial power chose. If the Rhodesian problem was 'a can of worms' in 1979, it remains so today, and Britain cannot deny its part in the process that led to these situations. Had Britain engaged as an interested party, it is possible that Zimbabwe could have achieved a different and more sustainable outcome.

It is thus, both legally and morally correct that Britain should face its obligation to be involved in the process of finding a better and permanent constitutional dispensation for the future situation of Zimbabwe. Some time has been necessary to come to a more measured judgement of the success of the conference and the constitution. Davidow, who found that 'The more I studied it the more impressed I was with the diplomatic victory that had been achieved in London', added a cautionary note, observing that '(I)n retrospect, Lancaster House appears to have been an easier victory for good sense than in reality it was. What is absent from the historical perspective is the fog of uncertainty, confusion, and misperception that hung over the conference, preventing most there from obtaining a clear view of what was actually happening' (Davidow, 1984: 17). The key words here may be 'diplomatic victory'. Making a constitution to serve as the foundation of a new state is arguably *not* best done in the context of achieving a cease-fire and an end to war. Strategic action, timing, and forcing the pace dominated the Lancaster House conference: getting a result before the convenient conjunctures unravelled. The price that the disputing parties paid for this was a constitution very close to their own, especially with regard to the long-term protection of property, including land and pensions. This was the consequence of accepting a British guarantee of an assisted transitional process, the cease-fire, the temporary direct government by Britain, and the externally supervised election followed by international recognition.

For the Patriotic Front, the price of a transition offering a real, but not totally secure, chance to survive and compete and win an election, was ultimately a take-it-or-leave-it constitution. This hard line was made possible by the fact that Lord Carrington made it understood that he could always adopt the 'Second-Class Solution', namely recognizing the Internal Settlement and a continuation of the war. This was impossible for the Front Line States, which had suffered and were suffering Rhodesian attacks, and were not prepared to provide continued support to the PF forces.

It is no surprise that Britain's priority lay in pursuing its own interests and seeking to rid itself of the Rhodesian albatross. But, given the long-term outcomes, it seems fortunate that both Namibia and South Africa were able to pursue their constitution-making within the contacts and timeframes more within their control, albeit being surrounded by agreed principles as well as powerful international and regional influences and players (Tshuma, 2001: 45).

Two particular aspects of the constitution-making process are important: first, the protection of commercial farmland, which Section 16 of the Constitution provided for in great detail and length; second, the issue or group of minority rights (apart from the property rights of the white minority), which the process energetically avoided. One aspect of the land issue, not mentioned in the Constitution, is the complex and significant involvement of so many actors in the effort to prevent disagreement on this matter from breaking up the conference. By early October 1979, Carrington had obtained Muzorewa's acceptance of the British constitution. He had also got most of the African presidents to find it acceptable. By that time, Renwick points out, 'The Front's objections had been whittled down largely to the question of land' (1997: 41). Britain rejected suggestions for a fund, modelled on the Kenyan Million Acre Scheme. In its view, 'What was required for food production in Rhodesia was to keep European farmers there, not to encourage them to leave, to allow time for African commercial farming to develop'.

The PF had proposed wide powers of land acquisition and discretion on compensation, to enable it to use its sovereignty, once elected. This would enable it to achieve the major changes in land ownership for which it was fighting and which were its main recruiting plank. This proposal was not accepted. Section 16 of the Constitution only allowed either a piecemeal, market-based process of land reform on a willing-seller, willing-buyer basis, or the compulsory acquisition of *under-utilized land* in limited circumstances, by payment of prompt and adequate compensation *freely remitted* to any country of the former owner's choice.

This created the most serious impasse of the conference, and the PF leadership threatened to walk out. Their position attracted sympathy and some support from various sources, and the threat of a break-up generated considerable activity by those who had invested a great deal in the prospect of an agreed outcome. Carrington, sticking to the dominatant strategy, announced that the conference would continue, without an agreement on the Constitution, to deal with the transitional arrangements. He met with the Muzorewa delegation and announced that he proposed putting a British governor into the country to take full responsibility for the transitional government.

This hectic period and the various actors involved were among the most controversial aspects of 'the fog of uncertainty, confusion and misperception that hung over the conference' to which Davidow referred. These aspects constituted no part of the formal documentation or record of the constitution-making process, but continued to be the source of, or explanation for, the continued and increasingly bitter conflict. Carrington himself put out various suggestions of international and British assistance for significant reform and development in the agricultural sector. The Commonwealth Secretary General, Ramphal, worked with others to find a way ahead. US Ambassador Kingman Brewster, who told the PF leaders that 'the Americans would help with land development', played an important role. Davidow was of the opinion, regarding these activities, that '[P]erhaps the most significant involvement of a supporting actor was that of US Ambassador Kingman Brewster' (1984: 65). President Carter authorized Brewster to convey to the British, the Front Line States and the PF a pledge of US assistance should Lancaster House result in success. The wording of the US commitment was convoluted and cautious, reflecting the Carter administration's concern that it might face Congressional criticism for participating in a 'buy' out of white landlords or for opening the US treasury to land-hungry peasants.

Nkomo reported what he felt were encouraging private discussions to his legal team. He was advised by his party that significant land reform was essential for the credibility of a PF government, and was asked to obtain clear written commitments from those making promises to fund land development. Later he informed the team that there was no chance of any clear written commitment being forthcoming. To quote Davidow again, 'The US offer of October 15 did not significantly add substance to Carrington's pledge of a few days before, but it did present Nkomo and Mugabe with a face-saving way out of the impasse which finally, on October 18, they took' (Davidow, 1984: 65).

Nkomo announced the PF's readiness to re-join the conference. The wording is interesting with hindsight. Refusing to accept the constitutional provisions on land excluded the PF from the next stage of the process. Nkomo in his memoirs states, 'Neither the Americans nor the British would tell us how much they would put up, but the principle was a useful one' (Nkomo, 1984: 196). Announcing the situation to the press, he noted the British and US assurances on land issues, since they 'go a long way in allaying the great concern we have over the whole land issue... We are now able to say that if we are satisfied beyond doubt about the ... transitional arrangements, there will be no need to revert to discussions on the Constitution, including those issues on which we reserve ... our position' (*Financial Times*, 19 October 1979). Like the assurances being given, the PF's response was somewhat convoluted and cautious. However, it brought it back to the conference table, saved the timetable, and contributed to the Lancaster House miracle.

A significant section of the ongoing analysis of Zimbabwe's post-independence history has continued to dwell on land as a vital issue. Land was, and remains, a problem of such fundamental importance that it deserves a place in the heart of the country's Constitution. The 1980 Constitution gave land such a role, and the ongoing concerns, whether within or outside Zimbabwe, continue to center on it. These include the present government, its radical and often anarchic War Veteran and Youth Militia supporters, the MDC official opposition party, Zimbabwe's neighbouring states, concerned states, and organizations in and beyond Africa. The Abuja Agreement of Commonwealth Ministers that sought, without success, to find a solution to Zimbabwe's 'controversial land reform programme', sums up the matter. The communiqué issued by the meeting stated 'that as a result of historical injustices (a) Land is at the core of the crisis in Zimbabwe and cannot be separated from other issues of concern to the Commonwealth such as the rule of law, respect for human rights, democracy and the economy' (ibid.).

Thus, land remains fundamentally connected to more 'traditional' constitutional issues. The process of finding a constitutional solution has been long and so far without success. It involves an extensive range of actors and methods, the most recent of which has been the attempt to involve civil society and the population at large.

Group Rights?

The fact that, like many other states, Zimbabwe has a variety of peoples, some minorities with varying senses of identity and language, is a matter outside constitutional attention, apart from the interest in white-owned farmland and the recognition of certain overall elements of customary law and tradition. Given the dramatic tensions between the two major political parties in the war of liberation and the group identities attached thereto, whether mythical or real, this omission is noteworthy. The brutal events in South West Zimbabwe in the 1980s, before the 1987 Unity agreement between (PF)ZAPU and ZANU(PF) that led to the creation of the unified ZANU(PF) and the end of political pluralism at that time, further highlight this omission. There are a variety of possible explanations for this, but here it is intended to make a somewhat limited contribution on a minor non-event connected with the Lancaster House conference.

A conflict studies specialist, Professor John Burton, sought to persuade officials that the issue of relations between the different groups ought to be part of the agenda. The suggestion went nowhere, whether because he made it to the wrong people or because officials considered it an unnecessary deviation. It is almost certain, however, that had he made the suggestion to either of the Patriotic Front parties or the Muzorewa incumbents, they would have given it even shorter shrift. Most Zimbabwean (as opposed to Rhodesian) politicians have long regarded the suggestion of inter-tribal tensions as politically incorrect. This is partly because of the past reality of 'divide and rule', based upon the emphasis on tribal differences. It may also stem from the deep desire for 'Unity' generated during the anti-colonial war. It might also be suggested now that in the intense heat of confrontational politics in Zimbabwe of the past few years, involving more national, social, economic, and governance issues, differences have undergone a considerable homogenization and are increasingly matters of cultural rather than political (and potentially constitutional) interest.

Post-Independence Constitution-Making and Popular Involvement

The legislature which, until the 2000 elections, was overwhelmingly controlled by the government party ZANU (PF), made many of the important constitutional amendments, among them the abolition of racial representation, the establishment of an Executive Presidency, and the relaxation of restraints on land reform and resettlement. Thus, the process involved largely party policy and parliamentary procedure, though the interesting debates took place both in and outside the party and parliamentary fora. Civil society did not choose to organize or become actively involved with these issues. Mandaza points out that this was equally true of such serious issues as 'the tragedy of Matabeleland', which remained largely removed from the public domain in Zimbabwe until much later (Mandaza, 2001: 48).

The focus here is on the more complex process that has surrounded constitution-making since 1999, and, in particular, the popular calls for, and the government's response to, the demand for a constitutional review. The government's response was to establish a Commission of Inquiry 'to inquire into and carry out a comprehensive review of the present Constitution and to make general and specific recommendations for consideration by the President'.[2] For reasons considered below, the National Constitutional Assembly (NCA), the main civil society organization debating and promoting constitutional reform, did not support the Commission. Instead, it made its own parallel proposals.

THE CONSTITUTIONAL COMMISSION AND ITS WORK

The President set up the Constitutional Commission under the Commissions of Inquiry Act. The NCA was critical of the Act because it gave the President the sole discretion on whom to appoint, and giving no role to civil society. In the event, the President appointed 241 people to the Commission in addition to the 150 serving MPs appointed as *ex officio* members, 148 of whom were from the ruling party. This created a body of over 400 persons. The Commission had no international members, but had provision for a two-day international conference, on the Making of Zimbabwe's New Democratic Constitution. A variety of experts attended the conference to discuss the draft being prepared for submission to the President. The group did not see the draft at the event, as it was not complete.

The opening address at the conference was given by the retiring Commonwealth Secretary-General, Emeka Anyaoku. Anyaoku stressed the importance of the constitution-making process as essentially a Zimbabwean one, applauding the fact that 'It is the people of Zimbabwe and their government that have decided of their own volition to embark on this process of constitutional reform' (*SAPES*, January 2000: 19). He emphasized the point: 'There is a well-founded suspicion in Zimbabwe and in Africa as a whole, of anything smacking of superior wisdom from the outside. No other continent has suffered so much from the solicitude and pontification of others'.

The NCA pointed out that, under the Commissions of Inquiry Act, the President had no obligation to publish the Commission's findings. The NCA saw this as putting the President above the people in the constitution-making process and undermining the representative nature that the conference should have.[3] In particular, the Act did not require the President to refer the results to a referendum. The NCA also pointed out that the period for the Commission's work was too short for a proper process to inform and educate the public on a highly complex set of issues, and to allow the Commissioners to engage in effective consultation. (The Commission was set up at the end of April 1999 and was required to submit the draft Constitution to the President by 30 November 1999, but it took some time for it to become operational.)

Independent observers tended to conclude that the interplay between officials and NGOs improved the process. The minority of government critics on the Commission appeared to be unrestrained in the range and directness of their comments, and this was the case in the many consultative meetings. (The Commission held over 4,000 meetings throughout the country, and received

7,000 written submissions.) The print media provided an effective forum for the effective projection of both points of view, and debates took place on radio and television. The polarization of the debate after the establishment of the Movement for Democratic Change as a political party during the course of the Commission's work was of concern to the Centre for Democracy and Development (CDD), which observed the process. It led to frequent and extremely abrasive exchanges between the Commission's spokesperson and NCA leaders who became MDC officials. Whether the coincidence of the MDC launch was deliberate or fortuitous, the launch failed to concentrate the debate on the constitutional issues, but was part of a different though equally important political agenda to do with President Mugabe's continuation in office. The CDD Report confirmed that '[t]he desire to limit or curtail the powers of the President has been the single most important factor giving rise to and subsequently driving the initiative for constitutional reform'.

The debate that took place beyond the Commission, such as at the regular and well-attended meetings convened by organizations such as SAPES in Harare, informed and stimulated formal Commission discussions. In sum, public discussion of the constitutional question appeared to be a real, participatory discussion. A noted Zimbabwean political scientist, admittedly closely involved with and committed to the Commission's work, went so far as to suggest that it generated 'a virtual national discourse of the kind seldom experienced in post-colonial Africa' (Mandaza, 2001: 43). The more pointed question is whether the ultimate outcome was one that came, as most people thought it should, from below rather than from above. There were a range of criticisms of the substance of the draft, but the main concerns concentrated on the proposals relating to the Presidency and its powers, in particular, the perception that the proposals did not properly reflect the demand for a non-executive president and an executive prime minister responsible to parliament expressed by the public.[4] The more serious criticism was that the process was ultimately in the hands of the President, subject only to the possibility of a draft being put to the people in a referendum.

The Constitutional Commission process was certainly a major initiative for Zimbabwe; civil society was able in a relatively short time to raise the level of political interest and involvement among the population, which appeared to have lost interest in politics and to have accepted the permanent dominance of one party. Also noteworthy is the fact that the governing party was prompted by NCA demands in setting up the Commission. This makes it all the more important to ask why the process apparently went so wrong, became so polarized, and generated so little consensus. Mandaza attributes part of the problem to the two very different approaches to constitution-making by lawyers as compared with political scientists (*SAPES*, 14(4): 43–9). He approves of Issa Shivji's explanation that 'Constitution-making is a process of constructing a political consensus around Constitutionalism. It is a process by which rulers derive legitimacy', and argues that the Commission did 'almost everything required in consensus-building, but the NCA/MDC...withheld their support at the referendum'.

The NCA, whatever their alleged ulterior motives, clearly opposed the Commission as a restrictive, insufficiently participatory, and insufficiently predictable process. Lovemore Madhuku, an NCA spokesperson, summed this up with the words, 'An undemocratic process in constitution-making is no good for the country' (ibid.). The NCA participated in the informal discussions and maintained a critical commentary on the Commission's work and outcome. They found the referendum draft unacceptable, in particular the provisions relating to the acquisition of land, which Madhuku suggests added little to the powers under the 1992 Land Acquisition Act and were inserted as camouflage to distract from more important issues, such as the President's discretionary powers. Mandaza's analysis is correct in the simple sense that the NCA/MDC did not see the Commission's provenance, composition or possible outcome as a process of consensus building in which they could believe. It could not offer them enough to compensate for the risks of losing their identity by involving themselves in a system seen as arbitrary, corrupt, and antithetical to their interests.

This connects with a more fundamental question: the extent to which the attempt to create a new constitution with popular support was aimed at re-establishing state power to enable the governing party to carry out the liberation of the land, for which it had gone to war. It is arguable that, by 1997, the incumbent party was on notice that its period of 'liberation legitimacy' was under threat. By 1999, and even more so after the 2000 referendum, the possibility of its losing power without achieving a major reform in land should have been seen as a clear threat. In addition, given the other omissions and commissions over the previous twenty years for which the government and its officers might be held responsible, the situation called for a serious decision either to accept the possibility of a change of government or to make constitutional amendments that would preclude or pre-empt a change.

THE EMERGENCE OF A CIVIL SOCIETY WITH CONSTITUTIONAL CONCERNS
In this context, it is necessary to consider briefly the process that brought about that change in what one might call the 'Informal Constitution' of Zimbabwe and the unexpected prospect of the ZANU(PF) coming to the end of its time in power. What brought the long period of one-party dominance to the brink? The process has changed parts of the country's social and economic make-up, and has turned an essentially quiescent, passive population that initially enjoyed the highly positive outcome of independence into a self-confident, critical, mass movement. At the same time as Zimbabwean civil society was tolerating the new state elites of the 1980s, it was gathering expertise and experience and exploiting the opportunities of the social benefits. In March 1990, in the wake of the merger of ZANU(PF) and (PF)ZAPU, the country went to the polls to elect the first Executive President and a new Assembly. In spite of the announcement that the party would not seek to set up a formal one party state, many saw the situation as reinforcing that trend *de facto*. The public thus saw the formation of the Zimbabwe Unity Movement (ZUM) by Edgar Tekere, a former ZANU(PF) leader, and its electoral challenge as a significant test of the nation's attitude to the dramatic change in the balance of the informal constitutional structure. Consequently, the perceived mismanagement of the 1990 election and the recurrence of election-related violence suggested that there was a serious threat to achieving democracy in Zimbabwe. This was seen as threatening in a new way, as 'the 1990 elections were held at a time of widespread disenchantment with the authorities, particularly in urban areas where problems such as unemployment, shortage of transport, lack of housing and inflation had become con-

spicuously burdensome' (Moyo, 1992: 2; see also Gibbon, 1995; Bond and Manyanya, 2002).

The lack of real change in either Zimbabwe's inherited colonial economic structures or its economic fortunes by the end of the 1980s meant that, by the early 1990s, it faced external pressures to commit itself further to economic neo-liberalism. Accordingly, in 1991, behaving as the 'economically-well-behave-country' status to which it aspired, the government voluntarily undertook its own Economic Structural Adjustment Programme (ESAP), the implementation of which coincided with and stimulated the emerging maturity and assertiveness of civil society in the country, in particular the trade union movement. By this time, a vibrant range of human rights, women's, war veterans' and special interest NGOs had emerged and consolidated. An increasingly confident independent press, served by a resilient corps of local professionals, had established its credentials with such exposures as the Willowgate motor vehicle scandal. The scene seemed set fair for Zimbabwe to move into its next stage of constitutional development, with a healthy interaction between the state and a vigilant civil society.

At this time, the government, given its overwhelming parliamentary majority, could legally and politically amend the constitution as it wished. The first sign of this came in response to the land issue raised in the 1990 elections. By the end of 1990, the government enacted a constitutional amendment extending its power to acquire land and designate it for resettlement as well as to change the level of compensation payable. This provoked an *extra curia* response from Chief Justice Gubbay, which raised the long-standing, but until then relatively healthy, tension between the executive and the judiciary several notches.

The role of the Zimbabwean courts in the constitutional process has been important and instructive, and deserves greater attention than can be given here, but the issue is worth dwelling upon briefly.[5] The Chief Justice suggested 'it must not ... be assumed that an affirmative vote of one hundred members will enable Parliament to pass a constitutional Bill which goes to the extent of damaging or destroying the very foundation or structure of the Constitution' (Gubbay, 1991). The assertion of the 'Essential Features Doctrine' underlines a fundamental cleavage between those Zimbabweans who believe that democracy and constitutionalism rest exclusively in the sovereignty of the people and their elected representatives, and those who assert a higher status for certain immutable features of the Constitution. Given the history of Zimbabwe and the fact that the doctrine was given its first public hearing in connection with protecting land, it may be no surprise that the subsequent and intensifying clash between a ZANU(PF) executive and the Chief Justice took the disastrous course that it did. Economic democracy, and particularly the 'Democratisation of the Land' is a theme that Zimbabweans, including many, but by no means all, lawyers, have championed for generations.[6]

Thus, between 1991 and 1997, three processes relevant to the constitutional debate were running in parallel and in contradiction in Zimbabwe: (i) the promise of land reform, which necessarily implied interference, essentially with white farmers' rights; (ii) the ESAP liberalization program; and (iii) the growing assertiveness of extra-parliamentary criticism of the government and the ruling party. The ESAP had achieved many of its objectives by 1994: 18,000 government jobs had gone and the wage bill had dropped; the government had removed controls on foreign exchange and prices; tariff reduction was at a better rate than the WTO's expectations; the government had reduced trade restrictions and deregulated the labor market. By 1997, the World Bank found Zimbabwe's progress 'highly satisfactory'. On the other hand, the changes were painful enough to evoke in an escalating series of civil protests. Particularly noteworthy were the 1993 riots against bread price increases, the 1995 strike in Harare, and the strikes of civil servants in 1996 and private sector workers in 1997.

The long honeymoon period of 'Liberation Legitimacy' was coming to an end, in spite of (or because of) the unification of the two major parties. In Parliament, radical party members complained that the government was failing to implement land reform. Some suggested that it was time for a new leadership. In the streets, organized groups, including a newly organized section of the War Veterans, were complaining of prices, corruption, and cronyism. One source of complaint was a recent and largely unexplained act of generous 'compensation' by the government to many of its own, for injuries or disabilities from the liberation war. This infuriated the 'Vets', who disrupted a judicial inquiry into the matter. The backdrop was beginning to unfold to the 'shocking' scenario that came with the Constitutional Referendum followed by the 2000 general election, after which many proclaimed things would 'never be the same again'.

But it is arguable that Zimbabwe was experiencing a pattern of governance and constitutional order that appeared stable as long as the fundamental issues of the economy, including demands for land reform, did not force their way to the surface. And Zimbabwe was about to be caught between a 'rock and a hard place', the rock being the governing party with a military background that has inherited and refined the authoritarian instruments of Rhodesia, the memory of the colonial past and the knowledge that it has not fulfilled its 'revolutionary' promise, while enjoying the wealth of the incumbent elite, and is therefore determined to retain power, and the hard place being the product of good and bad developments in the country's social and economic life, the good being the remarkable growth of a civil society determined to see a less corrupt and more humane government. A combination of the energy and talent of Zimbabweans and capacity-building support from a range of international agencies promoting and supporting good governance has brought about this situation. Significant among these developments was strengthening the integrity and cohesion of the trade unions.

Unhappily, neither the informal nor the conventional constitutional structures are able to provide a framework to manage peacefully the inevitable conflict between these two forces. The confrontation between the two became physical in 1997. In November, President Mugabe, after having refused to talk with the strident War Veterans, met them, and without provision in the national budget or prior notice, promised to pay them each a Z$50,000 lump sum gratuity and a Z$2,000 monthly pension. As a result, the Zimbabwean dollar devalued in the span of four hours from 10 to 30 to the US dollar. In December, the ZCTU organized the first National Stay-away. Industrial action was repeated during 1998. In February 1999, a National Working Peoples Convention spurned government-inspired initiatives.

This was the context of the attempt to debate and create a new constitution – a context that was clearly not ideal, but was pressed forward by both civil society and government. One result, which was decried by many dissatisfied with both the government and the modified Lancaster House Constitution, was that the constitution-making process became involved with the rapidly deteriorating political confrontation. Thus, a 'No' vote on the proposed constitution was characterized by the opposition as a vote for the removal of the President. Inclusion of an enhanced provision on land acquisition in the proposal made this association stronger. It also laid the basis for the allegation that the real architects of the 'No' vote, and thus the new opposition party, were a combination of white farmers and foreign, particularly British, interests seeking to preserve the post-colonial status quo.

This situation set the scene for the subsequent relations between ZANU(PF) and its supporters and fraternal regional neighbours on the one hand, and the MDC, civil society, their allies and the international critics of ZANU(PF) activities and projects on the other. The determination to democratize put Zimbabwe's other democratic credentials into serious doubt, whether related to respect for the rule of law, the independence of the judiciary, the protection of individual liberty, or freedom of association and speech. It has also led to increased economic hardship and a dramatic economic downtown. On the other hand, the MDC's insistence on challenging the government of ZANU(PF) has earned it praise for its determination, courage, and loyalty, despite accusations of treason and betrayal regarding the land reforms for which they fought. Two elections brought Zimbabwe some notoriety, smart sanctions, and suspension from the Commonwealth. But has the MDC made its election to Parliament work for its supporters? Has it taken the obligation to find a democratic solution seriously enough? Has it failed to take full and responsible advantage of the constitutional reform process? Has it jeopardized the principles of social justice upon which it was founded, by accepting convenient alliances in the pursuit of a single-issue program concerned with one man?

The situation has raised questions of the prospects for good governance in the entire region. Is it possible to find a constitutional solution in what appears to have become an anarchic situation? Is this a situation where the emerging right to democracy, the advancement of international law and standards, and actors from further afield can help to find a way forward? The century-old tussle in Zimbabwe has repeatedly resisted what seems like a stable solution, apart from those claiming success, put in place by authoritarians acting from one dominant position or another. Can the answers be found for the many problems that resurface? Can the country still achieve a balanced and productive reform of land? What are the legitimate rights of groups such as the comparatively wealthy white minorities? Do they enjoy the right of association and to participate in politics? Should they be regarded as citizens? Connected with this, and again this has been dramatized by the British imperial connection, is the legitimacy, in a globalized world where developing states require assistance for a range of financial, moral, or political needs, of intervention for 'democracy'? Does the 'right to democracy' provide a basis for such activity? If so, to what degree? The current actions by the Commonwealth against Zimbabwe may be something of a landmark in this respect, but what constructive constitutional solution can be made out of it?

Conclusions: Conflict Resolution and Constitution-Making

In the context of the complex background, a number of tentative lessons emerge from the Zimbabwean constitutional experience, including the general issues of military conflict, constitution-making and peace-making, and consensus building. Other lessons cover the structure and substance of the process, public participation, representation, timing, participation of the international community and the role of international law. The military nature of the Zimbabwean conflict had a significant effect on the process, in both the pre- and post-independence era. It conflated the peace-making process with formulating the constitution and the transition to peace, and accounted for the 'acceptance' of a constitution that is not conducive to the long-term resolution of conflicting interests, nor to the constitution's stability. 'Lancaster House' became a pejorative term when referring to the Constitution, and, selectively, a convenient explanation for not respecting some of its most fundamental elements.

The duration of the military conflict and the failure of 'constitutional' negotiations have made military culture an important part of the 'politics' of the process. The intensity of the war, including its specific contemporary ideological dimension, meant that the rhetoric was as brutal as the fighting. Black Nationalists expressed their cause in largely communist terminology, which made it extremely alien to the white minority, even when it was dramatically modified by 'reconciliation-speak' after 1980. This possibly accounts for the 'distance' the white minority maintained from the new nation, something that the new national leadership frequently deplored.

The Zimbabwean experience suggests that the constitution-making process is of limited use to peace-building or conflict-resolution processes. But the 1980 process probably accounts for a greater reservoir of resentment than of consensus. Smith, whose Rhodesia Front was overwhelmingly returned in the white seats in 1980 and represents some of the deepest suspicion among whites, regarded it as an act of betrayal by both South Africa and Britain. Mugabe made it clear that, despite his dramatic reconciliation statement immediately after his victory in 1980, he considered the deep entrenchment of protecting white farms to be a total denial of the essential cause of the liberation war. In view of the history of Rhodesian land resettlement, it would seem to be an issue for separate, or at least differently time-framed, negotiations. In addition, given the events in southwest Zimbabwe in the 1980s, minority rights, beyond the property rights of white farmers, might have been included in the Bill of Rights. The pattern of support for the opposition party suggests that regional and language, and not merely tribal, identities might be as relevant in Zimbabwe as in Europe. Both the 1980 and 1999/2000 constitution-making exercises suggest that co-ordination between constitution-making and peace-making is useful, but preferably not their coincidence.

It would clearly have been an advantage had the 1999 review exercise lasted longer, been better resourced, and allowed more time for public education and debate. Nevertheless, time and debate would not have cured its essential defect, since the problem lies in its provenance and its controllers. The same, ironically, was true of the criticism of the Lancaster House process.

Managing the expectations of the public, the elite, and the leadership arising from the new constitution is important. The referendum result was a shock to

President Mugabe and his government. It also became clear to Mugabe that if radical reforms, such as land reform, were to be undertaken, they would need to be carried out before a change of government. At the other end of the historical spectrum the post-1980 scenario created expectations of continuity among the farmers which the country has not realized, and a confidence in the permanence of constitutional guarantees that took too little account of the possibility of continued injustice. Here again, some greater degree of participation by those whose status, wealth or whatever is in contention in a changing constitutional scene, should help put expectations into a more manageable situation.

In 1980, Britain's insistence on its unique control of the process best served the short term. Earlier attempts had failed, possibly due to some ambiguity on the side of the British. Though ex-rulers must be involved in the independence situation, their closeness to later processes, as is true of other external actors, is not helpful in most cases. The 1999 process was clearly made more difficult by the real or alleged involvement of Britain and other 'donors' in the debate. Similarly, the UN and other global intergovernmental organizations are likely to, and should, seek a role. But it should be a controlled role in promoting and realizing constitutional values. The processes of constitution-making in both the broad and the narrow sense should make repeated references and appeals to international and comparative law. The use of human rights conventions in national documents and international legislation, as well as in jurisprudence, has had an important role in the Zimbabwean process, especially in constitutional development through the courts. But Zimbabwe also demonstrates the limits of these norms.

Where substantial and fundamental issues, such as devolution and regional autonomy, are the subjects of strong claims which the constitution may be able to deal with, should they be part of the substance, as well as discussed, debated, and aired in the process? An issue that has arisen in Zimbabwe in a very real form is the substantive issue raised by the former Chief Justice: the Doctrine of Immutable Principles. This debatable proposition is of the greatest importance in developing constitutional democracies. It is important to determine clearly if this is or is not a part of the Constitution. Leaving it to the courts alone is a recipe for heroism and not for the preservation of the rule of law or judicial independence.

Notes

[1] One is reminded of the many other agreements and treaties meant to bring peace and support to a new order that seem only to have nurtured an unresolved conflict. See Steven Ratner's reference to E.J. Hobsbawm's description in *Nations and Nationalism since 1789* of the explosive (ethnic) issues of 1988–92 in Europe as 'The eggs of Versailles and Brest Litowsk ... still hatching.' Ratner (2000).

[2] Proclamation no. 6 of 1999, S.I. 138A of 1999.

[3] The author acknowledges with thanks, the comments and information on the international meeting with the Commission provided to him by Professor Muna Ndulo and Dr Michael Pinto-Dushinsky, who participated on behalf of International IDEA.

[4] Amy Tsanga has argued that there were differing views on this and that the criticism exaggerates the position. *SAPES*, Feb. 2000 p. 9.

[5] For an up-to-date comprehensive work on the substance of the Constitution, see Linington (2001), on this issue, pp. 352–371 in particular.

[6] See, for example, Tshuma (2001: 126–32) who argues the necessary but curing effect of the 1992 Land Acquisition Act's explicit ousting of the Court's jurisdiction, which he regards as defective in the Constitutional amendment. The same author, commenting on section 16 of the Lancaster House Constitution, states 'For black Zimbabweans, property rights were a political construct of the colonial state and no attempts at insulating them from government interference as an inherent human right could give them legitimacy.' Ibid. p. 43.

15

DOUGLAS G. ANGLIN

The African Peer Review of Political Governance: Precedents, Problematics & Prospects

The peer review process is the 'heart' of NEPAD (Gelb, 2002: 26)

THE provision in the New Partnership for Africa's Development (NEPAD) for peer reviews of governance practices is not only its most innovative and distinctive feature but also its most crucial. It may not be too much to suggest that how the review process functions in practice could make or break NEPAD. Yet, not every stakeholder is persuaded that peer review is feasible or even desirable. The response to the initial announcement ranged from profound scepticism to outright alarm. While some were persuaded that the scheme was destined to fail, others feared it would succeed. Among ruling elites, many were quick to recognize the potential threat peer review, particularly of political governance, posed for their regimes and themselves personally. The very idea of holding heads of state accountable to each other, let alone to their own people, for the way they chose to rule their countries was anathema. Hence the concerted efforts to capture, control and, if possible, cripple the peer review mechanism before it became fully operational.

In the case of civil society, NEPAD got off to a shaky start, from which it has yet to fully recover.[1] Many claimed that NEPAD was neither 'new', a genuine 'partnership', 'Africa'-inspired, nor 'development'-oriented. The concerns of social critics focused on the undoubted shortcomings of NEPAD's neo-liberal prescriptions, a critique that, at times, was also used to discredit the peer review process. Yet, given a modicum of political will, peer review might conceivably offer a promising prospect that, over time, sufficient political space might be opened up for popular forces to effect meaningful changes in policies and perhaps regimes. Admittedly, the early prognoses were not encouraging, and responses to developments in Zimbabwe have not improved matters. Nevertheless, it is too early to write peer reviews off. As with NEPAD and the African Union (AU), peer review is very much a 'work in progress'. It may take some years before even an interim verdict on it is out.

The Policy Environment

NEPAD is the outcome of a sober assessment of where Africa stood at the outset of the new millennium as well as of what realistically needed to be done to check the disastrous downward trends. As the Secretary-General of the Organization of Africa Unity (OAU) lamented in 2002,

> ... it is no secret to anyone that Africa, our Continent, has up to now, remained the least developed in the planet. All socio-economic indicators are in the red, thus portraying Africa as the only economic space whose growth has remained constantly negative. This state of affairs ... verges on catastrophe.[2]

In reviewing the lengthy list of earlier promising OAU (and UN) initiatives – among them the Lagos Plan of Action (1980), the African Charter for Popular Participation in Development and Transformation (1990), and the Cairo Agenda for Action: Relaunching Africa's Economic and Social Development (1995) – a principal concern has been the inability (or unwillingness) of OAU members, despite their initial enthusiasm, to implement their solemn undertakings. Two policy directives, in particular, have emerged from this exercise in soul-searching.

The first was scarcely new. It was to take more direct charge of the continent's destiny – a sentiment that has found wide resonance within civil society. The insistence on African ownership of its agenda for recovery was indicative of the depth of dissatisfaction with prevailing policies imposed from abroad. It also testified to growing public acknowledgement that Africa shared some responsibility for its predicament and that, ultimately, its salvation lay in its own hands. Hence, the renewed emphasis on collective self-reliance, and especially domestic resource mobilization.[3] This did not preclude continued reliance on the international community for enhanced support, though now it was expected to be on the basis of a new 'partnership of equals' forged with the donors, providing for shared commitments and mutual accountability (Mbeki, 2002a; NEPAD, 2001: paras 148–9).

The second lesson, rooted in decades of disappointment, viewed the decision to accord precedence to economic development over good governance as a strategic blunder. Conventional wisdom had long contended that, until a country had met its pressing development needs, it could ill afford to indulge in the luxury of democracy. This was the underlying rationale for a one-party state. Typical of the times, no mention of democracy found its way into the landmark 1980 Lagos Plan of Action. NEPAD reversed these priorities. 'Development is impossible', it confidently declared, 'in the absence of true democracy, respect for human rights, peace and good governance' (NEPAD, 2001: para 79).

This was not the first occasion that the relevance of democracy to development had been noted. As early as 1988, in the course of a World Bank brainstorming session in Kenya,[5] African advisers had argued the case for good governance forcefully and effectively. Then, in 1990, with the resurgence in demands for political freedom and democratic reforms, the African Charter for Popular Participation in Development and Transformation added the voices of civil society, and urged the 'imperative necessity' of a mechanism to monitor compliance with it.[6] Also, in 1990, the OAU Summit asserted that 'democracy and development should go together and should be mutually reinforcing'. A host of other OAU (and UN) documents and declarations took up similar themes. Thus, in 1996, the OAU's Yaoundé Declaration attributed Africa's economic plight 'particularly to the failure of our countries to provide good governance'.[7]

Yet, regrettably, none of these initiatives was pursued with vigour. One by one, they died of 'benign neglect'. Not until NEPAD asserted categorically that good governance was a prerequisite for sustainable development (and privileged access to enhanced aid), and prescribed a mechanism – peer review – designed to encourage compliance, did the issue attract the serious attention of governments. Even so, while the international community formally endorsed NEPAD, resistance from Africa's old guard mounted. As late as mid-2002, President Moi of Kenya contested the claim that political reform should take precedence over economic programmes. More disturbing, at a caucus of SADC heads of state in July 2002, 'Mugabe openly challenged the NEPAD conception of good governance', and received the warm support of the presidents of the Congo, Malawi, Namibia, and Tanzania.[8] Although the political opponents of peer review relied on the sanctity of national sovereignty to sustain their case, undoubtedly a more immediate concern was the perceived threat to their personal career prospects.

Precedents: OAU Peer Monitoring

Although peer review, NEPAD-style, marks a potentially significant advance in promoting good governance, Africa did not lack experience of earlier political initiatives involving peer judgements of state behaviour, commonly in response to specific events or actions. In contrast to peer review,[9] 'peer monitoring' has typically been less structured, less comprehensive in its coverage, and less intrusive. Although it has manifested itself in various guises and contexts, its focus has been on three principal issue areas. First and foremost have been lapses from constitutional rule, notably military coups, particularly when accompanied by assassination. In such cases, self-interest ensures that African governments join in denouncing the perpetrators, at least at the outset. Condemnation in the other two issue areas – fraudulent electoral practices and human rights abuses – has been more problematic, especially for leaders with dubious democratic credentials.

UNCONSTITUTIONAL RULE
Independent African states have experienced over 100 military coups. Although routinely deplored, after a decent interval most military regimes have been able to count on recognition and reception back into the OAU fold with a minimum of fuss.[10] Since the democratic revival of the 1990s, however, coups have encountered growing intolerance, with Commonwealth African countries assuming a lead.[11]

Commonwealth
The action of the military regime in Nigeria in executing Ken Saro-Wiwa and his Ogoni colleagues prompted Commonwealth leaders, then meeting in New Zealand, to adopt a robust Action Programme giving teeth to the landmark Harare Declaration proclaimed four years earlier. So enraged were African leaders, led by Nelson Mandela, by Abacha's calculated act of defiance that they immediately suspended Nigeria's membership of the Commonwealth. 'If Africa refrains from taking firm action against Nigeria', Mandela warned, 'then talk about the renaissance of Africa is hollow'.[12] At the same time, members drew up a checklist of sanctions to apply progressively 'particularly in the event of an unconstitutional overthrow of a democratically-elected government'. Members

also instituted a watchdog committee, chaired by Zimbabwe and including South Africa and Ghana, with a mandate to deal with 'serious or persistent violations' of the Harare principles.[13] Although the territorial reach of the Commonwealth Ministerial Action Group (CMAG) was not restricted to Africa, initially its focus was on the military administrations in Nigeria (1995–9), Gambia (1995–2001), and Sierra Leone (1995–2001).[14] Since then, the principal African concern of the Commonwealth has been the Zimbabwean conundrum.

ORGANIZATION OF AFRICAN UNITY

The OAU was slower than the Commonwealth in waking up to the continued prevalence of coups d'état. Not until the Burundi coup in July 1996 did the issue engage members centrally. Previously, fearing a repetition of Rwanda, the OAU, especially its East African members led by Julius Nyerere as facilitator, had sought to mediate between the Tutsi-led army and the majority Hutu population. However, pressed by Nigeria and South Africa to defuse the 'extremely dangerous and highly explosive' situation, the OAU Central Organ, in a last-minute effort, 'warned [the Tutsi], in no uncertain terms, against ... any attempt to take power through illegal means' as this 'will not be accepted by Africa and will be strongly condemned and opposed by the OAU'. Should a coup occur, it called on Africa and the international community to 'isolate completely' and 'impose sanctions' on those responsible. Moreover, the OAU served notice that if (Tutsi) obstruction to its offer of security assistance continued, the 'only other option' would be a pre-emptive 'humanitarian intervention' by a multinational force (OAU Central Organ, 1996a).[15] Instead, within hours, the Tutsi military took pre-emptive action on its own, deposing the Hutu president in a bloodless coup. In response, a hastily assembled regional summit resolved to 'exert maximum pressure,' including 'economic sanctions,' on the 'illegal' regime, an action the OAU fully endorsed.[16]

As in the case of Burundi, the overthrow of Sierra Leone's democratically elected government on 25 May 1997 was not entirely unexpected. Nevertheless, the shock unleashed a flood of denunciations. Not only did it occur on Africa Freedom Day, it was also the eve of the annual OAU summit in Harare. At the opening sessions, President Mugabe, as chair, insisted that 'democracy must be restored in that country as a matter of urgency', while Secretary-General Salim Ahmed Salim castigated the coup as 'an unacceptable attempt to defy history'. South Africa's ambassador saw it as another one of Africa's 'ugly spots that people just throw as mud in your face'. He added that 'we are taking it upon ourselves to say enough is enough. We are not going to tolerate this kind of behaviour on our continent.'[17]

OAU deliberations culminated in adoption of the Harare Declaration that 'strongly and unequivocally' condemned the Sierra Leone coup, and called on Africa and the world 'to refrain from recognizing the new regime and lending support in any form whatsoever to the perpetrators'. Moreover, in an OAU first, it appealed to the Economic Community of West African States (ECOWAS) to intervene militarily 'to restore constitutional order' to the country,[18] which its monitoring group (ECOMOG) succeeded in doing, though only after eight months. Reflecting on the OAU's forceful response to the Sierra Leone coup, Stan Mudenge, Zimbabwe's foreign minister, commented,

It was a major affront to an Africa bent on the path of democratization. The message from the OAU leaders ... was clear. Africa would no longer tolerate military coups. Although the trend has been clear for some time, its express articulation at Harare was an historic benchmark for our continent.[19]

Nevertheless, little action was taken to follow up the Harare Declaration. The OAU Central Organ did appoint a Committee on Unconstitutional Changes, but it failed to pursue the matter energetically, possibly because there were no coups in 1998 to prod it into action.[20]

That changed in 1999 with three coups within a month,[21] though only the palace coup in Niger aroused keen interest. The reaction there was in marked contrast to January 1996 when Col. Baré Maïnassara seized power in Niamey. At that time, Benin and Mali were almost alone in denouncing him.[22] Now, three years later, his assassination in the course of a counter-coup created an outcry. As a result, in 1999 OAU members, led once again by South Africa and Nigeria, both new democracies, expressed their 'grave concern' at the resurgence of coups d'état and called on the OAU's Central Organ to 're-activate as a matter of urgency' its Committee on Unconstitutional Changes. 'As from this conference', President Chiluba of Zambia declared, 'those who took power by force [will] be excluded and prevented from sitting alongside democratically-elected presidents'.[23] In the event, at Mbeki's suggestion, the heads of state decided that governments that 'came to power through unconstitutional means' within the past two years would be granted a further year to organize democratic elections and 'restore constitutional legality'. Once again, the motivation driving these decisions was the need to restore Africa's international credibility. As Salim Ahmed Salim explained, 'We must in word and deed endeavour to improve the image of a continent in permanent crisis'.[24]

Of the three regimes on probation, Niger and Guiné-Bissau held timely elections deemed 'peaceful and democratic'.[25] Comoros, on the other hand, failed to meet the deadline before the OAU heads of state assembled in Lomé in July 2000 (and in Lusaka in July 2001), and was barred from participation, along with Côte d'Ivoire whose coup had taken place only six months earlier.[26] This shortened period of grace was consistent with the timetable the OAU Central Organ's Committee on Unconstitutional Changes of Government had recommended and the Lomé summit adopted (OAU, 2000a, b). However, when it came to incorporating the proposed procedure for dealing with illegal regime changes into the African Union's constitution, the six-month reprieve before sanctions (other than suspension which was automatic) could be imposed was eliminated.

With the adoption of the African Union (AU) in July 2002, Article 30 of its Constitutive Act came into effect. 'Governments', it asserts, 'which shall come to power through unconstitutional means, shall not be allowed to participate in the activities of the Union.' In the event of such a challenge, the approved procedure provided that the OAU shall immediately condemn the action, 'convey a clear and unequivocal warning that such an illegal change shall not be tolerated or recognized', and urge a speedy return to constitutional order. Meanwhile, the Secretariat shall gather relevant facts and establish 'appropriate contacts' with the perpetrators in order to ascertain their intentions. If the regime refuses to end its illegality, the Assembly must immediately apply a series of travel, trade, communications, and other sanctions.[27]

In practice, states have treated the term 'unconstitutional means' as a euphemism for a military coup. Nevertheless, they recognized that it was applicable to a broader range of illegal actions, political as well as military. The Committee on Unconstitutional Changes was the first to formulate a comprehensive definition of situations that qualified as unconstitutional. Its report, as revised by the OAU in 2000 and adopted by the AU in 2002, identified three situations in addition to 'military and other coup d'états against a democratically-elected government', namely, intervention by mercenaries to replace a democratically elected government; replacement of democratically elected governments by armed dissident groups and rebel movements; and refusal by an incumbent government to relinquish power to the winning party after a free and fair election.[28]

Perhaps because of the reputation of OAU members for failing to match the vigour of their actions to the fervour of their rhetoric, the AU instituted a special pledge to 'enforce strict adherence' to its decisions on unconstitutional changes of government.[29] This undertaking was put to the test even before it formally entered into force. Following the December 2001 Madagascar presidential election, the opposition candidate, alleging the results were rigged, unilaterally proclaimed himself the victor and (twice) hastily installed himself in office. The OAU responded that the election had not resulted in 'a constitutional and legally constituted government', without specifying the nature of his crime. Instead, the presidency was declared vacant pending a fresh election. Meantime, the pretender was barred from attending OAU/AU meetings.[30] Not until July 2003, by which time the former incumbent had fled the country and the challenger had won a convincing majority in the National Assembly elections, did the AU regularize his status.[31]

In the end, the OAU resolved to restrict its definition of unconstitutional governmental changes essentially to coups, and thus forgo consideration of other relevant undemocratic practices and abuses of human rights (OAU, 2000b: para A2). However, it did oversee two other programmes: one focused on electoral democracy and the other on the protection of human rights. Both employed peer monitoring to check the actions of regimes bent on repressing their people.

ELECTIONS

While democracy is much more than elections, popular participation in elections is an indispensable element in the democratic process. Since the 1990s, periodic pluralist elections have become an accepted part of the political culture and *de rigueur* in most of Africa.[32] Civil society demanded them and donors promoted them, while political leaders and parties recognized their instrumental value in acquiring access to state power and assets. Admittedly, not all regimes have been equally committed to democratic norms. Yet, most have at least reconciled themselves to the need to respect certain electoral formalities and endure the prying presence of foreign observers. At the same time, too many have demonstrated skill and success in managing and manipulating elections without undermining their credibility too openly.

Peer monitoring intruded into three stages of the electoral process: establishing common continental standards, observing the conduct of elections, and responding appropriately to malpractices detected. Of these, observation has clearly been the principal thrust.

Norms

The Namibian election of 1989 was crucial in imprinting the principle of 'free and fair' elections (independently monitored) as the source of government legitimacy and authority. Yet, what precisely this term implied in practice became a lively subject of debate, with each country setting its own standards, with or without international assistance. Inevitably, this resulted in wide variations in the measures adopted and, especially, in the actual conduct of elections. However, it was not until the late 1990s that moves were taken to introduce some uniformity in electoral practice. The most significant of these initiatives was the SADC Parliamentary Forum's success in producing an election manual and securing its adoption by all member states. The OAU followed in 2001 with its own code of conduct governing democratic elections.[33] AU members endorsed this unanimously, ironically at the same time as they were defending the legitimacy of Zimbabwe's controversial presidential election.

Observation

OAU initiation into election monitoring began with the 'liberation' elections in Zimbabwe, Namibia, and South Africa. In 1980, its observer mission in Zimbabwe comprised only three OAU officials and their stay in the country was restricted to five days.[34] In Namibia in 1989, the team was equally modest, though members were deployed in the field four months in advance, thus enabling them to follow closely the campaign leading up to the polling in November. While financial constraints were a constant factor in limiting numbers, even more important were the restrictions imposed by the South African Administrator. He contended that, with a substantial Front Line States Observer Mission already operational in the country since April 1989, anything more than a token OAU presence was unnecessary. This prompted five OAU members – Egypt, Kenya, Nigeria, Tanzania, and Zambia – to open their own observer offices in the capital.[35]

Organizationally and operationally, the OAU Observer Mission in South Africa differed markedly from its predecessors. Following authorization by the OAU's Ad Hoc Committee on South Africa, an initial complement of 13 peace observers arrived in the country in November 1992. Originally conceived of as a 'preventive deployment' exercise, the mission's immediate preoccupation was monitoring the violence. Nevertheless, its fundamental mandate remained to promote conditions conducive to free and fair elections. By the time of the 1994 elections, the contingent numbered over a hundred.[36] Although a relatively modest presence considering the vast army of international observers in South Africa, it still constituted a significant contribution, comparing favourably with that of the Commonwealth.

At the time, liberation elections were one-off affairs, and the deployment of observers in them was not intended as a precedent for generalizing the practice. Moreover, their purpose was to ensure that the departing 'colonial' authorities did not rig the results, not to check on the conduct of OAU members. Yet, with the greater respectability election missions acquired as a result of the Namibian experience and the wave of democratic change sweeping the continent, the OAU soon found itself caught up in a new growth industry (see Anglin, 1989–90, 1990–2, 1998).

Following the liberation elections, the focus of attention shifted to 'reconciliation' elections held in the aftermath of civil wars, and then to 'transition' elections as military or one-party regimes gave way to pluralist politics. Soon, with OAU monitoring a routine feature in the great majority of African elections, establishment of an election observation unit within the OAU Secretariat became a necessity to cope with the demand. By 2000, the OAU had mounted over 90 observer missions (in 39 countries), with many more since then (Rugumamu, 2001)

Initially, the OAU was reactive, only responding to government requests. By the mid-1990s, however, with Japanese and other donor support, it was actively marketing its observer services. As Salim Ahmed Salim explained, the OAU viewed this 'as an encouragement to our member states in their efforts towards democratization'. In the process, it acquired considerable experience and expertise. Moreover, if account is taken of the continental network of observers deployed by sub-regions, governments, and civil society, the pool of African talent available for election service was quite substantial. Nevertheless, Salim was acutely conscious of the operation's continuing 'limitations and shortcomings', and urged that OAU's role should be 'further enhanced'. The African Union has since repeated the call and undertaken to 'reassess and where necessary strengthen the AU and sub-regional election monitoring mechanisms and procedures' (OAU, 1997: 54; NEPAD, 2002a: para 13) At the same time, the OAU at its final session in July 2002 spelt out the principles that should govern African elections and provided guidelines to enable the AU to become 'fully engaged' in 'observing and monitoring elections in our member states' (OAU, 2002a: sec. v).

Response

Although the AU Secretariat now has the 'right to decline invitations to monitor elections which in its considered view do not measure up to normative standards', to do so would be exceptional (ibid.).[37] The primary responsibility of an election-monitoring mission is to assess the mass of often conflicting evidence and respond appropriately. A range of possibilities exist. What the outcome is depends on the adequacy and accuracy of the available facts and opinions as well as the integrity of the observers and their customary reporting practices.

Customarily, observer groups issue one or more reports, publicizing them widely. They vary greatly in their coverage, criticisms, and conclusions. Some simply lay out the facts, while others pronounce a verdict on the validity of the exercise overall. OAU practice has been to say little or nothing publicly, especially anything critical, presumably for fear of causing offence and risking diplomatic repercussions. Thus, in the case of Zimbabwe's presidential election in March 2002, the 24-member OAU observer mission monitoring the event issued no public statement.[38] On occasion, the OAU has felt less constrained, notably in the 2000 Zanzibar elections. In its report then, the OAU Observer Team regretted that:

> it is unable to endorse the Zanzibar Elections as being conducted freely and peacefully and as representative of popular opinion, and hereby calls on the Zanzibar Electoral Commission to espouse the cardinal principle of transparency and credibility in the conduct of Elections in Zanzibar.[39]

The 2001 Madagascar presidential election is a second instance of OAU observers rejecting election results outright. Faced with rival versions of the vote count, neither of which had been independently verified, the OAU declined to certify either.[40] Admittedly, such examples are rare. More common are situations where observer missions have deemed undemocratic elections legitimate when clearly they were not.

What has accounted for the willingness of some missions to under-report their observations and fudge their conclusions? While clearly not solely an African phenomenon, certain features are distinctive to the continent. The core problem has been the politicization of the monitoring process. This manifests itself in two ways. First, observers from elsewhere in Africa may feel constrained, personally or politically, in the exercise of their independent judgement. In particular, they may be reluctant or fearful to criticize other African governments too openly. As President Mugabe once explained: 'The spirit of brotherliness prevails even where wrongs are recognized, and taking measures against a brotherly state is not easy.' In this same spirit, South Africa's Foreign Minister declared emphatically that condemnation of Zimbabwe by Pretoria 'will never happen so long as this [ANC] government is in power'.[41] Reinforcing this cultural trait are powerful pressures to conform to politically correct opinions in the wider interests of African solidarity.[42]

Secondly, self-interest may subtly influence monitoring authorities. Precedents that might rebound adversely on African regimes on some future occasion are carefully avoided. Moreover, African monitoring has had its roots in liberation elections, with OAU and other African watchdogs understandably seeing themselves as the political custodians of the interests of liberation movements. The keen partisanship of that era has added to the difficulty of adapting to a culture of scrupulous impartiality.

HUMAN RIGHTS

Former Secretary General Salim Ahmed Salim was wont to remind OAU members that 'Africa, which has suffered for so long from the gross abuse of human and peoples' rights, should be in the forefront of the struggle for the sanctity of human life and for the promotion and protection of human rights.' Yet, as experience in Zimbabwe and elsewhere demonstrates, few issues are as sensitive as human rights, especially with the prospect of peer reviews of current practices. Although OAU members routinely reaffirm their commitment to respect human rights, the reality is often very different. Moreover, when confronted with grave violations of human rights, ruling elites typically seek refuge in the sanctity of sovereign rights. All too often, the OAU has also readily accepted that some horrendous event, however deplorable, was nevertheless a matter of domestic jurisdiction.[43]

Not every African leader has contended that national sovereignty is absolute. In response to the Amin regime's brutality in Uganda, President Nyerere exploded with a blistering indictment of the OAU and his fellow presidents. 'The whole of Africa', he declared,

> cries out against the atrocities of the colonial and racist states ... But when massacres, oppression, and torture are used against Africans in the independent states of Africa, there is no protest from anywhere in Africa. There is silence even when such crimes are perpetrated by or with the connivance of African governments and the leaders of African states ... The OAU never makes any protest or criticism at all. It is always silent. It is made to appear that Africans lose their right to protest against

state-organized brutality on the day that their country becomes independent ... the OAU acts like a trade union of the current heads of state and government, with solidarity reflected in silence, if not in open support for each other. (OAU, 1975)

Nearly a quarter of a century later, President Mandela, in his valedictory address at the OAU summit in Ouagadougou in June 1998, took up the torch. Arguing the case for strengthening OAU powers to cope with domestic crises, he stated bluntly: 'We must all accept that we cannot abuse the concept of national sovereignty to deny the rest of the continent the right and duty to intervene when, behind those sovereign boundaries, people are being slaughtered to protect tyranny'. Unfortunately, his words largely fell on deaf ears.

Despite the earnest efforts of Secretary General Salim to persuade OAU members to live up to their obligations to protect victims of gross human rights abuses, the response was disappointing.[44] As for Secretariat officials, who were nominally responsible for 'monitoring the human rights activities in member states', they lacked the financial and human resources for this monumental task.

African Commission on Human and Peoples' Rights[45]
The African Commission on Human and Peoples' Rights (ACHPR) is the one African institution with a clear mandate to peer review the human rights records of OAU (now AU) member states. Although modeled on the UN human rights system, ACHPR is distinctively African. Along with an infusion of 'positive African cultural values', the Commission's code of rights recognized 'not only individual but also peoples' or group rights; not only civil and political rights but also socio-economic rights; and not only rights but also duties' (Heyns and Viljoen, 1999: 428). Among the 'measures of safeguard' that enabled ACHPR to 'ensure the protection' (and not just the promotion) of human and peoples' rights in Africa were four peer monitoring 'protection activities': open accountability sessions, periodic state reporting, focused investigations, and complaint procedures (OAU, 1981: art. 45(2)).

ACHPR traditionally devoted the opening days of its biennial sessions to public sessions where commissioners, along with governmental and non-governmental observers, raised issues concerning the state of human rights on the continent. In some cases, their deliberations eventuate in resolutions, though the countries 'named' commonly pay little or no attention to them. On one notable occasion in 1998, the Rwandan regime publicly executed 22 alleged *génocidaires* in open defiance of a Commission appeal for delay. This provoked a second, equally ineffective, protest expressing outrage at this blatant violation of the African Charter on Human and Peoples' Rights.[46]

A second monitoring mechanism obliged states to submit biennial reports on their human rights policies and practices. These accounts tended to be of uneven quality and excessively factual, if not fictional and uncritical. ACHPR officials appraised the accounts first, after which Commission members examined representatives of the state concerned in open session with NGO observers present. By avoiding confrontation and engaging in 'constructive dialogue', commissioners have sought to assist the reporting state to improve its performance. Unfortunately, little was done to follow up on the deficiencies noted and recommendations made. In any case, the record of compliance in reporting remains appalling, even worse than that of the UN Human Rights Commission.

Ironically, so strapped is the Commission for funds that, if all reports actually arrived on schedule, ACHPR would be incapable of coping with the flood.[47]

Thirdly, there were on-site inspections headed by commissioners since, unlike members of the UN's Commission on Human Rights, they were appointed as independent experts. As in the UN, visits were of two types. Country-specific missions assessed the overall human rights situation or probed a particular problem. Thus, in June 2002, a fact-finding mission spent six days in Zimbabwe investigating reported human rights abuses.[48] In addition, there were thematic special rapporteurs delving into such issues as prisons and conditions of detention, the rights of women, and summary, arbitrary, and extra-judicial executions. The work of the first has been exemplary.

Finally, if a state had 'good reason to believe' that another African state has violated Charter rights, it could raise the matter with the Commission (and now the AU). This has rarely, if ever, been done, presumably because it was considered politically incorrect. Alternatively, an individual or group of individuals (or an NGO) could address a complaint against a government to the Commission, which, in private session, pronounced on its admissibility and merit. Although approval by the OAU/AU Assembly was formally required before rulings were published, permission has been granted regularly, though rarely promptly.

Of the 42 such 'communications' considered during 2001–2, ACHPR reached a substantive decision on only one. This dealt with a litany of Ogoni allegations against the Abacha regime in Nigeria, and underscored the system's strengths and weaknesses. On the positive side, the judgement was both inclusive and conclusive. The Nigerian government was deemed to have violated eight separate Articles of the Charter for failing to protect the rights of the Ogoni people over a range of first and second-generation rights.[49] On the other hand, the process had dragged on for nearly six years, by which time Abacha had died and Obasanjo had emerged from prison to become president. More serious, ACHPR could not hold Abuja accountable as it lacked the power to make binding decisions. Thus, any hope of financial or other redress rested in the uncertain hands of the Nigerian judiciary, or conceivably the benevolence of the post-Abacha government. Whether the AU will be able or willing to rectify this omission remains unclear. Meanwhile, the Commission sought to compensate for the lack of a legal remedy by establishing an African Court of Human and People's Rights. Although the Protocol finally entered into force on 25 January 2004, the Court is not yet in operation two years later.[50]

Verdicts on ACHPR have typically been harsh, unduly so. Admittedly, its performance has not matched the importance of its mandate, in part because it has been 'routinely starved of resources' (and is unlikely to fare any better under the AU) and, at times, has 'functioned erratically'.[51] Also, while the Commission was empowered to pass judgement on the human rights record of African states, its inability to remedy the injustices victims have suffered has enabled the perpetrators to escape with impunity. Nor have the time and efforts devoted to assessing state reports and keeping the OAU/AU informed translated into meaningful human rights reforms on the ground. Nevertheless, ACHPR can fairly claim modest success in peer monitoring, as well as the potential for improvement.[52]

On the eve of the OAU's transmutation into the AU and of Salim Ahmed Salim's retirement following a decade of productive leadership as Secretary-General, he reflected on the:

steady but definite contribution in the inculcation and strengthening of the culture of democracy and the respect of human rights. The rejection of unconstitutional changes of government, the willingness of member states to have their elections monitored as well as the reproaches often made on violations of human rights are some of the gradual steps being taken to institutionalize these values. (Salim, 2001)

In each of these three respects, peer monitoring has proved a key component for intervening in areas traditionally considered internal affairs. Human security concerns had begun to intrude on regime security. Clearly, the greatest progress had been made in coping with coups, presumably because ruling elites had a direct interest in discouraging them. Remarkably, for nearly four years, no attempt to seize power had succeeded, and no military regime remained in office south of the Sahara.[53] Sadly, in March 2003, that enviable record was shattered with the overthrow of the coup-prone Central African Republic regime,[54] followed by São Tomé and Guiné-Bissau. As for election monitors, although they are still accepted grudgingly by some, by the time the OAU had handed over to the AU, their presence had become an established part of electoral practice. Only in human rights did serious doubts remain about the commitment of African governments. Even so, the experience ACHPR had gained, especially with state reporting, offered useful lessons for NEPAD as it set about fashioning a unique peer review system of its own.

Problematics: African Peer Review Mechanism (APRM)

The incorporation of a peer review component into NEPAD came relatively late in the process leading up to its launching. Indeed, nowhere does the NEPAD document refer to 'peer review' directly.[55] This is curious considering its centrality to NEPAD as well as the scale of the undertaking and the contemplated degree of intrusion into African society. Substantively and methodologically, APRM represents a significant advance over OAU peer monitoring. Operationally, it comprises four related but separate focal areas: democracy and good political governance, economic governance and management, corporate governance, and socio-economic development. Of these, the first is the most distinctive and innovative. It is also the most critical to the success of NEPAD (and hence, the principal focus of this study). As Alex de Waal has pointed out, the political peer review initiative involves 'a wholly new practice that has not been tried anywhere in the world' and 'holds the potential truly to set NEPAD apart from its predecessors'.[56]

NEPAD first considered how best to monitor state performance at the inaugural meeting of its Heads of State and Government Implementation Committee (HSGIC) in October 2001. It resolved to 'set up parameters of good governance to guide their activities at both the political and economic levels' and to 'consider and adopt an appropriate peer review mechanism and code of conduct'.[57] This did not prove easy. With the G8 summit in Kananaskis in June 2002 rapidly approaching, HSGIC members were under intense pressure to present it with concrete proposals as a measure of the sincerity of Africa's intentions. In the event, the Committee succeeded timorously in adopting two key documents. Drafters of the first, the 'Declaration on Democracy, Political, Economic and Corporate Governance' (*Declaration on Governance*), intended it as a 'strong statement of reaffirmation by African leaders of their strong commitment to the principles of good governance'. The second provided for an 'independent, effective, professional and credible' African Peer Review Mechanism (APRM).[58]

Two weeks later, the G8's *Africa Action Plan* welcomed the two documents, especially the peer review proposal, as 'an innovative and potentially decisive element' in ensuring NEPAD's success. The G8 also undertook to support African efforts to overcome their limited institutional capacity, which, along with an uncertain political will, posed perhaps the most serious problems for NEPAD in promoting good governance. Then, in July 2002, the inaugural session of the Assembly of the African Union in Durban confirmed its 'commitment to the principles and core values' contained in NEPAD's *Declaration on Governance* and urged members not only to adopt it but to accede to the APRM as well.[59]

Meanwhile, to confuse matters, the AU summit added its support to that of the OAU for a parallel peer review process known as CSSDCA (Conference on Security, Stability, Development, and Cooperation in Africa). CSSDCA arose out of the Africa Leadership Forum of the 1980s, which Chief Olusegun Obasanjo had spearheaded. Its strategic vision was encapsulated in its 1991 *Kampala Document* which, following a Ministerial Conference in Abuja in May 2000, the OAU had endorsed in its 'CSSDCA Solemn Declaration'.[60] Subsequently, the OAU created a CSSDCA Unit within its Secretariat and convened the first biennial Standing Conference of Heads of State and Government on CSSDCA in Durban in July 2002. It also reaffirmed 'the centrality of the CSSDCA Process as a policy development forum, a framework for the advancement of common values, and as a monitoring and evaluation mechanism for the African Union'.[61] Finally, the OAU approved a Memorandum of Understanding to enable signatory states to register their acceptance of CSSDCA's 24 core values, 46 commitments, and 50 performance indicators.[62] As the name suggests, it embraced four inter-linked issue areas or 'calabashes', of which the Stability calabash was the most relevant.

Despite Obasanjo's active promotion of CSSDCA, and generous Nigerian and South African funding, it remained marginal to mainstream OAU concerns. As Obasanjo explained, it 'threatened the status quo and especially the power positions of a few governments whose domestic hold on unscrupulous power rendered them vulnerable and insecure'. For this reason, it was never more than a minor complication in the controversies that raged around peer review.[63]

RESISTANCE

CSSDCA was not alone in suffering a political backlash. NEPAD, too, encountered an ominous resurgence in resistance to its peer review package, led by those who saw themselves as the intended targets. While there were early intimations of a strong desire to rein in peer reviews,[64] once their full import sank in, opposition hardened. Matters came to a head in July 2002 during a 'tension-filled' inaugural of the AU Assembly when a 'titanic battle' ensued for control of NEPAD's soul. The 'first deadly blow against the reformists' agenda' came when Muammar Gaddafi persuaded (with ample inducements) a majority of African leaders to expand the Implementation Committee from 15 to 20, and rotate its membership,[65] thus dealing the NEPAD 'a potentially severe blow'. Inevitably, it meant the inclusion of 'countries with doubtful democratic credentials or ambitions', notably Libya, and the possibility of excluding the five founding members. It also had 'a marked negative effect on external perceptions of NEPAD'.[66]

Although NEPAD was an OAU/AU initiative, its precise relationship with the umbrella organization became a matter of continuing controversy. Initially, Mbeki envisaged that the link would be purely nominal, a view that was fiercely contested. Instead, the majority decided that full and final integration into AU would best serve their interests. NEPAD was similarly unsuccessful in securing acceptance of its claim that it, rather than AU, should conduct and control political peer reviews (Cilliers, 2002b; 2003: 14). Fueling this struggle has been a fundamental contradiction. While African ruling elites commonly committed themselves publicly to onerous human rights and related obligations, most actively opposed intrusive measures intended to ensure their implementation. Peer review, in particular, was judged an obstacle to their continued retention of power. 'This threat to domestic power', one observer of the 2003 AU summit in Maputo recounted, 'is why the battle, and it was a ding-dong battle, over how to integrate NEPAD into the AU was waged'.[67]

A further dimension of the tension within the AU that impacted on NEPAD was the mounting resentment of Pretoria's leadership. The critics' motivations ranged from personal pique and ideology to fears of regional hegemony. Peer review provided a popular outlet for expressing diverse grievances. Gadaffi's outbursts stemmed in part from the fact that, as the self-appointed father of the AU, he was outraged that the inaugural ceremony should have been held in Durban rather than in Sirte. Similarly, not even all Mbeki has done to prop up the Zimbabwe regime sufficed for Mugabe to forgive Pretoria for the humiliation he felt at being marginalized following Mandela's arrival on the African stage. In addition to these bitter rivalries, Gadaffi and Mugabe also voiced ideological objections to NEPAD. Gadaffi characteristically rejected the 'new partnership' as a project of Africa's 'colonialists and racists', while Mugabe shared the concerns of many NGOs that Mbeki's economic agenda was too similar to the Washington Consensus. As his forthright Minister of Information declared, NEPAD was simply a 'modern type of imperialism'.[68]

Perhaps even more significant was the rising tide of discontent among less vocal AU members at the dominant role of South Africa (and, at times, Nigeria), which seemed destined to benefit the most from NEPAD. As one commentator has recalled, there was a 'popular assumption and misconception about the APRM that it was a monster created by the relatively more powerful African nation states and their leaders to arm-twist, or … whip the smaller and weaker nation states into line'.[69] Many countries with weaker economies had experienced the dire consequences of opening the floodgates to aggressive South African entrepreneurs (black and white), and were fearful that those in positions of power in NEPAD would pursue their national interests at the expense of regional and continental solidarity.

A particularly distressful incident that helped to galvanize opinion was Pretoria's clumsy (and initially unsuccessful) attempt in July 2002 to block the appointment of retiring OAU Secretary-General Amara Essy as Chair of the AU Commission. Apart from alienating West African and francophone states, the intervention triggered an unprecedented outburst of anger directed personally at South Africa's Foreign Minister during a caucus of African Foreign Ministers in September. What made this 'extraordinary attack' more remarkable was that Amara Essy led it.[70] Mbeki found himself no longer in command of the situation – with potentially profound consequences for the peer review's prospects. Nor did his standing improve greatly when, in July 2003, Côte d'Ivoire was persuaded – in circumstances not fully explained – to withdraw Essy's nomination. Although the old guard lost this battle, it remained as determined as ever to assert a veto power. It was not a promising beginning.[71]

MECHANISM

NEPAD's Implementation Committee was assigned the onerous task of developing suitable 'mechanisms for reviewing progress in the achievement of mutually agreed targets'. Amplifying on this mandate in March 2002, the Committee (HSGIC-2)

> stressed that an effective African Peer Review Mechanism [APRM], designed, owned and managed by Africans, must be credible, transparent and all-encompassing, so as to demonstrate that African leaders are fully aware of their responsibilities and obligations to their peoples and genuinely prepared to engage and relate to the rest of the world on the basis of integrity and mutual respect. (NEPAD, 2001: para 201)

To implement its peer reviews, NEPAD established four institutions. Capping the structure in succession to HSGIC is the APR Forum which held its inaugural session in February 2004. A self-selected Committee of Participating Heads of State and Government, it comprised the 15 states – now 26 – signatory to the APRM Memorandum of Understanding. The Forum's principal responsibility is conducting 'peer reviews', which it does through a 'constant dialogue' with the country under review.[72]

Panel of Eminent Persons

In May 2003, almost a year prior to the launch of the APR Forum, HSGIC took the first concrete step in activating the peer review process by appointing an expert Panel of Eminent Persons (APR Panel) and calling it into session in late July.[73] To qualify, members must be Africans of 'high moral stature and demonstrated commitment to the ideals of Pan Africanism' who have 'distinguished themselves in careers that are considered relevant to the work of the APRM'. At the same time, it is necessary to ensure a 'broad regional balance, gender equality and cultural diversity'.[74] The seven Eminent Persons are charged with responsibility for the overall management and direction of peer review operations and, in particular, for ensuring their 'independence, objectivity and integrity'. Initially, the intention was that the Panel should serve as 'final arbiter in any dispute relating to the interpretations of the APRM agreements', but peer review opponents succeeded in excising this provision.[75]

APR Secretariat

The African Peer Review Secretariat was set up in South Africa in June 2003. Functioning under the supervision of the chair of the APR Panel, it provides secretarial, technical, co-ordinating and administrative support services, including selection of 'partner institutions' to conduct reviews. From the first, it encountered major staffing problems. When its Executive Secretary, Dr. Bernard Kouassi, assumed duty at the beginning of 2005, his staff numbered a mere ten.[76] Currently, the APR Secretariat operates as a unit within the NEPAD Secretariat, though both are destined for early integration into the AU Commission in Addis Ababa. Part of the delay in opening the APR Secretariat office arose out of the intense controversy over the form it should take and its degree of autonomy. With a job specification calling for professional competence, operational capacity and political impartiality, the choice was not only critical but highly contentious. Three agencies were short-listed: the Economic Commission for Africa, CSSDCA, and NEPAD's own Secretariat.

The credentials of the UN Economic Commission for Africa were impressive. It alone was a functioning entity, possessing the required human, technical, and financial resources, and actively involved in promoting peer review. Located in Addis Ababa, it had a long history of constructive collaboration with the OAU. Its report, *Compact for African Recovery*, was 'the most intellectually substantive' contribution made to NEPAD, providing it with a clear roadmap, while its multi-volume Governance Project has laid the foundations for an effective peer review process.[77] In its determined bid for the job, the ECA could count on Mbeki's enthusiastic support and, initially, Obasanjo's. Moreover, the Implementation Committee at its June 2002 meeting recommended that the Secretariat be 'located in the ECA' rather than the OAU, as envisaged earlier.[78] It was on this basis that NEPAD sold its peer review proposal to the G8 a fortnight later. Subsequent adaptations and reinterpretations of its provisions generated considerable controversy and confusion.

Shortly after Kananaskis, doubts concerning the ECA's suitability surfaced. At the Durban summit, in July 2002, Obasanjo abandoned his support for the ECA and joined in the popular chorus. Conscious of the mounting revolt of the old guard against peer reviews, he resorted to the trendy argument that, as a UN body, the ECA was 'not "African" and, in any case, represented the interests of the North and of the donor community'.[79] For the nervous ruling elites, fearful of the ECA's strict standards and anxious to keep peer review under firm AU control, the appeal found a ready response. Besides, unrivalled as ECA's reputation was as the continent's 'premier expert community on economic issues', the same could not be said of its expertise on sensitive matters of human rights and democratic governance (de Waal, 2003: 469; Cilliers, 2002b: 5).

Meanwhile, as an alternative to the ECA, Obasanjo was promoting CSSDCA. It had pioneered the concept of peer review in Africa, and was the first to propose a mechanism for implementing it. With the adoption in July 2000 of a 'Solemn Declaration' on CSSDCA, the OAU summit reaffirmed 'the centrality of the CSSDCA Process ... as a monitoring and evaluation mechanism for the African Union'.[80] The first meeting of CSSDCA's Standing Conference also contributed to its credibility with NEPAD's critics.[81] Besides, as Obasanjo's brainchild, it could count on solid diplomatic and political support. Nevertheless, the fact that CSSDCA had no physical presence, apart from an embryonic unit within the AU Commission, made it difficult to treat it as a serious contender.

This left only one real option, apart from the AU Commission itself. This was the NEPAD Secretariat, a nascent group that Mbeki had set up in South Africa with funding and seconded personnel from a handful of supportive states. Although NEPAD was a mandated initiative of the AU, it aspired to a semi-autonomous status for itself and the proposed APR Secretariat.[82] Yet, in view of the intensity of opposition to any meaningful peer review, this appeared politically a non-starter, likely to precipitate full incorporation into AU. To add to the tension, the Durban summit was unable to settle on a site for APRM.

In the circumstances, Obasanjo's approach was to seek to harmonize NEPAD and CSSDCA, while insisting that the harmonization should not be at the expense of the latter. As Chris Landsberg noted, 'Obasanjo appears to have identified political peer review as the ideal role for CSSDCA.' He conceded, however, that, since the AU lacked the necessary capacity and competence to deal with economic governance, reliance on the ECA for that task was inevitable. Meanwhile, the ECA continued to campaign strongly, rightly stressing its strength in capacity-building and its ability to provide the 'analytical and technical underpinnings' the circumstances demanded. Although reconciled to limiting itself to an economic focus, it remained convinced that its forthcoming report on the state of governance in 28 African countries gave it a distinct competitive advantage even with respect to political governance.[83]

The controversy burst into the open in November 2002, a week before a critical meeting of HSGIC-5. Pretoria chose to announce, contrary to earlier understandings, that NEPAD would not undertake political peer reviews. Instead, as the AU's designated 'socio-economic programme,' NEPAD would confine its peer reviewing to economic performance.[84] This action struck at the heart of the partnership forged at Kananaskis, where NEPAD leaders had undertaken to institute a peer review process embracing political as well as economic governance. The apparent retreat prompted Canadian Prime Minister Chrétien, as G8 chair, to write to Mbeki (privately) on 1 November 2002 to express his concerns and seek clarification. In a feisty (highly public) reply, following a lengthy debate on 3 November, Mbeki explained, with some impatience, that the NEPAD was not abandoning political peer reviews, just transferring control to the AU.[85]

The NEPAD-AU compromise provided for a comprehensive two-tier system. Despite confusing explanations designed to sweeten the bitter pill, its essence was a division of labour between NEPAD and the AU, with the former retaining responsibility for economic peer reviews and the latter handling the political hot potatoes. However, during a 'transitional' period – originally one year, subsequently extended for an additional three years ending in July 2006,[86] and now unspecified – the APR Secretariat would initiate 'comprehensive' operations involving 'both political, and economic and corporate governance'. Once 'the AU structures are set up', the AU will 'take over' NEPAD and assume direct responsibility for monitoring 'implementation of [AU] decisions' on political governance.[87]

Mbeki's clarification 'did little to restore the trust and optimism that had previously existed'(Cilliers, 2003: 1). Considerable uncertainty persisted on two points. The first was whether, following the integration into the AU of the APR Secretariat, it would retain any residual responsibility for peer reviews. While peer reviews of economic and corporate governance would likely survive in practice, the prospects for NEPAD reviews of political performance seemed more problematical.[88] Secondly, although HSGIC-5 'called on the AU to establish a mechanism and, where necessary, develop capacity through which the implementation of its decisions can be monitored' (HSGIC-5: para 14), the form the AU's projected 'peer review' secretariat would take remained unclear. Early indications were, however, that the AU process might bear limited resemblance to peer review under NEPAD.[89]

Technical support

Plans for the transition, and possibly beyond, called for 'a competent Secretariat that has both the technical capacity to undertake the analytical work that underpins the peer review process and conforms to the principles of the APRM'. HSGIC-2 went further and called for 'an independent, credible African institution, separate from the political process and structures' to conduct technical assessments. In the event, it was found necessary to authorize the Secretariat to engage the services of 'African experts and institutions that it considers competent and appropriate to act as its agents'.[90]

Two forms of assistance have been sought. As the Secretariat had 'minimum capacity' on its own to carry out its mandate, it drew upon a pool of African technical expertise to maintain 'up-to-date background documentation' on developments throughout the continent. Secondly, APR Partner Institutions have been assigned to the multi-discipline Country Review Teams that conduct the technical assessments in countries under review. Thus, the ECA (now restored to favour) is responsible for economic governance and management and the African Development Bank(ADB) for banking and financial standards). As for corporate governance and socio-economic development, the APR Panel selects Partner Institutions or individuals appropriate to each situation.

In the special case of democracy and good political governance, there was no obvious choice. Accordingly, HSGIC-5 recommended that, pending the ultimate integration of the ARPM with the African Union, the AU organs responsible for democracy, political governance and human rights – now referred to as Strategic Partners – should conduct the assessments. This, in effect, imposed a 2–tier system, one for political peer reviews and another for all other areas. Yet, while the African Commission on Human and Peoples' Rights was well-established, the AU's Peace and Security Council was inaugurated only in May 2004, and the Pan African Parliament and the Economics Social and Cultural Council (ECOSOCC) first met in March and May 2005 respectively. Hence, it may be some time before they are in a position to contribute effectively to the peer review process.[91] So far, with the possible exception of ACHPR, no AU institution has played any part in the peer review process, and may not do so prior to the AU taking over, whenever that might be.

The confusion and crisis of confidence generated by the controversy over political peer reviews arose out of the inherent impossibility of reconciling the demands of AU members, the assurances given to the G8, and successive conflicting statements intended to 'clarify' the situation. African regimes opposed to peer review may well persist in their efforts to render peer review ineffective, though some appear to have already concluded that their best hope of restraining the enthusiasts is to sign on and work to protect their interests from within. Worrying as this is to Cilliers, he concedes that NEPAD's action in succumbing to elite pressure was 'inevitable and politically necessary'.[92]

PARTICIPATION

For the present, responsibility for peer review remains with NEPAD, with participation on a voluntary basis. AU members wishing to submit to the regime must first sign two memoranda of understanding (MoU). The first binds them to uphold the AU's 2002 *Declaration on Governance* as well as APRM principles and practices, notably acceptance of technical assessments and country review visits. In addition, participants undertake to draft a customized Programme of Action specifying the 'standards and goals' mutually agreed to, along with the timetable for achieving them. In doing so, signatories are required to 'ensure the participation of all stakeholders'. Finally, they undertake to 'contribute fully' to funding the APRM – a matter of no small significance – and pay all in-country costs.[93]

To assist countries to meet their preparatory obligations, the APR Secretariat mounts Support Missions, headed by an Eminent Person and consisting of technical experts in the four focus fields. The culmination of their Mission is the negotiation and signing of a second, more comprehensive MoU detailing, among other things, the scope, objectives and modalities of the proposed Technical Assessments and the Country Review Visits. Once this step is concluded, the peer review process is ready to begin.[94]

In October 2002, Ghana became the first country to offer to undergo a peer review. By early 2006, 26 states, including 80 per cent of the members of the HSGIC, had signed the initial MoU[95] (half the AU members still remain outside the peer review process). Several more states have intimated that they are likely to sign on soon. Yet, even if they do, half of those eligible will still remain outside. When questioned on the APRM's modest numbers, Professor Wiseman Nkuhlu, chairperson of NEPAD's Steering Committee, responded that 'not every African leader is democratic'. Earlier, an AU spokesperson offered a fuller explanation:

> Not all the presidents have got the same views and understandings in respect of NEPAD. Some are going to take time to get on board, some are going to walk with it, some are going to crawl, and others are going to run with it. Some are going to wait to see what they can gain before joining NEPAD.[96]

Although officially NEPAD encourages all AU members to volunteer for peer review, no pressure is applied to comply. There may even be a certain reluctance on the part of some to admitting members whose commitment to APRM is suspect.

From the first, NEPAD was conceived of, in the minds of some, as a self-selected 'coalition of the willing'. Yet little has survived of that concept, apart from limiting APR Forum membership to states acceding to the peer review process. Contributing to this outlook was an acute awareness of Africa's negative image as one undifferentiated collection of chaotic, corrupt, and collapsed states,[97] along with the tendency to paint all Africa with the same brush. This failure to discriminate was deeply resented by a number of countries, led by South Africa, which objected to being lumped in with the Congos, Liberia, Somalia, Sudan and Zimbabwe, especially when that tag carried with it adverse economic consequences. This prompted a group of like-minded countries committed to restoring the continent's credibility rating, to band together in a 'club of the willing' to promote peer review.[98] Their approach had three principal merits: the committed minority of AU states rather than the hostile majority would exercise operational control of peer review; the focus would be on mutual support in raising standards of governance rather than on settling for the lowest common denominator; and those states prepared to fast track their reforms could do so. As one observer commented, instead of a single large convoy ploughing on at the pace of the slowest, states capable of greater speed could form up their own fast convoys.[99]

Nevertheless, the initiative aroused suspicions. Opposition focused on the alleged 'exclusive' nature of the 'club'. Admittedly, in differentiating among AU states, NEPAD departed from OAU practice of respecting the sovereign equality of all members, especially in matters of governance and development. But no state was excluded unless it so chose. All that membership required was agreement to abide by the club rules.[100]

Actually, the critics appeared less interested in joining than in denying the right of others to reap the benefits of membership. Having failed in their initial bid, they now sought to safeguard their interests by ensuring that the AU, rather than the peer review participants, administered the process.[101] Among small, weak states, an added concern was the role of the larger, more powerful players. They were perceived of as dominating NEPAD, and in a position to benefit most from it. There was also fear that donors would accord excessive weight to peer review ratings in allocating aid. Certainly, the clear intention was that there would be winners and losers. Regimes with good governance records were expected to attract aid (and investment). On the other hand, alarmist rumours portraying a system of triage in which failed states would simply be abandoned, were ill-founded.

Process
Two related assumptions underlie the APRM, and are crucial to its success. The first is that, despite the open invitation, states choosing to participate will not only be motivated by a genuine desire to improve the quality of their governance practices, but will make the necessary effort and welcome the assistance of their peers in doing so. Secondly, on enlistment, countries will be at 'different levels of development' and will require 'differential support programmes' appropriate to their particular circumstances. For this reason, NEPAD does not lay down pre-determined standards for accession, but rather has 'a commitment to move towards common standards and practices'.[102] This necessitates a clear understanding of the indicative criteria for assessing regime conduct.

Indicators
Following protracted deliberations, NEPAD agreed in March 2003 on suitable indicators of good governance when it adopted its 'operative guidelines' for the APRM.[103] With respect to economic and corporate governance, the task was relatively straightforward. In addition to the readily available range of quantitative measures, eleven thematic standards and codes of conduct had previously been adopted.[104] By contrast, the selection of acceptable political indicators for good governance was highly contentious. Not only were fewer relevant objective (quantitative) measures available, but the indicators that best captured the diverse dimensions of the political process were the subjective (qualitative) ones. [105] A second source was the AU's *Declaration on Governance*, which is the basic

compendium of AU principles and core values. Included in that Declaration is an undertaking on the part of all parties to it to adopt 'clear codes, standards and indicators of good governance at the national, sub-regional and continental levels'. So far, the AU has made limited progress fleshing these out. Moreover, as Cilliers (2003: 7) points out, '[t]he objectives and standards that relate to democracy and political governance all refer to existing [OAU/AU] undertakings', which are already binding on all African governments whether or not they are peer review signatories.[106]

With respect to technical support for the APR Secretariat, as early as March 2001 the ECA had developed 'indices for good governance based upon benchmarks that reflect the norms of good governance'. Also, its ambitious Project on Monitoring Progress in Good Governance in Africa has led to two dozen country studies to date. In October 2002, the ECA presented a paper, 'APRM: Core Indicators for Tracking Progress' to a NEPAD workshop on peer review and to a Committee of Experts that reports to African development ministers. The governance indicators are grouped in three broad categories: political representativeness and rights, institutional effectiveness and accountability, and economic management and corporate governance. With its acknowledged technical superiority, the ECA is now involved with the technical aspects of economic governance and management.[107] As for democracy and political governance, early evidence suggests that the APRM will rely on independent technical consultants to provide the technical assessments.[108]

Criticism of the proposed indicators has come from two sources: those that favoured lowered or even no common standards, and those that argued for different, specifically 'African', standards. The former were mainly regimes that were sceptical of the whole NEPAD enterprise on grounds of either ideology or self-interest, and regularly resisted efforts to set strict political standards.[109] Thus, Theo-Ben Gurirab, then Namibian Prime Minister, declared that NEPAD has 'no business dealing with political, security and conflict resolution issues,' adding defiantly: 'I shall, with due respect, consign [the peer review mechanism] to the dustbin of history as a sham.'[110]

The demand that, in devising indicators, account should be taken of sociocultural diversity, within Africa and globally, has undoubted merit, though the motives that inspired it may have less to commend them. Appeals to Africanize the principles of good governance are scarcely new,[111] especially in countering universal claims of Western cultural norms. 'We are faced with the challenge,' Mbeki declared, 'of infusing our traditional systems and institutions into modern processes in a manner that does not dilute our democracies but also in a way that does not marginalize these traditions and customs.' Although NEPAD is formally committed to 'global standards', their most outspoken critics, particularly Mugabe, often resort to cultural arguments as a convenient excuse to justify flagrant violations of political rights.[112] Even President Obasanjo, one of the architects of NEPAD, has been unable to resist the temptation. In a sharp rebuke to European Union election observers, he dismissed their allegations of widespread fraud during the 2003 elections, arguing that 'our culture and environment [are] different' from the European Union.[113]

The peer review process comprises two phases and, within them, five stages.[114] The phases are investigating governance in the designated state and assessing aspects that require improvement. In addition, it is necessary to monitor compliance with the agreed changes. Throughout, the aim of the operation is reformative rather than punitive, supportive rather than confrontational, and more concerned with the direction and pace of change than the point of departure. No attempt is made to rank the performance of states, though Prime Minister Chrétien initially had anticipated a report-card style ranking. 'One will be number 1', he announced, 'and one will be number 53'.[115]

Investigation

Once the MoU on Technical Assessments is signed, the APR Secretariat is in a position to proceed with the peer review. Stage 1 is essentially preparatory, involving desk research with a view to identifying the principal issues for subsequent scrutiny. In anticipation of this, the APR Secretariat is required to maintain, on a continuing basis, 'extensive database information' on all participating countries in order to prepare background documentation for visiting missions, and to track the progress of countries in terms of performance indicators. The target country, too, will be actively preparing for its Country Visit by assembling its Self-Assessment Report on the basis of responses from stakeholders to an exhaustive APRM questionnaire. At the same time, it will be preparing a first draft of a Programme of Action indicating how it proposes to implement the AU's *Declaration of Governance* and other commitments, and within what timeframe.[116]

Armed with this information, the Review Team is ready to embark upon an on-site inspection, with a view to identifying areas for improvement (Stage 2). In doing so, it is expected to accord priority to the 'widest possible' range of stakeholders, including civil society. Although country reviews are of different kinds and serve different purposes – base, periodic, requested and pre-emptive – the most significant is the base review.[117] It establishes initial benchmarks and best practices (with timeframes) against which to measure future progress during the course of subsequent periodic reviews planned for every two to four years. The standards adopted are objectives towards which the state undertakes to strive over time rather than 'hurdles that [have] to be cleared'.

During the course of Stage 3, the Review Team assembles its findings, with particular attention to four issues:

- Is there the [political] will on the part of the government to take the necessary decisions and measures to put right what is identified to be amiss?
- What resources are necessary to take corrective measures?
- How much of these can the government itself provide and how much is to come from external sources?
- Given the necessary resources, how long will the process of rectification take?

Prior to submitting its draft report, the Review Team will hold discussions with the government in question to ensure factual accuracy and to elicit its comments. These are appended to the final Report.[118]

Assessment

The assessment phase begins when the Panel of Eminent Persons receives a draft Team Report. After reviewing it and adding its own recommendations, the Panel passes it on to the the APR Forum (Stage 4) for its deliberations and ultimate decision on the follow-up action 'deemed necessary'. In June 2005, on the

first occasion APRM reached this stage, President Obasanjo outlined the procedure to the heads of state of the participating governments (including the two
governments under review). 'Today, the APR Panel will present to us the
Country Review Reports of Ghana and Rwanda'.

> We will allow some time to hear the comments of our brothers from Ghana and
> Rwanda as well as questions and comments from all of you. We will then give you time
> to study these reports in your respective countries and, at our next Forum [in August
> 2005], we will be able to undertake the peer review. In other words, Ghana and
> Rwanda will present to us their own plans for the implementation of their Programmes
> of Action, their concrete needs and expectations in the political, financial and human
> resources domains. We also hope to benefit and learn from the current best practices
> in Ghana and Rwanda as highlighted in the reports. This interaction constitutes the
> essence of this whole process.[119]

Since government leaders are likely to react differently when confronted with the
judgement of their peers, the APRM has prescribed courses of action for three
distinct circumstances. If the government concerned evinces a 'demonstrable
will to rectify the identified shortcomings,' then it is 'incumbent' on Forum
members to 'provide what assistance they can' as well as to marshal additional
resources from within Africa and beyond. In the absence of the political will to
reform, the Panel should attempt 'everything practicable' to engage the state in
'constructive dialogue, offering in the process technical and other appropriate
assistance'. Finally, if the regime is still recalcitrant, the Forum could 'as a last
resort' 'put on notice' that its 'collective intention' is to proceed with 'appropriate [but unspecified] measures by a given date'. The hope is that the interval
might 'concentrate the mind' of decision-makers, and afford a 'further opportunity for addressing the identified shortcomings under a process of constructive
dialogue'.[120]

Although these guidelines, first adopted in 2002, have yet to be tested, it
seems unlikely they will be as originally envisaged. Peers may be prepared to
offer some support, but the role of peer pressure has been played down, and any
threat or resort to sanctions can be ruled out. As one analyst has claimed, when
first mooted, NEPAD was

> seen as a means for African states to ensure compliance with good governance princi-
> ples, challenging national sovereignty. Since then, it has become increasingly a consci-
> entisation tool, aiming only to raise awareness in those countries that have self-selected
> to join it. (Cilliers, 2003: 3, n.11).

The intention is that assessment reports should be tabled publicly in all relevant
AU and other African institutions (Stage 5), thus underscoring the importance
of public disclosure in maximizing the impact of peer review. Initially, a delay of
six months was prescribed. Later, publication need only occur 'in a timely
manner'. Finally, all mention of time was dropped.[121]

Implementation
After years of effort, the road map to good governance is laid ahead with great
care and clarity, with each stage in the peer review process clearly signposted
along the way. Already, the first few adventurers have set out on their journey,
confident of reaching their goal. How have they fared so far, and how rough has
the road been in practice?

Predictably, implementing the APRM has posed a greater challenge than had been expected, thus reinforcing public scepticism about the whole enterprise. Press statements, such as President Obasanjo's in July 2003, announcing the intention to 'conduct the first reviews during the second half' of the year, have proved over-optimistic and have required regular revision.[122] Nevertheless, the peer review programme is now on track and gaining momentum. The institutional structure is in place and operational. The Panel of Eminent Persons is fully functional, with its members spreading out across the continent, assisting countries to prepare for or participate in the exercise. The APR Secretariat, while still seriously handicapped by limited staff, capacity and resources, is performing more effectively, bolstered by its ability to access appropriate expertise in partner institutions.[123] AU members have come forward in acceptable numbers, and are responding well to the need to designate a National Focal Point to co-ordinate their country's efforts and discharge its APRM responsibilities.[124]

A schedule of countries offering to be reviewed has been established. Although Ghana was keen to be first, from the outset APRM's intention was to begin with 'at least three countries' to secure a 'good spread'. As Nkuhlu explained, 'If we praised Ghana on everything, people would dismiss this review mechanism and say it is a [matter of] people scratching each others' backs'.[125] Accordingly, he sought to persuade countries with poorer performance prospects than Ghana to take part in the first pilot exercise. In February 2004, the first cohort of four was named: Ghana, Rwanda, Kenya and Mauritius. Since then, all four have received Support Missions (in 2004) and submitted the requisite Self-Assessment Reports and National Programmes of Action to the APRM. Subsequently, Country Review Missions have visited Ghana and Rwanda and submitted their reports to the APR Forum. Meanwhile, the calendar of countries for review in 2005–6 has been announced, with four of the fathers of NEPAD – Algeria, Nigeria, Senegal and South Africa – plus Mali and Mozambique listed.[126] Nevertheless, despite this promising beginning, peer review is still very much a 'work in progress', and likely to remain so indefinitely, subject to regular review, revision and resistance.

COMPLIANCE
The focus in the post-peer review phase is on ensuring that the policies and practices of participating states conform to agreed governance values, codes, and standards (*APRM*, para. 2). While the expectation is that peer review volunteers are sincere in implementing their time-bound Programmes of Action, inevitably some will fall behind in meeting their obligations. APRM's role is still to encourage and assist states to comply fully, and thereby reap the benefits of peer review. A range of incentives and other levers of influence are available for this purpose. These are principally of three kinds: peer pressure, civil society monitoring, and enhanced partnerships.

A key component of peer review is the 'sharing of experiences and reinforcement of successful and best practices, including identifying deficiencies and assessing the needs of capacity building'. Hence, the preference for the term 'peer learning'. Nevertheless, states in agreeing to undergo peer review 'accept that constructive peer dialogue and persuasion would be exercised, where necessary'. Inevitably, this may involve a measure of subtle pressure, even 'soft persuasion' (ibid.: para 3; NEPAD, 2003a: paras 24, 26) The concern is not that the pressure may be inappropriate, but rather the difficulty of persuading peer states to resort to it, particularly if it sets an inconvenient precedent. At best, peer pressure may encourage compliance, but cannot compel it.

The minimal involvement of civil society (and many OAU member governments) in drafting the NEPAD documents was a costly error of judgement, as it has greatly complicated the task of enlisting necessary popular support. Progress, though not insignificant, is still uneven. In too many cases, the rhetoric of participation has continued to obscure the persistence of exclusion, especially of women.[127] Until this neglect is rectified, the full weight of civil society organizations (CSOs) will not be available to play a constructive role monitoring African regimes and serving as the conscience of the continent.

Enhanced partnerships

As with peer pressure, civil society initiatives have their limitations, especially in countries with embryonic civil society networks. Hence, in order to provide sufficient incentive for participating states to honor their promises, NEPAD appealed to the G8 democracies for financial inducements. In their *Africa Action Plan*, the G8 responded:

> [W]e each undertake to establish enhanced partnerships with African countries whose performance reflects the NEPAD commitments. Our partners will be selected on the basis of measured results ... The peer review process will inform our considerations of eligibility for enhanced partnerships. We will each make our own assessments in making these partnership decisions.[128]

With countries that have not met the NEPAD standards, but are 'clearly committed to and working towards' such targets, the G8 are prepared to form limited partnerships. However, their offer does not extend, except in 'situations of humanitarian need', to working with regimes which 'disregard the interests and dignity of their people'.[129] The significance of these measured interventions was, as Gelb pointed out, their 'signalling effect ... to investors and ODA contributors, inducing them to attach increasingly lower risk premiums to resource flows to well-performing member countries' (Gelb, 2002: 31).

Of the three instruments for inducing compliance, peer review is the least intrusive, but also the least efficacious; civil society could potentially make a real difference, but has yet to decide whether it is prepared to take on a watchdog role; and enhanced assistance 'talks' the loudest, but alarms those for whom African ownership of the NEPAD is sacrosanct.

Prospects

Launching NEPAD has been a monumental task, requiring states and institutions to accept radical changes in entrenched patterns of behaviour. Moreover, although the peer review process has only begun, it has already undergone significant modification and will, no doubt, continue to evolve in response to experience and conflicting pressures from its diverse stakeholders. With the NEPAD riddled with so many ambiguities, it has been difficult to discern where peer review is headed.[130] Meanwhile, its core of dedicated supporters is well aware that the success of the project largely rests with three constituencies: the AU and its members, civil society, and the development partners. Securing and retaining their active co-operation will prove critical.

CONSTRAINTS

African Union

With a majority of the AU member states sceptical about the NEPAD enterprise, if not outright hostile, President Mbeki and his fellow founders have, in the words of one informed observer, had to fight a fierce rearguard action 'barricade by barricade' in an effort to salvage their vision of good governance as the key to development. Ensuring NEPAD's survival has necessitated a series of costly concessions to the AU on control of the political process. Money is also a constraint. As Obasanjo reported to the Maputo summit, 'Funding remains one of our greatest challenges'. Peer review participants are committed to funding the operation during the transitional period but, once NEPAD is fully integrated into the AU, the APRM may have to depend on handouts from the regular AU budget. 'It is critical,' Dr Nkuhlu has warned, 'that NEPAD is established ... with its own secure funding.' Otherwise, it could 'suffer the fate of many of its predecessor initiatives: sound on paper, but with no dedicated resources'.[131]

Civil society

'Public scrutiny', we are told, 'is the most likely factor to affect change and corrective actions' – precisely what civil society sets out to do. Yet, NEPAD's relations with it (and, by association, APRM's) began with alienation on the part of the non-governmental community and lack of interest on the part of most governments. This led Cilliers to the pessimistic conclusion that APRM would be 'a closed, state-to-state process with no room for non-official input or consultation, apart from the ability to comment on country reports', as and when released (Cilliers, 2003: 3, 14; 2002b: 6). In practice, the outlook has not been as dismal as was first feared. Increasingly, NGOs have been reassessing their options and cautiously exploring opportunities for productive engagement, though too few are yet active participants. At the same time, peer review participants, encouraged by the APRM, appear more receptive to reaching out to stakeholders for support. Nevertheless, a recent ECA study has characterized the nascent partnership with civil society as still 'skewed, intermittent, *ad hoc* and ill-timed, resulting in largely low level and contradictory contributions'.[132] Whether the relationship can ever realize its full, fruitful potential will largely depend on two related factors: the strength and sustainability of civil society organizations and networks on the ground, and the democratic instincts and resolve of the political leadership. In too many cases, CSOs still suffer from limited capabilities and institutional weaknesses as well as from repressive environments.

From the outset, APRM identified three promising roles for civil society. The first was sharing in drafting the internal Self-assessment Report and Country Programme of Action. As MoU signatories, participating states are obliged to 'ensure' the inclusion of civil society, along with other stakeholders, in the process. Secondly, in their research, Country Review Teams must also consult widely with 'representatives of civil society organizations', among them the media, academia, business, trade unions and professional bodies.[133] In both instances, significant progress has now been made, at least judging by the first cohort of states, all of whom, except Rwanda, can claim to have well developed civil society organizations. Particularly prominent during APRM visitations have been the many workshops organized under diverse auspices and conducted in regional centres as well as in the capital. Nevertheless, much more could and should be done by all parties. To neglect the potential contribution of civil society would be tragically short-sighted. As Gelb has argued, the public should be involved 'at every stage in the peer review process, including the formulation of targets for the next period of assessment'. Otherwise, he fears the exercise will have 'limited political legitimacy'.[134]

The third role for civil society, and arguably the most important, is monitoring the policies and practices of states between periodic visits, and not just during reviews. CSOs are also needed to mobilize the African public to provide critical support for peer review principles. With peer pressure from above problematical, ongoing informed pressure from below is vital. How seriously CSOs are prepared to take up this challenge and undertake this onerous watch-dog function could well prove crucial in deciding the fate of the peer review initiative. One encouraging development is the action of seven African research NGOs, operating under the umbrella of the African Human Security Initiative, in issuing a 'Shadow Review' Report measuring the level of compliance with APRM standards of (ultimately) eight countries, all candidates for peer review. The first (on Ghana) was launched in Accra in February 2005, in advance of the APRM's Country Review Mission. The release of other country studies will similarly be timed to maximize their impact.[135]

While peer review signatories are committed to promoting 'vibrant civil society organizations', most have yet to learn how to relate to them.[136] What is required is for NEPAD leaders themselves to muster the confidence and courage to join in strengthening civil society. According to Gelb (2002:, 29):

> For the NEPAD peer review mechanism to be credible both within Africa and outside, it is critical that heads of state of participating countries be subject to domestic political pressures in favour of improving governance. If governance is to improve in these societies, a demand for it must be constructed: improved governance will not emerge automatically.[137]

Development partners
Two occurrences could conceivably derail NEPAD's partnership with the G8, though the chances of that happening appear minimal. The first is if the G8 were to allow national interests to override their undertakings as donors to rely on peer review outcomes to guide them in allocating or withholding 'enhanced' aid.[138] In order to ensure that G8 members honor their commitments on aid levels and development cohesiveness, NEPAD has insisted that accountability be mutual. In response, the existing NEPAD/G8 Dialogue has been transformed into a unique Africa Partnership Forum (APF) with broadened scope and expanded high-level political representation.[139]

Secondly, if the AU were to introduce further unilateral revisions to the terms of the partnership, the G8 might eventually reconsider the arrangement. In Cilliers' opinion,

... the emerging nature of the APRM is a far cry from the original intention of President Mbeki ... The difference between that intent and the present structures and process reflect the extent of the compromises that had to be made ... [T]he effective removal of political and good governance components from NEPAD ... contradicts the original purpose and content of the APRM as contained within various NEPAD documents and communicated to Africa's development partners.[140]

As Canada's Minister of Trade reminded South Africans in 2002, the G8's partnership was with NEPAD, not the AU. He also warned that the promise of $6 billion in extra annual aid was 'conditional on all NEPAD elements' functioning, including good governance and peer review. Evidently, the G8 were not excessively alarmed, as their summit took no action on the matter, and even postponed the planned review of their own *Africa Action Plan* to 2005.[141]

CREDIBILITY

Ensuring the political impartiality of the peer review process poses a problem. Although the composition of the Panel of Eminent Persons is reassuring, the loss of its role as final arbiter on APRM agreements was not. More serious is the involvement of heads of state in the assessment of country reports, inevitable as this is in a peer review system. For their judgements to carry credibility, it is critical that they should detach themselves as completely as possible from past, often long-standing personal and political relationships. To minimize conflict of interest, Gelb argues (2002: 34) that 'engagement with non-state actors is likely to be very helpful – in the African context – for maintaining the "measure of independence"', which is required for the process to function effectively.

In addition to formal peer reviews, African states can express their collective opinion on the policies of other governments by adopting consensus statements or in bloc voting. Yet, all too often, the primary purpose of such actions is to demonstrate African solidarity and power rather than to uphold AU principles. Frequently, the price of unity is a refusal to condemn gross violations of accepted norms. Thus, in March 2003, African members of the UN Commission on Human Rights voted together (with only Uganda abstaining) in opposing renewal of the mandate of the UN Special Rapporteur on Human Rights in Sudan, despite the appalling conditions in that country and the solemn commitment of all AU members to 'promote and protect human and peoples' rights' there.[142] Since then, failure to speak out when certain brother regimes commit horrendous crimes against African humanity has become almost routine. 'Silence and solidarity' have taken over as guiding principles.

In an attempt to rationalize their actions, African states commonly distinguish between the standards practised at home and the contradictory policies pursued elsewhere on the continent and overseas. Only with respect to their own domestic actions do African leaders concede that they are accountable to fellow heads of state. Whether they condemn, condone, or collude with the Mugabe regime, they consider their actions as irrelevant in peer review assessments.[143] Convenient as the claim may be, it has not gone unchallenged, at least not by civil society. As long as AU members are unwilling to 'call their counterparts to task on contentious issues' of foreign and domestic policy, doubts will persist concerning the convictions of some ruling elites.[144]

AU PEER MONITORING

Although the July 2006 deadline for the end of the transition has been effectively lifted, the intention to proceed with NEPAD's 'complete integration into the AU structure and processes' remains (AU, 2003a; Cilliers, 2003: 2). As a result, there is still some residual uncertainty concerning the future of African peer reviews of political governance, institutionally and programmatically. However, AU peer monitoring will continue, building on precedents and practices inherited from the OAU rather than NEPAD.

Conceptually and structurally, the two approaches are quite distinct. Unlike NEPAD (and individual AU members), the AU's legal status entitles its Assembly (by consensus or two-thirds vote) to intervene in a member state, uninvited, in 'grave circumstances, namely, war crimes, genocide and crimes against humanity'.[145] The Assembly is also empowered to impose explicit punitive measures on a delinquent member, if it fails to comply with an AU policy or decision 'without good and reasonable cause'. Sanctions could involve 'the denial of transport and communications links with other member states' – a serious matter for landlocked states – and 'other measures of a political and economic nature'. To do so, the Assembly must first set a date, which, if defiance persists, will 'trigger the sanctions regime'.[146]

Although these provisions mark a dramatic break with past OAU policy, the missing element is the necessary political will to make them work. Moreover, before AU monitoring can become operational, the AU Commission will need to acquire the requisite capabilities and expertise. However, in two areas of earlier OAU concern useful actions continue: curbing coups d'état and election fraud. In the third area – protection of human rights – little if any improvement is evident. Practice and profession continue to diverge widely.[147]

The one issue where near-unanimity exists is opposition to the military subversion of democratic regimes. Since the overthrow of the Central African Republic government in March 2003, which ended four years free of coups, there has been a worrisome 'resurgence of the scourge'. This prompted the AU's Central Organ, following the São Tomé 'mutiny' in July 2003, to order an 'in-depth' review of the 2000 Lomé Declaration with a view to strengthening its effectiveness.[148] Existing procedures provide for a three–step strategy: suspension, restoration, and sanctions.[149] In the series of cases of unconstitutional regime change that the AU has dealt with so far, it promptly barred the usurpers from participation in AU activities, and initiated negotiations and mediation to speedily restore constitutional order. In São Tomé, these efforts succeeded within a week (Seibert, 2003), in Guiné-Bissau within two weeks. In other cases, such as Comoros in April 2002, Madagascar in January 2003, the CAR in March 2005 and Togo in April 2005, it has taken the verdict of National Assembly elections to settle the competing legitimacy claims. At the same time, the AU Assembly has shown great reluctance to 'immediately apply sanctions', as required with states refusing 'to restore constitutional order'.[150]

On paper, there has been a burst of activity in promoting democratic elections. Following reports by the OAU Secretary General, the AU adopted statements in July 2002 on 'Principles Governing Democratic Elections in Africa' and 'Election Observation and Monitoring'.[151] These led to the creation of a Democratization and Election Monitoring Unit within the AU Commission and the convening, along with South Africa's Independent Electoral Commission, of an African Conference on Elections, Democracy, and Good Governance in Pretoria in April 2003. The 'Conference Statement' and its 'Guidelines for African Union Electoral Observation and Monitoring Missions' were submitted to the Maputo summit which merely encouraged AU members to 'study and implement' them.[152]

Conclusion

In itself, peer review is not a panacea for Africa's ills. It is, however, a vital link in the chain of reforms needed if the continent is to progress along the path to sustainable development and ultimate poverty reduction. Meanwhile, the best hope of prodding African regimes into adopting acceptable governance practices appears to rest with civil society and the peer review pioneers. This requires the active engagement of civil society in establishing 'parallel processes to hold African governments and leaders accountable'. Whether such initiatives succeed in making a significant difference will depend as much on the receptivity of African regimes to dialogue as on the efforts of the CSOs themselves. Similarly, the exemplary effect, as an incentive to others, of heads of state submitting their personal and political reputations in office to the scrutiny of colleagues will only be adequate if it can clearly be shown that peer review pays, especially in terms of enhanced assistance and productive investment. Ultimately, the challenge comes down to the need for 'a deep and genuine commitment by African leaders and their governments at every level to reform'. That is what peer review sets out to achieve (Cilliers, 2003: 14).[153]

With the completion of the APRM's first cycle, prospects for peer review of political governance have improved, and are now better than could have been expected. But the future is far from assured. Many difficulties and dangers still lie head. Now is not the time to relax, but rather an opportunity to build upon the successes to date. The cause continues to be well worth pursuing with renewed energy, even if the final outcome must still be regarded as problematic.

Notes

[1] The communiqué of the Harare conference of Southern African NGOs (25 September 2002) dismissed peer review in one sentence. NGOs rightly felt they should have been consulted.

[2] Amara Essy. 'Statement,' 76th OAU Council of Ministers, Durban, 4 July 2002.

[3] Trevor Manuel, South Africa's Finance Minister, urged 'an unwavering commitment to domestic resource mobilization' (*Business Day* [Johannesburg], 6 December 2002).

[4] Although this view is 'now generally acknowledged', support for it is not universal. See Chabal (2002: 447–50, 455, 460–61); Kaufmann and Kraay (2002); Abrahamson (2000).

[5] Although, initially, the Bank sought to preserve its non-political credentials, it did acknowledge the crucial importance of good governance, World Bank, (1989: xi, 15, 22, 30, 192).

[6] Appendix II: 7–10, 17–18). According to Peter Anyang' Nyong'o, 'this was the first time that the official documents discussing Africa's development agenda conceded that democracy was a cardinal issue' ('From the Lagos Plan of Action to NEPAD (2002: 3)).

[7] OAU (1990; 1996, para. 7).

[8] 'Moi's plea to African leaders', *East African Standard* (Nairobi), 29 June 2002; *Daily News* (Harare), 11 July 2002.

[9] 'Peer review refers to the systematic assessment of the performance of a state by other states (peers), by designated institutions or by a combination of states and designated institutions' (ECA, 2002: 18). See also Mbeki (2002b: 3).

[10] African Development Bank (2001: 111). Following Doe's bloody coup in Liberia, he was excluded from ECOWAS and OAU summits (*Africa Contemporary Record* [hereinafter *ACR*], XIII (1980–81: 64–5).

[11] Anglin (1996–98): A54–56. The 19 (now 18) African members of the Commonwealth account for over half the population and GDP of sub-Saharan Africa.

[12] Sampson (1999: 549). Mandela added that Abacha was 'sitting on a volcano, and I am going to explode it under him'. Up to this point, he had supported Thabo Mbeki's policy of 'quiet diplomacy', but now (along with Mugabe) called for expulsion. Mbeki remains wedded to 'constructive engagement' (Callard, 2003: 26).

[13] 'The Millbrook Commonwealth Action Programme on the Harare Commonwealth Declaration', Queenstown, New Zealand, 12 November 1995, para.3–4.

[14] Flight-Lieutenant Rawlings, who twice seized power in Ghana by force, held elections in December 1992, thus escaping surveillance. Instead, Ghana became one of the watchdogs.

[15] Ethiopia, Tanzania and Uganda had offered troops. A fortnight earlier, the OAU Summit affirmed that such action 'can in no way be considered as an interference in the internal affairs of [Burundi], but flows from a fraternal and genuine concern to prevent yet another African tragedy of epic proportions' (AHG/Res.257 [XXXII], 10 July 1996).

[16] Joint Communiqué, 2nd Arusha Regional Summit on Burundi, 31 July 1996 (UN doc. S/1996/620, 2 August 1996, Appendix); OAU Central Organ, 1996b. Sanctions were imposed from July 1996 to January 1999. Their initial severity caused the Burundi people great hardship.

[17] *ACR*, XXVI (1996–98), pp. A105–7; Welile Nhlapo (1997) See also *Africa Research Bulletin: Political Series* (hereinafter *ARB*), June 1997, p.12712.

[18] OAU doc. CM/Dec.357 (LXVI), 31 May 1997. The resolution should not to be confused with the 1991 Harare Commonwealth Declaration. Ironically, it was the Nigerian dictator, General Abacha, who was assigned responsibility for restoring Sierra Leonean democracy. The resolution on coups was not retroactive.

[19] Addis Ababa, 25 February 1998 (SABC 'Dateline Africa', 26 February 1998).

[20] The rebel capture of power in Congo-Brazzaville in October 1997 did not count.

[21] Niger (9 April), Comoros (30 April) and Guiné-Bissau (6 May). The committee was initially designated the Committee on Anti-Constitutional Changes, and comprised Gabon as chair, Ethiopia, Lesotho, Libya and Nigeria, representing Africa's five recognized regions.

[22] *Financial Times* (London), 29 January 1996, p.4; *ARB*, February 1996, p.12146. In July 1996, Baré Maïnassara made a futile attempt to acquire some legitimacy by staging a blatantly rigged presidential election. In the course of the count, he dissolved the Independent National Electoral Commission and appointed a successor body, which promptly declared him victor (*ACR*, XXVI (1996–98), pp. B138–40).

[23] OAU docs. CM/Dec.483 (LXX), 10 July 1999 and AHG/Dec.142(XXXV), 14 July 1999; PANA, 'Coup makers slated at OAU summit', 13 July 1999.

[24] AFP, 'African leaders resolve not to recognize coup regimes,' 14 July 1999. President Obasanjo of Nigeria argued that 'Africa's reputation as a continent at war against itself must be arrested' (*SADC Now* 3 (2), August 1999).

[25] Salim Ahmed Salim, OAU Secretary-General, PANA, 9 March 2000.

[26] 'OAU ministers meeting begins in Togo,' BBC Africa News, 7 July 2000; 'Minister Dlamini Zuma to lead AU delegation to Comoros, 16–17 July 2003,' SA Department of Foreign Affairs, 15 July 2003. Elections were not held until March and April of 2002.

[27] AU, 'Rules of Procedure of the Assembly of the [African] Union' (hereinafter Assembly Rules), ASS/AU/2(I)-a, Rules 4.1(g), 36, 37; Constitutive Act of the African Union (hereinafter 'Constitutive Act'), 11 July 2002, Art.23. OAU (2000a) (p.5) called

on the Secretary-General to enlist the support of African leaders and personalities in exerting 'discreet moral pressure' on the perpetrators. Sanctions were to be 'limited and targeted'.
28 OAU (2000b: 3–4). 'All types' of unconstitutional changes – 'anywhere in the world' – were condemned as 'anachronistic'.
29 NEPAD (2002b) (hereinafter *Declaration on Governance*), President Obasanjo proposed the Declaration, and the AU reaffirmed its commitment to it and encouraged members to adopt it (ASS/AU/Decl.1 [I], Durban, 10 July 2002.
30 'Report of Secretary-General on the Situation in Madagascar', 6th Session of OAU Central Organ at Summit Level, Addis Ababa, 21 June 2002, Central/MEC/AHG/2 (VI). The decision was based on Art.4(p) of the AU's constitution that called for 'condemnation and rejection of unconstitutional changes of government'. See Cornwell, (2003). This was not a military coup; the usurper was a civilian replacing an admiral who originally had seized power in a coup.
31 OAU (2003). 'Decision on the Situation in Madagascar', Maputo, Assembly/AU/ Dec.1 (II), 10 July 2003.
32 Among the core components of democracy that 'Africa undertakes to respect' are 'fair, open, free and democratic elections periodically organized to enable the populace choose their leaders freely' (*NEPAD* 2001: para. 79).
33 SADC Parliamentary Forum, (2001); OAU, 'Declaration on the Principles Governing Democratic Elections in Africa', AHG/Decl.1 (XXXVIII), Durban, 8 July 2002, based on the Secretary-General's report, CM/2256 (LXXVI).
34 The Commonwealth Observer Group included 17 Africans; four others were accredited independently. 'The OAU was restricted [by the British Governor] to a visit from only February 25 to March 1, coinciding with the actual polling. The observers arrived in a high state of annoyance because they were prohibited from witnessing the campaign itself' (Wiseman and Taylor (1981: 76, 111–17).
35 *Facts & Reports* (Amsterdam), 19 I, 5 May 1989, p.20; *ACR*, XXII (1989–90), pp.A26, 154 -55. OAU members were divided on whether states in arrears to the OAU Liberation Committee were eligible to nominate observers (*Namibian* [Windhoek], 12 July 1889, p.3). Also present and actively monitoring the election was UNTAG's Kenyan peacekeeping battalion.
36 Anglin (1995 : 524–25, 531n43, 536). For the election, each OAU member was asked to provide 'at least two observers'.
37 The OAU joined with the Commonwealth in not monitoring the Gambian presidential election in September 1996. Zimbabwe's foreign minister termed it 'consolidation of military rule in another form' (Anglin, 1998: 473n4).
38 In press interviews, the Tanzanian head of the OAU delegation gave a strongly favourable assessment of the election ('Calm reigned in Harare, says OAU mission', Tomric News Agency, Dar-es-Salaam, 14 March 2002 and 'OAU fails to defend position on poll conduct', *Daily News*, 15 March 2002).
39 'Elections in Zanzibar,' Statement of OAU, Dar-es-Salaam, 31 October 2000. Observers also noted 'the counting process was in some cases interfered with by the Electoral Commission officials and by some ruling party cadres'. The OAU took no further action in the matter.
40 OAU, 'Report of the Secretary-General on the Situation in Madagascar'. President Ratsiraka had banned international observers as interference in internal affairs. The two parties had their own local monitors.
41 *West Africa* (Lagos), 20 May 1996, p.770; *Business Day*, 4 March 2003.
42 'When Senegal said that the elections in Zimbabwe were not of good standard,' Foreign Minister Cheikh Tidianne Gadio stated somewhat bitterly, 'everybody thought the same. They said, "Oh, Senegal is the daring country; go ahead and say it". Then they would go and tell Mugabe, "You see, Senegal should not have said that. We have to stick together as one continent, one people". That's nice!'(interview on *allAfrica.com*, 5 March 2003).
43 OAU (1997: 53); Salim (2001) 'If the [Zimbabwe] government, that they elected, say

they are restoring order by their actions, I don't think it would be proper for us [AU] to go interfering in their internal legislation' (Desmond Orjiako, AU spokesman on BBC Africa, 24 June 2005).

[44] Salim was instructed to 'closely monitor' the 'persistence of flagrant violations of human rights in some regions' (OAU doc. CM/Res.1665 [LXIV], Yaoundé, 5 July 1996). Citing 'situations where mayhem and chaos prevail', he warned that the principle of non-interference could not apply to them (*ACR*, XXVI [1996–98], p.A106, Harare, 9 June 1997).

[45] This section builds upon Anglin (1996–98: A58–60). See also Cilliers (2003: 11–12). The constitution of ACHPR, along with its code of rights, is contained in the African Charter on Human and Peoples' Rights, which entered into force on 21 October 1986.

[46] ACHPR, 23rd Session, 'Final Communiqué', 29 April 1998, para.9.

[47] As of mid-2002, only 8 states were up to date with their reports, while 20 had yet to submit their first report, 12 of whom were overdue on 8 reports (ACHPR, 'Statistics on States Initial/ Periodic Reports,' October 2002). Only four reports were examined during 2001–2002 (ACHPR, *Fifteenth Annual Activity Report, 2001–2*, p.4). The African Charter on the Rights and Welfare of the Child (1999) has its own treaty supervisory body to examine state reports.

[48] 'Human Rights Group's Fact-Finding Mission Ends', *Herald* (Harare), 29 June 2002. ACHPR finally adopted the report in November 2003, but publication was held up at the insistence of Zimbabwe until May 2005 (ACHPR, 34th Session, 'Final Communiqué', 20 November 2003, para.16; Jean-Jaques Cornich and Nazeem Dramat, 'Zimbabwe had AU report for two years' [not one week as claimed], *Zimbabwe Independent*, 9 July 2004; 'Zimbabwe: Report of the Fact-Finding Mission, June 2002').

[49] ACHPR, *Fifteenth Annual Activity Report*, p.13 and Annex V; Movement for the Survival of the Ogoni People (MOSOP), *Press Release*, Port Harcourt, 20 June 2002. In May 2003, four 'Decisions on the Merits' were handed down, three against Sudan and one against Gambia – the host state (ACHPR, *Sixteenth Annual Activity Report, 2002–2003*, Annex VII).

[50] A separate Declaration to allow individuals to petition the Court is also open for signature. ACHPR has resisted pressure to integrate the Court into the proposed AU Court of Justice.

[51] *Rwanda: The Preventable Genocide* (Addis Ababa: OAU, 2000, p.245).

[52] Cilliers (2003: 11, 14). ACHPR now prepares and publishes its 'Concluding Observations' on state reports. Ominously, as of May 2005, the May 2003 report reviewing the special rapporteur mechanism has still not been dealt with. (*Sixteenth Annual Activity Report*, para.17, 31–32).

[53] Several current presidents, who initially came into office through coups, have hung up their uniforms and contested (often controversial) elections to legitimize their regimes.

[54] Cocks (2003: 16). After hesitating briefly, the AU decided not to invite CAR to its Maputo summit in July 2003. The Central African Economic and Monetary Union (CEMAC) officially recognized CAR's military regime on the basis of a promise to hold elections in January 2005 ('Central Africa backs coup leader', BBC African News, 4 June 2003; *Africa Confidential* 44(6), p.8, 21 March 2003).

[55] Of the diverse contributions to the final NEPAD blueprint, only the Economic Commission for Africa's *Compact for African Development* (31 March 2001) mentioned 'peer review' (pp.31, 37). Other inputs were South Africa's *Millennium Partnership for the African Recovery Programme* (MAP) and Senegal's *OMEGA Plan for Africa's Development*, which was melded into the *New African Initiative* (NAI) and, after further refining, emerged as *NEPAD* in October 2001.

[56] de Waal (2002: 471, 472). Though APRM is based on the OECD, the inclusion of a comprehensive peer review of political governance goes beyond OECD practice.

[57] 'Communiqué issued at the End of the First Meeting of the Implementation Committee,' Abuja, 23 October 2001, para.6. HSGIC comprised 15 (later 20) states, 3(or 4) from each of Africa's five regions. Included among them were the five 'initiating states' – Algeria, Egypt, Nigeria, Senegal, and South Africa – that constituted the

Steering Committee.

[58] NEPAD, 'Communiqué Issued at the Third Meeting of the Heads of State and Government Implementation Committee', Rome, 11 June 2002, paras.8–9 (hereinafter 'HSGIC-3'); *Declaration on Governance*; *The African Peer Review Mechanism* (hereinafter *'APRM'*), 10 June 2002, AHG/235 (XXXVIII), Annex II, 8 July 2002.

[59] G8 *Africa Action Plan*, Kananaskis, 27 June 2002, paras.7, 2.2–3; AU, 'Declaration on the Implementation of the New Partnership for Africa's Development', ASS/AU/Decl. 1(I), 10 July 2002b.

[60] *The Kampala Document*, Kampala, 22 May 1991; OAU Summit, 'CSSDCA Solemn Declaration', Lomé, 12 July 2000, AHG/Decl.4 (XXXVI); see also Deng and Zartman (2002).

[61] OAU Summit, 'Decision on the Conference on Security, Stability, Devolopment and Cooperation', Durban, 8 July 2002. AHG/175 (XXXVIII).

[62] *Memorandum of Understanding on Security, Stability, Development and Cooperation*, 8 July 2002. The original Experts' draft was modified following the second OAU-Civil Society Conference, Addis Ababa, 11–14 June 2002.

[63] Deng and Zartman (2002: xv). Cilliers (2003: 6, 9 and nn.38, 40, 44–45). The CSSDCA Unit is in the process of being transformed into CIDA.

[64] 'Communiqué Issued at the End of the Second Meeting of the Heads of State and Government Implementation Committee of the New Partnership for Africa's Development' (HSGIC-2), Abuja, 26 March 2002, paras.12, 20. Prior to October 2001, only a Steering Committee, consisting of the five initiating states, existed.

[65] 'SA loses battle to transform Africa,' *Financial Gazette* (Harare), 11 July 2002. Only Nigeria, Senegal, South Africa and a few other states dissented.

[66] 'Declaration on the Implementation of the New Partnership for Africa's Development', 10 July 2002; Cilliers (2002a: 1, 16, 17). Angola, DR Congo, Ghana, Kenya and Libya were duly appointed. Libya's appointment was held up, reportedly in the hope that Gaddafi would be satisfied with the chair of the UN Commission on Human Rights ('Secret ballot, Libya elected chair of UN Human Rights Commission', *UN News*, 20 January 2003). It ended up with both.

[67] 'Given a chance, Nepad might take root', *Business Day*, 13 July 2003. At the 9 March 2003 Implementation Committee meeting, 'heated discussions' on good governance had ensued (Angola Press Agency, 'Prime Minister back from NEPAD summit', 10 March 2003).

[68] 'SA loses battle to transform Africa'; 'AU: More than a presidents' trade union', *East African* (Nairobi), 1 July 2002; 'African leaders on collision course over NEPAD', *Zimbabwe Independent*, 5 July 2002; 'The George Dubya [Bush] of Africa', *Sunday Times* (Johannesburg), 13 July 2002. Libya was bankrolling Chad, Madagascar, Sudan, Swaziland, Zambia, Zimbabwe and possibly other AU members (*Africa Confidential* 43(22), p.8, 8 November 2002).

[69] Salisu Na'inna Dambatta, 'African peers in self-review', *Daily Trust* (Abuja), 24 May 2005; Reg Rumney, 'South Africa – the New Colonial Power?', *Mail and Guardian*, 8 March 2004.

[70] 'SA loses battle to transform Africa'; 'Africa blasts SA for NEPAD dominance', *Sunday Times*, 22 September 2002; 'George Dubya of Africa'.

[71] 'Top AU official in the firing line', *Sunday Times*, 29 June 2003; 'Debating a continent in conflict', *Star* (Johannesburg), 11 July 2003; Cilliers (2002b: 7); 'Great Lakes security summit: SA given the cold shoulder', *Mail and Guardian* online, 6 June 2003.

[72] 'Communiqué Issued at the End of the First Summit of the Committee of Participating Heads of State and Government in the African Peer Review Mechanism (APR Forum), Kigali, Rwanda', 13 February 2004; Obasanjo, address to 3rd Summit of the APR Forum, Abuja, 19 June 2005.

[73] 'Communiqué Issued at the End of the Seventh Summit of the Heads of State and Government Implementation Committee', Abuja, 28 May 2003, para.22 (hereinafter 'HSGIC-7'). The 4 men and 3 women were: Marie-Angelique Savane (Senegal) (Chairperson), Adebayo Adedeji (Nigeria), B.A. Kiplagat (Kenya), Graça Machel

(Mozambique), Mourad Medelci (Algeria), Dorothy Njeume (Cameroon) and Chris Stals (South Africa). On the socio-economic implications of the Stals appointment, see Callard (2003b: 26–27).

[74] *APRM*, paras.6–7. Initially, it was required that, collectively, the expertise of Panel members embrace the areas of 'political governance, macro economic management, public financial management and corporate governance'. This condition was dropped by the time the appointments were made (Cilliers, 2003: 6, nn4, 20).

[75] *Ibid.* (6, n.4); *APRM*, para.7. The Panel is enjoined to exercise oversight of the APRM with a view to ensuring 'the independence, professionalism and credibility of the process' (*ibid.* para.10).

[76] *Economist*, 15 November 2003, p.22; *NEPAD Newsletter* (Nairobi), no.75 (25 January 2005), p.3. As a South African, Professor Wiseman Nkuhlu, headed NEPAD's Secretariat, it was logical that a francophone West African should head the APR Secretariat.

[77] De Waal (2003: 469); Project on Monitoring Progress towards Good Governance (Cilliers, 2002b: 4, 5 and n.18). ECA regularly attended HSGIC sessions and other NEPAD meetings.

[78] *Ibid.*, p.4; 'HSGIC-3,' para.9; Cilliers (2002a: 17).

[79] Cilliers (2002b: 4, 6). 'An important factor in understanding this shift is the increasingly precarious domestic situation in Nigeria in the run-up to presidential elections' (p.4).

[80] Cilliers (2002a: 17; 2002b: 1, 5). 'Time to put flesh on Nepad's bones', *Business Day*, 17 October 2003, 'Mbeki's volte-face has battered Nepad,' *Mail and Guardian*, 8 November 2002.

[81] Cilliers (2002a: 15–16). See above, notes 64, 65. Mbeki joined Obasanjo in offering CSSDCA $500,000, though with no great enthusiasm (Cilliers 2002b: n20).

[82] HSGIC-3, para.13. As of November 2002, only South Africa and Algeria were financial contributors (NEPAD: 'Report to the Heads of State Implementation Committee, July-October 2002', 3 November 2002, sec. F [hereinafter 'NEPAD Report']). Cilliers (2002b: 4). The APR Secretariat and the CSSDCA Unit within the AU Commission were instructed to 'work closely' to harmonize and align their two units (APRM, 'Organisation and Processes', 9 March 2003, para.4.4).

[83] 'Report of the Twenty-first Meeting of the Committee of Experts of the Conference of African Ministers of Finance, Planning and Economic Development', Sandton, South Africa, 16–18 October 2002, para.74; ECA (2004).

[84] SAPA, 'Pahad is right over peer review mechanism: Mbeki', 30 November, 2002; SA Government Communications, 'Media Statement: NEPAD Peer Review Mechanism,' 1 November 2002.

[85] 'Mbeki Letter – 'Work of AU separate from mechanisms of Nepad," *Business Day*, 18 November 2002. The reply to Chrétien was dated 6 November. On 19 November, the day following publication of Mbeki's reply, the Canadian Trade Minister, then in Johannesburg, warned that G8 support for NEPAD was 'conditional on NEPAD functioning' ('Canada insists on peer review for NEPAD', *Business Day*, 20 November 2002).

[86] The new transition period was for 3 years 'as from July 2003, or until such time as the relevant structures of the African Union are fully operational, whichever comes first' ('Declaration on the Implementation of the New Partnership for Africa's Development', Assembly/AU/Decl.5 (II), para.27 (ii), 12 July 2003).

[87] *Ibid.*; NEPAD: 'Communiqué Issued at the End of the Fifth Summit of the Heads of State and Government Implementation Committee, Abuja, 3 November 2002' (hereinafter 'HSGIC-5'), paras.11, 13, 14; 'Nepad to institute political peer review system after all', *Business Day*, 7 November 2002; Mbeki (2002b: 1–4); IRIN, 'Support for Nepad blueprint may be weakened', Johannesburg, 29 November 2002. The NEPAD Secretariat had ambitions to play a 'facilitator, catalyst and support role' in implementing NEPAD ('NEPAD Report', p.8).

[88] *Ibid*; 'Media Statement'; 'Mbeki Letter'.

[89] Mbeki stressed that, 'in the context of the AU, "peer review" has been mentioned only

in the context of NEPAD'(Mbeki, 2002b: 3). Experience during the transition period and the reaction of AU members to their baptismal peer review would no doubt have some influence on AU practice.

[90] HSGIC-2, para.14; APRM, 'Organisation and Processes', para.4.1; *APRM* (2002: paras.10–11). 'Every review exercise ... must be technically competent, credible and free of political manipulation' (para.4).

[91] HSGIC-5, para.16; 'Organisation and Processes', paras. 3.8, 5.1, 6.1–6.4, 7.4; Cilliers (2002: 10,14). Curiously, the reason given for a transition period was that, at that time, the Peace and Security Council, the Pan African Parliament and the Economic, Social and Cultural Council (ECOSOCC) did not exist. Other Strategic Partners are the ADB, ECA and the UN Development Programme's Africa Bureau.

[92] Cilliers (2003: 2, 6–8). Cilliers argued that, since NEPAD has failed to prevent its integration into the AU, it should strive to capture the AU by insisting that membership of the Peace and Security Council should be restricted to APRM participants. In fact, 14 of the 15 PSC members all but Botswana, are peer review volunteers.

[93] NEPAD, *Memorandum of Understanding on the African Peer Review Mechanism*, NEPAD/HSGIC/03–2003/APRM/MOU, 9 March 2003, paras.18–26; *Guidelines for Countries to Prepare for and Participate in the African Peer Review Mechanism*, NEPAD/APRM/Panel3/guidelines/11–2003/Doc.8, paras.29–40; NEPAD, 'Country Self-Assessment for the African Peer Review Mechanism', October 2004. Initially, formal ratification, in addition to a signature, was required, but later abandoned, presumably to entice more volunteers (Cilliers, 2003: 1, nn.4, 5).

[94] NEPAD, *Guidelines for Countries*, paras.16–20; *Memorandum of Understanding on Technical Assessments and the Country Review Visit*, NEPAD/HSGIC03–2003/APRM/Guidelines/Outline, 9 March 2003.

[95] Those volunteering were: Algeria, Angola, Benin, Burkina Faso, Cameroon, Republic of Congo, Egypt, Ethiopia, Gabon, Ghana, Kenya, Lesotho, Malawi, Mali, Mauritius, Mozambique, Nigeria, Rwanda, Senegal, Sierra Leone, South Africa, Sudan, São Tomé, Tanzania, Uganda and Zambia. The most notable absentee is Botswana, an HSGIC member (Dan Moabi, 'Whither Botswana?: Botswana's stand on peer review unconvincing', *Mmegi/Reporter* [Gaborone], 24 March 2005).

[96] *Sunday Times*, 15 June 2003; Thaninga Shope-Linney, Abuja (*This Day* [Lagos], 29 January 2003). Other reasons for delay are that some countries 'want to get their houses in order first', they are devastated by war, or waiting till after an election ('A Challenging Road Ahead for the Peer Review Mechanism', Inter Press Service [Johannesburg], 7 January 2005).

[97] 'African peoples have begun to demonstrate their refusal to accept poor economic and political leadership. These developments are, however, uneven and inadequate' (*NEPAD* 2002b: para.7).

[98] On the concept of 'NEPAD as a club', see Gelb, (2002: 26–28).

[99] *Ibid.* I am indebted to Edwin Willer for this analogy. See De Waal (2003: 467–68).

[100] *APRM*, para.5. Gelb argues persuasively for a (low) minimum standard of governance for membership but, to maintain the credibility of the peer review process, exclusion from benefits or membership for 'free riders' that fail to live up to their undertakings to improve (2002: 27–28).

[101] 'Part of Nepad's problem is ... the difficulty in managing the tension of inclusivity to be Africa-supported and yet exclusive and elitist to be successful' (Mills, 2003).

[102] Obasanjo (2002: 22); *APRM*, para.17; Cilliers (2002b: 4) For each of the 9 APRM objectives under the theme of Democracy and Political Governance, there are lists of existing standards, indicative criteria and (a total of 41) indicators.

[103] 'Objectives, Standards, Criteria and Indicators', NEPAD/HSGIC-03–2003/APRM/Guidelines/OSCI, 9 March 2003, pp.5–15.

[104] 'Communiqué issued at the end of the Sixth Summit of the Heads of State and Government Implementation Committee' Abuja, 9 March 2003, para. 24 (hereinafter 'HSGIC-6'); HSGIC-2, para. 14; NEPAD *Declaration on Governance*, paras. 18–19; Cilliers (2002a: 16, n89).

[105] UNDR (2002: 36–41) lists 8 (unhelpful) objective indices compared to 43 subjective concepts grouped under 11 indicators within three broad headings: democracy, rule of law and government effectiveness, and corruption.

[106] NEPAD *Declaration on Governance*, para.14; *NEPAD* calls for 'clear standards of accountability, transparency and participatory governance'(para.49).

[107] *Compact for African Recovery*, pp.10, 38; ECA (2002: 19); ECA, 'Measuring and Monitoring Progress in Good Governance in Africa' (September 2002); 'Report of the Twenty-First Meeting of the Committee of Experts', para.25; Cilliers (2002a: n 92; 2003: 7). See World Bank (2002b), which measures six dimensions of governance: voice and accountability, political stability, government effectiveness, regulatory quality, rule of law and control of corruption.

[108] Among the 16 members of the Ghana Country Review Mission were a South African Professor of Human Rights Law and a Nigerian and a Kenyan Professor of Political Science. Only one ECA member of staff was included (APR Secretariat, 'Brief Report Issued at the End of the African Peer Review Mechanism Country Review Mission to Ghana', 4–16 April 2005, p.2).

[109] An exception was Botswana, whose Foreign Minister urged that peer reviews should focus solely on political governance and shelve plans for economic reviews which, he claimed, were adequately dealt with by the World Bank and similar institutions ('Merafhe defends Botswana's NEPAD stand', *Mmegi/Reporter* [Gaborone], 14 March 2005).

[110] 'Prime Minister rejects NEPAD "peer review"', *Namibian*, 7 April 2003. The Namibian business community favoured adoption of APRM ('NCCI asks government to reconsider peer review', *Ibid.*, 16 July 2003).

[111] The 'Ouagadougou Declaration' (10 June 1998) called for 'effective democratic systems, taking into account the social-cultural realities of our states', while the Declaration on the Political and Socio-Economic Situation in Africa (11 July 1990) affirmed the 'right of our countries to determine ... their system of democracy'.

[112] SAPA, 'Build African democracy, Mbeki tells Botswana', 11 March 2003; *NEPAD*, para.79. As early as June 1997, Mugabe cautioned that democracy should be 'judiciously pursued', whereupon Kofi Annan responded that such thoughts were 'truly demeaning of the yearning for human dignity that resides in every African heart'. 'Human rights', he added, 'are African rights' (*ACR* XXVI [1996–98], p.A110).

[113] BBC Africa News, 'Nigerian leader slams EU', 25 April 2003. A year earlier, he had accused donors of insisting on 'extraneous standards' ('Obasanjo warns against imposition of foreign standards on Africa', *This Day* [Lagos], 26 March 2002).

[114] *APRM*, paras.18–25; Cilliers (2003: 3–4). Of the 5 stages outlined, 3 fall within phase 1 and 2 within phase 2.

[115] 'PM urges ranking system for Africa', *Toronto Star*, 11 April 2002, p.22. Mbeki indicated that there might be 'in some cases, even ranking among countries' (Mbeki, 2002b: 3).

[116] *APRM*, para.12; *Guidelines for Countries*, para. 21; 'Country Self-Assessment'.

[117] Cilliers (2003: n.10; *APRM* (paras.14, 19) lists 'government, officials, political parties, parliamentarians and representatives of civil society organizations (including the media, academia, trade unions, business, professional bodies)'.

[118] *APRM*, paras.14, 20–23; Cilliers (2002b: 4). Gelb employs the metaphor of 'a "path" towards best governance practices, rather than a "bar" to be "jumped over"' (Gelb, 2002: 28).

[119] Address to 3rd Summit of APR Forum, Abuja, 19 June 2005. Obasanjo is Chairperson of the AU, HSGIC and the APR Forum.

[120] *APRM*, paras.24–25; *Guidelines for Countries*, paras.25–26. Gelb has urged adoption of a 'yellow card/red card' system under which a state that persisted in violating its obligations would receive 'warnings followed by suspension of membership' (Gelb, 2002: 31, 32). 'Naming and shaming' is unlikely to influence the most intransigent offenders.

[121] *APRM*, para.25; Cilliers (2003: 6, n.11); ECA (2002: 18); Gelb (2002: 31); 'Organisation and Processes,' para.7.17.

[122] 'Progress Report of H.E. Chief Olusegun Obasanjo ... Chairperson of the NEPAD

Heads of State and Government Implementation Committee', Assembly/AU/Rpt(II), Maputo, 12 July 2003, p.5. Cilliers calculated that the 'first results' could be expected 'some 18 months after the start of the Mechanism', assuming no further delays and problems and 'a common will and cooperation unparalleled in African history' (2003: 13–14).

[123] Ross Herbert considers it urgent that the APR Secretariat acquire 'well-qualified staff and not rely on consultants' (David Mageria, 'Peer review taking longer than expected', *Independent Online*, 19 April 2005).

[124] 'Communiqué Issued at the End of the First Summit of the Committee of Participating Heads of State and Government in the African Peer Review Mechanism' (hereinafter APR Forum-1), Kigali, Rwanda, 13 February 2005, para.24–5; *Guidelines for Countries*, para.34. 'It is critical that the work of the APR Focal Point is inclusive, integrated and co-ordinated with existing policy-decision and medium-term planning processes' (*ibid.*).

[125] 'No "back scratching" for Nepad peer review', *Mail and Guardian* online 27 June 2003. He even suggested choosing a country like South Africa that may think it is doing everything right just to see how rigorous this process is', and added: 'Nothing is sacred'.

[126] *APRM*, para.25; *Guidelines for Countries*, para.25; Abimbola Akosile, 'Beyond a Civil Society Shadow Report', *This Day* (Lagos), 1 March 2005.

[127] 'Despite an outcry from civil society organizations, the [Ghana] government appointed a civil society panel without consultation or the involvement of the two major confederations of NGOs' ('Will NEPAD and APRM work?' *News from Africa* [Nairobi], 24 February 2005).

[128] Obasanjo, Kananaskis, 27 June 2002; 'Further support beyond [humanitarian needs] though, must be targeted at reinforcing progress in line with the principles, standards and goals of NEPAD' (NEPAD Secretariat, 28 June 2002).

[129] G8 *Africa Action Plan*, 27 June 2002, paras.4, 7–8. In their response, the African leaders emphasized that APRM 'should also apply to the partnership commitments' ('Statement issued by four African leaders of the Nepad Steering Committee', Kananaskis, 27 June 2002, para.17).

[130] *Business Day*, 5 November 2002.

[131] 'NEPAD Report', 2002, p.9; NEPAD, 'Progress Report', 2003, p.8; HSGIC-6, para.7; Cilliers (2003: 12–13); 'Organisation and Processes', sec. 8; APR Forum-1, paras.15, 26.

[132] Ernest Harsch, 'Civil society engages African plan', *African Renewal*, 18: 3 (April 2005), pp.10–12; ECA (2005: para.1.7); Verwey (2004: sec.4).

[133] *APRM* paras.18–19; *Memorandum of Understanding*, para.22; *Guidelines for Countries*, paras.20(ii), 22; 'Organisation and Processes', paras,7.8–7.9, 7.11. Stakeholders include 'trade unions, women, youth, civil society, private sector, rural communities and professional associations'.

[134] 'Brief report issued at the end of the African Peer Review Mechanism Country Review Mission to Ghana', 4–16 April 2005, paras.5–9; Gelb (2002: 29).

[135] Abimol Akosile, 'Beyond a Civil Society Shadow report', *This Day*, 1 March 2005.

[136] NEPAD, *Declaration on Governance*, para.15. Obasanjo called CSOs 'soldiers of development' and expected them to play a 'major role' in the peer review process (*East African*, 17 June 2002)

[137] He added that the 'first and most important' thing that can be done to improve credibility is that NEPAD leaders 'allow, indeed encourage, domestic political pressure *in favour of improving governance* within participating countries, so that a demand for improved governance is encouraged and nurtured' (Gelb, 2002: 34).

[138] The Bush administration has largely ignored its own eligibility criteria on human rights and political reforms in certifying Côte d'Ivoire, Eritrea and Rwanda under the US Africa Growth and Opportunities Act (Human Rights Watch, 2003).

[139] HSGIC-6, para.20; Cilliers (2003: 2, 12); 36th Session of the Conference of Ministers of Finance, Planning and Development, Addis Ababa, 'Ministerial Statement,' 1 June 2003, paras.4–7, 27–37. APF comprises 20 NEPAD and 19 donor governments as well as 9 African and 6 international institutions. It held its first meeting in November

2003 and the second in April 2004 ('African and Western policy makers refine agenda for continent's developments in Maputo', *eAfrica* [Johannesburg], v.2, May 2004).

[140] He claims that the intent and content of NEPAD were inevitable and should have been anticipated. Nevertheless, 'the damage could not have been more severe'.

[141] John Fraser, 'Canada insists on peer review for Nepad', *Business Day*, 20 November 2002; G8 Chair's Statement, Evian, 3 June 2003, para.2.

[142] Freedom Quest International (2003); AU, 'Constitutive Act', art. 3(g).

[143] African states have complained that they are being held 'hostage' for Mugabe's excesses. Yet, in acting in solidarity with Harare, they would appear to be willing hostages (Akwe Amosu and Charles Cobb, '"Don't hold Nepad hostage over Zimbabwe" says Minister', *allAfrica.com*, 27 March 2002; BBC Africa News, 'African leaders seek aid', 26 March 2002). African leaders are not blamed for Mugabe's actions, but for their response to them.

[144] 'Zimbabwe Nepad's 'acid test,'' *Mail and Guardian* online, 6 July 2003 and 'Zimbabwe the "first litmus test for NEPAD,"' *ibid.* 5 August 2003; Southern Africa NGO Meeting, Harare, 'Communiqué', 25 September 2002; IRIN, 'Southern Africa: Civil society coalition calls for end to forced evictions in Zimbabwe', Johannesburg, 23 June 2005. BBC News, 'Africa rejects action on Zimbabwe', 24 June 2005.

[145] AU, 'Constitutive Act', Arts.4(g)(h), 7.1. A constitutional amendment to Art.4(h), seeking ratifications, adds 'a serious threat to the legitimate order to restore peace and stability to the member state of the Union upon recommendation of the Peace and Security Council' to the list of 'grave circumstances'. It is unlikely to be adopted.

[146] *Ibid.*, Art.23.2; Assembly Rules, 4.1(g), 36.

[147] The AU awarded Gambia the honor of hosting the 2006 AU Assembly despite President Jammeh's notorious hostility to the press and journalists (*Reporters sans frontières*, 'Shock at African Union's decision to let President Jammeh host 2006 summit', 10 February 2005). In response to appeals to halt the bulldozing of thousands of squatter shacks in Zimbabwe, the arrest of tens of thousands, and the rendering of hundreds of thousands homeless, a spokeperson said the AU had many more serious problems to consider (BBC News, 'Africa rejects action on Zimbabwe', 24 June 2005).

[148] AU Central Organ, 93rd Ordinary Session, Addis Ababa, 24 July 2003, 'Communiqué', Central Organ/MEC/AMB/COMM. (XCIII), para.A6. One concrete proposal is that perpetrators of unconstitutional change be barred from elections organized to restore constitutional order.

[149] AU, 'Constitutive Act', Art.30; 'Assembly Rules', 37.4. The provisions are not retroactive.

[150] AU, 'Constitutive Act', Art.37.5.

[151] 'Declaration on the Principles Governing Democratic Elections in Africa,' AHG/Decl.1 (XXXVIII), Durban, 8 July 2002.

[152] AU Executive Council, Maputo, 4–8 July 2003, 'Report of the Interim Chairperson on the Proceedings of the African Conference on Elections, Democracy and Good Governance', EX/CL/35 (III), Annexes I and II; AU Assembly, 'Decision on the Report of the Interim Chairperson on the Conference on Elections, Democracy and Good Governance', Maputo, 12 July 2003, Assembly/AU/Dec.13 (II).

[153] Nkuhlu has pointed out that Ghana is doing most things right but is not attracting much foreign investment.' ('No "back scratching" for Nepad peer review', *Mail and Guardian* online, 27 June 2003).

Bibliography

Abel, Richard, *Politics by Other Means: Law in the Struggle Against Apartheid, 1980–1994*. New York: Routledge, 1995.

Abrahamson, Rita, *Disciplining Democracy: Development Discourse and Good Governance in Africa*. London: Zed Books, 2000.

Abreu, A. 'Gender Integration into Policies, Programmes and Budgets in Mozambique.' Paper presented at the Inter-Agency Workshop on Improving the Effectiveness of Integrating Gender into Government Budgets, Marlborough House, London, 2000.

African American Institute, *African Women in Politics: Together for Change, Three Struggles for Political Rights*. New York: African American Institute, 1995.

'Africa on the Internet: An Annotated Guide to African Web Sites.' [available at: http://www.uneca.org/aisi/nici/africacontent.htm].

African Charter for Popular Participation in Development and Transformation. Arusha, 16 February 1990. UN doc. A/45/427, 22 August 1990. Appendix II.

African Development Bank. *African Development Report, 2001*. London: Oxford University Press, 2001.

Africa Research Bulletin: Political Series. Oxford: Blackwell Publishing.

Afrobarometer, 2001 [available at: http://www.afrobarometer.org]

Agranoff, Robert, 'Asymmetrical and Symmetrical Federalism in Spain,' in *Evaluating Federal Systems*, ed. Bertus de Villers. Dordrecht: Martinus Nijhoff, 1994.

Ahikire, Josephine, *Decentralization in Uganda today: Institutions and Possible Outcomes in the Context of Human Rights*, International Council on Human Rights Policy Decentralization, Local Government and Human Rights. Project 116–Stage One: Survey of the Issues, Spring 2002.

Alailima, P.J., 'Engendering the National Budget in Sri Lanka,' paper presented at the Inter-Agency Workshop on Improving the Effectiveness of Integrating Gender in Government Budgets. London: Marlborough House, 2000.

Allot, A., *New Essays in African Law*, London: Sweet and Maxwell, 1970.

Alster, Gordon, 'Radio's Peacekeeping Potential in Humanitarian Crisis,' in *Somalia, Rwanda, and Beyond the Role of the International Media in Wars and Humanitarian Crisis*. ed. Andrea Bartoli et al. Dublin: Crosslines, 1995.

Amin, Samir, 'Preface', in *Popular Struggles for Democracy in Africa*. ed. Peter Anyong Nyong'o. London: Zed Books, 1987.

Amin, Samir, 'Peace, National and Regional Security and Development,' in *Breaking the Links – Development Theory & Practice in Southern Africa*, ed. Robert Mazur. Trenton, NJ: Africa World Press, 1990.

Andrews, Penelope E., 'Spectators at the Revolution: Women and Rights in the New South Africa,' in *The Post-Apartheid Constitutions: Perspectives on South Africa's Basic Law*, eds. Penelope E. Andrews and Stephen Ellmann. Athens, OH: Ohio University Press, 2001.

Anglin, Douglas G., 'International Election Monitoring: The African Experience,' *African Affairs* 97, 389, October (1998).

Anglin, Douglas G., 'International Monitoring in Africa: From Bullets to Ballots,' *African Contemporary Record* XXIII (1990–92).

Anglin, Douglas G., 'International monitoring of the transition to democracy in South Africa, 1992–1994,' *African Affairs*, 94, 377, October (1995).

Anglin, Douglas G., 'International Monitoring: The African Experience and Contribution,' *African Contemporary Record* XXII (1989–90).

Anglin, Douglas G., 'Monitoring Human Rights Observance in Africa: Assessing the Impact.' *African Contemporary Record* XXVI (1996–98).

Apter, David, *The Gold Coast in Translation*. Princeton, NJ: Princeton University Press, 1958.

Archer, R., *Markets and Good Government: The Way Forward for Economic and Social Development*. UN Non-Governmental Liaison Service, 1994.

Armstrong, Alice, ed., *Women and Law in Southern Africa*. Harare: Zimbabwe Pub. House, 1987.

Armstrong, P., 'Human Rights and Multilateral Development Banks: Governance Concerns in Decision Making,' *88 Am. Soc'y. Int' L' LL Proc.* 277 (1994).

Aryeetey, Ellen Bortei-Doku et al., *The Right to Development in Ghana*, Cambridge, MA: Francis Xavier Bagnoud Centre for Health and Human Rights, Harvard School of Public Health, and The Hague: Ministry of Foreign Affairs of the Netherlands, 2003.

AU, *Declaration on Democracy, Political, Economic and Corporate Governance*, AHG/235 (XXXVIII), Annex I, 18 June 2002a.

AU, 'Declaration on the Implementation of the New Partnership for Africa's Development.' ASS/AU/Decl. 1 (I), 10 July 2002b.

AU, *African Peer Review Mechanism*. AHG/235(xxx viii), 10 June 2002c.

AU, 'Declaration on the Implementation of NEPAD.' ASS/AU/Decl.5 (II), 12 July 2003.

AU Assembly, 'Decision on the Report of the Interim Chairperson on the Conference on Elections, Democracy and Good Governance.' Maputo, 12 July 2003. Assembly/AU/Decl.13 (II).

AU Executive Council, 'Report of the Interim Chairperson on the Proceedings of the African Conference on Elections, Democracy and Good Governance.' Maputo, 4–8 July 2003. EX/CL/35 (III), Annexes I and II.

AU, 'Rules of Procedure of the Assembly of the [African] Union.' ASS/AU/2(I)-a.

Austin, John, *The Province of Jurisprudence Determined: and the Uses of the Study of Jurisprudence*. London: Weidenfeld and Nicolson, 1954 (1st edn 1834).

Ayisi Agyei, J. 'African Women: Championing Their Own Development and Empowerment – Case Study, Ghana,' *Women's Rights Law Reporter* 21, Spring (2000).

Baden, S., 'Gender Issues in Agricultural Market Liberalisation.' in *Bridge Report No. 41*. Brighton: Bridge IDS, 1998.

Baden, S., 'Gender, Governance and the Feminisation of Poverty.' Prepared for the UNDP conference on Women and Political Participation: 21st Century Challenges. New Delhi, 1999.

Bakkar, I., 'New Direction in UNDP: An Overview', paper presented at the Inter-Agency Workshop on Improving the Effectiveness of Integrating Gender in Government Budgets. London: Marlborough House, 2000.

Banerjee, N., 'Taking Gender Budgets to the Sub-national and Community Levels,' paper presented at the Inter-Agency Workshop on Improving the Effectiveness of Integrating Gender in Government Budgets. London: Marlborough House, 2000.

Barkan, Joel D., 'Protracted Democratic Transitions in Africa,' *Democratization*, 7, 3 Autumn (2000).

Barkan, Joel D., *Emerging Legislatures in Emerging African Democracies*, Washington DC: World Bank, 2003.

Barth, Fredrik, *Models of Social Organization*. London: Royal Anthropological Inst., Occasional Paper No. 23, 1966.

Baxi, Upendra, 'Voices of Suffering, Fragmented University and the Future of Human Rights.' *Transitional Journal of Law and Contemporary Problems* 8, 125 (1998).

Bayart, Jean François, *The State in Africa: The Politics of the Belly*. London: Longman, 1993.

Beall, J., 'Urban Governance: Why Gender Matters.' Paper prepared for Gender in Development Division, UNDP, 1996.

Bell, Derrick, 'Racial Realism – After We're Gone: Prudent Speculations on America in a Post Racial Epoch.' *St Louis University Law Journal* 34, 393 (1990).

Benda-Beckmann, Franz, 'Scapegoat and Magic Charm in Development Theory and Practice.' *Journal of Legal Pluralism and Unofficial Law* 28, 129 (1989).

Berlin, Sir Isaiah, *The Crooked Timber of Humanity*. New York: Knopf, 1990.

Bertrand, Claude-Jean, *An Arsenal for Democracy: Media Accountability Systems*. Creeskill, NJ: Hampton Press, 2001.

Bhalla, Surjit S., *Imagine There's No Country: Poverty, Inequality and Growth in the Era of*

Globalization. Washington, DC : Institute for International Economics, 2002.

Blackden, C.M., 'Paradigm Postponed: Gender and Economic Adjustment in Sub-Saharan Africa.' Technical Note: Human Resources Division. Washington, DC: World Bank, 1993.

Blackden, C.M. and C. Bhanu, *Gender, Growth, and Poverty Reduction: Special Programme of Assistance for Africa, 1998 Status Report of Poverty in Sub-Saharan Africa.* Washington, DC: World Bank, 1998.

Bond, P. and M. Manyanya, *Zimbabwe's Plunge.* Durban; University of Natal Press, 2002.

Bratton, Michael, 'Africa's Second Elections,' *Journal of Democracy*, 9, 3 July (1998).

Bratton, Michael and Nicholas Van de Walle, *Democratic Experiments in Africa.* Cambridge: Cambridge University Press, 1997.

Brock, Karen, Rosemary McGee, and Richard Ssweakiryanga, *Poverty Knowledge and Policy Processes: A case study of Ugandan national poverty reduction policy.* Brighton: Institute of Development Studies at the University of Sussex, 2002.

Buchanan, James M., 'Politics, Property and Law: An Alternative Interpretation of Miller v. Schoene,' *Journal of Law and Economics* 15, 439 (1972).

Budlender, D, ed., *Engendering Budgets: The Southern African Experience.* Harare: UNIFEM, 1999.

Budlender, D., 'Taking Gender Budgets to Sub-national and Community Levels.' Paper presented at the Inter-Agency Workshop on Improving the Effectiveness of Integrating Gender in Government Budgets, Marlborough House, London: 2000.

Budlender, D., R. Sharp, and K. Allen, *How To Do a Gender-sensitive Budget Analysis: Contemporary Research and Practice.* London: Commonwealth Secretariat and AusAid, 2000.

Budlender. G., 'Justiciability of the Right to Housing – The South African Experience.' [available at: www.lrc.org.za]

Callard, Richard, 'A Betrayal of Democracy,' *Mail & Guardian* (Johannesburg) 14 March 2003a: 26.

Callard, Richard, 'Setting NEPAD's Compass,' *Mail & Guardian* (Johannesburg) 27 June 2003b, pp. 26–7.

Cantori, Lewis and Andrew Ziegler, eds., *Comparative Politics in the Post-Behavioural Era,* Boulder, CO: Lynne Rienner, 1988.

Carnoy, Martin, *The State and Political Theory.* Princeton, NJ: Princeton University Press, 1984.

Carothers, Thomas, 'The End of the Transition Paradigm.' *Journal of Democracy*, 13, 1 (2002).

Cass, Ronald, 'Property Rights Systems and the Rule of Law.' Boston University School of Law Working Paper No. 03–06 in *The Elgar Companion to Property Right Economics,* ed. Enrico Colombatto. Northampton, MA: Edward Elgar Publications, 2003.

Chabal, Patrick, 'The Quest for Good Government and Development in Africa: Is NEPAD the Answer?', *International Affairs* 78, 3 (2002).

Chambers, Robert, 'Rural Poverty-oriented Monitoring and Evaluation. Simple is Optional,' Brighton: Institute of Development Studies, University of Sussex, 1978 (mimeo).

Chambliss, W.J., 'Types of Deviance and the Effectiveness of Legal Sanction,' *Wisconsin Law Review* (1967).

Chambliss, William and Robert B. Seidman, *Law, Order and Power.* Reading, MA: Addison-Wesley Pub. Co., 1971.

Chaskalson, Arthur, 'Human Dignity as a Foundational Value of our Constitutional Order,' *South African Journal of Human Rights* 16 (2000).

Chikulo, B.C., 'Decentralisation in Centralism: An Analysis of the Zambian Experience 1964–1981,' in *Issues in Zambian Development.* eds. K. Osei-Hwendie and M. Ndulo. Rosbury, MA: Omenan, 1985.

Chikuwa, J., *Zimbabwe: The Rise of Nationhood.* London: Minerva, 1988.

Chomsky, Noam and Edward Herman, *Manufacturing Consent: The Political Economy of the Mass Media.* New York: Pantheon, 1988.

Chuen, Tan Soo, 'The Rule of Law: Imperialist Baggage or Heritage?' *Ethos* [available at: www.ethos.com.my/magazine/vol3].

Cilliers, Jakkie, *Peace, Security and Development in Africa?* Occasional Paper 60, Pretoria: Institute for Security Studies, 2002a, August.

Cilliers, Jakkie, *NEPAD's Peer Review Mechanism*. Occasional Paper 64, Pretoria: Institute for Security Studies, 2002b, November.

Cilliers, Jakkie, *Peace and Security through Good Governance: A Guide to the NEPAD African Peer Review Mechanism*. Occasional Paper 70, Pretoria: Institute for Security Studies, 2003, April.

Cocks, Tim, 'CAR: Don't hold your breath for democracy,' *Mail & Guardian*, 8 March 2003.

Colson, E. *Seven Tribes of Northern Rhodesia*. Manchester: Manchester University Press, 1957.

Commission on Gender Equality, *Redefining Politics: South African Women and Democracy*. Johannesburg: CGE, 1999.

Commonwealth Secretariat, *Commonwealth Declaration Issued by Commonwealth Heads of Government, 1971–1991*. London: Commonwealth Secretariat, 1993.

Commonwealth Secretariat, *Best Practice Guidelines for National Human Rights Institutions*. London: London Commonwealth Secretariat, 2001.

Commonwealth Secretariat, *Report of the Commonwealth Regional Workshop on Strengthening National Ombudsman and Human Rights Institutions*. London: Commonwealth Secretariat, 1998.

Commonwealth Secretariat, *Protecting Human Rights: The Role of National Institutions*, London: Commonwealth Secretariat, 2000.

Constitution of Uganda. Kampala: Government Printer, 1995.

Constitution of Zambia. Lusaka: Government Printer, 1991.

Constitution of Zimbabwe. Harare: Government Printer, 1996.

Consultative Business Movement, 'Regions in South Africa: Constitutional Options and their Implications for Good Governance and a Sound Economy' (unpublished), Johannesburg: CBM, 1993.

Cornwell, Richard, 'Madagascar: First test for the African Union.' *African Security Review* 12, 1 (2003).

CSSDCA, *Kampala Document*, Kampala, 22 May 1999.

Cusack, K., *Violence Against Women and Girls*. Report of National Study of Violence. Accra, 1999.

Davidow, J., *A Peace in Southern Africa*. Boulder, CO: Westview, 1984.

Decisions of the Commission on Human Rights and Administrative Justice (Ghana) 1994–2000). Accra: CHRAJ.

d'Elgelbronner-Kolff, F.M., Hinz, M.O. and Sindano, J.L., eds., *Traditional Authority and Development in Southern Africa*. Windhoek: New Namibia Books, 1998.

Demery, L., 'Gender and Public Social Spending: Disaggregating Benefit Incidence.' Paper prepared for the World Bank. Washington, DC: World Bank, 1996.

'Democracy and Rule of Law Project,' Roundtable on the rule of law at the Carnegie Endowment [available at: www.ceip.org/files/events.asp?p=1&EventID=380].

Deng, Francis M. and I. William Zartman, *A Strategic Vision for Africa: The Kampala Movement*. Washington, DC: Brookings Institution, 2002.

Desai, Ashwin, *We Are the Poors*. New York : Monthly Review Press, 2002.

de Sousa Santos, Boaventura, 'Towards a Multicultural Conception of Human Rights,' *Zeitschrift Für Rechtssoziologie* 1,1 (1997).

De Vos, Pierre, 'Grootboom, The Right of Access to Housing and Substantive Equality as Contextual Fairness,' *South African Journal of Human Rights* 18 (2001).

de Waal, Alex, 'What's New in the "New Partnership for Africa's Development"?', *International Affairs* 78, 3 (2003).

Dewey, John, *Theory of Valuation*. Chicago: University of Chicago Press, 1939.

Dia, Mamadou, *Africa's Management in the 1990s and Beyond: Reconciling Indigenous and Transplanted Institutions*. Washington, DC: World Bank, Directions in Development

Series, 1996.

Diamond, Larry, 'Africa: The Second Wind of Change,' *Times Literary Supplement* 2 July (1993).

Diamond, Larry, 'Class Formation in the Swollen African State,' *Journal of Modern African Studies* 25 (1987).

Diamond, Larry, 'Democracy: Africa's Second Liberation,' *Africa Report* 37, 6, November/December (1992).

Dicey, A.V., *Introduction to the Study of Law and the Constitution.* 10th edn London: Macmillan, 1959.

Dickerson, F. Reed, *The Fundamentals of Legal Drafting.* Incorporating *Legislative Drafting*, 2d. edn Boston, MA: Little, Brown, 1986.

Diver, Colin S., 'The Optimal Precision of Administrative Rules,' *Yale Law Journal* 93, 65 (1983).

Dollar, D., R. Fisman, and R. Gatti, *Are Women Really the 'Fairer' Sex? Corruption and Women in Government.* Policy Research Report on Gender and Development. Working Paper Series No. 4. Washington, DC: World Bank, 1999.

Dore, I., 'Constitutionalism and the Post-Colonial State in Africa: A Rawlsian Approach,' *St Louis University Law Journal* 41, 1302 (1997).

Dresang, D. 'The Zambian Civil Service: A Study in Development Administration.' Ph.D. dissertation, University of California, Los Angeles, 1971.

Driedger, Elmer A., *The Composition of Statutes*, 2nd edn, Toronto: Butterworth, 1983.

Driedger, Elmer A., *The Composition of Legislation*, 2nd edn, Ottawa: Dept. of Justice, 1976.

Driedger, Elmer A., 'The Preparation of Legislation,' *Can. Bar Review* 31, 33 (1953).

Dugard, J., 'Public International Law,' in *Constitutional Law of South Africa*, ed. M. Chaskalson et al. Kenwyn : Juta, 1996.

Dutch Directives for Regulations, *Official Journal* 1993, 230 (Stert. 1993, 230).

Dworkin, Ronald, *Law's Empire*. Cambridge, MA: Belknap Press, 1986.

ECA, *African Governance Report*. Addis Ababa: Economic Commission for Africa, 2004.

ECA, *African Governance Report*. Addis Ababa: Economic Commission for Africa, 2005a.

ECA, *Compact for African Development*. Addis Ababa: Economic Commission for Africa, 2001, 31 March.

ECA, *ECA and Africa. Accelerating a Continent's Development*. Addis Ababa: Economic Commission for Africa, 1999.

ECA, *Strategies for Promoting Effective Stakeholder Participation in the African Peer Review Mechanism*, Addis Ababa: Economic Commission for Africa, 2005b, 14 April.

ECA, *What NEPAD Implies for African Policy Makers*, UN doc. E/ECA/Cm.1/2, Addis Ababa: Economic Commission for Africa, 2002, 30 September.

Economist, 15 November 2002.

Eriksson, Lars D., 'Making Society through Legislation' in Wintgens, 2002.

Erturk, K and S. Esmin, 'Impact of Government Budgets on Poverty and Gender Equality.' Paper presented at Inter-Agency Workshop on Improving the Effectiveness of Integrating Gender in Government Budgets. London: Marlborough House, 2000.

Esmin, S., 'Gender-sensitive Budget Initiatives for Latin America and the Caribbean: A Tool for Improving Accountability and Achieving Effective Policy Implementation.' Prepared for the 8th Regional Conference on Women of Latin America and the Caribbean – Beijing plus five. Lima, 8–10 February 2000.

European Charter of Local Self-Government. Council of Europe Treaties. ETS No. 122 (1985).

The European Institute for the Media, Media and democracy, <http://www. eim.org/MaDP.htm>http://www.org/MaDP.htm.

The European Convention for the Protection of Human Rights and Fundamental Freedoms, 213 UNTS 221, ETS 5.

Evans, Peter B., ed., *Livable Cities? Urban Struggles for Livelihood and Sustainability*. Berkeley, CA: University of California Press, 2002.

Fenrich, J. and T. Higgins, 'Promise Unfulfilled: Law, Culture, and Women's

Inheritance Rights in Ghana,' *Fordham International Law Journal* 25, 259, December (2001).

Field, Martha, 'The Differing Federalisms of Canada and the United States,' *Law and Contemporary Problems* 55 (1992).

Fischer, Stanley, Remarks at the World Economic Forum, Davos, 27 January – 1 February 2002.

Freedom House, *Freedom in the World, 2001, 2002* [available at: http://www.freedomhouse.org/research/survey2002.htm].

Freedom Quest International, 'Khartoum's Human Rights Record Rehabilitated,' 16 April 2003.

Friedman, S. and D. Atkinson, eds., *The Small Miracle: South Africa's Negotiated Settlement*. Cape Town: Ravan Press, 1994.

Friedman, Thomas L., *Lexus and the Olive Tree*. New York: Farrar, Straus and Giroux, 2000.

'From the Lagos Plan of Action to NEPAD: The dilemmas of progress in independent Africa.' Renaissance South Africa Programme, Continental Experts Meeting, Pretoria, 17–19 June 2002.

Fuller, Lon, *Morality of Law*. New Haven, CT: Yale University Press, 1969.

G8 *Africa Action Plan*. Kananaskis, 27 June 2002.

'G8 Chair's Statement,' Evian, 3 June 2003.

Galanter, Marc, 'The Modernization of Law,' in *Modernization: The Dynamics of Growth*, ed. Myron Weiner. New York: Basic Books, 1966.

Gathii, James Thuo, 'Neoliberalism, Colonialism and International Governance: Decentering the International Law of Government Legitimacy,' *Michigan Law Review* 98, 1996 (2000).

Gelb, Stephen, *South Africa, Africa and the New Partnership for Africa's Development*. Johannesburg: Edge Institute, 2002.

Gertzel, C., C. Baylis and M. Szetfel, *The Dynamics of the One Party State in Zambia*. Manchester: Manchester University Press, 1984.

Ghai, Yash, ed., *Law in the Political Economy of Public Enterprise: African Perspectives*. Uppsala: Scandinavian Institute of African Studies, 1977.

Ghai, Yash, 'The Rule of Law, Legitimacy and Governance.' *International Journal Soc. of Law* 14, 179 (1986).

Gibbon, P, ed., *Structural Adjustment and the Working Poor in Zimbabwe*. Uppsala: Nordiska Afrikainstitutet, 1995.

Gluckman, M., *Politics and Ritual Tribal Society*. Manchester: Manchester University Press, 1965.

Gluckman, M., *The Judicial Process Amongst the Barotse of Northern Rhodesia*. Manchester: Manchester University Press, 1967.

Goldin, Ian, Halsey Rogers, and Nicholas Stern, *The Role and Effectiveness of Development Assistance: Lessons from World Bank Experience*, A research paper from the Vice Presidency of the World Bank. Washington, DC: World Bank, 2002.

Gopal, G., *Gender and Law: East Africa Speaks*. Washington, DC: World Bank, 1999.

Gouldner, Alvin, *The Coming Crisis of Western Sociology*. New York: Basic Books, 1980.

Government of Ghana, *Economic Recovery Programme*. Accra: Government Printer, 1983a.

Government of Ghana, *Budget Statement*. Accra: Government Printer/Ministry of Information, 1983b.

Government of Ghana, *Budget Statement*. Accra: Government Printer/Ministry of Information, 1998.

Government of Ghana, *National Programme for Economic Development* (revised). Accra: Government Printer, 1987.

Government of Ghana, *Budget Statement*. Accra: Government Printer/Ministry of Information, 1999.

Government of Ghana, *Yellow Book*. Accra: Government Printer/Ministry of Information, 2001a.

Government of Ghana, *Budget Statement*. Accra: Government Printer/Ministry of Information, 2001b.

Gower, James, *Modern Company Law*. London: Sweet and Maxwell, 1965.

Griffiths, John, 'Is Law Important?,' *N.Y.U. Law Review* 54, 339 (1976).

Grimwood, C. and R. Popplestone, *Practical Social Work*. London: Macmillan, 1994.

Grote, Rainer, 'Rule of Law, Rechtsstaat and Etat du Droit,' in *Constitutionalism, Universalism and Democracy – a Comparative Analysis*, ed. Christopher Stark. Baden-Baden: Nomos, 1999.

Gunetilleke, N. 'Improving the Effectiveness of Integrating Gender into Government Budgets.' paper presented at Inter-Agency Workshop on Improving the Effectiveness of Integrating Gender in Government Budgets. London: Marlborough House, 2000.

Gutmann, Amy and Dennis Thompson, 'Why Deliberative Democracy is Different,' *Social Philosophy & Policy* 17 (1994).

Gyimah-Boadi, E., 'The Rebirth of African Liberalism,' *Journal of Democracy*, 2, 2 (1998).

Habermas, Jürgen, *Between Facts and Norms: Contributions to a Discourse Theory of Law and Democracy*, trans. William Rehg. Cambridge, MA: MIT Press, 1996.

Habermas, Jürgen, *Theory of Communicative Action*. Boston, MA: Beacon Press, 1984.

Handbook on Journalism Ethics – African Case Studies [available at: www.misanet.org/publications.html].

'Harare Commonwealth Declaration,' issued by Commonwealth Heads of Government, London: Commonwealth Secretariat, 1991.

Hart, H.L.A., *The Concept of Law*. Oxford: Clarendon Press, 1961.

Hart, H.L.A., and A. Sachs, 'Legal process,' Harvard Law School, unpublished, 1972.

Hatchard, John, *Individual Freedoms and State Security in the African Context: The Case of Zimbabwe*. Harare: Baobab; London: James Currey, 1993.

Hatchard, John, 'Developing Governmental Accountability: The Role of the Ombudsman,' *Third World Legal Studies* 215 (1992).

Hayek, F.S., *The Road to Serfdom*. Chicago: University of Chicago Press, 1944.

Hearn, Julie, *Foreign Aid, Democratisation and Civil Society in Africa: A Study of South Africa, Ghana, and Uganda*, Discussion Paper 368. Brighton: Institute of Development Studies at the University of Sussex, 1999.

Heyns, Christoff and Frans Viljoen, 'An Overview of International Human Rights Protection in Africa,' *South African Journal of Human Rights* 15, 3 (1999).

Hoffman, G., 'Das vergassungrechtliche Geboty der Rationalist in Gestzgebungsverfahren. Zum "inneren Gesetzgenuigsverfahren" im bundesdeutschen Recht,' *Zeitschrift fur Gezetsgebung* (1990).

Holmes, M. et al., 'Governance and Poverty Reduction,' draft document produced for the World Bank. 2000.

Homans, George Caspar, *The Nature of Social Science*. New York: Harcourt, Brace, 1967.

Human Rights Watch, *The Oil Diagnostic: An Update*. New York: Human Rights Watch, 2001a.

Human Rights Watch, *Bush Trip to Africa*, Briefing paper. Washington, DC: Human Rights Watch, 7 February 2003.

Human Rights Watch, *Protectors or Pretenders, Government Human Rights Commissions in Africa*, Washington, DC: Human Rights Watch, 2001b.

Hume, Ellen, 'The Media Missionaries: American Support for International Journalism.' (May 2002) [available at: www.ellenhume.com/articles/missionaries1_content.html].

Huntington, Samuel, *The Third Wave: Democratization in the Late Twentieth Century*, Oklahoma City: Oklahoma University Press, 1991.

Ilbert, Courtenay, *The Mechanics of Law Making*. New York: Columbia University Press, 1914.

Information for Development ('infoDev'). World Bank. [available at: www.infodev.org].

Instituciones, cambio institutional y disempeno economics. Mexico: Fundode Cultural Economie, 1985.

Institute for International Communication and Development. [available at: www.iicd.org].

International Monetary Fund, *International Financial Statistics, Yearbook*, various years.

International Monetary Fund, 'Good Governance and Development.' *I.M.S. Polc.* 1997.

Inter Parliamentary Union (IPU), *An Assessment of Developments in National Parliaments, Political Parties, Governments and the Inter Parliamentary Union Five Years after the Fourth World Conference on Women.* Geneva: IPU, 1999.

Inter-Parliamentary Union (IPU) Women in National Parliaments, 2002. <http://www.ipu.org/wwn-e/classif.htm>http://www.ipu.org/wwn-e/classif.htm

Jackson, Robert and Carl G. Rosberg, *Personal Rule in Black Africa.* Berkeley, CA: University of California Press, 1982.

Johnson, A.W., 'Fiscal Arrangements in a Multi-tier State: The Canadian Case and How it Relates to South Africa's Interim Constitution.' Paper presented at International Roundtable on Democratic Constitutional Development, Pretoria, 17–20 July, 1995.

Johnson, Barnabas D., 'Ten Principles Governing Law and Law-Making,' in Seidman and Seidman, 1994.

Joseph, Richard, 'Africa, 1990–1997: From Aberatura to Closure,' *Journal of Democracy* 9, 2 (1998).

Kalathil, Shanthi and Taylor C. Boas, *Open Networks, Closed Regimes; The Impact of the Internet on Authoritarian Rule.* Washington, DC: Carnegie Endowment for International Peace, 2003.

Karam, A., ed., *Women in Parliament: Beyond Numbers.* International IDEA Publication, Handbook Series 2. Stockholm: International Institute for Democracy and Electoral Assistance.

Karl, M., *Women and Empowerment: Participation and Decision Making.* London: Zed Books, 1995.

Kaufmann, Daniel and Aart Kraay, *Growth without Governance.* World Bank Research Working Paper. Washington, DC: World Bank, 2002, July.

Kayonde Eso, 'The Role of the Judge in Advancing Human Rights,' in Commonwealth Secretariat, *Developing Human Rights Jurisprudence.* Vol. 3. London: Commonwealth Secretariat, 1991.

Kedzie, Christopher R., 'Communication and Democracy: Coincident Revolutions and the Emergent Dictator's Dilemma.' Rand Corporation study. 1997 [available at: www.rand.org/publications/RGSD/RGSD127/].

Kelsen, Hans, *General Theory of Law and State*, trans. A. Wedburg. New York: Russell, 1961.

Kesselman, M., 'The State and Class Struggle Trends in Marxist Political Science,' in *The Left Academy*, eds. Bertell Ollman and E. Vernoff. New York: McGraw Hill, 1982. Reprinted in Cantori and Ziegler, 1988.

Kidder, Robert L., *Connecting Law and Society: An Introduction to Research and Theory.* Englewood Cliffs, NJ: Prentice-Hall, 1983.

Klare, K., 'Legal Culture and Transformative Constitutionalism,' *South African Journal of Human Rights* 14 (1998).

Klug, Heinz, *Constituting Democracy: Law, Globalization, and South Africa's Political Reconstruction.* Cambridge: Cambridge University Press, 2000.

Kritz, Neil, 'The Rule of Law in the Postconflict Phase: Building a Stable Peace,' in *Managing Global Chaos; Sources of and Responses to International Conflict*, eds. Chester A. Crocker et al. Washington, DC: United States Institute of Peace Press, 1996.

Kronman, Anthony, 'Precedent and Tradition,' *Yale Law Journal* 99, 1029 (1990).

Levy, Brian, 'Participatory Governance: Africa's Development Frontier.' paper presented at conference on Social and Economic Aspects of Liberalization and Globalization, University of Toronto, 14–20 April 2002.

Levy, Brian, *Patterns of Governance in Africa.* African Region Working Paper Series 36. Washington, DC: World Bank, 2002.

Lewis, Peter, 'Economic Reform and Political Transition in Africa: The quest for a politics of development,' *World Politics*, 49, 1, (1996): 92–196.

Leys, Colin, ed., *Politics and Change in Developing Countries: Studies in the Theory and Practice of Development.* London: Cambridge University Press, 1969.

Leys, Colin, *Underdevelopment in Kenya: The Political Economy of Neo-Colonialism.*

London: Heinemann, 1975.

Liebenberg, Sandra, 'Violations of Socio-Economic Rights: The Role of the South African Human Rights Commission,' in *The Post-Apartheid Constitutions: Perspectives on South Africa's Basic Law*, eds. Penny Andrews and Stephen Ellmann. Athens OH: Ohio University Press, 2001.

Lindblom, Charles E., *The Policy-Making Process*. Englewood Cliffs, NJ: Prentice-Hall, 1963.

Lindblom, Charles E., 'The Science of "Muddling Through",' *Public Administration Reviews* 19 (1959).

Linington, Greg. *Constitutional Law of Zimbabwe*. Harare: LRF, 2001.

Linz, Juan J. and Alfred Stepan, *Problems of Democratic Transition and Consolidation: Southern Europe, South America, and Post-Communist Europe*. Baltimore, MD: Johns Hopkins University Press, 1996.

Lippert, Lawrence and Marie Lippert, *The Matabeleland Travels of Marie Lippert, 21 September – 23 December 1891*, trans. Eric Rosenthal, ed. D.H. Varley. Cape Town: Friends of the South African Library, 1960.

Lipton, Michael, 'Key Variables in Village Studies,' in *Village Studies in the Third World*, ed. B. Dasgupta. New Brunswick, NJ: Transaction Books, 1978.

Llewellyn, Karl, 'Some Realism About Realism – Responding to Dean Pound,' *Harvard Law Review* 44, 1222 (1931).

Llewellyn, Karl. 'The Normative, the Legal, and Law Jobs: The Problems of the Juristic Method,' *Yale Law Journal* 49, 1355 (1940).

Longwe, Sarah and Roy Clarke, 'Towards Improved Leadership for Women's Empowerment in Africa. Measuring Progress and Improving Strategy,' 1999. Unpublished document.

Lowe-Morna, C., 'Strategies for Increasing Women's Participation in Politics.' Paper prepared for the Commonwealth Ministers responsible for women's affairs fifth meeting in Trinidad, 1996.

Lowe-Morna, C., 'Gender Budgeting: From Rhetoric to Reality.' Paper prepared for the UNIFEM Women's Budget Workshop, South Africa. 1998.

Lowe-Morna, C., 'Conflict Resolution, Reconstruction, and Transformation from War Torn Societies.' Paper presented at United Nations Workshop on Beijing plus five Future Actions and Initiatives. 1999.

Loxley, J., 'Political and Policy Considerations in Alternative Budgets: The Alternative Federal Budget of Canada.' Paper presented at Inter-Agency Workshop on Improving the Effectiveness of Integrating Gender in Government Budgets. London: Marlborough House, 2000.

Lugard, F.D., *The Dual Mandate in British Tropical Africa*. Edinburgh: Blackwood, 1992.

Machangana, Keboitse, 'A Case Study of Programmes to Empower Women in Politics in a SADC Country,' in SADC, 1999.

Mainga, M., *Bulozi Under the Luyana Kings*. London: Longman, 1973.

Makgetla, Neva and Robert B. Seidman, 'Legal Drafting and the Defeat of Development Policy: The Experience of Anglophonic Southern Africa,' *Journal of Law and Society* 5, 421 (1987).

Mandaza, Ibe, 'Constitution-making in Southern Africa: The Zimbabwean Experience,' *SAPES*, 14, 4 (2001).

March, James and John P. Olsen, *Rediscovering Institutions: The Organizational Basis of Politics*. New York: Free Press, 1989.

Mathew, George and Panchayatri Raj, *Institutions and Human Rights in India*, International Council on Human Rights Policy Decentralization, Local Government and Human Rights, Project 116–Stage One: Survey of the Issues, Spring, 2002.

Mbeki, Thabo, 'Africa's New Realism,' *New York Times*, 24 June 2002a.

Mbeki, Thabo, 'Critics ill-informed about peer review,' *ANC Today* (Johannesburg), 2(45), 8–14 November 2002b.

McGee, Rosemary and Andy Norton, *Participation in Poverty Reduction Strategies: A synthesis of experience with participatory approaches to design, implementation and monitoring.*

IDS Working Paper 109. Brighton: Institute of Development Studies at the University of Sussex, 2000.

Media Intervention in Peace Building in Burundi, March 2002. [available at: http://www.usaid.gov/regions/afr/conflictweb/pbp_report/case6.pdf].

'Media Law Reform in New Democracies,' *USAID Democracy Dialogue* July (1998). [available at: http://www.usaid.gov/democracy/techpubs/dialogue/ddmedia_final.pdf].

Media Monitoring Project, 'Biased? Gender, Politics and the Media,' in Commission on Gender Equality, 1999.

Meinjes, S., S. Hassim, and C. Albertyn, 'Women's Participation in Election Processes: SA in Global Perspectives.' Paper presented at the Electoral Institute of South Africa (EISA) roundtable discussion. Braamfontein: 23 February 1999.

Meredith, M., *The Past Is Another Country: Rhodesia, 1890–1979*. London: André Deutsch, 1979.

Mhina, E.H., 'Experiences in GBI Research and Advocacy with Government Agencies in Tanzania.' Paper presented at Inter-Agency Workshop on Improving the Effectiveness of Integrating Gender in Government Budgets. Marlborough House, London, 2000.

Migdal, Joel S., *Strong Societies and Weak States: State-society relations and state capabilities in the Third World*. Princeton, NJ: Princeton University Press, 1988.

Mills, Greg, 'Focus on realistic goals for Africa,' *Business Day*, 10 June 2003.

Minear, Larry et al., *The News Media, Civil War and Humanitarian Action*. Boulder, CO: Lynne Rienner, 1995.

Mkandawire, Thandika, 'Incentives, Governance and Capacity Development in Africa,' in *Capacity for Development*, eds., Sakiko Fukuda-Parr, Carlos Lopes, and Khalid Malik. London: Earthscan Publications, 2002.

Mkandawire, T. and C. Soludo, *Our Continent Our Future: African Perspective on Structural Adjustment*. Dakar, CODESRIA and Trenton, NJ: Africa World Press, 1999.

Moore Jr., Barrington, *Social Origins of Dictatorship and Democracy*. Boston, MA: Beacon Press, 1966.

Moore, Mick, 'Political Underdevelopment.' Paper presented at Conference on 'New Institutional Theory, Institutional Reform and Poverty Reduction', London School of Economics, September 2000.

More Instruments and Broader Goals: Moving Towards the Post-Washington Consensus. United Nations University/WIDER, Helsinki, 1998.

Morris-Hughes, E., S. Esim, and H. Coulombe, 'Gender Equity Concerns in Public Expenditure: Methodologies and Country Summaries.' Paper prepared for the World Bank. 1995.

Morrison, Herbert, in the House of Commons, *Hansard*, Vol. 423, col. 850 (1954).

Motara, Shireen, 'Women's Participation in Voter Registration,' in Commission on Gender Equality, *Review of the 1999 Elections – A Gender Perspective*. Cape Town: CGE, 1999.

Movement for the Survival of the Ogoni People (MOSOP). *Press Release*. Port Harcourt, 20 June 2002.

Moyo, Jonathan, *Voting for Democracy*. Harare: University of Zimbabwe, 1992.

Mtintso, Thenjiwe, 'Women in Decision Making: A Conceptual Framework,' in Commission on Gender Equality, *Redefining Politics: South African Women and Democracy*. Pretoria: CGE, 1999.

Mubako, S.V., 'Single Party Constitution – A Search for Unity and Development,' 5, *Zambia Law Journal* 67, 5 (1973).

Mudenge, S.I.G., *A Political History of Munhumutapa, c. 1400–1902*. Harare: Zimbabwe Pub. House, 1988.

Murdock, Graham, 'Base Notes: The Conditions of Cultural Practice,' *Cultural Studies in Question*. eds Marjorie Ferguson and Peter Golding. London: Sage, 1997.

Murphy, J., *Mainstreaming Gender in World Bank Lending: An Update*. Washington, DC: World Bank, 1997.

Museveni, Y., *What is Africa's Problem?* Kampala: NRM Publications, 1992.

Mutua, Makau Wa, *Human Rights: A Political and Cultural Critique*. Philadelphia: University of Pennsylvania Press, 2002.

Mwanakatwe, J.M., *The End of the Kaunde Era*. Lusaka: Multimedia Publishers, 1994)

Nana Wereko Ampem II, 'The Role of Chiefs and Chieftaincy in the Development of a Democratic Constitution of Ghana.' Paper presented to International Roundtable on Democratic Constitutional Development, Pretoria, July 17–20 1995.

Narayan-Parker, Deepa, ed., *Empowerment and Poverty Reduction, A Sourcebook.* Washington DC: World Bank, 2002.

Ndulo, M., 'The Democratic State in Africa: The Challenges for Institution Building,' *National Black Law Journal* 16, 70 (1998).

Ndulo, M., 'Customary Law and the Zambian Legal System,' in *The Individual Under African Law*, ed. P. Takirambudde. Kwaluseni: University of Swaziland, 1982.

Ndulo, M., 'Liability of a Paramour in Damages for Adultery in Customary Law,' *African Social Research* 28, 179 (1981).

NEPAD, 'Communiqué Issued at the End of Fifth Summit of Heads of State and Government Implementation Committee.' Abuja, 3 November 2002a.

NEPAD, *Declaration on Democracy, Political, Economic, and Corporate Governance.* AHG/235 (XXXVIII), Annex I, 18 June 2002b.

NEPAD, *Guidelines for Countries to Prepare for and Participate in the Africa Peer Review Mechanism*, NEPAD/APRM/Panels/Guidelines/11–2003/Doc.8.

NEPAD, *Memorandum of Understanding on the African Peer Review Mechanism*, NEPAD/HSGIC/03–2003/APRM/MOU, 9 March 2003a.

NEPAD, *Memorandum of Understanding on Technical Assessment and the Country Review Visit*, NEPAD/HSGIC-03–2003/APRM/Guidelines/Outline, 9 March 2003b.

NEPAD, 'Report to the Heads of State Implementation Committee, July-October 2002.' 3 November 2002.

NEPAD Newsletter, Nairobi, 25 January 2005.

New from Africa, (Nairobi) 24 February 2005.

New Partnership for Africa's Development, October 2001.

Nhlapo, N., 'Accommodating Traditional Forms of Governance in a Constitutional Democracy: A Motivation.' Paper presented at the International Roundtable on Democratic Constitutional Development for South Africa, Pretoria, 17–20 July 1995.

Nhlapo, N., 'The African Family and Women's Rights: Friends or Foes?' *Acta Juridica* 135 (1991).

Nino, Carlos S., *The Constitution of Deliberative Democracy*. New Haven, CT: Yale University Press, 1996.

Nkomo, J., *The Story of My Life*. London: Methuen, 1984.

Norris, Pippa, 'Giving Voice to the Voiceless: Good Governance, Human Development, and Mass Communications.' [available at: http://ksghome.harvard.edu/~.pnorris. shorenstein.ksg/ACROBAT/Voice.pdf.]

Norris, Robert and Patrick Merloe, *Media Monitoring to Promote Democratic Elections, An NDI Handbook for Citizen Organizations*. Washington, DC: National Democratic Institute, 2002. [available at: http://www.accessdemocracy.org/NDI/usr_search.asp? SearchType=adv&DocURL=doc&DocType=0&RC=0&TS=54&Author=0&Publisher =0&Date=0&keywords=&submit1=Search%21].

North, Douglass C., 'Institutional Change: A Framework for Analysis,' in Sjostrand, 1993.

North, Douglass C., *Structure and Change in Economic History*. New York: W.W. Norton, 1981.

North, Douglass, C., L. Alston, and T. Eggertsson, *Empirical Studies in Institutional Change*. Cambridge: Cambridge University Press, 1996.

Nowrojee, Pheroze, 'Public Enterprise in Kenya,' in Ghai, 1977.

Nwabueze, B.O., *Ideas and Facts in Constitution Making, The Morohundiya Lectures, Faculty of Law University of Ibadan*. Ibadan: Spectrum Books, 1993a.

Nwabueze, B.O., 'The Constitution as Law,' in *Ideas and Fact in Constitution Making, The Morohindiya Lectures, Faculty of Law University of Ibadan*. Ibadan: Spectrum

Books, 1993b.

Nwabueze, B.O., 'Dangers of Absolute and Total Power', in *Ideas and Fact in Constitution Making, The Morohindiya Lectures, Faculty of Law University of Ibadan*. Ibadan: Spectrum Books, 1993c.

Nwabueze, B.O., 'Our March to Constitutional Democracy,' *Law and Practice*. August (1989).

Nzongola-Ntalaja, *Revolution and Counter-Revolution in Africa – Essays in Contemporary Politics*. London: Zed Books, 1987.

Nzuwah, Maryawanda, 'Local Government Structures, Management and Elections in Zimbabwe.' Paper delivered at International Roundtable on Democratic Constitutional Development, Pretoria, 17–20 July 1995.

OAU, *African Charter on Human and Peoples' Rights*. CAB/LEG/67/3/Rev. 5. Addis Ababa: OAU, June 1981.

OAU, *African Charter on the Rights and Welfare of the Child.*

OAU, Central Organ, 25 July 1996a (UN doc. S/1996/594, 25 July 1996, Appendix).

OAU, Central Organ, 5 August 1996b (UN doc S/1996/628, 5 August 1996, Appendix).

OAU, 'Communiqué of the Seventh Ordinary Session of the Central Organ at Heads of State and Government Level.' Addis Ababa, 3 February 2003.

OAU, 'Declaration on the Framework for an OAU Response to Unconstitutional Changes of Government,' AHG/Decl.5 (XXXVI), 11 July 2000a.

OAU, 'Decision on Unconstitutional Changes of Government in Africa.' CM/2166 (LXXVII), AHG/Dec.150 (XXXVI), 12 July 2000b.

OAU, 'Declaration on the Political and Socio-Economic Situation in Africa and the Fundamental Changes Taking Place in the World,' AHG/Decl.1 (XXVI), 11 July 1990.

OAU, 'Declaration on the Principles Governing Democratic Elections in Africa,' AHG/Decl. 1 (XXXVIII), Durban, 8 July 2002.

OAU docs. CM/Dec.483 (LXX), 10 July 1999 and AHG/Dec.142 (XXXV), 12 July 1999.

OAU, 'Elections in Zanzibar.' Dar-es-Salaam, 31 October 2000c.

OAU, *Introductory Note to the Report of the Secretary-General*. Addis Ababa, 15 May 1997.

OAU, 'The OAU Meeting in Kampala: An Official Statement,' Dar-es-Salaam, 25 July 1975.

OAU, *Memorandum of Understanding on Security, Stability, Development and Cooperation*, 8 July 2002.

OAU Summit, 'Decision on the Conference on Security, Stability, Development and Cooperation, Durban, 8 July 2002, AHG/175 (XXXVIII).

OAU Summit, 'CSSDCA Solemn Declaration.' Lomé, 12 July 2000, AHG/Decl.4 (XXXVI).

OAU, 'Yaoundé Declaration: Africa Preparing for the 21st Century.' AHG/Decl.3 (XXXII), 10 July 1996.

Obasanjo, O., 'G8 Summit: African Leaders' Response.' Kananaskis, 27 June 2002.

Obasanjo, O., 'Africa in Today's World,' paper presented at Africa Leadership Forum, Ota, Nigeria, 24 October – 4 November 1988.

O'Brien, Donal., 'Saints and Politicians,' in *Sub-Saharan Africa*, ed. Christopher Allen and Gavin Williams. New York: Monthly Review Press, 1975.

Ocran, M., 'The Rule of Law as the Quest for Legitimacy,' in *Law in Zambia*, ed. M. Ndulo. Nairobi: East Africa Publishing House, 1984.

Oder Commission (Uganda Commission of Inquiry into the Violation of Human Rights), *The Pearl of Blood*, Kampala: Government of Uganda, 1994.

Oloka-Onyango, J., 'Beyond the Rhetoric: Reinvigorating the Struggle for Economic and Social Rights in Africa,' *California Western International Law Journal* 1, 68 Fall, (1995).

Oloka-Onyango, J., 'Human Rights and Sustainable Development in Contemporary Africa: A New Dawn, Or Retreating Horizons,' *Buffalo Human Rights Law Review* 6, 39 (2000).

Osei-Hwedie, B.Z., 'Awakening of Civil Society: In Defense of Transparency and

Accountability, The Case of Zambia,' *Africa Notes* (Institute of African Development, Cornell University) 5, Jan/Feb (2003).

O'Siochru, Sean, 'Rethinking Media and Democracy: What about "Democratic Media",' *The Bulletin of the European Institute for the Media* (1997) March.

Ott, Dana, 'Electronic Media in Promoting the Formation of Democratic Political Regimes in Africa.' 1998. [available at: www.firstmonday.dk/issues/issue3_4/ott/index.html]

Otto, Jan Michiel, 'Toward an Analytical Framework: Real Legal Certainty and Its Explanatory Factors,' in *Implementation of Law in the People's Republic of China*, eds. Jian fu Chen, Jan Michiel Otto, and Yuwen Li. The Hague: Kluwer Law International, 2002.

Oukasie Development Trust, *The Year of Transformation and Delivery*, Annual Report January–December 1997.

Oukasie Development Trust, 'Voices from Oukasie: From Resistance to Development,' *The Legal Resources Centre Review* 1 (1995).

Oxner, Sandra E., 'The Quality of Judges,' in *The World Bank Legal Review: Law and Justice for Development*, ed. Rudolf V. van Puymbroeck. Washington, DC: International Bank for Reconstruction and Development, 2003.

Oye Lithur, N., 'Constitutional and Other Statutory Provisions on Women's Rights in Ghana,' paper presented to Commission on Human Rights and Administrative Justice (March 2000).

Palley, Claire, *The Constitutional History and Law of Southern Rhodesia, 1888–1965.* Oxford: Oxford University Press, 1966.

Palmer, R., 'Lawyers and Land Reform in South Africa: A Review of the Land, Housing & Development Work of the Legal Resources Centre (LRC).' September 2001. [available at: www.lrc.org.za]

Palmer, V. and S. Poulter, *The Legal System of Lesotho.* Charlottesville, VA: Michie Law Publisher, 1972.

Pareto, Vilfredo, *The Mind and Society: a Treatise on General Society.* New York: Harcourt, Brace, 1935.

Paul, J.C.N., 'Developing Constitutional Orders in Sub-Saharan Africa: Unofficial Report.' *Third World Legal Studies* (1988).

Phimister, Ian, *An Economic and Social History of Zimbabwe 1890–1948: Capital Accumulation and Class Struggle*, London: Longman, 1988.

Pipkin, Hannah F., *The Concept of Representation.'* Berkeley, CA: University of California Press, 1967.

Poplova, Maria, *Legal Thought and Russian Objections to the Rule of Law Doctrine.'* (special report), 2003.

Porter, Michael, *The Competitiveness of Nations.* New York: Free Press, 1998.

Pound, Roscoe, *Law as Engineering.* New Haven, CT: Yale University Press, 1942.

Pound, Roscoe, 'Law in Books and Law in Action,' *American Law Review* 44, 12 (1910).

Pound, Roscoe, *Social Control Through Law.* New Haven, CT: Yale University Press, 1942.

Poverty and Inequality in South Africa, Report Prepared for the Office of the Executive Deputy President and the Inter-Ministerial Committee for Poverty and Inequality, 13 May 1998.

'Progress Report of the H.E. Chief Olusegun Obasanjo. Chairperson of the NEPAD Heads of State and Government Implementation Committee,' Assembly/AU/Rpt (II), Maputo, 12 July 2003.

Przeworski, Adam et al., 'What Makes Democracy Endure,' *Journal of Democracy* 7, 1 (1996).

Ranger, Terence, Jocelyn Alexander and JoAnn MacGregor, *Violence and Memory: One Hundred Years in the Dark Forests of Matebeleland.* Oxford: James Currey, 2000.

Ratner, Steven, 'Does International Law Matter in Preventing Ethnic Conflict?' *New York University Journal of International Law and Politics* 32, 3 (2000).

Reid, J.P., *A Law of Blood: The Primitive Law of the Cherokee People.* New York: New York

University Press, 1970.

Renwick, R., *Unconventional Diplomacy in Southern Africa*. New York: St Martin's Press, 1997.

Report of the Constitutional Review Commission. Lusaka: Government Printer, 1995.

Report of the Kenya Constitutional Review Commission. Nairobi: Government Printer, 2001.

Republic of Zambia, *Report of the National Commission on the Establishment of a One-Party Democracy in Zambia*, (Chona Commission), Lusaka: Government Printer, 1972.

Robson, William Alexander, *Nationalized Industry and Public Ownership*, 2nd edn, London: G. Allen & Unwin, 1962.

Rodden, J. and S. Rose-Ackerman, 'Federalism Preserves Markets,' *Virginia Law Review* 83, 1573 (1997).

Rose, Arnold, 'Sociological Factors in the Effectiveness of Projected Legal Remedies,' *Journal of Legal Education* (1959).

Roth, G. and C. Wittich, eds., *Economy and Society*. Berkeley, CA: University of California Press, 1978.

Rubin, Edward L., 'Law and Legislation in the Administrative State,' *Col. Law Review* 89, 369 (1989).

Rubin, Edward L., 'Legislative Methodology: Some Lessons from the Truth-in-Lending Act,' *Geo. L. Rev.* 80, 223 (1991).

Rugumamu, Severine M., 'State Sovereignty and Intervention,' *Conflict Trends* (Durban), 4 (2001).

Russell, Sir Alison, *Legislative Drafting and Forms*, 4th edn. London: Butterworth and Co, 1938.

Rye, Dick, 'Inter-Governmental Relation Structures Responsible for Financial and Fiscal Management.' Paper presented at Internatioanl Roundtable on Democratic Constitutional Development, Pretoria, 17–20 July 1995.

SA Government Communications, 'Media Statement: NEPAD Peer Review Mechanism,' 1 November 2002.

Sachs, Justice Albie, 'Impromptu Remarks on Differences between Constitutional Adjudication in the USA and South Africa.' Lecture given at Harvard Law School, Cambridge, MA, 26 April, 2000a.

Sachs, Justice Albie, 'Social and Economic Rights: Can They be Made Justiciable?' *SMU Law Review* 53 (2000b).

SADC, *Women in Politics and Decision Making in SADC: Beyond 30% in 2005.* Report of the Proceedings of a Conference held in Botswana, March/April 1999. Gaborone: SADC, 1999.

SADC Parliamentary Forum, *Norms and Standards for Elections in SADC Region*, Windhoek: SADC, 2001, March.

SADC Parliamentary Forum, *The SADC MPs Comparison on Gender and Development in Southern Africa*. Windhoek: SADC Parliamentary Forum, 2002.

SADC Gender Unit and SARDC, *SADC Gender Monitor Issue 2*, 'Monitoring implementation of the Beijing Commitments by SADC Member States', Harare: SARDC, and Gaborone SADC, 2001.

Salim, Salim Ahmed, *The Challenge Facing Africa in the Coming Decades*, Addis Ababa, December 2001.

Sampson, Anthony, *Mandela: The Authorized Biography*. New York: Alfred Knopf, 1999.

Samuelson, Paul, *Economics: An Introductory Analysis*, 13th edn, New York: McGraw Hill, 1989.

Santos, Soliman, *Local Government and Human Rights: A Philippines Perspective on the Feasibility of Their Interface in Policy and Practice*, International Council on Human Rights Policy Decentralization, Local Government and Human Rights, Project 116–Stage One: Survey of Issues, March 2001.

Sassen, Saskia, *Global Networks: Linked Cities*. New York: Routledge, 2002.

Sawer, Geoffrey, *Law in Society*. Oxford: Clarendon Press, 1963.

Schaffer, B.B., 'The Deadlock in Development Administration,' in Leys. 1969.

Schiller, Herbert I., *Mass Communications and the American Empire*, 2nd edn, Boulder,

CO: Westview Press, 1992.

Schneider, Hartmut, *Participatory Governance: The Missing Link for Poverty Reduction*, OECD Development Centre Policy Brief No. 17. Paris: OECD, 1999.

Schultz, Alfred, 'The Social World and the Theory of Social Action,' in *The Philosophical Problems of the Social Sciences*, ed. David Braybrooke. Englewood Cliffs, NJ: Prentice-Hall, 1965.

Sedler, Robert, 'Constitutional Protection of Individual Rights in Canada: The Impact of the New Canadian Charter of Rights and Freedom,' *Notre Dame L.R.* 1191 (1984).

Seibert, Gerhard, *Coup d'état in São Tomé e Príncipe: Domestic Causes, the Role of Oil and Former Buffalo Battalion Soldiers*. Pretorian Institute for Security Studies, Occasional Paper, 10 October 2003.

Seidman, Ann, *Apartheid, Militarism and the US Southeast*. Trenton, NJ: Africa World Press, 1990.

Seidman, Ann, ed., *Natural Resources and National Welfare: The Case of Copper*. Papers presented to conference held in July, 1974. New York: Praeger Publishers, Inc., 1975.

Seidman, Ann and Robert B. Seidman, *State and Law in the Development Process: Problem-Solving and Institutional Change in the Third World*. Basingstoke: Macmillan and New York: St Martin's Press, 1994.

Seidman, Ann, Robert B. Seidman, and Nalin Abeysekere, *Legislative Drafting for Democratic Social Change*. London: Kluwer Law International, 2001.

Seidman, Ann, Robert B. Seidman, Nalin Abeysekere, and Judy Seidman. 'Assessing Legislation: A Manual for Legislators.' [available at: http://www.bu.edu/law/lawdrafting].

Seidman, Ann, Robert B. Seidman, and Theodosio Uate, 'Assessing Legislation to Serve the Public Interest: Experiences from Mozambique,' *Statute Law Review* 20 (1999).

Seidman, Ann, Robert B. Seidman, and Janice Payne, eds., *Legislative Drafting for Market Reform: Some Lessons from China*. New York: St Martin's Press, 1997.

Seidman, Ann, Robert B. Seidman, and Thomas Waelde, eds., *Making Development Work: Legislative Reform for Institutional Transformation and Good Governance*. London: Kluwer Law International, 1998.

Seidman, Robert B., 'Justifying Legislation: A Pragmatic, Institutionalist Approach to the Memorandum of Law, Legislative Theory and Practical Reason,' *Harvard Journal of Legislation* 29, 1 (1992).

Seidman, Robert B., 'Law, Development and Legislative Drafting in English-Speaking Independent Africa,' *Journal of Modern African Studies* 19, 133 (1981).

Seidman, Robert B., 'Perspectives on Constitution-Making: Independence Constitutions for Namibia and South Africa,' *Lesotho Law Journal* 3, 35 (1987).

Seidman, Robert B., 'The Reception of English Law in Africa Revisited,' *Eastern African Law Review* (1969).

Seidman, Robert B., *The State, Law and Development*. London: Croom Helm, 1978.

Seidman, Robert B. and A. Seidman, ' The Political Economy of Customary Law in the Former British Territories of African,' *Journal of African Law* 44 (1984).

'Seminar on Media Ownership in Central and West Africa.' [available at: http://www.wacc.org.uk/publications].

'Seminar on the Political Economy of Media Ownership in Southern Africa.' [available at: http://www.wacc.org.uk/publications].

Sen, Amartya Kumar, *Development as Freedom*. New York: Knopf, 1999a.

Sen, A., 'Democracy as a Universal Value,' *Journal of Democracy* 10, 3 (1999b).

Sen, A., 'Role of Legal and Judicial Reform in Development.' Paper presented at World Bank Legal Conference. Washington, DC. 5 June 2000.

Senapaty, M., 'Government of India Budget 2000–2001 and Gender,' paper presented at Inter-Agency Workshop on Improving Effectiveness of Integrating Gender in Government Budgets. London: Marlborough House, 2000.

Serote, Phetu, January-Bardill Nozipho, Sandra Liebenberg and Jacqui Nolte, *A Report on What the South African Parliament Has Done to Improve the Quality of Life and Status of Women in South Africa*, 1996.

Seth, Leila, 'Social Action Litigation in India,' in *The Constitution of South Africa From a Gender Perspective*, ed. Sandra Liebenberg. Community Law Centre, University of Western Cape and Cape Town: D. Phillip, 1995.

SGTS & Associates, *Civil Society Participation in Poverty Reduction Strategy Papers*, Report to the Department for International Development Vol. 1: *Overview and Recommendations*. London: SGTS & Associates, 2000.

Shaw, T.M., *Alternative Futures for Africa*. Boulder, CO: Westview Press, 1982.

Shihata, Ibrahim F.I., 'The World Bank and "Governance" Issues in its Borrowing Members,' in *The World Bank in a Changing World* eds. Franziska Tschofen and Antonio R. Parra. Boston, MA: M. Nijhoff publishers, 1991.

Short, E., 'The Commission on Human Rights and Administrative Justice.' Paper presented to a workshop organised by the Uganda Human Rights Commission and Commonwealth Secretariat, 1997.

Simeon, Richard, 'The Structures of Inter Governmental Relations.' Paper presented at International Roundtable on Democratic Constitutional Development, Pretoria, 17–20 July 1995.

Singer, Joseph, 'The Player and the Cards: Nihilism in Legal Theory,' *Yale Law Review* 94, 1 (1984).

Sjostrand, Sven-Erik, ed., *Institutional Change: Theory and Empirical Findings*. Armonk, NY: M.E. Sharpe, 1993.

Solum, Lawrence, 'Equity and the Rule of Law,' in *The Rule of Law: NOMOS XXXVI*, ed. Ian Shapiro. New York: New York University Press, 1994.

Sparks, Allister, *Tomorrow is Another Country: the Insider Story of South Africa*. New York: Hill and Wang, 1995.

Stapenhurst, R., *The Media's Role in Curbing Corruption*. Washington, DC: World Bank Institute, 2000. [available at: http://www.worldbank.org/wbi/governance/pubs/mediacurb.htm].

Stiglitz, Joseph, *Globalization and Its Discontents*. London: W.W. Norton & Co., 2002.

Stiglitz, Joseph, *More Instruments and Broader Goals Moving Towards the Post-Washington Consensus*. Helsinki: UNU/WIDER, 1998.

Stoddard, M., 'South Africa's Elections: Establishing Democracy at the Grassroots,' *Fletcher F. World Affairs* 21 (1997).

Swamy, A. et al., 'Gender and Corruption.' Paper produced for the World Bank. Washington, DC: World Bank, 2000.

Szentes, Thomas, 'Socialism in Theory and Practice,' in *Breaking the Links – Development Theory & Practice in Southern Africa*, ed. Robert Mazur. Trenton, NJ: Africa World Press, 1990.

Tamanaha, Brian Z., 'The Lessons of Law and Development Studies,' *American Journal of International Law* 89 (1970).

Taylor, Vivienne, *The Marketisation of Governance: Critical Feminist Perspectives from the South*. Cape Town: SADEP, University of Cape Town, 2000.

Thomas, Melissa, 'The Rule of Law in Western Thought.' [available at: http.//www1.worldbank.org/public sectore/legal/western.htm].

Thornton, G.C., *Legislative Drafting*, 3rd edn, London: Butterworth, 1987.

Thring, Henry, *Practical Legislation. The Composition and Language of Acts of Parliament and Business Documents*. Toronto: Little Brown, 1902

Thurow, Roger, 'In Impoverished Niger, Radio Provides Missing Links in Chain of Development,' *The Wall Street Journal*, 10 May 2002.

Trachtman, Joel P., 'The Applicability of Law and Economics to Law and Development: the Case of Financial Law,' in Seidman et al., 1998.

Tripathi, S.M., *The Human Face of the Supreme Court of India: Public Litigation in the Apex Court*. Varanasi: Ganga Kaveri Pub. House, 1993.

Trubek, David and Marc Galanter, 'Scholars in Self-Estrangement: Some Reflections on the Crisis in Law and Development Studies in the US,' *Wisconsin Law Review* (1974)

Tshuma, Lawrence, *A Matter of Injustice, Law and the Agrarian Question in Zimbabwe*, Harare: SAPES Books, 2001.

Tuori, Kaarlo, 'Legislation between Politics and Law,' in Wintgens, 2002.
United Nations, *Beijing Platform for Action*. New York: United Nations, 1995.
United Nations, *Millennium Declaration*. New York: United Nations, 2000.
United Nations Division for the Advancement of Women, *Women and Decision Making in 2000*, October 1997.
United Nations, Universal Declaration of Human Rights UN GAOR, 3rd. Sess., U.N. Doc. A/810 pmbl. (1948).
United Nations, International Covenant on Economic, Social, and Cultural Rights, G.A. Res. 2200A (XXI), U.N. Doc. A/6316 (1966), 993 UNTS 3, 1966, 16 December.
United Nations, International Covenant on Civil and Political Rights, 999 UNTS 171, 1966, 19 December.
UNDP, *Governance for Sustainable Human Development*. A UNDP Policy Document. New York: UNDP, 1997a.
UNDP, *The Africa Governance Forum Conceptual Framework*. New York: UNDP, 1997b.
UNDP, *Governance for Sustainable Growth and Equity*. Report of International Conference. New York: UNDP, 1997c.
UNDP, *Human Development Report*. New York: Oxford University Press, various issues.
UNDP, *Integrating Human Rights with Sustainable Human Development*. A UNDP Policy Document. New York: UNDP, 1998, January.
UNDP Bureau for Development Policy, *UNDP Thematic Trust Fund: Good Governance*. New York: UNDP, 2002.
UNDP, *Women's Political Participation and Good Governance: 21st Century Challenges*. Report of the meeting held in New Delhi. New York: UNDP, 2000.
UN Economic and Social Council, *Limburg Principles on the Implementation of the International Covenant on Economic, Social and Cultural Rights*, E/CN4/1987/17.
UNOMSA (UN Observer Mission in South Africa), Final Report to the Secretary-General, *A Democratic Non-Racial and United South Africa*, 26 May, 1994.
UN Secretary-General, *Causes of Conflict and the Promotion of Durable Peace and Sustainable Development in Africa*. Report to Security Council. New York: United Nations, 1998.
Uphoff, Norman, *Local Institutional Development: An Analytical Sourcebook with Cases*. West Hartford, CT: Kumarian Press, 1986.
USAID Centre for Democracy and Governance, 'The Role of Media in Democracy: A Stategic Approach', <http://www.usaid.gov/pubs/ads/200/200sbc.pdf>http://www. usaid.gov/pubs/ads/200/200sbc.pdf.
USAID Centre for Democracy and Governance, 'Program Options in Conflict Prone Areas,' USAID Office of Transition Initiatives, <http://www.usaid.gov/ hum%20response/oti/focus/media.html>http://www.usaid.gov/humresponse/oti/focus/ media.html
Valdivieso, C. and M. Fong, *Gender Analysis in the CAS Process*. Washington, DC: World Bank, 1997.
Verwey, Len, *Nepad and Civil Society Participation in the APRM*. IDASA Occasional Paper. Johannesburg: Institute for a Democratic Alternative for South Africa, 2004.
Wach, H. and H. Reeves, 'Women's and Gender Budgets: an annotated resource list,' in *Bridge Bibliography No. 9*. Brighton: IDS, 1999.
Wade, H.W.R., *Administrative Law*. Oxford: Clarendon Press, 1959.
Warnock, Kitty and Nikki van der Gaag, eds., *Reducing Poverty: Is the World Bank's Strategy Working?* London: The Panos Institute, 2002.
Weber, Max, *The Theory of Social and Economic Organizations*. New York: Henderson & Parsons, 1947.
Weingast, Barry R., 'Constitutions as Governance Structures: The Political Foundations of Secure Markets,' *Journal of Institutional and Theoretical Economics* 149 (1983).
Weingast, Barry R., 'The Economic Role of Political Institutions: Market-Preserving Federalism and Economic Development,' *Journal of Law, Economics and Organization* April (1995).
Westhuizen, Christie van der, 'The AU's Peace and Security Council,' *Global Insight*,

Johannesburg, 42, January (2005).

White, Lucie E., 'To Learn and Teach: Lessons from Driefontein on Lawyering and Power,' *Wisconsin Law Review* 699 (1988).

Widner, Jenifer A., *Building the Rule of Law: Francis Nyalali and the Road to Judicial Independence in Africa*. New York: Norton, 2001.

Williams, David V., 'The Authoritarianism of African Legal Orders: A Review and Critique of Robert B. Seidman's *The State, Law and Development.*' *Contemporary Crises* 5 (1980).

Williams, Michael M., 'Nkrumahism as an Ideological Embodiment of Leftist Thought Within the African World,' *Journal of Black Studies* 15, 117 (1984).

Williamson, John, 'What Should the Bank Think About the Washington Consensus?' Background paper for World Bank Development Report, 2000. Washington DC: Institute for International Economics, 1999 July.

Wintgens, Luc J., *Legisprudence: A New Theoretical Approach to Legislation*. Oxford: Hart Publishing, 2002.

Wiseman, Henry and Alastair M. Taylor, *From Rhodesia to Zimbabwe: The Politics of Transition*. New York: Pergamon Press, 1981.

Wolfensohn, James D., 'Foreword' in *The World Bank Legal Reviews: Law and Justice for Development*, ed. Rudolf van Puymbroeck. Washington, DC: World Bank, 2003.

World Association of Christian Communications, *Ownership and Control of the Media and Citizen's Access: Consolidated Report of WACC's Media Ownership Programme, 1997–2000*. Kennington, London: WACC, 2001.

World Bank, *African Development Indicators*. Washington, DC: World Bank, 2002a.

World Bank, *Governance Matters II*. Washington DC: World Bank, 2002b.

World Bank, *Decentralization and Governance; Does Decentralization Improve Public Service Delivery?* Washington, DC: World Bank, 2001, June.

World Bank, *Entering the 21st Century: World Development Report 1999/2000*. New York: Oxford University Press, 2000a.

World Bank, *Can Africa Claim the 21st Century?* Washington DC: World Bank: 2000b.

World Bank, *Engendering Development*. Washington, DC: World Bank, 2000c.

World Bank, *Poverty Reduction Strategy Sourcebook*. Washington, DC: World Bank, 2000d.

World Bank, *World Development Report, 1996: From Plan to Market*, Washington, DC: World Bank, 1997a, June.

World Bank, *World Development Report 1997, The State in a Changing World*, Washington DC: World Bank, 1997b.

World Bank, *Governance: The World Bank's Experience*. Washington, DC: World Bank, 1994a.

World Bank, *Adjustment in Africa*. Washington, DC: World Bank, 1994b.

World Bank, *Governance and Development*. Washington, DC: World Bank, 1992.

World Bank, *Sub-Saharan Africa: From Crisis to Sustainable Growth*. Washington, DC: World Bank, 1989.

World Bank, *World Bank Country Report: Ghana*. Washington, DC: World Bank, 1983.

World Bank, *Country Study. Ghana: Policies and Program for Adjustment*. Washington DC: World Bank, 1984.

World Bank Institute, *The Right to Tell: The Role of Mass Media in Economic Development*. Washington, DC, July 2002c.

Wunsch, James S. and Dele Owolu, 'Foundations of Centralization: The Colonial Experience and the African Context,' in *The Failure of the Centralized State: Institutions and Self Governance in Africa*, ed. Wunsch and Owolu. Boulder, CO: Westview Press, 1990.

Yusuf, A., 'Reflections on the Fragility of the State Institutions in Africa,' *African Yearbook of International Law* 2 (1994).

Zimba, L., 'The Origins and Spread of One-Party States in Commonwealth Africa and Their Impact on Personal Liberties; A Case Study of the Zambian Model,' in *Law in Zambia*, ed. M. Ndulo. Nairobi: East African Publishing House.

Index